With the odds stacked against him making a c
and despite an injury-hampered rise in first-gr
Roberts was widely acclaimed as the best front-rower in the world in
the late eighties. There was acrimony and even bomb threats when he
left his humble working-class South Sydney surrounds to play with the
'silvertail' club Manly in 1989, a move that made him league's highest-
paid player ever at the time.

Three years later he was broke and broken.

By 1995, having once again overcome insurmountable odds, and
amidst further controversy, he signed with Rupert Murdoch's Super
League, while seeing out his commitment to the ARL flagship club
Manly. That year he was almost crippled with a knee injury, but played
through to the grand final.

At the same time he became arguably the world's first high-profile
sportsman to voluntarily confirm his much-rumoured homosexuality,
subjecting himself once again to the litany of abuse that has seemed to
follow his every move. This time, however, there was the acclaim and
certainty that he had done great good and that right was on his side.
And with that knowledge, and the support of scores of admirers and
mentors, came the peace and happiness that had eluded Ian for so long.

This is his story, told extensively in his own words and those of
his friends, family and team-mates, the story of an ordinary man with
an extraordinary talent and the courage to finally live his life honestly.

Paul Freeman was born and raised in Tasmania. After graduating as a Bachelor of Arts, he moved to Sydney to find greater personal freedom and to study and to pursue a career as an actor.

After several years of sporadic work in theatre, film and television, he worked briefly in management within the video and then the fashion industry, before he began to work and be published as a freelance writer and photographer.

He photographed his friend Ian Roberts for the inaugural issue of *Blue* magazine in late 1994, and after acting in a confronting play dealing with homosexuality which toured Sydney's high schools, he spent much of 1996 writing *Finding Out*, his first book.

PAUL FREEMAN

IAN ROBERTS

FINDING OUT

RANDOM HOUSE
AUSTRALIA

Writing the biography of a young, living, known homosexual has its pitfalls. Due to current defamation laws, the identity of several people in this book had to be altered so that their association with Ian, which may now be an embarrassment to them, does not encourage them to seek litigation. It was never the intention of the book to out or to embarrass anyone, and, where possible, this has been avoided.

Random House Australia Pty Ltd
20 Alfred Street, Milsons Point, NSW 2061
http://www.randomhouse.com.au

Sydney New York Toronto
London Auckland Johannesburg
and agencies throughout the world

First published in 1997
This edition published 1997
Copyright © Paul Freeman 1997

National Library of Australia
Cataloguing-in-Publication Data
Freeman, Paul, 1960- .
  Ian Roberts: finding out.

Includes index.
ISBN 0 09 183 337 X

1. Roberts, Ian, 1965- . 2. Rugby League Football -
Australia - Biography. 3. Gay men - Australia - Biography.
4. Gays - Australia - Identity. I. Title.

796.3338092

Design by Yolande Gray
Typeset by Midland Typesetters, Maryborough, Victoria
Printed by Griffin Press, Adelaide

10 9 8 7 6 5 4 3 2 1

CONTENTS

ACKNOWLEDGEMENTS

I would like to acknowledge the assistance and co-operation, and the support and encouragement of the following people:

Ian Roberts, Julie Free, Kylie Corbett, Ray and Jean, and Paul Roberts, Frank Cookson, David Johnson, George Piggins, Mario Fenech, Craig Coleman, Ben Widdicombe and The *Sydney Star Observer*, Neil Halpin, Darren Hadland, Daniel Lane, *Rugby League Week* and Australian Consolidated Press, Steve Mascord and the Fairfax Library, Tom Brock, Terry Hill, Dawn Stenning, Theo Lianos, Lee Slattery, Shane Goodwin, Penny Douglas, Michael Gorman, Julie Kalya, Myriam Loda, Sally Freeman, Louise Freeman, Ross Johnson, The State Library of NSW, Jane Palfreyman and the staff at Random House, and Ian Heads, a true gentleman of League.

FOREWORD

When Paul [Freeman] and I first seriously discussed doing a book about my life, I knew there was a story to tell, but I wasn't sure I'd be able to be open enough to tell it properly. It's been quite a process of emotional exploration and self-assessment. I've learned a lot about myself through the grillings Paul gave me, and through thinking about the journey I have been on so far.

Many opportunities came my way during much of that journey, such as rugby league, which I didn't seem to have the capacity to enjoy properly. Whenever something was happening in my life that was positive, there always seemed to be a negative overshadowing it, stopping me from being content. In particular, there have been a couple of major disasters that were real eye-openers for me, and which nearly destroyed me financially and emotionally. In the end, though, I was pointed in the right direction by these challenges, towards truth. People and events in my life were like pointers. Although knowing him was immensely painful in the end, Blake showed me what strength and endurance through pain and prejudice really was. Without the love of people like him, I wouldn't be who I am today, and I certainly wouldn't be having my story told.

It took me too long a time to realised that if I had the courage to really *like* who I was, everything else would fall into place, and I wouldn't keep inviting disaster to happen. I now know that, in the end, whether directly or indirectly, each of us is responsible for a lot of what happens in our life, good and bad, and that it is up to each of us to take control, even when the odds against us seem too great.

It took me too long to realise that I was weighed down by a burden that I shouldn't have had to carry, a problem that wasn't really *my* problem. I hope that by telling my story I can prevent someone else having to carry this unnecessary burden for too long. I hope it is of help to

some kids out there punishing themselves, then they should really be celebrating their lives with as much esteem as everyone else.

Looking back over my life, while doing the book, I realise that obviously not everyone will be as lucky as I have been to have the support and love of a good family to get them through things. But not everyone, thankfully, has their life scrutinised under a microscope. When people always say to me, 'Its been easier for you to come out because of who you are, but *I* could never do it in *my* situation,' I laugh to myself and say to them, 'Look, believe me, if I can do it, anyone can!' So I also hope that my story will inspire those sorts of people—especially the people who think their high profile and responsibilities prevent them, because they don't!—to stand up and provide the gay role models that future generations of Australian truly and obviously need.

Ian Roberts
Townsville, March 1997

*D*ear Ian

I haven't wrote before because I feel bad doing it … I really admire you. You always look so happy. And one day I want to be just like you. I can't understand why I feel so dirty. About myself being gay.

I am writing to you both as a friend and under the compulsion of the Holy Spirit of God to warn you of the results you will experience if you continue to live as a homosexual. This also applies to your friends and associates of the same persuasion … God did not create man for that purpose. In Romans Chapter 1 verses 24–28 you will be able to see for yourself where you stand with God at the present time … I believe through the Holy Spirit you are going to become a very ill young man and will eventually die as a result of it before your time. If you want to talk more about this subject do not repeat do not hesitate to get in touch with me at the following address …

Here's a poem a friend gave me. I hope it touches you like it did me

> **If you dare to be different**
> **and you do not join the crowd**
> **If they laugh at your honesty**

and taunt you if you're proud
When they talk of you in whispers
and criticise the things you say and do
Do not fear them but forgive them
for they are more afraid than you ...

I just wanted to say that without a doubt you have made a difference, a huge difference. If I can be frank, I had never come out to anybody till one night we were talking about football and Manly and the subject slipped to you and the next thing I know I am coming out to them. It was a great experience, a feeling/emotion I will never forget, with all good consequences. They are crazy, but more importantly great friends ...

In one fell swoop you have given tens of thousands of young kids a role model, a reason to feel good about themselves, a reason to look after themselves, a reason to respect themselves, a reason to be safe. There were at least a 1000 letters of complaint when the Courier-Mail *ran the story, with a vicious tone that shocked the editor. But there were at least 3000 letters of support ...*

I am a great fan of yours and would very much like to meet you.
I'm not trying to convert you—heaven forbid, I'm Anglican, fondest
regards, Father Anon Anon ...

In the past month two young gay men personally known to us
have suicided. A recent US Health Department survey revealed
that gay and lesbian youth comprise 30% of successful teen sui-
cides. The problem is not homosexuality, but homophobia. Self-
disclosure is by far the most effective weapon against that ...

I was dismissed from the UK army on the grounds that I am gay ... I have no doubt people such as you can achieve wonders in changing public perceptions ...

I want to send you my love and admiration. You made it all so effortless and straightforward. It was very different in my day. How I wish I were your age but I shall be 70 next year. We have much in common. I was a prop as well. God bless you ...

For years we have defended your honour and desperately tried to stop the gay rumours only because you denied them, but now we know the truth does it change our feelings and our respect for you? NO NO NO NO! We love you not only as a dear friend but as an extension of our family. Your sexual preference is of no importance to us. We love the person. We hope the end result of your decision will be a more fulfilling life a chance to be who you are and not who you think you should be. We all wish you a wonderful future a future hopefully the McDermotts will be part of, warmest love . . .

My wife Wendy and I both salute you. It takes a brave person to do what you did. Be proud and stand tall for who you are. May your life be filled with happiness and God's blessings . . .

Congratulations on outing. Wish I had the courage. Will, London . . .

You have inspired me to write a poem. You are great and gutsy . . . I am a GP who is somewhat older than you who has yet to find the courage to do what you have done. Straightforward courage and honesty have always been the mark of Australians. I believe you follow in the path of great Australian men . . .

It troubles me deeply that you can hold your head up while you spread the sickness and decay that is destroying this society and for which God will damn you. Shame on you for your weakness. I pity your family, but I can only assume they are to blame in many ways . . .

As a late blooming gay father of two teenage children, my body and soul rejoice at your openness and honesty. It makes me proud that I finally found the strength to be who I am. From a supporter . . .

I have always looked on rugby league as one of the last domains of the rugged Australian and I know the attitude of a lot of people at my club towards gays so I guess it can't have been easy . . .

Thank you for coming out. What you have done for gays is far greater than anything I can do. I came out in my church 15 years ago. They kicked me out but I found a church that would accept me. I am sure you would have to be aware that the negative feelings that come from the community come originally from the church. Therefore we must change the church attitude. But you are so right about homosexuality within the football community. About 30 years ago when I was younger and prettier I had sex with six males who were playing first grade and at least one was an international. I have a dream one day that at a given signal all gay and bisexual men will come out. Wouldn't the world get a shock when they saw who was there? Even in my lifetime there have been three prime-ministers who have been gay. Of course they all married ...

It was then that I attempted suicide. As a testament to my skill I survived. You gave me comfort that not all gays are the limp-wristed stereotypes that we are bombarded with. Your whole character combined with the stance you took makes the burden a lot easier to bear. You are helping lift the cross. I see the success that you are and I know that something else exists besides empty space and me ...

The decision to tell my mother has been painful. I am scared, for her reaction may be a negative one, yet it can only be positive because finally the weight I have been carrying around for years will be lifted. I work in a predominantly male, homophobic workplace. The more I see what strength it must take to continue to be yourself and be proud of yourself in the face of such resistance, fear and ignorance, the more strength I find within myself to be able to continue and not lose conviction to exposing the truth. I thank you from the bottom of my heart ...

The decency of all our children thanks to you is threatened and we have to be ever more vigilant that trends like these don't spread. You have used your position of respect and have abused it to the utmost. Squandered all the good chances you were given. How you can look people in the face is beyond me. I feel sorry for you, for your soul ...

I think what you have done is fantastic. The last four months I decided to tell my family. Like your family, they are supportive ...

Your despicable lifestyle choice has made my son decide to join your lot and I fear more than anything that he is lost to me and to decent living and God forever ...

You have brought a thought-provoking challenge to the public that shatters forever their stereotyping conventions ...

Your sexuality has caused some major upsets for me at my place of work, RSL and Diggers' Club I go to because I couldn't stand what people were saying about you. A few years ago I was screaming out for Manly and this guy said to me 'Hey! you're going for the wrong team. They're all a bunch of pooftas, especially that Ian Roberts.' I said very politely, 'You come here and say that to my face!' I think you're simply the best. You see, Ian, I have a gay brother. Unlike you he never had the guts to tell our parents who are now deceased. And that's why I'm so happy you told your parents . . .

I am a 30-year-old farmer and have wanted to write to you since *Blue* to thank you for the strength you have given me, and others like me, by your example. I had always considered myself bisexual, something I explained to my girlfriend before we got engaged. We are now married and expecting our first child. But the way you dispelled myths about lifestyles and footballers has empowered me to acknowledge that I am really a gay man who is married and not a bisexual. It has helped me to see myself for who and what I really am. Eight years ago I was disillusioned and left my job and home in Sydney and lost a good friend because I refused to be 'out' about our relationship. I came back home to the family farm, and don't regret doing that or getting married, but I now know that had you and your media profile been around back then I would have done what I should have done and not run away from myself. Being a married gay man is one thing, but in the country it is even harder with no opportunity for relief . . .

There are people from generations slightly older than you who were socialised to believe that it is all in their minds and haven't a clue why they have problems relating . . .

Your off-field moves have shown courage that a thousand warriors could never possess. The spectre of damaging what will be a successful professional sporting career because of my personal life bears upon me. Though, as you have created for yourself, I can see a coexistence of these two worlds . . .

Congrats for being so strong in your convictions. Stand tall. I am the parent of nine children. One of my sons recently stood tall. He had been sexually abused for many years by a so-called friend and school teacher. This man is a pedophile. I also have a son who is homosexual. I was insulted when people assume they are the same. My son is a kind and sensitive loving person. I know the pain a parent feels at first knowledge of it—but he like you does not make himself out to be anything else. I am proud to be his mother. I am sure your parents and family have the same feelings. I apologise for the narrow-minded people who will not accept it ...

The decision must have been extremely difficult but you truly are a trailblazer knocking down traditional stereotypes. It was interesting to see my teenage football-playing boys' reaction. At first disbelief. My eldest's comment was, 'But he plays football' and later 'But he doesn't look gay.' As I said, stereotyping. We had a good discussion. You will find many people who will take great delight in trying to knock you down but remember, mate, there are many around who respect you ...

While I'm heterosexual and not an advocate of your type, I can't help but feel the highest respect and admiration for you. I've been defending you against my mates in verbal slanging matches. In a team of great players you're one of the greatest ...

We find it ridiculous the way the fans have treated you. Good on you for doing it and here's to opening the eyes of footy fans world-wide.

Growing up in the country as part of a great footballing family and being gay has caused me much anxiety over the years. Your comments have made me feel much more comfortable about myself. Thank you. I am 46—never too old to learn, eh?

I am an 18-year-old school student in year 12 at [Catholic college] and I play football. People always tell me I've got ball skills like you and John Cartwright. I'm a masculine sort of guy. I'm not a pussy gay guy attempting to play a tough man's game. I don't act gay but just normal. I thought that I was the only guy that was gay and played football. I'm heaps confused about it all. No-one at all knows, not even my family. If my dad found out he would disown me and I'd be a disgrace to the family. I've got no-one to talk to. I don't know any gay people and haven't even had an experience of being gay ...

To someone like myself who gets shit from straight people for being gay and from gay people for following league and 'pretending to be straight', your recent words and actions have been a great comfort ...

But are you gay? Most of the people I know say you are gay, but I stick up for you.

My main area is counselling as well as having a number of gay friends and know of the trauma that is gone through by young people trying to be themselves. They suffer much and it is all so needless. I have also seen the suffering caused when parents rejected children and then children contract AIDS and there is no time to make up for lost years. Thank you for allowing yourself to be such a fine role model for children, sports people and the gay community and society in general. As people like you speak out, then some of these stupid taboos and attitudes can be broken. Please allow me to encourage and thank you for the work you do with sick kids. May your dreams come true. Reverend Anon ...

I am a straight female with no real interest in rugby league. But I'm sure your detractors will be loud enough and so I believe it is important that you know that a great many people support you and that we make at least as much noise. Appearing in *Blue* magazine is a brave and truly noble thing. I am truly proud of you. The suffering of future generations will be less because of your action. I have seen a great many gay men and women suffer from bigotry ...

My brother is gay and has had a terrible time dealing with it himself as he has found it to be so socially unacceptable. He had a number of gay friends who attempted suicide (some were successful). Why? When they came out to their families they were disowned. My family and my fiancé have been wonderful. We don't have a problem with him being gay. We are very concerned about the amount of drugs and alcohol he has consumed along the way. He thought it could help if he could blot out the feelings. Feelings don't go away that easy. Thanks to the profile of people like you supporting gays and lesbians it makes it just that little bit easier to be themselves. Pretending to be something you're not is never easy.

As you are a public figure I'd imagine it was particularly difficult, but that makes it particularly important ...

I woke up the next morning and I felt so dirty. I think it was because of what people would think of me. I never told anyone what happened between me and him. But they think I'm just a normal guy. But inside, I think different. When I read the article it made me feel good inside ...

All the courage you have displayed on the field as a footballer

is nowhere near as impressive as the courage you are showing in your life.

If it is the last thing I do, you are done for. You and your lot ...

She told me it is all my fault. When they die she tells me it will be me who send them to the grave. She dug up everything bad she could and threw it at me. We had arguments about her alcoholism and about how I was left at home alone every night for twelve years since I was four. Why does it get this bad? ...

It's midnight in this small country town where I run a take-away. I hear comments that are so pitiful they are not worth mentioning even. But they make me realise just how small-minded country people can be. The decision you have made makes me sad for you as I know you will have a hard time but then it makes me proud to see you live your life the way you want. In the country we can't do that. We have to play it straight. But we survive ...

I know you must have a lot of detractors because of the brave thing you have done. I just want you to know that you have admirers too ...

I think it's important to let people who are doing brave and wonderful things know that they are supported and applauded. Thank you for your courage, style and guts. Mate, you've made my job [counsellor] easier.

You are not even an animal. Your parents will disown you and you will die alone soon. AIDS will finish you in hell. There is no such word to hide behind as gay. Sodomist is what you are. SODOMIST. An arsehole bandit and an AIDS carrier. You are pure filth and will die SOON!

I am an old ex-rugby league player of yesterday, played for Queensland and against some of the great players, such as Clive Churchill, Don Furner, Harry Wells and many others. As a young man I was encouraged to follow in the footsteps of the great players and tried to apply myself to being a man on the field and also off the field. I heard about your decision to come out and announce you are a homosexual. What a disappointment that is to myself and sons as well as my many friends and the followers of rugby league. Having had a brush with this so-called lifestyle, or deathstyle, it left me feeling dirty and unclean. Homosexuality is a carrier of disease, death, violence, murder, and lacks compassion, it incites jealousy and is an abomination to God. One is not born with a genetic defect that leads them into this terrible way of living. People choose to go down this highway to Hell. Ian, I urge you to come out of it, these people will only use you and eventually destroy you. One day, you will have to stand before the owner-coach and chief and only selector of the heavenly team— this is the winning team, there is no runner-up. All other teams go into eternal damnation—this is not nice. There is a jersey just your size waiting. It does not fit anyone else. If you don't pick it up it goes into the fire with the one it was made for.

I am nineteen, soon to be turning twenty. I know you have more than enough on your plate. The thing is I think I am gay and I have not told anyone this. I noticed myself look at and liking other guys. I had girls chasing everywhere. See I am a fairly good looking guy so I've been told. My mates used to say you're mad for not getting into her . . . This one night me and a mate Brad . . . mucked around. We mucked around again in the morning. My heart was going mad. I was a bit nervous again. On the way back we didn't say much. He said we should be having sex with a girl and that it was wrong for us to be doing it. When I got home I felt really bad and upset for doing it mainly because I had a really good loving strong family upbringing and know wrong from right, and knew that wasn't right. That was it for two years. No-one would ever have expected me for maybe being gay. Still to this day I don't know what I call myself. See I was a bit of a rough nut at school, always doing crazy things, playing footie, just your average teenage bloke down the beach surfing, motorbike riding, the works. You are a huge fantasy of mine. I don't really know how gay life works 'cause I haven't really experienced it. I don't really like that way some guys carried on really feminine like. You will always be a fantasy of mine. I would like to try to lead a straight life, family and all. I am really confused and I hate it. I've got a 1000 things I want to ask you. Things I just need to *find out* somehow . . .

ONE
A FAMILY

*F*aded hues of autumn dance on the screen. A woman, pale and youthful. Blushed cheeks, skin translucent. Thick, flaxen hair. She is withdrawn. Fragile but warm. She dares an occasional momentary glance to camera.

Tumbling children envelop her. They peer eagerly at the viewer, vigorously performing. A handsome and strong father awkwardly guards the background. Sometimes he lifts and displays a child. The focus of this tale is the children.

The children flapping hands in a sea of flapping wings. Piccadilly. The children at the English seaside.

The happily drenched and dishevelled kids on the water's edge at Maroubra beach.

Healthy and vigorous, beautiful children. They age before our eyes, one moment clumsy, toddling and dependent, the next feisty.

One more aggressively claims his space for posterity. It is Ian. He is a gorgeous child, a thick mop of sun-blessed light brown hair crowning cheeky, narrow, smiling eyes. He is the clown with wild gestures. More extrovert, pushy, he plays the camera.

For a second he is seven, erratic and energised, with a bold performance on monkey bars, then a vaudeville exit, gesturing wildly. Then he is eight and running rings round the others on the sand.

Time has put its spin on the film and a sad twilight haunts moments that once sang in the full midday sun. Piercing white arrows *rain down the screen, chasing the film through the projector as they try to wipe the images completely. The film is tired. Happy times reads now like lost hopes, lost innocence. The effect is melancholic. An indefinable, yet gaping, sense of loss.*

The past of that family, those children, is our own.

The sheer vigour of unfettered happiness, of unfettered dreams gone, shattered by a too brilliant white light of reality.

Ian switches the film off and we are yanked back to a stark present. A more definable reality. 'Sorry, mate, it's pretty boring. We're just an ordinary family.' He's seen it many times. He was continuously shuffling in his seat, uncomfortable. Bored. Interjecting: 'This bit is nothing, it's just stuff-all. I'll find one bit ... here ... watch what I do here ... see!' He replays the shot that still amuses him, of him swinging from monkey bars, jumping down and running, arms flailing wildly, face expressive. Now there are gales of laughter. 'You can see it, even back then, can't you?'

'What?'

'You know!' He chuckles at what he sees now as evidence of an early and detectable, well ... over-exuberance, shall we say. But it's innocent exuberance, a healthy energy and an insatiable desire for action. He shows off, for laughs. He executes physical feats. He helps his sisters into the limelight of the camera. The moment the camera rolls, he crams it with life. He is definitely the rowdiest child.

Yet, for Ian, there is nothing remarkable that anyone can derive from watching this family footage, on this particular Australia Day long weekend in 1996, as we sit inside his sparsely furnished apartment, vertical blinds drawn against a brilliant day. Ian is recovering from a major knee reconstruction. It's the most complex of countless operations he has had over the years, to patch wear and tear. He retains a childish lack of interest in witnessing a day in which he is unable to cavort. He is impatient with his recovery. He is impatient and bored with everything. His knee is throbbing with pain. 'I hate this apartment. It's not home. That's why I'm not buying more furniture. There's no use getting stuff that doesn't suit the place I move to.' What little furniture there is in the vast chasm of a living room is of superb quality. Two chesterfield-style lounges, in comfortable, soft and faded imperial green leather. A solid French provincial sideboard. A massive, beaten old timber table. All proportionate to his giant frame, which is slumped in a sofa, his plastered knee placed carefully on the table. He is distracted, frustrated at his immobility.

Ian is dismissive of any interest in his family films. He is awkward about any flattery. 'Mate, we're just an ordinary family,' he mumbles quickly again. 'There's nothing special. We're close is all. A very close family.' Then, hardly missing a beat, 'Do you want to go up to the roof for a swim?' End of story ...

... Part of the beginning really.

Roberts is a Welsh name, Ray Roberts will tell you in a strong Cockney accent, despite having been in Australia for nearly three decades. Quietly spoken, Ian's dad will mumble too, and is understated if not encouraged. There is a reliable warmth, a dependability about him. The blushing beauty from the home movies is Jean. She busies herself from the moment you walk into their tidy comfortable home as a guest. She can't do enough to make you comfortable.

There something else about Jean. Etched into her face is a weariness. Challenges and pitfalls have taken their toll and left her brittle. She needs calm and serenity about her now. Ray is protective of Jean. He seems somehow weary too, but you won't hear it. These two will not complain about their lot. They are more grateful and content than they ever hoped to be. Their adopted country has been good to them and they are proud. Proud of their family. Proud of their lives. But their faces are etched with the stains of worry. They tell a different tale to the one Ray and Jean will tell. Like the aged home movies.

Ray and Jean Roberts are Londoners. Born when the Bow Bells lay silent during the war, they are still Cockneys. Ray's father was a demolition man, a consistent provider for his large family. But times were often hard. Hunger and going without were common. Adversity seemed to strengthen the Roberts, who remained tight-knit and loyal. The extended family remained close. Ray talks with nostalgia of a time back in London when he was younger. No-one in the family wanted for anything. There'd always be someone around to bail them out, a cousin, an uncle, a brother. He talks sentimentally of large and happy family gatherings on big occasions.

Ray has modelled his own fatherhood on lessons learnt in London. He has no elaborate philosophy on life. Work hard, provide for your family as best you can and love them all, unconditionally. This was his recipe for real family bonding.

Jean's mother died when she was a baby and she was raised by her grandmother in Lambeth. She has one brother, and two step-brothers from her father's subsequent re-marriage. She became a part of the Roberts' clan fairly early in life. She was a clerk at Lombard's Bank, and barely sixteen when she met Ray at a party in post-war ravaged London. Ray was working for the Water Board. He had already been a courier/waiter at the Ritz Hotel, and a merchant navy man. Soon he was a truck driver, with J. Lyons, tea merchants.

While the Marshall plan rebuilt Germany, a derelict London got a cheap rebuild. The British Empire was exhausted, drained. Refugees flooded the city, too, from troubled newly independent lands, impoverished ex-colonies. For Cockney youth there was a feeling of disenfranchisement. Preference in health and housing seemed to go to the new arrivals, and London felt burdened and bursting with strangeness. It looked and felt unfamiliar.

At seventeen, Ray and Jean were engaged. At nineteen they were married, and living with Ray's family in Totteridge Road, Battersea. Ray was stocky and muscular, a handsome man with a glint in his narrow eyes. And a damn good amateur boxer. Jean was the proverbial English rose in bloom. Precious and delicate. Beautiful.

Two days after Christmas 1961 came Julie, followed in February 1963 by Paul. Jean left the factory where she was working. The couple applied and waited for housing. 'You make your bed, you gotta lay in it,' says Ray about the tough times. 'Most Londoners worry about today. They live for now. You go to work this week. You live for this week. No planning.'

When Ian was born on 31 July 1965, there was no room at their hospital and Jean was shunted to Chelsea.

In 1966, the Australian government had a migration scheme, whereby £10 got you passage, hostel accommodation and the guarantee of a job. Since New Zealand didn't want drivers, the Roberts applied for Australia.

Then they finally got allocated a villa and moved into a housing estate. 'We wondered if we'd done the right thing,' says Jean, 'or would we always regret not going to Australia. We rang Australia House six months after moving and all our papers were still in order, so we came.'

In December 1966, aged 26, with three children and 200 pounds sterling, they sailed on the *Fairsea*, destined to be away for a minimum of two years. They left the roots of centuries, and the safety net of Ray's big extended family. Jean was still excited. 'We saw it as heading for a new adventure, a big adventure. It was terrible for those we left behind, but I knew we'd see them again. I loved it from the start.'

Ray was shocked on arrival. 'I used to do night work before I came, truck driving. Anyway, from the TV, Jean knew what to expect, except I worked nights. We got off at Woolloomooloo. We were picked up by a limo, a big Rambler, and they took us on a tour through the National Park. We thought, gee, this is all right.' But Fairy Meadow hostel did not live up to its name. 'I could've turned around then and gone home. They were dumps, the hostels at Wollongong. They said there was work for drivers. They put me down to work at Port Kembla steel works. They offered me $43 a fortnight! I was earning 43 quid a week in England, driving! And they wanted me to go under the furnaces to clean all the crap out!'

So Ray lied. He said he had work in Sydney and got the family shifted to Bunnerong hostel. Ray did endless job rounds and eventually got work at the ICI plant at Botany. He's been there ever since.

Jean enjoyed the spirit of adventure, the camaraderie of Bunnerong. 'We were with people who were in the same boat as us. There were people who'd lived in the hostel for years. Then, after eighteen months, I was pregnant and I wanted to go home. But we hadn't lived outside the hostel yet, and until we had we wouldn't have given it a chance out here.' So on 10 April 1970, Kylie was born and the family moved to a tiny brick semi at Maroubra Bay.

When Kylie was two, the family took a trip back to England, and Ray knew Australia was home and hope for his family. 'But we knew one of the things we had to change was living for the moment, like in London. We had to worry about tomorrow, where we never used to worry about money in the bank, which we never had to. Back in London with a big family, you never went without. In Australia whatever we've got is what *we've* gotten, what we've earned ourselves. The kids always had what we could give them. I'm not saying we were the best providers in the world.'

They were good providers. Worked hard. Took no risks. In isolation, the security of a tight-knit family was their strength. Ray would've liked to have bought a home for added security. 'We looked at houses, but we didn't want to look in Botany, near work. We looked at everywhere else except Botany. All industrial and stinking, we thought it was. We weren't Robinson Crusoes. There were thousands of other people in the same position, but we would never take the chance, not with four kids would I get myself into twenty-five years of debt.' Instead, Ray worked so that ten years down the track, he could safely buy a place. In Botany. 'I always worked shift,' Ray laments, 'ever since I been in Australia. We've not really had what you'd call a normal life, have we? When you're rostered on, whether it's a public holiday or weekend, you work!'

Ian was a bit of a handful for Jean. Stubborn from the start, as they say. 'I'd be pushing Kylie in the pram out shopping, and if Ian didn't want to go that way, there's no way you could make him go that way. I'd have to drag him along the ground, sometimes, so I could go the way I wanted to with the pram.' Julie adds: 'If Mum took him to the shops and wouldn't buy him what he wanted, he'd start hollering. He'd throw tantrums. He was so naughty when he was little. He was such a show-off too. He always wanted to be the centre of attention. He knew what he wanted, and that was it!'

When Jean had her hands full, Julie was in charge of Ian. 'I grew up thinking it was normal to go everywhere with your sister,' Ian recalls. 'Julie used to treat me like her little pet when I was four or five. I used to go round and find all these Coke bottles and go and change them. Do you remember when you used to get your money back for Coke bottles? I have this memory of my sister sitting there, like I'd get twenty cents—you'd get a lot of sweets for twenty cents. Then she used to divide them up, and then she'd eat hers and I wasn't allowed to eat mine and I'd have to sit there and watch her eat hers. Then she'd divide mine up and I'd end up with the sweets she liked the least!'

Maroubra Bay has bushland on a rocky coast, and a beach. Jean was able to keep a watchful eye out at first. 'He would happily collect bugs and play in the backyard on his own. Content for ages!' He wouldn't hurt a fly, Julie reckons. 'He was one of those kids who wouldn't harm a spider or an insect. He would collect them and he was fascinated by them, but he would always be careful to let them go.' But he outgrew the tiny yard, and the dilapidated fence with the rotting palings didn't contain kids hungry to explore. 'You didn't have to worry about your kids as much in those days,' says Jean, 'especially down that way. There was plenty for them to explore and not much harm to come to. I couldn't prevent them anyway. I'd look out and they'd be gone.'

Ian did things by himself. 'I loved going to the beach but I loved going alone. I was quite a loner when I was very young. I used to be out a lot on my own, doing the kinds of things most kids do—catching lizards, cutting my legs open and coming home with cuts all over me. I'd cut my legs climbing round the bushed area near the rifle range. I used to go up there inside the Commonwealth property with those signs around it. You're not supposed to go there but kids do. I was always out catching frogs and things, always come back covered in mud and get into trouble from my mum. Always. Every day!'

With an appetite for physical challenges, Ian remembers being an accident-prone kid, and a perpetual headache for his mother. 'If ever there was a kid that fell over at school and grazed his knee, that was me. If ever a kid bumped his head on the clothesline or fell off something, it was me. I always seemed to be getting cuts and that ... because I was clumsy. And I was fearless. I was five or six, I went out on my birthday. That day I ran round the rocks with my brother and I slipped and split my head open. My mum had to come and get me because I wouldn't come home. I thought I'd be in trouble. Mum used to freak when she saw where we would climb and explore.

I was thankful that she came, relieved that I wouldn't have to stay there all night. Other times, I would come home with my leg cut open or something and I wouldn't want to tell my mum. Then she'd notice and go "What's all that blood doing on your leg?" I was always getting hurt and trying to hide it.

'For some reason I remember this earache I had when we were living at Maroubra. I can recall just laying in bed quietly crying to myself and then my dad came in and turned the light on, and I remember feeling so relieved—I suppose everyone goes through it—and my dad said, "What's wrong, son?" He got me some aspirin and held me in his arms rocking me slowly while the pain-killers took effect, and I felt so safe, and I knew that nothing terrible was going to happen to me.

'My Dad always took time out to do things with me. He would come home from work and we would go out the front and play cricket or throw frisbee, or whatever, for hours. He taught me to tell the time. Me, sitting on his knee, and him, for hours and hours saying, "This is five minutes, ten minutes ..." He was very patient, still is. He was basically my best friend as a kid. I think I spent more time with him because I was often hanging out alone while my brother was always hanging out with his friends.'

Maroubra Bay Primary was a few doors up from home. From day one that would prove to be a disadvantage. 'I could run home. I ran home the first day of school and sat in the backyard next door. My dad couldn't get me out of the next door neighbour's yard because they had this security dog. The first time I met the dog, I just bowled up to it, and started patting it. It took a liking to me for some reason. I would jump the fence and sit with this dog in its kennel and no-one could get me. This dog was vicious!' How to keep Ian at school became Jean's nightmare. 'I used to take him to school and when I got home, I'd look out in the yard and he would be sitting out there. Playing in the dirt, with the beetles. He'd come home on his own. I started taking him to the police station—well, outside the police station—to threaten him that that's where he'd be if he didn't go to school!'

'I think I was a bit scared of school' is the way Ian remembers it. 'I was harassed because I didn't take much interest in it. I remember I was good at maths and that was what kept my head above water. I was hopeless at English and all that and spelling and things.' This was pretty much the case right through his school years at Maroubra Bay Infants, Maroubra Bay Primary and Maroubra Bay High. Ray never liked school, either. 'I never had any inclination and it wasn't where Ian wanted to be.'

When he did sort of settle in, he was a rebel who took on everyone's cause. Or a brat. A teacher's headache. There was always a glint of approval in his dad's eyes. 'He'd never get in trouble off his own bat. He got in trouble for someone else!' A wearied Jean recalls, 'He used to take on everyone's cause, didn't he? If he thought one of the kids was being hard done by, by the teacher, he would say so. "You can't do that!" Once, they had some do on at school where everyone took cakes and they put them in the middle to share. A couple of kids hadn't brought any, and they weren't allowed to join in the party, and Ian pipes up with "You can't do that"' He kicked up a bit of a fuss and Ray got summoned. 'I had to go up to the school, to see his teacher.'

The one good thing about school that Ian discovered was sport. He excelled, and he loved the challenge of mastering a new physical skill. According to Ray no matter what he tried to do, he was always good at it. 'He's always beaten me, even as a kid, at table tennis and that.' The little tike used to trundle down to the beach too, where he joined the Maroubra Tadpoles with his brother. Surf lifesaving for toddlers.

There was one presentation day embarrassment for the pommy immigrants once. Julie recalls, 'Ian was always winning everything. One day, we all went down to the beach for some presentation day, dressed and ready for a day at the beach. Well, everyone there was dressed up, and Ian was hauled up for some big presentation!' Tousled hair, a scruffy T-shirt and togs, and given a trophy as big as he was. 'We'd never been to anything like that before, but after that we knew how to dress for presentation day at the beach!'

In 1970, when he was four, Mr Riley from next door took his two boys to footy, and Ian tagged along to check it out. 'I joined a football club,' he announced at home after practice with the N-grade Maroubra Lions team at nearby Snape Oval. Ray thought football meant soccer.

Julie can't recall being startled by any early brilliant form from Ian at half-back. 'Ian was up the other end of the field throwing rocks and digging in the dirt! He wasn't that interested. I wasn't that interested either, but I can remember him strolling over one game, to where we were standing, to change his jumper.' Well, by the final, which they won, he was concentrating, and got Man of the Match, and Ray was getting used to the game.

In 1972, the Roberts moved to a housing commission flat in South Coogee, a working-class seaside suburb not far north of Maroubra. A couple of kilometres from the old place. Ian changed football teams and went to Maroubra Diggers. They used the same oval for training, and were in the same South Sydney Juniors competition. Paul played with that team, so it was easier if Ian did too. He was in M-grade that year.

His new coach was Dave Johnson. Dave was tough but fair with the kids, hearty working-class stock, all heart. Dave can find nothing controversial to say about the young Ian. 'It's hard, because with the other kids that Ian played with, I could say they were ... buggers, you know. They played up and did all these sorts of things, but Ian didn't fit into that category. Ian was pretty quiet, quite shy, a bit of a loner. Of course, on the field he was a different sort of person. He was a machine on the field, a smaller version of what he is now.'

Ray's pride is clear even if his hindsight is blurred a little by it. 'They used to call him the one-man team, and that was Ian. He'd do all the scoring, all the tries, all the tackling ... That's just the way he was. He always wanted to be the best.' And where did he get these skills? 'Not from us,' Ray and Jean chime in unison. Ray calls himself a 'Norm'—the sports version of a couch potato. But he wouldn't tell you even if he had been a brilliant sportsman. In his day he'd been an avid boxer, an amateur title holder in the UK.

Ray encouraged Ian's sporting inclinations. According to Julie, 'Mum and Dad were always prepared to get up at the crack of dawn to take them wherever they had to go. Dad travelled anywhere to where Ian was playing. That's just the way they are.' Even when Ian was only small, Dave noticed that 'he had already done laps around the oval before training started. Our kids used to hate going for a run around the oval. He was *always* running around the oval. He was constantly training—dedicated even then. Ray dropped him down, and Ray would be standing on the fence, or sitting in the car. He wasn't one of those parents that used to get on the field and scream out. But he always supported Ian and, you know, Ray was a tough sort of a fellow too. I know a couple of times when he was on the sideline, he would yell out.' But there was one incident where Ray got pretty riled at the opposing side's coach, who was a little too loud (and drunk) for Ray's liking. 'Ray was going to belt him, and the bloke was younger than Ray. But that is the sort of fellow Ray can be, like Ian. They can be cool, and they are quiet. But I would hate to be on the wrong side of Ray at the wrong time.'

There was another time that Dave thought Ray was going to lose his cool, when he took Ian off one match. 'I thought Ray was going to job me! He was bigger than me at that time and I thought my only chance was to slam the [car] door on his foot or something. (I was sitting in my car.) I said, "This is not the first time he's going to be taken off." Ray had been concerned that Ian wouldn't realise the reason he was coming off. He might have thought he was doing the wrong thing or something. But he had already scored quite a few points, and we were well in front, and I just thought I would pull him off and give somebody else a run.'

Ray concedes that 'ever since he was a kid I'd say—well, all fathers probably say it. I used to have a mate whose son played football and we'd both say it—"My son's going to play for Australia". I thought it of Ian for the simple reason he could never do enough!'

Even if Ian was sick, he would be dressed and ready to play, insisting on playing. Dave recalls, 'Once we were getting beat. I was reluctant to put him on, but I did. He scored the points and we won the game.' Ian is dismissive of such commendation. 'Any kid is like that.' Dave sees it differently. 'I know at times when he was fit, he was in such pain because he used to tackle himself to a standstill.'

Ian concedes and smiles at the memory of his determination. 'One day we had a game at Pioneer Park down Malabar way. I wouldn't have been more than nine or ten. Towards the end of the game I collapsed. Blacked out. I was at that stage where I was so exhausted that I couldn't get enough air into my lungs, and I was just standing there gasping for air. I was only a kid and you don't know why you're feeling like that. I just fell to the ground. Blacked out. Dave snapped me out of it.' He laughs. 'But I got back up and finished the game! At that stage I was playing second row or lock. And I wasn't very big then. For my age. I didn't start to shoot up till later. So I always used to have this fear, and every guy would know about it. When you used to play against teams that had big guys, and you'd gasp, "Uuuggh, *he* can't be *ten*! We can't play him! *Has he got a birth certificate!? Has someone seen his birth certificate?*"

'There used to be a guy nicknamed "Little Joe". He used to play for Mascot. Mate, the guy had a full beard at twelve years old. And when I got out there, even though I had that fear, I always used to feel like I had to be the one to tackle him, because unless I did, no-one else was going to do it.'

'And I used to be really superstitious as a kid. The things I used to do! Leading up to the games and that. Like, the way I packed my bag, or the way I'd get my clothes out of my bag! I'd have to put my right boot on first, put my mouthguard in and take it out about five times. Anything I had done the week before I had to try and remember so I could do it the same way again! It's just a kid's paranoia, I s'pose.

'And you know, it's quite strange. I think I used to feel really sorry for the club. Because remember the Diggers had never won a grand final. And they never did. We made two grand finals but we never won them. And it was just that drive to do something we hadn't done. And I used to feel sorry for Dave as coach because he never won a grand final.'

Dave was proud to lose fighting the clean fight. 'We played a game against Zetland once. Ian would remember it. It was a pretty spiteful sort of game. They knew he was the danger man, and they really hit him, really tried to put him out of the ground, virtually did put him out of the ground.' The South Sydney region bred them toughest and, some would say, roughest when it came to rugby league. They were working class, often poor. The football field was the only 'level playing field' many Souths people would know in life, the only place to fight the inequities in their lives. The Souths Junior teams were bred on this culture.

Dave remembers Souths' first grade team, under Ziggy Niszczot's captaincy. 'One night we went out to watch Souths play Manly, and I was told before the game to watch out for the fourth scrum. I waited until the fourth scrum and you should have seen the blue they started. It upset Manly, and Souths won the game!' That was in the rip-roaring days of all-in blues, when players would often converge into a fighting mass, when fisticuffs began on cue, a tactic to unnerve. 'You can't get away with it now. But in those days I actually had one kid taken to hospital after the game. This is when they went up to shake hands *after* the game!'

Ian thinks Dave was a bit over-protective of his wards. 'From Dave's perspective it probably looked rougher than it was. But I think he exaggerates how rough it was. You know how parents and that see everything the other team does, and get upset about it. The problem was we were a tiny team compared to everyone else. There was often nothing dirty about the game. It was just they could just pick us up and throw us around, we were such a small side. And then, if they did play dirty, Dad used to say, "Whatever they do, don't retaliate. Cop it sweet." So if someone hit me, I'd be looking over to the sideline, out the corner of my eye, to my dad, to see if he was watching. Kids do what they're told—good kids, anyway.'

Dave got sick of the kids copping 'a bit of stick' from time to time. 'We got jack of that one day, and one of the fellows had a relative who was mates with Tony Mundine [former Australian middleweight boxing champion], and so they arranged to have Tony Mundine's coach give them a few boxing lessons.' Mark Lyons, later a first-grader, was in the team. He was a champion amateur boxer at that time. Dave laughs at Ian's gall when he recalls, 'They put Mark in the ring, and they asked who else wanted to get in the ring with him, and they all rejected the offer. But then Ian said, "I'll go." So he went into the ring and copped a bit of a hiding, but the fact was, he went into the ring and he stayed there until the session was over.'

'Oh, it was horrible, mate.' Ian winces at the memory even now.

'Mark was a state champ and used to bash every bastard. Back then he used to fight quite a bit. He was a good guy, don't get me wrong. When we went for this boxing lesson, I'd never boxed. When you're fighting on the street you just, you know, throw punches. My dad never came to this but Mark's dad was there. They put me in the ring with Mark, and we had to warm-up, and all that, first, and I was sitting in the corner, doing whatever I was doing. And his father and his coach are over in his corner!' He's laughing now at the absurdity of it. 'We started fighting and I got the shit punched out of me. We had three rounds, and at the end of the rounds they had him in his corner, taking the whole thing really seriously, telling him all this stuff like, "Ian's got his guard down" and "You'll have to get in underneath him, and over the top of him", and I'm sitting there thinking "Fucking, *what*?" because I'm sitting there with a black eye, my nose is bleeding, my lip is bleeding, and they're discussing tactics like I know what I'm doing in the ring! It was hilarious.'

'Me and Mark had a couple of run-ins at training and that, over the years. He always used to act more tough than me. But even as a young kid I used to take the game pretty seriously.' And by this time Ian was captain of the side. 'Anyway, kids do funny things sometimes. During one game, Mark didn't go in and tackle someone. He just let the guy go, and I said to him, "Why didn't you tackle the guy?" And he said, "I didn't want to!"' Ian laughs. 'I got my back up. "Well fuck off! Get off the field then!" He said, "I'm not going." Then he started pushing me around. This was behind the try line. I was like "Mate, we're actually playing a game here. I haven't got time for this. Just get your bag and piss off." Of course, even though we were pretty competitive, I'd have to say that Mark is one of my best friends from rugby league.'

Dave recalls Ian as a 'very kind-hearted sort of kid. One of the things I used to do at training, I used to hold the ball and then I used to just run up slowly and then have all the kids come up and tackle me. I remember it well because the kids used to put everything into it. Punch, kick and really tear into me. So when they eventually got off me, and I had to drag myself off the ground, Ian was always there, asking, "Are you all right, Dave?" All the others had sort of gone back ready to line up and come back at me again, where Ian was always asking me how I was.'

By 1979, Ian had played eight years with the Diggers. Grand final appearances—two. Grand final wins—zero. Dave ponders, 'You know, maybe, if I'd just taught them to be a bit more aggressive, we could have ...'

There is a photo. It's Ian at thirteen. With his trademark cheesey, cheeky grin. A happy kid. He hugs another award. The Club Champion Shield. His sixth in eight years.

TWO

A SON'S SECRETS

A small, neat, perfumed room. The early seventies. Walls covered in pop-icon posters. Lurid, outrageous fashions on skinny, big-haired men. A teenage tabernacle. Ian, a tousled-haired seven-year-old, has invaded his sister's sacrosanct space. Door closed firmly behind him, he is wreaking havoc to candy striped sheets and puce pink terry-towelled bedspread. He is bouncing in rhythm to loud pop music, carried willingly along, with a smile. His performance reaches an ecstatic crescendo of sorts, when a thought takes him. He leans towards one of the posters. He places a gentle kiss, reverently, eyes open, on the glossy two-dimensional lips, as he usually does. And, as usual, they are not responsive. They smile dumbly back from the poster. Les McKeown, of the Bay City Rollers, resplendent in tartan flares, would remain forever oblivious to the favour just bestowed. And in the gravity of the moment, Ian realises that he will never get to really kiss Les, and he still remembers to this day how it made him miserable.

Music was big with the Roberts kids. At home, they would play and dance to records for hours. Ian was the extrovert, the performer in him escaping into the rhythm. 'Ian was a real clown,' says Julie. 'He's always been the same way. Whenever there were school plays he'd always want to be in them, whereas some kids, like me, would be "oh no don't pick me!" He was in *Tommy* one year. He played the Elton

John part. He was never embarrassed to get up in front of everybody and talk or whatever, whereas I was. Ian was different from me and Paul like that. He was fearless back then.'

Julie witnessed his frustration at what topped off his then-skinny frame. 'He had, like, afro hair as a young kid. If he tried growing his hair it would boof out, not like Michael Jackson, but curly. So he couldn't grow his hair long.' Not the go in a surfie suburb during the groovy '70s. Instead he relied on a gorgeous purple body shirt, his particular favourite, and platform shoes, to create a cool look back then. 'He was the skinniest of all of us kids. We were all big-boned except for Ian. But I don't think anyone picked on Ian, ever. I was always sticking up for Paul, but Ian always got on with everybody. Paul was a bit bigger, a bit plump, and people ribbed him. Ian could look after himself.'

From an early age he was volatile and self-defensive. 'I never copped abuse off people. When I was in third class I remember a couple of times I had fights with my brother's friends because they'd called me a "little shit" or something, so I'd have fights with them and get beaten up. In first form, I had a fight with a year 12 bloke. I hit him because he'd done something or another, tripped me I think. I was about thirteen and I was an idiot. If someone said something to me I used to lash out at them. Stand up for myself. And I was no angel.

'When I was about ten I had a fight with this guy, and the kid's dad comes round to my parents' place and tells my dad what I'd done, that I'd shot rocket shooters at his son. Anyway, Dad smacked the shit out of me saying, "You could have hurt that kid! Taken his eyes out!" I'll always remember the next words because I heard them again and again. "Being a man is being responsible for yourself and your actions. You've done that now, and I'm going to punish you for it." I remember that line about being a man just sticking with me and sticking with me for ages afterwards.

'My dad never liked me fighting. "Only fight as a last resort." But I used to be a bit fiery when I was young. "If you do have to fight," my dad would say, "at least go for the big guy." That way you look like you're not afraid of being hurt. And the fight becomes more of a cause. My father's word was law. When I was little he'd always be saying little things like "If you ever lie, your tongue will drop off." I used to run round at school telling everyone that, like it was the most important thing in the world.'

But pretty early on Ian had to start lying to his dad. 'Once dad caught me mucking around with a kid. We were doing, let's just say exploratory stuff—sexual, but we didn't think of it as that, back then. Dad asked me what I was doing. I made something up, and then I waited for something momentous to happen as punishment. Then the boy across the road told my brother what I used to get up to with his brother. We were about five or six. Paul would blackmail me, say he was going to tell Dad. I was terrified. I don't think Paul quite understood what was going on. I didn't even know what was going on. I thought that it was just a stage that naughty boys went through. I supposed I'd just come out of it when the time came for the next stage.

'At school me and one boy would always be sneaking off to the toilets. I'll show you mine if you show me yours type of thing ... I wonder if I was the ringleader? Even at an early age, there always seemed to be one person in particular that I liked, that I had a crush on, and wanted to be around.'

Ian didn't feel he needed to control these natural urges. As he grew older, he closed the door on them so no-one else could see. Like when he pursued his little crush on the Bay City Rollers, alone in his sisters' room. 'One strong memory I have is of the time I heard the words to Rod Stewart's song, "The Killing Of Georgie". I must've been nine maybe, and I went to Mum and Dad and asked them what "gay" meant. I think the song haunted me in a way. But it's just a blank when I try to think of how they explained it, even though I can remember really clearly my curiosity, and wanting to know.' The lyrics must have haunted Ian, with their story of Georgie disappointing his parents and being thrown out of home to fend for himself because he is gay. The boy ends up dead.

All he knew was he felt guilty about something. He atoned for his overall badness by trying to be the perfect brother and son, on the footy field and off. Everyone had to pull together in his close-knit family. 'When I got to about twelve or thirteen, I always used to take Kylie round with me, going fishing, the beach, everything.' Jean had started work at Qantas as a cleaner and Ian became Kylie's official minder. Kylie, who still refers to Ian by his nickname, Ern, recalls: 'Poor Ern, he would have to walk down to my school, after school finished, and pick me up first, so we could catch the bus home to Coogee together. Mum didn't have time to get me as she didn't get home early enough, and, because she started work so early, Ian had to take me to school as well. He never complained. Mum says that he was a bit jealous of me too, being the baby. I kind of took that away from him, kind of thing. But he never showed it. All youngest children are probably spoilt and, if anything, I was spoiled by him.'

'We used to go on these huge treks, even to the city on Ern's Dragster. He fixed a little seat up front for me so he could still pedal and steer. He took me everywhere on that bike. Ian was very into tropical fish at that stage. We used to go buying fish on his racer. I'd have to balance the fish in a plastic bag, while he was riding the bike home!'

'I felt like my sisters were my life,' Ian reflects. With his older brother there was an ongoing competitive struggle which you some-times get the impression Ian helped instigate. 'There was always a rivalry. I was competitive. But my sisters and me have always been really, really close. They spoilt me, and I'd do anything for them. My sisters were my best friends.' Julie would head family expeditions. 'We would always be going in to the museum in College Street, when Mum and Dad were at work of a Saturday afternoon, because it didn't cost anything. Ian just used to love it. He never got bored.' They trekked to the movies a lot too. *Jaws. Rocky. Superman.* One. The originals.

In first form, when Ern was in awe of some of the fourth form girls, he thought this must surely be the next stage in the process of growing up. And the end of his marked interest in boys. Then, wham! He experienced his first love. Gregory lived nearby at South Coogee. 'Greg was like me, a bit rough around the edges. He was really into different sports, and that, too. He was a bit of a tough kid, not like a street kid, but pretty tough. We were just like two soulmates. When I was twelve, we started staying over at each other's places. It felt pretty intense, even though, at the time, I didn't properly understand why.' Ian felt then, that the feelings and desires he had been experiencing were no phase. The two boys gave their love words, but it was their secret. 'We talked about our feelings, freely. We would tell each other how much we felt for each other. It felt so powerful, the whole experience. Knowing for sure what I was didn't bother me, because it felt so right and natural, the love we had, you know, and just the way we bonded. The intensity of it. It was so hard for us, though.'

With love came fear. Fear of discovery. Or fear that they might be stopped from seeing each other somehow. 'We always found excuses to sleep together for the night, for me to stay over. It amazes me, when I look back at those years, how we got away with it. I always felt like the passion would somehow show on my face, that people must somehow know, that people could see it in our faces.' But he stuck by his guns. 'Mum would ask questions like "Why do you spend so much time with him?" I'd go, "Because he's my friend."'

'I used to think they would find out. But Mum and Dad were pleased in a way. I was always such a loner in those days. If I wasn't playing with him, I'd be sitting at home on my own watching TV. So at least I had a friend. And really, it's always the last thing people think of, you know, the last thing they expect.'

Or the last thing they *want* to contemplate in their child. 'I remember Dad saying things about homosexuality like "It makes my skin crawl, the thought of doing ... you know." But then, my dad would always encourage me to judge people according to what sort of person they were, not according to their type. He was always trying to get me to think for myself. To make my own decisions and not be led by popular opinion. A lot of it would backfire on him later, but he would tell me that he and Mum would accept whatever friends I had and whoever I bought home.'

Ray's Uncle Charlie, back in London, had been a bachelor all his life. He and his 'friend', who became 'Uncle' Jack, lived together for many years and were an accepted part of the family, included together at big Roberts' gatherings such as Christmas. They didn't make a public show of their affection or speak of their love or embarrass themselves or anyone else. It wasn't talked about. It just was.

At the end of 1979, disaster struck. Ray and Jean bought a house in Botany. It was a bargain too good to turn down. Their own home.

A neat fibro cottage in a quiet street. But too far from Coogee for Ian.

'It was terrible when my family moved. It was really hard to see Greg. I couldn't just be at his place, and there was no excuse I could make to go there all the time, all that way. For months I was just so unhappy that I couldn't be near him as much.'

But you have to remain silent.

'We were at the mercy of other people, we were so young. And the worst part is you can't explain. You can't just say, "I miss the smell and the touch of Greg. I miss him because I love him." You just close over. You have to.' You learn to cry inside. Alone, you become resilient, or you build something that feels like resilience, but is really only a thin fragile shell around a marshmallow interior that hardens over time. 'I guess you get over things faster when you're young. One minute you think you'll die from having such strong feelings and the next the pain is gone. Not that Greg was the only guy, in those years, that I got close to.'

'Sometimes we'd go away on football trips and get billeted. That's how I met one guy, John. I was sharing a room with him. He had the bigger bed and just said, "Do you want to sleep in this bed too?" Then we started kissing and one thing led to another. You know what kids are like." '

In 1977, Ian went to Maroubra Bay High, across from the primary school, where there was more agressive talk of 'pooftas'. In high school it was definitely not a good thing to be.

'One of the sports coaches was always picking on the little guys about being sissies. There was this whole thing that big guys can't be gay, only small or sissy guys. Meanwhile, I was doing it with guys all through high school, with guys in the various sports teams. You get to judge people's interest by eye contact. Then you make friends with them . . . I was never once found out. I was always the best footballer, the best sportsman, never suspected. I probably tried even harder at sports. The hilarious thing was that the coach always tried to make an example of me. I was what everyone should aspire to, because I was just good at sport and had a go at everything and didn't whinge about things when the going got rough.

'An Asian guy, Jamie, used to get bagged by everyone in high school. There was a group of about four or five queers at school, gay guys who were more obvious, and everyone used to ridicule and bag them. And I used to feel real bad inside for not standing up for them. They never used to bag me and I just kept my mouth shut like a lot of others, I suppose. I remember thinking how I should speak up. I used to think they should be doing it to me too, because I liked guys as well. And half the time the guys that they picked on probably weren't even "doing it" yet.'

Ian didn't feel like he belonged anywhere. 'I didn't hang in any group in school, or out of school. I've always done my own thing. I never worried too much about being popular. I had a lot of friends at school, but no-one I used to mix with a lot. I was always friendly to the more obvious gay guys because I thought they were brave, the way the taunting they got seemed like it just deflected off them. Or they didn't let on that it bothered them, they were probably that used to it. I would say "g'day", or whatever. I used to really fancy one of them, actually.'

Kylie's gentle giant was Julie's saint. 'He never had to have, like, the "in" crowd around him. He didn't have to be with the "in" crowd. He was always the same, whether with girls or boys. He didn't care if it was the ugliest or daggiest girl, if he liked that person, it was because he liked that person. It wasn't because they were good-looking or smart, you know, he never cared.'

But he shared the feeling of isolation of most gay kids who realise they are different, even though they don't look or act it. They all manage in whatever ways they can. Feeling alone is the worst part. Like most adolescents, they're not sexually active. And can't understand why the more obvious 'sissies' don't have the good sense or good fortune not to be noticeable. Having the stereotype drummed in at high school is convenient for them. They can point out the gays who wear their sexuality on their sleeve like a pink triangle, and feel relieved that they are not so identifiable. But the really lucky ones are the kids who are in the middle of a hazy and confused adolescence through high school. Kids whose sexuality remains cloistered, so that they escape having to deal consciously with any sexual differences they may feel. Until later. After school. Or after they've left home. Or after they're married. And had kids. It probably all depends on a combination of the strength of their sexual orientation, their character traits, and the extent of their indoctrination during the socialisation process we call growing up.

Ian had a bold unfettered inquisitiveness and an independent spirit that was only encouraged by a loving home environment and a close connection with his dad. He felt the powerful pull of a homosexual identity very early on. Although he knew he was 'bad', according to what he absorbed from his surrounding world, he was safe as long as he hid that part, especially from the people he loved the most. And as long as he excelled in the things that made his dad proud. His biggest nightmare became letting his family down, having them suffer because of what he was.

Most self-aware gay kids would never consider revealing their identity to their parents. Like most, Ian is hazy about the exact incidents that dissuaded him. Idle comments from parents, seeing their reactions to things, hearing their answers to questions about gay songs perhaps, serve as indicators that sex talk is hard enough, without moving into taboo areas. But for some kids who, for one reason or another, divulge their secret while still minors under the law, the consequences can be pretty dire. Being rushed off to some archaic psychiatrist for archaic electro-shock therapy was still a prospect in the '80s. And, apart from other means of control parents exercised in order to 'correct' their kids, it is estimated in 1996 that more than a quarter of Australia's 6000 known gay homeless youth were thrown out when their parents found out they were homosexual. Many end up fleeing to Sydney from suburban and country towns, looking for help and acceptance. Every night 1500 have nowhere to sleep. Statistics of course cannot possibly reveal the real scale of the plight, or the individual horrors suffered.

A defining moment in Ian's gay social awareness occurred when he overheard the maths teacher talking about the Holocaust to another teacher. Ian's ears pricked up when he heard 'gay persecution'. 'I had never heard anything about it. It was like I had discovered this new and terrible secret. Some estimates put it at a million gays rounded up and slaughtered, only 50 years ago. And no-one taught it or talked about it the way they taught about the Jewish deaths. I wanted to know more. It pissed me off when I couldn't find out anything about it. It was like it never happened. That affected me.'

By late puberty, the Bay City Roller fan of old was feeling less celebratory, less exuberant. The things people said and did didn't always add up.

This was Sydney in the late '70s. As Australia was affected by what is generalised as the Sexual Revolution, people could get away with exploring their sexuality more, whether that was bisexuality or homosexuality. Part of the gay population became more bold. More visible. Some gays started to meet more safely at clubs and bars. Not just in secret, at toilets and parks, where they were open to attack. As people got in touch with all variations of heterosexuality and bisexuality, it got a tiny bit less revolting to be gay. Still illegal, but a tiny bit less revolting. A fearful conservative reaction resulted in a polarising of sexuality into 'us' and 'them' categories. The grey areas of bisexuality were shunted aside so that, once again, the real 'menace' of homosexuality could be isolated. The first Mardi Gras erupted into violence as the police tried to stop it as an illegal march. Arrests were made, and the names of those arrested were published by the *Sydney Morning Herald* so everyone knew just who these pooftas were.

A trickle of information and a lot of misinformation reached high schools down Maroubra way. But gay stereotypes were always confirmed. In the paper. On the TV. It always seemed to be 'them'. Either screaming fanatics being dragged off camera, or outrageous, costumed 'weirdos' performing lewdly *for* the camera. So you could look and say, 'Yes, that's right. That's them. That can't be me.' Or 'There's been some terrible mistake. I am a freak of nature. By some disgusting aberration, I am sexually attracted to my own sex, even though I'm not like "them". Yuk. What will I do? Well, apart from keep it quiet for a start.'

The four teenage boys came out of the Hoyts Cinema Complex in George Street into darkness and rain. Wearily bent frames scurried and dodged through the downpour as the boys darted across the street, through hostile traffic.

Once there, three looked round for a missing Ian, in time to see him on the narrow median strip, trapped in a sea of swishing metal, and staring blankly like an animal caught in headlights. Then he was down! Flat! Sprawled, hands hugged closely at his side, along the narrow cement platform that barely saved him from cars hissing by. Nervous and helpless as a million tyres spat filthy soup in his face.

On the other side, the three stared dumbfounded for twenty seconds. Then Ian stood, his front filthy and soaked, and crossed the road.

'Wadja do that for?'

'Look at your clothes, man.'

'Wadaryu gunna do now?'

A clumsy grin on a daubed face, he makes out he was kidding around. A silly prank, they thought.

He walked in at home a mess ... Jean wasn't shocked. A sigh, maybe.

The main thing for Ian was no-one had guessed. He was just a joker, a crazy joker.

He convinced himself he wasn't afraid.

As he grew older, it wasn't unusual for Ian to be playing some prank or getting into trouble. He was the kid who would leave a bath running and flood the house. He could be somewhat accident prone, and at the worst possible times.

Once, when the family lived at Coogee, Paul came back from a ten-day holiday camp.

'He was filthy,' Jean recalls. 'But almost as soon as he walked in the door, Ian started a fight with him. As soon as Paul and Ian got together they'd fight.'

There was a struggle. Paul got his arm caught between chairs. Ian came down on it. Crunch. It was straight to the hospital, where Jean was mortified at having to front with a stinking and filthy son. Ian wasn't popular, just as he wasn't popular after the eighth grade school dance.

'This guy we used to call Big Bird got us some drink,' Ian remembers. 'Cinzano. There was five of us, and we had three bottles of

Cinzano. I was about thirteen or something, so you can imagine. We must have been close to death. And I *hated* alcohol. I absolutely hated it! But you'd hear so much about it, and that's always been my problem—I have a really curious nature. And I didn't know how it was going to affect us. So we were doing it in gulps of five.

'We were passing these bottles around. I didn't even get to the social. We were walking up this hill to the school and we were spewing our hearts up. All over the teachers' shoes too, when we got to school. BBBAAAARRRRHH!! They took me home. Two of them dragged me to the door. My mum opened the door. She looked at me. "Arrghh." She sank. Like "What have you done now?" I got suspended from all school formals forever.

'Apparently when I was blind, at home, I kept mumbling, and all anyone could make out was "Big Bird", "Big Bird". No-one knew what I was on about. Dad asked me later "Who is this big bird?" They were thinking "What, is he talking *Sesame Street* or has he seen a big bird? Has a big bird scared him or something?" My grandmother was out from England and she was taking pictures of me throwing up in this bucket. Laughing her head off.'

Kylie ran round, screaming, 'Leave him alone, leave him alone! He's going to die! He is going to die! Don't take a photo, don't take photos of him! How can you do that when he's going to die. Is he going to die? ... Ian, Ian ... Is he all right?'

'I had the dry heaves for hours.'

When he was old enough, money became Ian's hobby. He saved his dollar notes in an album. He did the paper round. Then there was McDonald's, where the real trouble started. He couldn't wait to be old enough to work there. He started at the Kensington store. Julie remembers: 'He'd come home and say, I made this many patties today, in an hour, and it's beef patties and it's all 100 per cent beef. He used to work, work, work, because he wanted to get money, money, money.'

'I really enjoyed working there,' he reflects. 'I used to work all these incredible hours. You know how you get double time and a half? I used to work there Boxing Day, New Year's Day, Christmas Day. I didn't care when it was.

'I did everything but I would *never* do the French fries. I used to tell the bloke "I can't do French fries!" I'd always get someone else to do them, because I used to think I was going to burn myself from the fat. I thought I would put my hand in the boiling fat. I never told anyone that. It would sound too stupid to be believed.

'Then came the time when I was serving a woman, one day. I took her order and I was getting her a thickshake when she screamed out, "Oh can I have fries as well?" I had the thickshake in my hand when she said that, and IT started when I went and got the chips. I had these chips, and then I've started shaking, and the chips are going everywhere, and the drink spilt and splashed on the woman, and this woman was there going "Woooaahhhh", and trying to get away from me. Later, I was sitting in the manager's office because the lady had reported me, going "This boy's being silly." I apologised. I was really embarrassed and said "I tripped" or something, because they didn't know.'

Know about IT, that is. IT was a new thing bothering Ian. Now it was keeping the boys thing secret, and keeping IT secret. He didn't mean for it to become a secret, but that's how it panned out. 'I've always eaten cereals at night. One night when we were still living at Coogee, I was sitting on the lounge eating, and my dad was lying on the floor sort of between my feet. Watching television. All of a sudden, I just started wobbling, and all the milk and shit started going all over my dad's back! He yells, "What are you doing, you silly bastard? What are you doing, cut it out!" Julie remembers the incident. 'We thought he was showing off, and that's why he would do it.' So it was a bad thing, this thing, too, and he kept it to himself.

Ian explains what it was like. 'You know when you're lying down, and you jump straight up, how dizzy you get? It was kind of like that, at first, but much more intense. I used to think I was having dizzy spells. When we moved to Botany, I used to have these dizzy spells, where I'd jump up, then I'd fall over, collapse and bash my head against the furniture, or the wall or something. Once, when there was no-one home, I was watching TV and I went into the kitchen to get something, and halfway through the corridor I fell over and smashed my forehead against the wall. I was lying there on the floor. The dizzy spell thing was still happening, except by this stage it had started to get worse, so I was just laying there. Sometimes I'd feel bad and quiver, but I was still aware of what was going on. It wasn't painful at all, but I used to do some stupid things.

'I learnt to sense when it was coming on. I'd start to feel it through my body. I can't explain the feeling, I just knew, and I would start to lose sense of my brain. Then I'd lose control of things I was holding or doing with my body, for about ten or twenty seconds. I kind of went blank while my arms did whatever they wanted. Like I would just throw something I was holding. I would lose all control. Because at this stage no-one believed me, they thought I was being a dickhead. So, if I ever felt it coming on, and I was holding something hot, I would make sure I would put it on the ground, then I would go and sit down on the floor or something. It was quite embarrassing. I started to know to get myself out of trouble, because I'd spill coffee over myself and hurt myself sometimes. In the end, I was doing this up to twenty times a day!

'At first I tried to tell mum and dad, but because I would come right quickly at that stage, and I wasn't having frequent attacks, they thought I was having them on. I was always pulling pranks after all "Stop making a fool of us", they'd say. Or "You're just showing off". I thought I was going a little crazy. A little mad.'

Mind you, he didn't exactly try to tell them too hard. Ian was a bit ashamed of his weakness. He thought it could mean trouble, he was better at secrets than trouble. In fact he went to extraordinary lengths to conceal his pain and fear. 'I used to burn myself in the shower sometimes. Have the hot on and not be able to turn the cold on. But nothing too bad happened.'

He couldn't escape it. 'At school, during an exam once, my arm just started shooting all over the place. My pen ripped though the exam paper and tore it and crumpled it up. Walking down the stairs between classes, I had it happen halfway down. My arms started shaking and my legs gave way, and I just crashed down the stairs. Then I made out like I had tripped.'

His crisis management was pretty primitive. Rule One was 'Be brave'. Rule Two was 'Ignore it and hopefully it will go away'. He did his best to absorb the affliction into his daily routine. 'It isn't anything,' he told himself. 'It's just part of me, something I do. It's nothing.' The thought that it really was *something* was too terrifying to contemplate.

But Julie was watching. On the school holidays at the end of 1979, she was around the most. They would go to the beach together. She knew something was troubling him whenever he raced off all of a sudden. With a much younger Kylie, Ian could just get her to knock him back to his senses if ever he started to go 'strange': 'Because he knew when he was about to have it, he'd go "Hit me out of them", and me, being young, tried to do what he said!' Julie wasn't as easily manipulated. 'After a few months,' Ian recalls, 'Julie picked up that I was doing it that often. She'd see me go and sit down in a corner somewhere and say, "What are you doing that for?" and I'd say "It's nothing, I'm just tired." But she could see that I used to get like a really blank stare on my face.'

By Christmas, 1979, 'Julie knew that I wasn't mucking around and for a while leading up to Boxing Day, every time it used to happen, she would say, if someone was around, "Look! He's doing it now!" or, if I started to get clumsy, she'd say, "He's going to do it now, you watch". She used to get really upset because she was the only one that believed me. On Boxing Day, I was changing records at my auntie's place when Julie screamed out: "HE'S DOING IT, HE'S DOING IT." As she was saying that, I was scratching the needle right across the record, and she burst into tears. That's the first time Mum and Dad actually knew there was something wrong.'

Ian's family huddled around him. Everyone seemed to be crying. This must be serious, he thought. So now he really tasted panic. He cried too. His heart raced with the terror that swept through him. Is this dying-type serious? Ray and Jean were berating themselves for not realising sooner.

And Ian hated the real fuss. That sort of attention made him nervous. The attention you get when something is wrong. 'I was relieved I wasn't mad, that I hadn't been imagining things all that time. But I don't know what was worse. When my mum got upset, I realised the importance of what was happening.

'We went to the doctor and he said, "Your condition is nerves. There is not much you can do."

'We went to another doctor, a specialist, at Matraville. They were doing all these tests, and he was talking to Mum and Dad, and as he was talking I said, "It's going to happen! It's going to happen!" And he actually saw it.'

January 2, 1980, was when it happened big time. It was early morning, and the family were all in bed when the house shuddered violently from what felt like the clumsy footsteps of a giant. Seconds later Paul burst through the door of his parents' room, 'IAN'S SHAKING THE BED, DAD! HE'S SHAKING THE BED!' Ray and Jean rushed into the boys' room. Ian lay convulsing furiously, his body contorted, his face convulsed with panic. Ray had seen such a convulsion, in the navy. 'The doctor had warned what could happen to Ian, so when it happened first, and he was in bed, all I had to do was make sure he didn't fall out.'

Ian still shudders at the memory of his helplessness. His utter terror. 'I couldn't talk or anything. I remember going into it and jumping around all over the place. My brother grabbed me, saying "What's the matter?" and went off to get Dad, and Dad came in and was holding me down. Then he took me off the bed and put me on the floor. I was exhausted, really exhausted, once it had finished. I have never been that exhausted. It probably only went for a few minutes ... Then, after I'd been on the floor a while, it happened again! And I remember screaming: "DAD, I DON'T WANT TO DIE! I DON'T WANT TO DIE!"'

Ian had seen death. Once. At camp, a boy had drowned. Ian was there when his body was pulled from the water. Blue and still. Eyes wide open, staring blankly, just like he did when his thing attacked him. At home after the drowning, Ray tried to get him to talk about it. But he never would.

The ambulance came. Ian was still, totally spent. Frozen in fear. There was an eerie stunned quiet. A calm after the storm. The ambulancemen came into Ian's room. 'How many fingers am I holding up?' one of them asked. He held up three fingers.

'Tell him three, Ian! Tell him three!' Kylie instantly pleaded. She had to save her brother.

'They carried me out and I was coming in and out of consciousness. My dad got into the ambulance and he held my hand tight. As soon as he held my hand, I felt warm and safe. As I came in and out of consciousness, I saw my dad. He would talk to me and even though I was terrified and I still thought I was going to die, I felt safe.'

At the Prince of Wales Hospital in Randwick, a series of tests was carried out. And experiments with drug dosages. Everyone was frightened and on edge. Defensive. Julie cracked more than once. 'The nurse was writing her report and I was watching her like a hawk to make sure they knew what they were doing. She was saying Ian's eyes rolled back and all this stuff, and I felt like she was exaggerating the way she was describing it, and I said, "They did not! Don't make him out to be some ... epileptic!"'

But he was. When he was admitted to hospital, the admitting diagnosis read 'Epilepsy for investigations'. And the nurses kept fit charts.

1500hrs—fit of arms and legs shaking for 10 sec. Eyes rolling from side to side. Patient standing on feet ... not aware of surroundings ...
1830—fit of arms and legs ... nostrils flare ...
2005—lasted 20 seconds. Fixed facial expression—stepping from side to side standing upright—steadied by father—would have overbalanced if not held ... slightly dizzy for 30 secs after attack ...

When the doctors asked questions to establish the history of the illness, Ian didn't divulge too much. He didn't want to make more of this than he had to, or make it look like he'd been aware of his problem as long as he had. Hospital reports summarised the months and months of Ian's secret, making it official. It all appeared so elementary on paper. The report by the staff paediatrician, Dr Berdoukas, written in February, and sent to Dr Krejci, the family doctor in Coogee, read:

Ian was admitted to this hospital on January 2 subsequent to a generalised convulsion. For three months subsequent to a head injury four months ago he had had episodes lasting approximately 5 seconds and about 2–5 a day where he had absences. During these attacks he either stared blankly into space or had rhythmical movements of his arms and legs. He was aware of his surroundings and could hear people speak to him but he couldn't answer and they sounded distant. During his hospital admission he had further convulsions. However, a CAT scan was negative and the EEG [electroencephalograph] showed bilateral temporal focus. He was commenced on Tegretol 200mg twice a day to increase to 600mg twice a day ...

I reviewed him on 29th January 1980 and he had been quite well except that he had 3–4 very short turns ten days prior ... and he had lost his balance the day before. He takes his tablet religiously and initially had a fair bit of drowsiness with them ... I have organised for him to have another serum tegretol level done in three weeks time and I will review him again ...

Ian is having quite a few problems in adjusting to having epilepsy and for this reason I am asking for fairly frequent reviews to help him cope with this.

The family were in shock. Ian was in shock. 'I thought somehow I'd made the whole thing worse. The attacks were mild when the thing was my secret. After all, it was when everyone found out that they became worse. It was like a nightmare when everyone was involved and worried. And a nightmare having a doctor standing there telling you what you could and couldn't do in your life, from now on. I had to be supervised everywhere. There was to be no more football. I couldn't do this anymore. I couldn't do that anymore—things I had been doing and taking for granted for years. I wouldn't be able to drive. I couldn't become an electrician, which was what I had been thinking of doing. It was like being given a prison sentence.'

There were post-mortems all round. Ray berated himself. He thought back to the time, in London, he was babysitting the kids. He was watching TV. Ian was eighteen months and had climbed upstairs. The next second he was downstairs again, having fallen through the bannister, hitting the bottom head-first. In peak-hour traffic Ray had driven like a madman. Over traffic islands and down the wrong side of the road, to hospital. A thorough check-up at the time revealed nothing but a broken tooth. And Ian was always getting concussion in football. He was famous for playing with it. And then not remembering playing. Now this. Maybe this was related. Maybe *he* had ruined his son's potential, Ray thought. And he felt for his son.

As parents, Ray and Jean had to be positive. Jean recalls, 'We told him that Tony Greig [the cricketer] was an epileptic, and we used to say, "You're all right. Nothing's going to change. You can still do whatever you want to do". But he was very traumatised by the whole experience.'

Outpatient treatment monitored Ian's turns and his tegretol levels. On 29 February, 1980, Dr Berdoukas wrote to Dr. Krejci: *Things seem to have settled down, and everybody seems to be accepting Ian's problem much better in the family, and, in particular, Ian seems to be much more accepting of it.*

July 16, 1980: *I find him very well and I think he and his father are adjusting well to his problems.*

Julie didn't think he adjusted. 'After the epilepsy, his whole personality changed. He just wasn't the same Ian. He was quieter, more introverted. He wasn't as crazy. He didn't muck around as much. He did do his Mick Jagger performance at my wedding though, which was that year.'

It wasn't just the epilepsy, however. It was all of his adolescence. The physical challenges. The emotional challenges. It was all troubling. In 1980 he was a known epileptic. And still a secret homosexual. And there are no books or instructions on how to smoothly bottle up that big secret, because there is no way. Self-denial was out of the question. But the pressure felt like it was pushing in on him. And what is the physics of that? For every action, there is an equal and opposite reaction. There had to be an outlet.

THREE

A SPORTING CHANCE

Ian couldn't let his epilepsy get in the way of sport. Sport was all he had, it seemed. So he ignored his condition and simply didn't tell anyone. He was adamant that no-one should know.

Ian was set adrift in 1980, too, when the Maroubra Diggers folded. Dave Johnson recalls, 'We just couldn't get the team back together again. A couple of the fellows went back to rugby union, and one of our best footballers became a professional surfer.'

For boys like Ian, Dave and the team were a big part of their lives. Ian respected Dave like a second father. And, more importantly, Dave respected him. Dispiritedly, he played E-grade with 'Kenso', Kensington Rugby Juniors, that year, still in the same Souths Juniors comp.

The medical monitoring continued. In fact it continued for years.

January 15, 1981. Dr Berdoukas to Dr Krejci: *He seems to be having daily absences ... on the day I saw him he had an episode where he lost consciousness completely for a few seconds and fell to the floor ... it is worthwhile increasing his dosage in an attempt to reduce his 'turns' rather than adding new drugs at this stage.*

Ian trialled for Mascot in '81. This was the team with the biggest guys, the team that had been the Diggers' nemesis. The coach, and later president of the club, was Frank Cookson. Wily Frank personified that South Sydney working-class paradox you find in the real triers that the breed produced in the '50s and '60s. Humility mixed with a quiet confidence. He is a working-class gentleman of the first order, a

44

quiet listener when you're speaking on your subject, but he pelts along on when he's on his, reeling off dates and incidents as though he's reading them out. In a monotone, and never allowing himself to stray into emotion, he tells a good yarn and you don't recognise the hyperbole until much later.

'The first time I saw Ian, he came to the trials in a bloody Coogee Bay jumper! And everyone else was wearing Mascot jumpers! I said, "With the jumper you've got on, you'd want to stand out as a player!" And he did. He played very well.

'He could play the game, that's for sure, and I knew who he was, but I didn't put it together till later. I remembered I saw him play against Mascot at Kenso oval the year before, and we beat them in heavy weather. He used to play lock forward for Maroubra Diggers and they'd never won a comp. As a matter of fact I felt sorry for them—the only times they got to a grand final, they played Mascot!'

Frank and Mascot were big time for Ian. He had found another surrogate father in Frank, whom he quickly relied on and trusted wholeheartedly.

In '81, Ian played in D-grade. Still a forward, but at prop for the first time, where Frank decided he could utilise Ian's tenacity—even though he was considered exceptionally tall and lean for that position.

The prop is a complex position, demanding physically and mentally. Former Test prop Kevin Ryan once said, 'The prop has to look after his hooker, tie up the middle in defence, take the ball up, back up other forwards, and get rid of the ball, and the only secret to success is to be fit and hard.' A good prop will attract a lot of opponents, so forward movement and off-loading become arduous. Attitude is crucial. 'It's all mental. They have to realise they are in the position which controls the game. It's really the place where the thinkers have to be.' The rewards for a good prop? A feeling of power, control, and invincibility. Ian needed to feel all those things in his life.

'The first year he played,' Frank recalls, 'one of his mates who was a good year older than Ian won the best and fairest by a good margin, and beat Joey Thomas (who later played first grade and City of Origin). We were a bit concerned that Ian didn't get a trophy, because every game he played, he wasn't the best player, but he was *always* consistent. Just the one standard, all the time! So they put up a trophy that year for the most consistent player!'

Ian showed his medical condition no mercy. He continued his punishing football regime and was an impatient outpatient, continually trying to shrug the whole thing off. On 14 December 1981, Dr. Berdoukas wrote: '*Extremely fit—training for football ... Getting an apprenticeship at ICI*'.

In Frank's opinion, 'Playing in a good team allowed him to do more. I mean, when he was playing in a team where one player is good, you expect him to bash and barge and do this and that. At Mascot, he was more relaxed in his game, I feel. Playing with good players brings out the best in good players too. Of course, he did get to be an outstanding player, probably the following year, I think, when he played D-grade again, and Neil Haywood coached him. I was president of Mascot at the time, so I saw him play just about every week, and he was starting to really excel.'

Ian became a footballer who was driven. Who, or rather what, was driving was another question altogether. 'He was like a lot of kids in those days,' Frank reckons. He was totally dedicated to the game. One part of the season he got picked to play as fullback for Australia in the union side, the schoolboys' union competition. He knocked it back just to play his club football.

'We used to train them pretty hard. That's part of the deal. If you didn't train, no matter what happened, you didn't play, irrespective of who you were or what you were. A couple of blokes used to slack off, or turn up late at times, so the whole team had to do extra, half a training session extra, to make up for these blokes. Some of them used to whinge doing the extra if someone was a couple of minutes late, but I never got a word out of Ian. He always copped it. He was a very, very good trainer.'

'Ian was that dedicated, to get himself fit, he would often go on a road run to Brighton, or Dolls Point or something [from Botany]. Take his dog with him. Half bull terrier and half I don't know what, a bloody big lump of a thing, though! ... It used to go with him and it would only get halfway and it would get tired, so he had to pick it up and carry it! And he'd carry it and run, too!'

'Looking back,' Ian says, 'I think in some ways, Frank was the best coach I have ever had. He had a real sense of professionalism. He also had a real sense of fairness.'

Frank knew that to hone good footballers, he had to hone self-discipline. 'I knew blokes with the ability to make it that don't train properly. When it comes to the pinch they don't have what it takes to go on with it. Look at Kieran Perkins and those people. That's ten hours a day or something. And tennis players, gettting off with jet lag and playing the next day. They're playing tremendous tennis in ten or twelve countries in three months! That's the difference between the good ones, the good ones that are going to make it, and the good ones that are not.

'I look and say, right, there is a person with outstanding potential. He must realise it himself. And maybe if he didn't have that little extra ability, he might drop off. There are many who might be satisfied at what they have achieved at certain levels. But, if you have that bit extra, well, you have got to go all the way, I think.'

All the way to wherever your drive pushes you.

'Ian was born with this drive,' Dave Johnson reckons. 'He was born to be a good footballer. I believe 90 per cent of your play you are born with. And Ian was born with that natural ability to be able to read a game.'

He could also translate natural ability into any sport. Ian and Kylie did karate together at St Matthew's Church, around the corner in Botany, where Bill Kerr, one of the highest ranking practitioners in Australia and a work colleague of Ray's, took classes. Ian loved karate and dedicated himself to it for a while. There was a challenge to master complex technical skills. He was a good basketballer too and Frank remembers 'a question mark hung over whether he played football or basketball, at one stage'. However, Ray advised him to stay with football.

Football had become a big part of Ian's relationship with his dad, part of their special bond. 'Maybe I pushed a bit hard,' Ray reflects. 'I mean, he probably blames me for some of the things that he does. I used to say to him, "If you do anything, if you can't do your best, don't bother starting." But it's not like we haven't said that to all of the kids. Just from that little seed, it's just grown from there. But Ian was always a bit hard on himself. He'd always made certain he was good, at anything, and if he wasn't good enough, he'd practise and he'd practise until he was. He never got disheartened when he got beaten. He'd always know he'd done his best. With football, though, I just don't think Ian wanted to get beaten.'

Ray's adages were full of good efficient advice. And Ian was devoted to earning Ray's approval, to being seen as a good boy, to proving himself in the eyes of the respected authority. He was compensating because he thought deep down he was 'bad'. He needed to prove himself worthy—to others and to himself. It didn't matter that that meant busting his gut. He couldn't stand not being able to participate well. If he was sick, or injured, he was impatient. Illness was his Achilles heel. It could cost him his salvation. The limitations his epilepsy sought to impose only increased his determination to ignore any constraints. Kylie was worried by what came across like a kind of lunatic bravado. 'It was pretty scary when we were at the beach. We used to go to the beach all the time, and Ern would be out in the water, without a care, way out in the water! We were petrified that he would have a seizure. We used to watch him all the time.

'We learnt his medication by heart. Every morning we would be "Ian, have you taken your tablet?" Every morning! All of us!

'In the end, he said, "I'm not taking any! I don't need it any more, I'm not taking it!"

'And he didn't take it! He just sort of said, "I'm all right now", and that was the end of the story as far as he was concerned. We were the ones freaking!'

October 18, 1982, a letter to Dr G. Wise, paediatric neurologist, Prince of Wales, from Dr Berdoukas, read:

He maintained fairly good tegretol levels until recently when he started to lapse taking his therapy ... following a week when he went away and did not take his tablets. He was wondering whether he might be able to stop treatment and that possibly there will not be a recurrence of the fits. I have organised another EEG.

Ian was his own masochistic coach. He set his finish line further and further away. Not that he ever realised he was doing it, or what he was running towards. Or away from. People can get chased by their own drive. As Keiran Perkins once said of his swimming career, 'I've always wished I had a fast-forward button, so I could just hit that button and get to the end of it. I wish it was all over.'

He attacked any perceived shortcoming. To balance his growth upward, he joined a gym. He experimented with diet. He wanted lean muscle. He wanted to keep his speed and agility, and increase his explosive power, his strength. Jean was under strict supervision in the kitchen. 'When he really started getting into training, he started getting into all this calorie business. He used to tell me exactly what I had to make him for his breakfast. I used to have to cook these horrible buckwheat pancakes. All dry and no fat! He would have half a dozen eggs, but you'd have to take the yolk out. He used to make all those drinks with powders.' Ray rolls his eyes, raises his heavy brow and tosses his head back in a gesture of exhaustion at Ian's fanaticism. 'Even when he was still reasonably young, he had to have what he wanted, rather that what we had, for meals.'

It paid off. He was on his way, according to Frank. 'He mainly missed the '83 season. So he played a second year of C grade and he was pretty much on his way by then. In 1981 he was a good player. By 1984 I thought he was a player that would go at least to first grade. I had no doubt about that. He was a very good defensive player, but for the first time, unloading the ball, he had people who could run off him.' He was practising and developing skills. Mario Fenech, who was a few years ahead of Ian at Mascot, first saw Ian in '81. 'I likened him to a young foal that's just been born, with gangly legs. I said to Craig Coleman that Ian was going to be a great player of the future. He was thin, but like a young foal, was going to develop into a great athlete, very mobile, very strong. Then my belief was confirmed a year or two later when he looked like he was going to be very good. Ian had that rare quality of being quite strong, while looking gangly, with a strong will and constitution.'

Props were mostly squat and sturdy looking. For Frank, Ian's irregularity combined with his ability was an achievement at the same time as it was a bit of a chuckle. 'Here, you have got this big gangly kid who used to remind you of that bloke in the bloody *Adams Family*, the way he used to get around, because he wasn't graceful off the field, he had big feet, long legs, and he didn't look coordinated, even though he was.'

Ray and Ian only ever told one official about Ian's epilepsy, and then only because he was touring, playing Matthew Shield representative football, and someone had to know. But Frank saw that Ian was battling handicaps, besides his build. 'He had a lot of concussion in football. He evidently used to get it when he was just a kid too. All the way through he's been plagued by it. People don't get it as much as he did, and once you start getting it all the time ...'

Ian fought injury like he fought sickness. Frank reckons he almost willed his body to repair itself quickly. 'His recuperative powers from injury were astronomic! I remember when he first came to Mascot. He did his ankle in on a Saturday. Healing usually takes three to four weeks. He would be back on the field the next week! This was a ligament injury in his ankle! And ligaments don't recover overnight. And he was back the next week!'

In 1983, the first chink appeared in Ian's football armour. 'It was a game at Kensington Oval. I remember tackling someone and he spun round and trod on my foot ... CRACK! It just snapped!' He laughs. 'I looked at my ankle, and it was sitting at right angles to my leg! I was thinking "Oh-Oh! What have I done?" A trainer came over and he was saying, "It's OK, it's OK." You get to a point where you are in so *much* pain you don't even know that it's pain, you know what I mean? And he says, "You've just twisted your ankle. You'll be all right." And he moved my ankle back into place and it didn't hurt that much. He taped my foot up, with that white tape all over the boot, trying to support my ankle with the tape. He said, "You should be right now. Get on with the game!"

'I thought, "Well, this can't be right!", because at that stage I can start to feel my leg swell or whatever happens in there. I was in tears, too, but I'm thinking, "Everyone is watching me" and I didn't want them thinking I was a wimp. So for about probably 30 seconds I tried to get back into the play. I'm hopping round the field on one leg. I couldn't *get* anywhere!

'Finally, they took me off, and left me on the side of the field.

Eventually a proper doctor comes along and says, "Look! He's obviously broken his ankle!" They had to cut my boot off, my foot was so swollen.'

That knocked Ian out for the rest of the season. 'They would have won that year if he had played,' according to Frank. 'It would have been the difference between winning and losing. We won C grade the following year that he played, that I coached them. In 1984.'

By 1985, Ian had played in nearly every junior representative title, Matthew Shield at thirteen, S.G. Ball at fifteen, and President's Cup in both 1984 and 1985. Jersey Flegg was the only rep competition he missed.

Throughout 1985 it was football and little else. First it was B grade on Saturdays. Then he played for Souths Juniors in President's Cup representative football. Souths made the final against Penrith. Then he played A grade for several games on Sundays, still playing B grade each Saturday.

He moved up to the under 23s, as they were then, for four games, then up into reserve grade for three games. All the time he was being watched. And groomed.

Ian finished the 1985 season with Mascot, playing with the B grade side he had begun the season with. Not only that. They made the grand final and won it. Ian was awarded Man of the Match. Not only that. The A grade side also made the final and Ian was picked in the side to play, the day *after* the B grade final! Not only did they *also* win the final, but Ian was awarded Man of the Match for that game too. A young Terry Hill watched in awe, that weekend. 'I have never seen anything like it in my life! It is still talked about to this day at Redfern Oval, and around Souths.' Ian had just entered Souths Juniors' folklore.

In August 1983, Dr Berdoukas reported that Ian's medication had ceased in May, and that there had been no further episodes of epilepsy. Two further electroencephalographs had been normal. He expressed confidence that Ian was completely well, and was not likely to be troubled further by epilepsy.

Ian was getting far enough away from the horror now, to be able to laugh at it. There's a lighter side to having a fit in the middle of the road in pouring rain, or falling down the stairs at school, then trying to act cool while pretending you tripped. There's a lighter side to trying to explain tearing up an exam paper. And Ian found it. Now, he quite enjoys relating the bizarre rituals he had invented to avoid detection, and some of the odd situations he got into trying to cover his tracks. He starts. 'Honestly, mate, I could tell you some hilarious stories.' Then he does, chuckling to himself for ages first before he can proceed. He wanted to work so badly enough at fourteen that he invented ways of maintaining his job at McDonald's. But the risks associated with epilepsy still preyed on his mind.

'I'm still terrified of sharp things, knives. I don't run from them. I get a cold shiver sometimes and I just drop a knife if I'm holding it as if it's about to bite me. And heights! Because when we lived at Coogee I was always down the beach, I would never go to the rocks with all the blokes because I was always terrified that if I had an attack, that'd be it. I'll never trust myself near heights. I keep well away from the edge. I think I'm going to just throw myself over. It's the same thing, the cold shiver, the shudder, and I get a recall of some sort.

'Holding babies, that's another thing. I'm scared I'll do something to harm them. There's a thing at the back of your mind that you can't trust that it won't happen again, one more time.'

Ian shudders when he can't stand a thought he gets. It's like a waking nightmare flashing before his eyes. As for the epilepsy, it was as if his epilepsy was pounded into remission, by a sledge hammer will. The seizures had got milder, on the drugs, and then disappeared. This meant he could drive. And leave school and get a trade. Ian got an apprenticeship at Malabar Electrics and, three weeks into year 11, he left school.

He hated his new job. 'I was stuck out at Emu Plains for what seemed like forever, "chasing" all these housing commission places. You chase the bricks out of walls with a grinder, to put the pipes in the walls. I did that for months and months and months. I was basically a glorified labourer. Apprentices do all the shit work. I went to tech once a week at Randwick, opposite Centennial Park. I never actually got to work with electronics, the electrical side of things, except maybe 5 per cent of the time. Everything else was just running pipes up walls or pulling cables through pipes and garbage like that. It was hell. I didn't like it at all. It was good only because you got to meet people on the building sites and that.

'Anyway, after four years of apprenticeship, I qualified. I was twenty. Gradually, I was put in charge of jobs so I didn't have to do the lousy stuff. Basically, though, football was the thing that filled my life.'

He did all the usual stuff, if in a slightly unusual way. Like driving. 'Ian picked us up from the airport once,' Kylie smiles. 'While we were away he had bought this green thing, like an old Corolla. It was a manual, which he had never learnt to drive.' Ian recalls, 'I bought it from a bloke at work, and acted like I knew how to drive it. I must have looked a real idiot driving off. I stalled and jumped the whole way home. I just thought I'd pick up how to drive it as I went.'

'All the way back from the airport,' Kylie continues, 'it was kangaroo hopping. All the way from the airport to Botany! Ian just could not drive it. Mum was saying, "Ian! Will you stop this?! Stop being stupid! Will you stop this!?" Here we were in this beat up little car, kangaroo hopping all the way, bouncing up and down, with Mum screaming "Stop it, Ian", and Ian going "I can't! I can't!"'

Ian is chuckling. 'Mum was going, "Ian, this is a *hope*less car! What sort of car is this you've bought?!"'

Ian had his mates, but he kept his gay sex life a secret thing. Through Kylie he met a couple of Botany locals, Clem and Jo. They started going out a bit. At first they ended up at the clubs and pubs around the South Sydney area, where Ian sometimes wound up in fights.

'I didn't look for fights, not consciously. But I did some reckless things, with no concept of danger. And the weird thing is I hate fighting. I really do. Now, I avoid conflict at all costs. But when push comes to shove, there is a time to defend yourself.' Push just came to shove a lot more often for Ian, back then. 'Jo and Clem, and me, used to go to the Croatian Club. Their families were from Croatia. We were at this club once, when I was seventeen, and I got the shit kicked out of me. We somehow got caught in the middle of this brawl that was going on when I went to walk out of the club. I was going down the stairs and there is this big bloke standing in my way, and I was drunk. It was one of those few occasions I've really drunk. He wouldn't get out of my way and I said, "Mate, could you get out of my way?" He punched me in the head. And I was that drunk I didn't even feel it. I said, "Why did you hit me, you bastard?" and I pushed and kicked him down the steps, and I must've really hurt him because there were about twenty steps.'

The expletives rush in and crowd round the story. Too many to include.

'Next thing, all his fucking mates jumped on me and kicked the shit out of me. They were just kicking me and then when I picked myself up and got outside, as I staggered outside, every bastard was just kinging me. I wanted to go to the police because I was that stuffed up. When I got home, the next day, my mum came in and there was blood all over the pillow and Mum says, "What has happened to you?" because I had cuts and grazes everywhere. I was fucked. I've no idea how many people hit me, I lost count. There have been a few incidents like that. There's that many things, I just forget about them.

'When I was about sixteen, seventeen, eighteen, I used to get beaten up all the time when I used to go out. Me and my mates used to go out in Kogarah, St George, the Kogarah Golf Club, and all those sorts of places. I never used to let anyone say *anything* to me. I wanted to fight everyone. All the time. Over anything! If anyone ever laughed at me I would challenge them . . . I would never hit anyone first, though.'

It was an unconscious thing, but fighting proved he wasn't weak. Backing down from a challenge, any challenge, was unthinkable. His epilepsy humiliated him, as did the weakness society traditionally associated with his sexuality. He felt increasingly embattled and defensive. Fighting was part of his battle for self-approval, the same way that having to excel at everything physical was. It was also a rebellion of sorts, and a release of frustration.

Inside, Ian was a confusion of unformed and unanswered questions about self-worth and self-respect, and masculinity. Bits and pieces of a grand puzzle swirled around his subconscious mind. They formed and re-formed endless fleeting patterns which would change just before he had time to read them. Late adolescence was a confusing time for this homosexual who was revered by everyone around him as the epitome of macho heterosexuality.

'I look back now at my younger days and I can see now there was a battle going on inside the whole time. It would always be important for me to hold it together on the outside. Blend in and that. I think that's why I handled my epilepsy the way I did. I expected myself to live up to a certain standard. I was always trying to run from having to deal with what I thought was me being a fake. I knew I wasn't— well, I thought I knew—but other people would have freaked out or been let down because of me.'

He thought he handled the problem easily and that he was in control of the situation. At least he knew and accepted the truth about himself. So he was much further along than those homosexuals or bisexuals who shut that side of themselves away, without even knowing it.

There were just occasional short-circuits, that's all.

'I was still with Mascot when I walked up Oxford Street one night and these guys were having a go at this old gay bloke. I had a go at them, told them to leave him alone. I was a bit pissed. They told me to piss off but I wasn't going to go. I went over and started furiously pushing them off this guy. Next thing *I'm* the one being bashed up! But this guy, he must've been about forty-something, he didn't help me. I had a fight with these three blokes and I got the shit kicked out of me! I got up and I had a bloody nose and he was just standing there. And they left, laughing. And I said, "Thanks a bloody lot. You just stood there and watched me get the fucking shit kicked out of me!" And he said nothing. Like he just stood there in some sort of shock, like a stunned rabbit. To me it was just a simple kneejerk reaction to lash out. Hit back.' Angry at how others seemed to accept their allotted position at the bottom of the pile, Ian's fists prevented him from seeing that he was doing the same thing in many ways.

Any threat to his family made Ian catatonic with rage. He saw his family as innocents. 'We were at the front of Souths' Juniors, one night. We'd just had a Mascot presentation. I was going to put my mum, dad, Julie and Ken [Julie's husband] in a taxi. Ken walked up the road to get a cab, and while we were waiting these guys came out of the club. I was only sixteen. That will give you an idea of what an idiot I was. My dad was standing off to the side somewhere and I was standing with my mum and sister.' Julie recalls, 'One of the footballers who'd come out of the club made some crude remark to me and Ian leapt to my defence and told him to get lost. Then the guy foolishly said, "What are you going to do, ya pipsqueak?" and shoved Ian and that was all Ian needed. He just charged at this guy—who was much bigger—picked him up and dumped him down on the stairs and then pinned him to the ground and thumped him. The guy had no idea what had hit him. I was so upset, because I didn't want to be the cause of anyone getting hurt plus, of course, Ian was out numbered—not that that worried him at all.' Ian continues: 'I jumped up and I went over and jumped on this Maori bloke's back. My dad had to fight because he had seen what was happening and had come up saying, "What's going on here?" and one of the blokes actually kinged my dad! That's when I tackled that bloke and went wild on him. That's what I was like.'

Fighting and living to tell the tale run in the family. But the big soft kid surfaced as often as the angry and confused one when Ian found himself in environments where he didn't feel he was being challenged. 'I think he was very relaxed when I was around him,' says Frank. 'He got on well with the players. He was always part of a prank. He would always be involved in a joke. He had a very dry sense of humour. He used to laugh at jokes other people didn't think were so funny. He thought things were funny before he gave you the punch line. You'd miss out on the joke sometimes he'd be laughing so much. He was always down at the Mascot Hotel. When I had them, he would've been sixteen, seventeen, so they weren't much drinkers. But they did socialise together. He would come up to the pub to meet people. He was sociable. He went out with his team-mates and was part of the team.

'He was never a great drinker, but when he did get drunk, he got drunk! They had to carry him home on the night he won his first comp in D grade.'

There is a loud burst of laughter from Ian. 'I was doing my Mick

Jagger impersonation at one stage, on one of the tables, legless. Then I got taken home. And my dad got my brother to hold me while he hosed me off in the garden. I was paralytic.'

Eventually, Ian and co. gravitated to some of the really cool inner city clubs. They discovered the Exchange Hotel, and Ian found a passive outlet where he could rebel and revel in an accepting subterranean nightlife without giving himself away.

In its heyday, the Exchange Hotel, on Oxford Street, attracted fringe dwellers. An eclectic mix of people who dared to be different—drag queens, punks, leather. With the latest music, and a party atmosphere, it lured the liberal-minded mainstream. Gays, bis and straights. Lots of girls. It was the type of place that inevitably attracted the curious too. Because the sexuality of the club was mixed, closeted gays could get away with going there under the guise of being cool and hip. This was 1981.

Ian was still at school when he started going there. When he went with guys like Clem, he pretended to be freaked out by the drag queens and 'weirdos'. Secretly, he was the most nervous and excited he had been. At the Exchange he could flirt with his homosexuality right under the noses of his mates. He could be in an environment that didn't require anything of him. This was real fun. Everyone cool. Never fights. People at peace. Ian saw other homosexuals who were not living in secret, but living and loving openly. He began to relax as he connected with an alienated part of himself. He could actually socialise with other gay men without having to feel embarrassed or ashamed.

Ian identified strongly with the new music of this subculture. This was the time of a new wave of tolerance being expressed in a dance beat, the time of Boy George. 'I was wrapped in music by Depeche Mode. I used to get geed up because I identified with where they were coming from. What they were saying felt like it was so much a part of me. Their lyrics maybe don't even mean anything. But it all felt very important to me at the time.' Through the synthesised popping and clanging, and reverbed voices, came a definite message for an isolated young gay man.

Gay youth like Ian, struggling to understand and avoid prejudice in the '80s, adopted Depeche Mode's 'People are People', released in March 1984, as their own peace and love anthem. The lyrics read like a homosexual's lament, even though the band claimed, in interviews, that their music was not directed at, or reflective of, any gay experience. But references to senseless bashings stemming from prejudice, and appeals for justice and equality certainly struck a chord with most gays.

Here was a kind of tribal music. It was so reflective of the still timid voice of Ian's alter-ego, it almost hurt. And he could release some of that hurt on the dance floor. Loving this music was his protest, his acknowledgement of the simmering issues that he didn't yet have the means to consciously explore. He would sing the praises of the band to people in his everyday life for years to come. It was like a coded admission of his sexuality.

Ian adopted the dress code that went with the sound, with his new knowledge. Of course he hid the grungey military jackets and tailored suits in the car boot, so no awkward questions got asked at home. As it was, he got 'Where on earth are you going dressed like that?' in reaction to the little that Ray and Jean did get to see. Ray used to say 'Clothes don't make the man' and 'It doesn't matter what you wear or what you own, I will always be proud of you as long as you're a good man. That's all that counts.' But he was saying that in response to nagging kids wanting all the trendy clothes. Ray probably would've baulked if he'd seen some of Ian's get-ups in the early '80s.

The hidden outfits, the music, The Exchange. This was how Ian dared. His partners up to then were closeted, because there's an unspoken conspiracy of silence between closeted gays. It's worked for thousands of years. 'This sex we've just had didn't happen. I don't know you. You don't know me. We weren't here.' But even so, word starts to get around when the conspiracy leaks, and people talk about what goes on at 'that' place Robbo goes to.

Rumours started at Mascot. Frank thinks he 'knew'. 'I mean, I didn't *know* but I didn't give a damn, so what? I thought. He used to drag a few of the players down to the Exchange with him and they would stir him, you know, "Do you know what this place is, Robbo?" and they'd give him a bit of a bag about it, but you know, they went there, and enjoyed it, too. He used to tell us the Exchange was a fifty-fifty joint. I've never been there. On a cruise once we ran into girls who went there and loved it because all the guys knew how to dance.'

Ian went on trips and cruises with the guys from Mascot. 'I had quite a bit of fun on one cruise. There was a waiter who was serving us. I kept looking at him, and he kept looking back, and towards the end of the trip I just said "Why don't you come out?" They're not supposed to go to the bars, so I met him out on deck somewhere. Then we ended up in his cabin. But I would see all these girls as well, to keep everyone happy.' Keep them off the scent.

But he didn't always try that hard, as Frank recalls. 'Once we all went to Hawaii for a fortnight. We all went out for the first night there. Him and an Aboriginal kid, Brad Webb, who played with us, left the club we were at and went off exploring the town and ended up at some place. Brad told me it was a gay night club. "Of all the night clubs in Honolulu and we found the only bloody gay one on the first night!" We had a laugh about it. They used to make a few jokes about it. I made a few jokes about it myself! Ian came home after only a week, from that holiday. He had been diving and seeing this and seeing that. He's done all he wanted to do, so he came home early.'

In 1982 Ian met a guy through football. Alex. Perfectly Ian's type. Lean, creamy pale skin. Athletically gawky. A rough nut. 'Alex and I used to do a heap of stuff together outside of football. He was into lots of different sports, and I learned all these new skills just because I wanted to spend time with him. He loved horseriding, so I loved horseriding. He loved abseiling, so I started abseiling. He wanted to scuba dive. So I learnt scuba diving.

'One weekend we went away to go rock climbing. We stayed in this motel. We used to always wrestle. He was wrestling with me at the motel and he had his knees on my shoulders and I couldn't get him off. Then he kissed me. He took his shirt off and started kissing me more. I just panicked. It went that far, then it stopped. I know he wanted to go on with it. And I stopped because I felt like he was doing it just because we were close friends. To please me. He must've known I had a crush on him. I just pretended I had to go to the toilet. Then I went outside. I was frightened. I felt like I was in love with Alex for two years. It was the shock that he would go all the way. For me. I didn't really regret walking away. I didn't feel right about it. I thought it would ruin our friendship. I didn't think he was fully homosexual, but guys can be like that. To him, it would have been a good friend he was having sex with. He didn't have a problem with it.

'They always reckon that closeness with guys doesn't happen but it does. It happens with women all the time. They are allowed to explore their sexuality with another woman without it being dirty. For Alex, it wouldn't have been dirty. At that stage we knew each other really well. I mean, for me it was quite natural, but for him it would have been the same as when I have slept with women because I liked them, not because I was lusting after them. And the thing is, it's easier for people to accept that two girls might not be full-on gay, but can have sex, or that a gay guy can have sex with a woman, but a guy who is mostly straight isn't supposed to have sex with a guy. Well, I guess Alex felt free of all that crap. I guess it was me that didn't. For some reason I felt protective of him, and scared of what would happen to our friendship.'

By 1984 Ian was accustomed to unrequited love, or secret love. Love that you feel, but you're not allowed to have. He found it scary to be confronted with the possible consummation of his love for Alex.

Human sexuality has been so maligned, it frightens many. It's been so institutionalised that it's beautiful to too few. Social conditioning tries to create rigid boundaries.

At a time when we're finding out that even much of our personality is genetically determined, it seems more and more certain our sexuality is. And it's not as contained as human social structures and religious principles. It isn't neat and tidy. Unfettered humanity obeys only natural law, and natural law is less judgmental. Theories abound about homosexuality. Because science hasn't yet conclusively proven it to be genetic, and many require proof before they accept it is not just a form of deviancy in behaviour. Most homosexuals, like Ian, feel it. It's self-evident. When no amount of brainwashing, of fear, of subtle social pressure, can remove you from that 'undesirable' part of yourself, when you can't change yourself even though you don't identify with 'sissy' stereotypes, you don't need a theory to tell you it's genetic.

You just need some inner strength that is going to get you through the tunnel of adolescence and out the other end into the less stifling air of independent adulthood, sane. How is it that Peter Allen captures it in that wrenchingly beautiful song? 'Don't cry out loud, just keep it inside. Learn how to hide your feelings.'

The mere fact that you have spent some considerably painful time trying unsuccessfully to eradicate it, praying for it to go away so you can be like everyone else, while going to great lengths to hide it, is proof enough that you didn't freely adopt it ... that it can't just be 'corrected'. But human institutions absorb things much more slowly than the human mind.

Even some gay people prefer to think of their sexuality as their choice, their own mighty rebellion against an upbringing founded on thousands of years of human conformity. Sure, the release from enslavement of women, and the sexual revolution of the '60s, opened up the way for more homosexuals to be brave enough to choose to live homosexually, that is, to *not* get married and pretend to live happily ever after. But the actual sexual inclination that warrants that choice is most likely intricately woven into the fabric of our being. What environmental factors can effect is an unnatural suppression of a natural tendency. The social processes we are made to practise from the day we are born can even enable some homosexuals to avoid a conscious knowledge of their sexuality, until a momentous experience jolts them out of their dream at last, forcing them to confront a sometimes shocking reality. If they choose to live in denial even after that happens, the consequences aren't always happy, for themselves or the society that convinces them to do it. The Roman Catholic church for one, has finally been forced to confront that.

Ian eventually came across theories of the genetic basis of human sexuality that adequately resolved any confusion or questions swirling round his head in 1984. Most of these theories get attacked and vilified. Only time will vindicate them. Kinsey, through his research, reported human sexuality on a scale of one to six, one being straight and six being gay. He reckoned that most humans sit at two or three on the scale, but get regimented by societal interference to act as sixes. He used the scale to explain the huge diversity of sexuality in humans.

Diversity to be glorified. Not shamed. People shouldn't be conditioned to be ashamed of their sexual dimensions, or to be repulsed by behaviour outside the acceptable role models provided by man-made traditions. Provided that behaviour doesn't involve the non-consenting participation of another. Against such conditioning, it is often the strength of the genetic pull of their homosexuality that enables some to realise it. For Ian, the realisation dated way back, too far to remember. All around him were the images of the 'right' way to be. Adolescence was like being on a 'down' escalator, and having to walk up, while everyone else seemed to be relaxing on the 'up' one. Ian knew he wasn't alone, but he was alone in struggling to be the Ian Roberts that only *he* was expected to be.

He knew the negative images of 'poofs' and 'sissies' and 'freaks' were an elaborate lie, because the guys he had sex with didn't fit those descriptions. But, like them, he used the stereotypes to advantage. 'There were always stories about me ever since I was a kid, and they've always been founded, too, because I was always messing around with guys!' In fact, the gay tag stuck to Ian like he was made of teflon. Guys would go: 'Yeah, sure thing, he's gay! Look at him, for fuck's sake. Does he look like a poof to you?' He had the less than slight matter of his size and fighting strength going for him too. There weren't many individuals who would try to openly humiliate him by accusing him of being gay. No-one was going to accuse him of being weak or wimpy. And he wasn't about to let them.

In fact, Ian tended to defend anyone branded as weak, whether because of their sexuality, their size, or any physical disability. He became friends with Lee Slattery, who was a small bloke struggling to play football at Mascot, partly because he felt protective of him. Lee was also the first straight mate to openly offer him unconditional friendship. He took up, in a way, where Alex left off. 'Except that Lee knew I was gay, and was really cool about it. He was a lot younger than me. He'd been at Mascot since he was a kid.'

Lee's family was friends with Bill Kennedy, the manager at Mascot who got Ian his first job as a sparky. When he was eighteen, in 1984, Ian started coaching Lee's team. 'I got roped into it, actually. The guy who was coaching them asked me to come down and give him a hand for a few weeks. Then he stopped coming! My first and last stint at coaching! I hated it, but we ended up making the semis and they weren't expecting to. Anyway, I got to know Lee well. And I remember one day, he must have seen me hanging round with one particular guy at one stage, and I told him ... or, actually, he told *me*! He just came out and said, "You and him are together, aren't you? That's your boyfriend." I was a bit shocked. He was only like fourteen. But it didn't bother him. It was such a strange relief in a way, him knowing.'

Lee was closely connected to that part of Ian which had always been about denying his sexuality. Mascot, football, those were the centre of Ian's life, to date. And here was this cheeky teenager who was a part of all that, who undersood all that, who intuitively under-stood Ian and was prepared to be his friend. For all the uncool people around Mascot, of course, the friendship was the subject of more rumours about Ian. 'Everyone used to think we were having it off, even though we weren't. Lee just didn't mind. I actually felt quite proud of him because people sometimes made fun of him when he was fourteen or fifteen if we ever knocked around together. It was quite hurtful to me, because I never wanted to be the cause of hurt to him. We spent so much time together, and some people were starting to know I was "funny". They knew I was going to "those" clubs and that.

'I had known my sexuality for so long, I was used to lying about it, trying to hide it because I just didn't want people to hate me. Lee was the first non-gay person who accepted it. It just wasn't an issue, maybe because he was so young. He stuck by me. People used to say to him, "You're getting a bit of a name, you spend so much time together, you and an older guy."

'Lee was my best friend and to this day I love him and his family. Whenever I had problems I could go and talk to him. He was just this wonderful outlet. I used to be able to tell him about everything, everyone I was seeing, John and Andrew, a gay couple I had met, and this, that and the other. He understood my whole life, not just bits and pieces of it.'

*

In 1984, the Wran Government in NSW passed a law which meant that Ian was no longer committing a crime when he made love. It didn't immediately change his life, or make it easier. But it was a beginning of hope. Hundreds of years of propaganda and misinformation had passed under the bridge since the teachings of Thomas Aquinas plunged a wavering Christianity into the depths of ignorance and fear about sexuality. He gave homosexuality a zero rating, ranking it alongside cannibalism, bestiality and eating dirt. Ironically, in those days, being declared a deviate either meant torment, or a life tucked away quietly minding your own business in a career in the church.

Homosexuality had been through rough trots prior to this. Rough trots were pretty cyclic. They still are. Gay marriage was made illegal in 342 in the Roman Empire. Mind you, in 1102, the London council was still trying to get across to the population how big a sin anal intercourse was, but the Archbishop of Canterbury stopped them from passing an edict against it. He said that it was so widespread that it couldn't be stamped out and nobody was embarrassed by it anyway. (At that stage the church hadn't yet quite decided just how evil it was. They were still split into teams, St Paul versus the gay clergy.)

So the law was reformed in 1984 but most people's minds weren't. Everything from verbal vilifiation to vigilante-type action against homosexuals went on as usual. Often only homosexuals noticed it. And fear of embarrassment prevented and still prevents the reporting of it. All of which meant that gays remained the number-one low risk target group for hate crimes.

FOUR
SOUTHS FIRST

Around October 1985, not long after his famous grand finals weekend, Ian told his dad he was chucking football in. 'I couldn't tell him why. I just knew I couldn't mix football with being gay. I'd started making friends who were openly gay. Well, they were living with their boyfriends, and not hiding behind other lives.' These were people who understood what Ian had experienced. Not that they sat around sharing experiences. They didn't have to. Their shared history was simply understood.

Ian was growing up. He was finishing his apprenticeship and had even mastered the manual car. 'I was feeling like I didn't want to have to keep sneaking around. I was going out heaps to the Exchange. I knew that if I got into firsts, it could get embarrassing, especially for my family.' He wouldn't forgive himself if they suffered on his account, 'but I couldn't bring myself to tell them, or any straight mates, apart from Lee.'

One night a year or so earlier, Ian had been at the Exchange with Kylie. There were a couple of guys there who he observed discreetly, and they were openly watching him. When he and Kylie left that night, they found a phone number and a message from the guys on the windshield of their car. 'Just throw it away, Ern!' Kylie said, and Ian had to look like he did just that. He screwed up the paper and threw it … straight into his pocket. Later, he called the number and that's how he met Andrew and John. They lived together in Redfern and were the first gay couple he had met. For a confused second, their relationship with Ian was sexual, a bit Chekovian really: Ian liked Andrew and John liked Ian, and Andrew was happy with his relationship with John. But they sorted it all out, and became good friends. 'I started hanging with them. They even used to come round home. They came to the football. Mum and Dad got to know them. Knew they were gay and got to know that they were just nice blokes.' By boldly confronting Ray and Jean with homosexual friends, Ian could achieve surrogate acceptance. '*See, aren't these gay guys nice people?*' He could watch Ray and Jean being warm and hospitable, and respect differences in others, just as they had taught him to do. But he stopped short of totally identifying with his gay friends. And if any fears about Ian's sexuality entered his parents' minds, which was ridiculous anyway, given his 'masculinity', they allayed them by reminding Ian how abhorrent it would be to them. 'I remember watching TV one day, and the video clip to the Bronski Beat's 'Small Town Boy' came on. It's the film clip with the gay guy watching a guy at the swimming pool, and Dad is watching as well, and going, "That's disgusting. That makes me feel sick, that does." I was just squirming inside.' In the video the gay ends up getting bashed by a gang. The police drop him home, and when it comes out that he's gay his father is disgusted and the guy has to leave town.

Still, the period marked the beginning of a coming of age for Ian. Some homosexual kids start asking themselves who their life is to be lived for. Who are they striving for, with their work and effort? They either tell their parents who they are, or run away and try to nurture 'family' relationships or relationships of their own. For many, it's not enough to be ambitious, and alone. After striving for so many years for approval from parents, it's easy for them to feel resentful of the fact that their parents are approving of a child they don't really know, and who they probably wouldn't approve of if they did. Tiny indicators of this, like Ray's idle jibe while watching the Bronski Beat, grew into strong reminders that Ian was striving for approval from someone who was disapproving. Ian found himself in a dilemma that couldn't find expression—a jumble of feelings and counter-feelings, of moods that can come and go over a period of years, and which may never be resolved.

Telling his dad he was quitting football was a sort of vague signal from Ian to Ray that he was having trouble growing up. But Ian wasn't secure enough to risk losing the approval of his family when there was nothing in his life that could come near to replacing them. The message Ray got was garbled and confusing. 'When I told poor Dad my decision about football, he didn't know what to do. He was so disappointed for me. My decision must have seemed irrational to him. He would corner me in the backyard. "You can't just throw away all the hard work you've done, son!" He kept at me and at me. And all I could think was, here he was, he'd been dragged all over the place for years with my football. He'd never complained. Both Mum and Dad had put up with so much.'

As for Ray he was bewildered. 'We didn't care about ourselves. If we had put ourselves out, we'd done that for all of them. But to make it to first-grade standard. That's something *he* did. And it takes dedication. I didn't want to see that work he'd done go to waste.' Ray could see that his son could set himself up through football. That's why he had encouraged Ian to pursue that sport over others.

Pressure was brought to bear from all quarters. Ian knew that both Frank Cookson, and his mate George Piggins, who was to coach Souths firsts in '86, put great stock in him. So did Ray. His boy had worked for a place in the firsts team. He had been groomed for it. Since he set the ball rolling with the Maroubra Lions, trophies and awards as a junior player had followed, along with team barbeques and functions and presentation evenings with seemingly endless speculation by his proud dad, and by proud coaches. By 1986, both Ian and his family were fully blooded South Sydneysiders.

Ray wanted success for Ian. Ian dreaded it for Ray's sake. He knew he didn't fit comfortably into the mould he had helped cast. He had always sought his dad's approval, but he had lied to get it and had to separate the two most important aspects of who he was. Hide them from each other. Now he was in a bind of classic proportions. The irony was, in order to get Ray's approval now, he risked eternal disapproval in the long term. The people to whom he owed the most could be hurt by his exposure on a very public platform.

There were no role models Ian knew of who he could look to for encouragement. He knew other first-graders were gay, and heard rumours from gay people all the time, but the signals he got from them seemed to advocate secrecy, denial, and heterosexual marriage, in order to avoid detection. Ian knew he couldn't be happy living like that. On the other hand, he wanted to follow his football through, not just for others, but for himself. It was his competitive fate. What football provided him with was as much a part of him as his sexuality. 'In the end, I think I didn't want to let anyone down, my dad, people like Frank, people who had put so much into me, with high hopes for me. But a big part of me wanted to see where I could go and I thought, if there's a way of doing this, I'll find it.'

At that stage, Ian wasn't to know how difficult that was going to be, or how much of an impact he was going to make. He would need to utilise all his emotional reserves to forge his way through the quagmire ahead. Naturally, he wouldn't take the easy way, but would open up a path that others would be able to follow, with ease, after him.

Once the proud bastion of struggling workers, immigrants and Aborigines, South Sydney was financially strapped by 1986. Winner of more premierships than any team since the league's inception in 1908, they hadn't won since 1971. This was not good in a game that working-class supporters were encouraged to think was their chance to get square. Football provided their only even playing field against the North Shore privilege of teams like Manly, known derisively as the 'Silvertails'.

In truth, league was always a business, while union, which was amateur, was where privilege really lived. League attracted men who wanted to be paid to play. It originated in England when workers, sick of missing out on weekend work shifts in order to play football, met in pubs and set up a competition that would pay them for their trouble. In Australia, this business was administered by the New South Wales Rugby League, and later the Australian Rugby League, and run by the clubs. The supporters were the consumers. The print media, and later radio and television, advertised the product, eulogising the game and its stars, inventing and feeding club rivalries. Giddying and tantalising headlines coloured an otherwise black-and-white world.

The Rabbitohs, as Souths became known in the days when club members would sell rabbits to raise money, had the reputation of being hard and desperate fighters who took no prisoners. Players were sometimes less than gentlemanly. Whatever you could get away with to unnerve an opponent or to put them off their game, if not out of it, you did. No-one dobbed. Souths were famous for this kind of backplay.

In 1986 league wasn't polished and sanitised with the slick and glamorous marketing that makes it the product it is today. But new technology, like video playback and close-ups that provided hard evidence of foul play, was having legal ramifications. Heads had started to roll, and players like Mario Fenech, Souths captain, were often seen as scapegoats in a clean-up of the game that was taking place in the mid-'80s.

George Piggins personified the spirit of old Souths. An ex-Test star, and former captain of competition-winning Rabbitohs, he was working class through and through and a self-made truckie millionaire. He returned to his beloved team in 1986 as coach, selling up his business and electing to work for a pittance, determined to return the underdogs to their glory days with his straight-shooting approach. Everyone revered George. In *Personal Best*, Mario Fenech wrote: 'He was very basic in his coaching techniques, but he was so honest and likeable ... Out of his own money he bought us new weights equipment, tackling pads and boxing gloves. He paid for new water bottles and ice drums. George even organised to have the showers in the dressing room scrubbed and steam-cleaned so we could have a wash after training. He was hell-bent on lifting the standard in the place. George wore his heart on his sleeve. How couldn't we perform for him? We were like his children.'

Craig 'Tugger' Coleman reminisces about the new start the team made in '86, 'We had a team full of young blokes, young willing blokes who just needed a bit of direction. They'd do anything they were told. And we had some pretty fiery blokes there, who could handle themselves pretty well.' George had also imported Phil Gould, in the twilight of his playing career, for his technical expertise. 'When Phil Gould spoke football,' recalls Tugger, 'we'd never heard that before. He was like an encyclopedia—Where have you been all these years?

we thought. George brought him in for that, I think. He knew he had a good ally in Gould.'

One of the things which kept Souths afloat was its fertile junior competition, which bred a stream of cheap and loyal talent. In '86 Frank helped Ian nut out his first contract—$26,000 a year—and Ian joined a team made up of plenty of Souths Juniors graduates. He was part of George's plan for the club's rejuvenation.

PIGGINS GIVES UNKNOWN GIANT A BREAK
The rawboned youngster has the ball-handling skills and tight play to go all the way, according to Piggins. (RLW February 1986)

The big fellow has been training as well as any of the senior players in the club and Piggins believes he has a very bright future. 'He's certainly big enough and he has the right attitude,' Piggins said last night. (Mirror, February 1986)

After a preliminary game against Wests at Redfern, the press were curious. Curious as to what George would do at Souths, and about this new young front-rower. Souths won their first match of the comp, against St George, 22–4.

BIG LURCH—HE'S A KNOCKOUT
South Sydney prop Ian 'Lurch' Roberts ... matched it with his big name opposites ... Driven by skipper Mario Fenech, the young fellow showed he is one of the finest prop prospects for years. Teammates did not take long to nickname him 'Lurch' after the club's former great front-rower John O'Neill. 'I was very nervous early but Mario Fenech, Phil Gould and Craig Coleman really helped me settle into the game.' (Phil Rothfield, Mirror, 8/3/86)

Ian remembers his first first-grade games as being harrowing: 'I was petrified the first half dozen games. I was thinking, "I just don't belong out here!" It's not panic, it's nerves. That's what people talk about, I guess, when they talk about experience. You lose those nerves the more experience you get. It's just another learning curve. It wasn't a fear of losing that I had when I first played with Souths. It was a personal fear. A fear of failure. Back then, if I played well, and we lost, I was happy. Whereas now if I play terrible and we win I'm happy and if I play good and we win, I'm even happier. Early on it's just your self you are trying to establish.'

GOOD TIMES AHEAD FOR SOUTHS' FANS

George Piggins believes Brad Webb and Ian Roberts can inject some of the '60s magic into the Rabbitohs ... after Souths stunning win over grand finalists St George at Redfern Oval. 'Souths are overdue to produce some outstanding talent ... Roberts could be the start of that revival ... They gave the fans something to cheer about. Not since the days of Bobby McCarthy, Ron Coote, Eric Simms and Paul Sait has Souths produced such outstanding talent,' Piggins said. 'He will go all the way in the game.' Piggins had no hesitation in naming Roberts as a future international. Former Test prop John O'Neill said, 'That was old Souths stuff and exciting to watch.' (RLW, 8/3/86)

'I didn't think I was good enough to be playing first grade, initially. In '85 I thought the only reason I had played any reserve-grade games was because there was a whole lot of injuries. I was basically filling in. I didn't think I deserved to be there. I mean, I played some decent footy. But when I used to play with Maroubra and Mascot, it was like you *are* the team. You really feel like you're a part of it. It wasn't just a personal thing. But when you're graded, all that evaporates. It's like primary school, starting from year one and working your way up. You get to sixth class and you're the top of the school. Then you go to first form at high school and you're a dickhead again. When you're put into first grade, even though it's a team sport, that's when I started to realise that it becomes personal. I was playing in a team, but I felt like I was playing on my own as well. I always worried and thought that I wasn't good enough to be there. I really thought it was just that 'Piggo' had ties with Mascot and knew of me, and I was lucky to get the break, that's all.'

South Sydney rekindled the glories of the past ... Piggins had every reason to be proud of his team. They stuck rigidly to his edict that

there was to be no brawling, and they had to concentrate on their
football. (Alan Clarkson, SMH, 9/3/86)

YOUNGSTERS TAKE ON THE DRAGONS
Roberts, a 20-year-old giant straight out of Souths' junior ranks, was
ready to take anything Saints hulking front-rowers Craig Young and
Pat Jarvis could throw at him in what is traditionally one of the fiercest
games of the season. 'If someone smashes me in the mouth I'll smack
them back,' said Roberts, who backs up his fighting words with a
towering physique. 'You can't let anyone get on top of you—it doesn't
matter if it's Craig Young or whoever. As soon as they see you flinch
a bit they've got you. You can't afford to take a backward step. The
whole thing is to keep coming at them and make them know you mean
business.' (Les Muir, Mirror 5/3/86)

First grade was like nothing else Ian had experienced before. The
game, the psyche of the players. Especially the players in his own team.
'I was like this twenty year old ... stick! And they're all geed up going,
"Mate! If the cunt sticks his finger in your mouth fucking bite the cunt
off. If he's in the bottom of the fucking scrum, *kick* the bastard!" you
know, and I'm sitting there, going "*What* have I gotten myself into?
Fuck, this just isn't *me*!"

'They'd all be, "If you get a fucking chance rip the guy's fucken
eyes out!" and I used to sit there, shaking, going, "ohhh, noo."

'But, those guys were older. Years later, I understood where all
that comes from. How much winning can determine you, to the point
where you'd do *anything*.

'When I first came to grade it was just at the end of that period
when guys just used to give it to each other. Stand toe to toe. And
Souths were renowned. Everyone like Mario, Dave Boyle, Les Davidson. They were tough. Les hits like a Mack truck!

'Special treatment was reserved for someone who'd left Souths to
play somewhere else. Then, they'd all say, "When that maggot gets the
ball, just give it to 'em. Kick him. Fucken' scratch him."

'All that was just starting to be phased out when I made grade.
Guys like Steve Menzies today, you know, who are just superb athletes,

fifteen years ago you wouldn't have seen players of that standard. They would have been cut in half in the backplay. People would get away with horrendous stuff. It was like, you know, just elbow some bloke in the head as they're walking by! Mind you, Steve is good enough that he would have got through that anyway.

'Backplay and stuff was just the way that the administration let the game run. A lot of people thought all that hard-head stuff was what the supporters were coming to see.'

And the press reported the lot so that it resembled an ongoing battle between warriors of mythic proportions:

STUNNER OF 42.—Steelers Wrecked by Rookie 'Lurch'
... all the talk after the match centred around that kid Roberts ... The 6ft 6in giant ... played himself to a standstill and topped South's tackle count with 42 bone-crunching hits ... 'Opposing forwards want to let me know I'm a rookie. They try to get me riled. But I try and cop it sweet and get on with my game. John O'Neill has taught me a lot about niggling and self-preservation.' (Ian Hanson, *Mirror* 16/3/86)

The bravado for the press was a bluff. The right attitude was crucial. Essential for survival. And for Ian, in more ways than one. At twenty, he was front-rowing against some players of awesome reputation and experience. The game was very hard on front-rowers, particularly new ones. Conventional wisdom had it that front rowers mature into the demands of the position in their mid-twenties, although this would change as younger players paved the way for teenage props in later years. Yet Ian displayed a remarkable maturity as well as exceptional ability in the position. Nothing, apart from experience, could prepare him to confront players with notoriety, not just fame. 'I'll never forget that first trial against Wests,' Ian reckons. 'I got almost knocked out just scrumming down! The guys at Wests just grabbed your head and bashed it against theirs for good measure. They were just animals, some of those guys. What's the name of that guy? ... I don't know, but he had a pointy head, and I've got this scar to prove it.'

He laughs and indicates what is now a small line above his eye, but which must have been a massive cut. Wests were the team legendary for their pre-game warm-ups under coach Roy Masters, when players would give each other genuine slaps to 'gee them up' before they went out to play. At least one memorable time, the warm-up in the dressing-room went terribly wrong and the trainers and officials had to break up an all-in team brawl!

Tugger dismisses any modesty Ian might express about his preparedness, and reckons that he could handle himself pretty well. 'On the field he was aggressive. If a fight broke out in the scrum, he'd just fly into them. His approach to tackling someone, well, he'd try and kill them when he hit them, try to break them in half! Off the field, he'd turn around and be sorry if he hurt someone!'

Ian personified what the League was looking for at the time, in order to finesse the brawler out of the game. He was a finely tuned athlete who could look after himself in any situation on the field. And being bred in South Sydney, where fighting was a conduit to survival, he had had his baptism of fire over the years. His physique accentuated that which is special to sport and sportsmen, something ideal which the press immediately homed in on. Naturally long limbed, he was powerfully muscled. In fact he was the personification of an ideal, tall, handsome, lean and graceful in his movements, and his ball handling in play.

He's big, strong and promising. He also seems to have cornered the rugby league pin-up market this season with some justification. As a President's Cup player last year who was thrust into first grade this season, Roberts has adapted amazingly well in a predominantly young South's side that runs on the high octane fuel of enthusiasm. (Ian Walsh with Ray Chesterton, *Mirror 3/5/86*)

And he was young and apparently squeaky clean, a good boy from a humble working-class family.

Ian immediately stood out among the others as a quiet, unassuming, uncomplaining machine of a player. He was like nothing else Mario Fenech had seen. 'Looking back on my career, and I've been playing professionally for fifteen years, something like 284 first grade games, and if you asked me to tell you three or four of the nicest people

I've met, Ian's name comes to mind. I've always found him to be on the quiet side, but when you got to know him, there was a great depth to him. He's a real good-natured bloke, not boastful, and in the environment of football you get a lot of people that mouth off a lot. You know, we're all quite verbal and joking and I must say I don't know anyone that doesn't like Ian. No easy feat in football! George had a very fatherly relationship with Ian. He was the coach but he was very fond of Ian as a bloke, everyone was, because Ian was honest. He came out more after a while, through the joking and the laughing, but he was always very quiet, whereas Craig Coleman and myself would be joking around.'

'We'd go up to the club after the games,' 'Tugger' recalls, 'and have a couple of beers. Ian used to stand there—he'd bring his sister along sometimes—he'd have a couple of orange juices and off he'd go. We used to think, "Oh, he's going home now." He'd always be back training the next day. Everyone likes him though. He's a likeable person. He's never got anything bad to say about anyone. Even though he kept to himself, he'd always be the first to say hello to you, and ask how your family was going and things. I never heard him bag anyone.'

Ian appeared on the cover of *Rugby League Week* on 26 March, with Mario and Tugger: ROYAL EASTER RABBITS—Three Secrets That Could Change Their Year.

A SALUTE TO THE BIG THREE *'I used to be a rake [Ian said]. I still am.' Looking up at the Rabbitoh, his only connection with the aforementioned garden implement can be in defence. Roberts simply rounds up attackers by the bundle. He does harbour a complex about his size though. As if 100kg were to be trifled with, Roberts wants more. 'I'd be happy at 102kg. I like the idea of being bigger. But I wouldn't go on a protein diet and put on fat as well. There's no point. Besides, I don't carry fat now.' Astonishingly, Roberts was near to offering his 190cm frame to basketball 12 months ago.*

Ian was flat-out flogging himself in those first years. He had to be running out front. To show he was meant to be there. That he deserved the accolades he received ahead of the older and more experienced players. Being found out as a fraud was a fear that would stay with him for years.

'Ian was quite fanatical about his weights,' Mario recalls. 'He prided himself on his body shape, and took a real interest in improving it all the time. He was one of the fittest athletes I've ever seen. We used to have this "beep" test, where you've got a 25 metre grid to run, and they've got this tape playing through speakers. And they go "right, stage one", BEEP—and the tape starts to beep slowly and you have to make your way to the other line and put your foot over the line. "Stage 2" BEEP, and the beep gets progressively quicker. And guess what? You keep going until you drop. Well, with Ian, they had to drag him off it! Team-mates and opponents could see the amount of work he did. He had the power of a gorilla. He had so many different things. In fact George, I can recall vividly, used to say to him that he was doing too much work! "You are doing too much work, because I want you to be fresh, to run the ball a bit more." But Ian would run the ball as often as you'd want. George felt that if he'd just cut back on doing 50 tackles a game, maybe do 40, he'd have that little bit extra to maybe get through the line and do whatever.'

Tugger Coleman was another player who was astounded by the effort Ian put into his training. 'He'd go to run the golf course at Eastlakes the day after a game! He was unbelievable! The Monday after the game was the hardest session. Nothing was a problem for him. He had no injuries because of the way he played, you know. Never complained or said anything. He'd just turn up, lead the runs, everything. He'd lead anything. I mean football-wise, there wasn't a thing he couldn't do. We used to have forwards pummelling punching bags. He punched like a mule, mate! Straight from the shoulder, he used to knock blokes across the floor at training. He could've been a fighter. He could've been anything he wanted to. To see how agile he was, a guy that size!'

George Piggins did feel the fatherly affection for Ian that Mario mentioned. Ian had that rare combination that all his coaches recognised, of sheer ability, dedication, a phenomenal physique and, most importantly, a good nature. It was this combination that the sports journalists would hone in on over the years, and come to respect. George was just the first to start harping on about it in the press. A decade down the track, he still eulogises Ian.

'Ian was more than a very talented footballer. It's easy to pick a good footballer. But it's not till you get them to first grade that you can tell by the way they conduct themselves whether they're going to make it or not. Like, if they want to get a heap of money in their pockets and head to the races, you know their football career's going to be short and limited. But a kid like Ian! He had everything. He never knocked himself about. The drink never got him. He put a lot into his football. He was dedicated and with that build he had a lot going for him. That and his ability. It was easy for Ian to be that superb type of footballer. I mean, at six foot four and seventeen stone, you've got a bit on them, haven't ya?'

'And you could tell by the way he conducted himself that he cared about other human beings. I remember one night at training, one of the young players there, he wasn't coming off the line and I wanted to demonstrate to him. I ran at him hard, and Ian was more concerned that I could've hurt the bloke, where someone else would just laugh if you did. He said, "Oh, you didn't have to be that bloody hard on him!" That's how he always was. He had concern for other people. Even at Mascot, he used to have a lot of feeling for the kids that couldn't play. When you're growing up, there's always that pecking order. The weakest one always gets picked on by everyone. Ian was the type that looked out for the little bloke.'

LURCH II—THE LAST OF THE STRAIGHTBACKS

So far, Ian Roberts is the Halley's comet of this '86 league season. At no other club has any first season first-grader made such an impact. 'He's got the world at his feet,' says [John O'Neill]. 'Lurch' ... 'I like him,' says the former Australian Captain [Ian Walsh], 'But he's got this kamikaze style of running which leaves him open. He's a big straight sort of a bloke and he's going to need to protect himself more when he runs the ball up. They'll be driving into him under the rib cage and he'll get hurt.'

To [Terry] Fearnley, last year's Australian coach, Roberts 'looks the goods. The only danger I see is if it's a case of too much too soon ... I prefer to see young players ... with a really solid foundation in lower grades. But he's good—and maybe Souths couldn't afford that luxury.'

After his booming start to the season (100 tackles in two games: versus Cronulla and Wests) the media have had him in their sights and in the past couple of days he has done interviews with 7 and 9.

'I'll be glad when that's all over,' he says. 'I appreciate the attention—but I suppose what it serves to do most is "gee up" my opposition.'

There's a nice mix of confidence and modesty in Roberts. Qualities of South Sydney stalwarts like Piggins ... and Lurch O'Neill shine through.

'There's something special about the place [Souths] ... a spirit and a harmony.' His formula for success. 'Establish yourself in the first ten minutes. Let them know that you're not going to back off ... My aim is to be going at the same pace, up and back, at the end of the game, as I am at the start.'

Young 'Lurch' Roberts is very much the new professional. Conscious of diet, a non-drinker, and prepared to give up hours each day to flay his body into the shape needed to play in the toughest competition in the world. 'My goals from Rugby League in the long term are to own a home, a car, have a good job ... For those, I'll give it everything I've got.' (Ian Heads, RLW 9/4/86)

For Ian, the press stories in those early years in firsts were like a glamorous movie version of his life. Crammed with superlatives, the adulation seemed to be about someone else—someone who was bigger, better, and often taller and heavier than he was! Someone superhuman. He personified a new breed for the commentators, and they were merely celebrating, in the mass of press items about him, as best they knew how.

LURCH ON THE REP PATH

Coach George Piggins ... declared Roberts was ready for representative honours after another powerhouse performance. 'I don't care how young he is—he's ready for it. He's good enough and tough enough.

I rate him the form front-rower in the Sydney premiership.' There wouldn't be too many arguments about Piggins' opinion of the rookie local junior who seems to keep on improving.

'I'm up against too many good props ... maybe next season.' There is no question he is the most promising young prop to emerge in Sydney since Steve Roach. Yesterday, Roberts topped the tackle count yet again—finishing up with 38 hits. (Phil Rothfield, Telegraph 13/4/86)

The press were always interested in any rising star who could sell papers, and George was proud to be able to provide them with one, and get in a plug or two about his clean-up of the team. As a businessman, George knew how to play the press to advantage. It was a marketing tool. Part of his job was to keep and attract sponsors, and bolster interest in the club from supporters. This was money in the coffers with which to buy and keep players and win competitions. Ian was very much a contributing factor in enabling Souths to whitewash its image. And getting him to rep football only reflected more prestige back on Souths, who, all rhetoric aside, had only lost one game so far out of seven.

ROBERTS CATCHES ARTIE'S EYE

Arthur Beetson ... one of the all-time great front-rowers, saw Roberts for the first time. 'He's a good kid and he's got something of everything. He has an outstanding physique, a good football brain, and covers a lot of the field. I am impressed with his capacity to work and his pace.' Prop forwards usually don't mature until around the late 20s but Roberts is an exception. (Geoff Prenter, RLW 13/4/86)

On Anzac Day, in the game against Canterbury, Ian got a particularly bad dose of concussion after being knocked out on the field. 'And it was such a pleasant experience, coming to. It's hilarious sometimes, when you get knocked out on the field. You come to, and you're lying on your back, so that when you open your eyes you haven't a clue where you are. I just woke up to this vast expanse of vivid blue sky, and I remember feeling really content, and I just said "Gee, it's such a beautiful day" to no-one in particular, and it was! It was one of those perfect warm still autumn days. I hadn't taken it in till then. Then the trainer came into focus, leaning over me, asking me if I was alright. He probably thought I was off with the pixies ... You get so used to it. There's so many games I can't remember. I've just played them instinctively, on auto-pilot. Heaps of guys do.'

The year before, he was knocked unconscious and revived in both the famous A- and B-grade grand finals, when he got man of both matches. 'The first few games of a new season are always a shock! The first few knocks to the head are really disorientating. When you're hit, you think, "What the hell was *that*!" Your head's not used to it. Then it becomes part of the routine again.'

Ian was selected to play for the annual seconds match between City and Country.

LURCH II SHINE IN SECONDS RUNAWAY
It's hard to believe Roberts is in only his first full season of grade football. He genuinely has to be considered a Kangaroo candidate. (Neil Cadogan, *RWL*, 21/5/86)

UNLIKELY HITMEN
Ian Roberts and Les Davidson are two of the most unlikely hitmen ... The juvenile juggernauts have been walking through their rivals for three months ... to set up their best chance for a premiership win in years. Roberts has such an innocent expression, a countenance so devoid of malice ... yet he is nicknamed 'Lurch II' after Souths fabled tough man. (Grantlee Kieza, *Telegraph*, 1/7/86)

Not all commentators were giddily outdoing each other with superlatives. A couple kept their feet on the ground. Ian Walsh was one who thought front-rowers should be blooded slowly and was a little disappointed with what he saw as Ian's too great a reliance on defence. Tackle counts meant little to Walsh.

FIVE
FEARFUL FAME

The gay rumours followed Ian from Mascot to firsts. That, and the fact that he became first grade's new golden boy, was bound to set tongues wagging. And create extra pressure for him. Tugger Coleman heard. 'You'd hear rumours, then you'd see him with an attractive woman. And you'd often hear rumours about anyone. I mean, not that we cared. Nobody gave a stuff because of who he was. He was doing a job for us, and he was doing a bloody good job. It was his personality too. It would have been different if he was a real bastard.' Mario French heard. 'I'm an old Redfern boy. You say nothing. You know nothing. You zip it. But there have been voices. You know what the Chinese whispers are like!' But according to Mario no-one openly discussed the issue. 'Like, I don't drink beer, and Ian doesn't very much either. But you can imagine, "What!? You don't drink beer?!" They'd laugh at me. I was called a "cat" and a "girl". It's the same thing [with being gay]. It's not part of the norm.'

George Piggins heard the same rumours going about. Unlike the others, George felt it was his duty to raise the matter. Ian was on the verge of greatness, as far as George was concerned, and, as a father would, George wanted to alert Ian to the pitfalls that he thought could topple him. Ian's new status obviously brought detractors as well as well-wishers to the fore, people who were happy to make his life uncomfortable. George was more concerned that other people would condemn Ian and make his life difficult. To even consider raising the

81

matter meant it was serious to George. No-one asked 'those' sorts of questions of a mate, and Ian didn't challenge the rules in any obvious way. He was a big, tough man. He spat. And he swore. In fact he swore a lot. He was one of the boys. George says, 'When blokes'd say to me Ian was a faggot, I'd say, "Well, you think he is, if you think you've got the ability, you tell him!" There weren't too many willing to walk up and tell it to him. There weren't too many blokes willing to take the chance.'

Ian recalls, 'George came to me a couple of times, worried about it. He warned me. I can't remember his exact words. "Mate, you've got to stop going to these clubs! You go to them, and you're getting yourself a bad name!" That sort of thing. I pretended I was cool about it all, but I was shitting myself.'

'I said "Look, Ian",' says George, ' "I couldn't care less if that's the way you are, but," I said, "you've got to be realistic that people will be cruel. The average Joe Blow that follows football will stick his head over the fence and yell out what he wants, and if you're gunna come out in the open, you have to be able to wear it. You'll have to decide the time to come out and say it, because you're the one who's gunna cop it." What he was didn't bother me in the sense that he's a bloke, he's a good style of young man. I mean the girls flocked after him. Now, you knew there had to be something dramatically wrong for him to ignore all that. You knew he wasn't that way because it was fashionable or because he wanted to be that way. You knew the gay thing wasn't a put-on thing. It was clearly that that was the way nature worked it out for him, he copped it sweet, and he went on with his life. I mean, I'm not sure which way it actually works, but to mine, it's got to be a defect to be born with the makings of a man and the emotions of a woman. But it doesn't mean you don't have the same rights as everyone else. It's like you're born with one arm. You get on as good as you can and people shouldn't blame you for it.'

George talked about his concerns with Frank Cookson. 'George told me that he said to Ian once "Are you gay?" and Ian had said "No, but I'm not offended by them either", which I thought was a brilliant answer. When George told me that I said "Serve you right for asking".' But as George said, 'Ian might have been frightened about his career, but I know there weren't too many people willing to call him it to his face ... They got a shock if they thought being homosexual and being weak were the same thing. I don't know why it was, but people at one time expected all homosexuals to be feminine and weak. Blokes got to the stage where they thought, "He's a big poof and I'm going to put him in his place! There must be a weakness in him because he's homosexual." Well, they got a terrible shock when he was willing to put his dukes up!'

The old sign outside the football world read 'No Poofs Allowed'. Footy is a man's world and poofs aren't men. That's reinforced from school onwards. Poof-hating has deep roots in our culture, bred on the historical ignorance and superstition of Christian and Anglo-Celtic morality. This is the culture that keeps boys *out* of touch with their feelings. Where big boys don't cry. And where sex between men, or any suggestion of it, is abhorrent.

Footy is a subculture of that culture. But because it's an all-boys contact sport, and the whole footy ethos can look uncannily homo-erotic, more effort has to be taken to counter any 'disgusting' associations of the game with homosexuality. And let's face it, the key image of rugby league in Australia for years was a statue of two men embracing. Blokes spend a lot of time in showers together. Every week, newspapers print action photos of males in struggling closeness with males. Comedians Roy Slaven and H.G. Nelson are always parodying the less-than-subliminal homo-eroticism in the game in their radio commentaries on JJJ's 'This Sporting Life'. All in all, there's bound to be a defensiveness.

Great lengths have to be gone to to counter any wrong impression. Just as the Christian status quo had to go to great lengths to market the suspiciously egalitarian communist movement as evil, it has done the same for years with homosexuality in all-male environments. Fear and ignorance drive the overreaction and abhorrence, supposedly a counter-attack against evil, with dire consequences for anyone who 'falls'. To put the 'correct' spin on blokish togetherness in sport, the footy culture helps society portray faggots as definitely unheroic, to distance them from the heroic ideals that surround the game. It's a logical knee-jerk reaction. A defence mechanism. If playing footy proves masculinity, then so too does poofta bashing, both verbal and physical. God forbid, and he evidently did, that anyone allow homos on the field. They're not fit to be present when real male bonding goes on.

In such a culture, poofs are the compulsory object of ridicule. Every real man is obliged to denigrate homosexuals. 'Cocksucker' and 'faggot' and 'poof' are everyday insults, along with 'cunt' and 'fucker', 'fuckwit' or whatever. There may not have been any poofs in football officially, but men never stopped talking about them, on or off the field, consciously and unconsciously. The language of the game is even anti-homosexual, when it isn't being misogynist. Homosexuals and women are discredited in the hysteria that surrounds proving manhood. You've got to go out and give it to the other team, fuck them right up, you've got to screw them, ram it up them, get on top of them. You insult the other team members with slurs about their sexual prowess, or about the sexual prowess of their girlfriends, wives or mothers. People who play badly, or who are opponents, can be girls, sissies, weaklings, dickheads, poofs, cocksuckers. It's all done in good fun, of course, but the underlying message is pretty clear.

It was just not allowed for a homosexual to be a hero or 'masculine'. Even history lessons in school were censored. You never learned that heroic men like Alexander the Great or Lawrence of Arabia were homosexual. No-one even mentioned it about the artists and intellectuals of history like Leonardo or Michelangelo.

To further justify the bad rap homos got, someone invented the contagion theory, or the One Bad Apple theory. You can catch it! You can't let poofs infiltrate men's ranks because it's contagious! They can force themselves on you with superhuman strength and then one whiff and you're gone. So poofs were not only weak sissies, but sinister, powerful forces who could seduce and convert big burly men at the drop of a hat. It wasn't safe for good boys to be around these ones. Gay murder defences often used this theory to good effect:

'The four boys were protecting themselves from unwanted superhuman advances of the "Big Sissy", Your Honour. It was horrible. It had lipstick on, and a skirt, and glared, Your Honour.'

'I stabbed him to death because he made advances toward me. My masculinity was threatened.'

As recently as December 1993, the NSW Supreme Court acquitted a man of murder on the grounds of self-defence, despite the fact his friends heard him say that he was going out 'to roll a fag' on the night in question. And since 1993 there have been 13 cases before the courts in which alleged homosexual advance has been offered as a defence, with still more awaiting trial. In 12 of the 13 cases the gay man was bashed pretty horribly before dying. In two cases, the accused were acquitted, and in several of the others they were convicted of the lesser charge of manslaughter. Of course society would never accept a woman's right to react in such a way after a man showed interest in her. A woman has a hard enough time trying to prove actual rape, let alone an unwanted advance. But for some peculiar reason, society has reserved for heterosexual men the right to go apeshit over another man even perving at him. This surely says something about society's lack of sexual maturity, and about men's utter fear of confronting sexual desires they might have for another man.

Despite the cultural aversion to homosexuality, tolerance wasn't unheard of in the men around Souths. One of Souths' stars back in the 1920s was not only generally known to be homosexual, but was also known to have lived with his lover for many years. Individually at least, men like Frank and George, Tugger and Mario display respect for a homosexual of Ian's calibre. Many men in professional football, from the South Sydney area, were from down-and-out backgrounds and had to struggle to get where they were. They knew tough times, ridicule and adversity, some of them. They knew what it was liked to be judged. Souths players came from ethnic minorities, from poverty, from Aboriginal families, and many of them knew prejudice in all its forms. Brad Webb had just laughed at ending up at a gay club in Hawaii when he went out with Ian. He didn't get all offended and violent. There was a grudging respect towards someone with the guts to be his own man, even when that meant challenging the rules of manhood. At least when the person doing the challenging happened to be an incredibly tall and strong front-rower!

From the start, Ian stood out as his own man. He didn't try too hard to live up to that macho image of masculinity, but he paid lip service to it. 'Once you made it to first grade, you were expected to act and live a certain way. Players weren't supposed to *be* anything else. You had this feeling that you were expected to be clean-cut, and toe a certain line. This was how a football player lived. This was how he behaved. You weren't supposed to let down this image that was held up to you.' At the same time, Ian's close and affectionate relationship with his father, the perfect role model of the man's man, helped him justify his independence. 'My dad taught me what being a man was and it's not about acting tough all the time.' Being gay, Ian would eventually come to test the masculinity of people, not by how they obeyed all the 'rules' of masculinity, but by their ability to be open, to be themselves in spite of what they might suffer in doing so. The people he gravitated to were individuals, despite the odds. For the most part, he found these people outside the football fraternity. And he especially avoided the men who shouted loudest about their masculinity. These were the ones who most often ridiculed people daring to live out their differences with pride, while they themselves hid behind a macho facade.

When he moved into firsts, the socialising didn't have the same innocence that it had at Mascot. Everyone was older, more adult. Gone was the naive adolescent frivolity and familiarity that junior football had. 'I used to go to football functions and that, and I could sense people were saying things about me. And I used to get knotted up and frustrated because I didn't have a comeback. I was always uncomfortable being around in situations like that.' Rather than conform, Ian found it easier to avoid them. He was never intimidated enough to go to the extent of other players attracted to men, who closeted themselves in a marriage and confined their homosexual activities to discreet meetings with call-boys, or other anonymous encounters. Acting as though it never happened, or ridiculing 'poofs' to protect their cover. While Ian didn't blame guys who lived that way, there was always an obstinate part of him that either couldn't or refused to bend entirely to rules that didn't seem fair or right.

In 1986 the very words 'homosexual' and 'gay' still had connotations of otherness. For many, they still have, suggesting some

Ray and Jean's
wedding day.

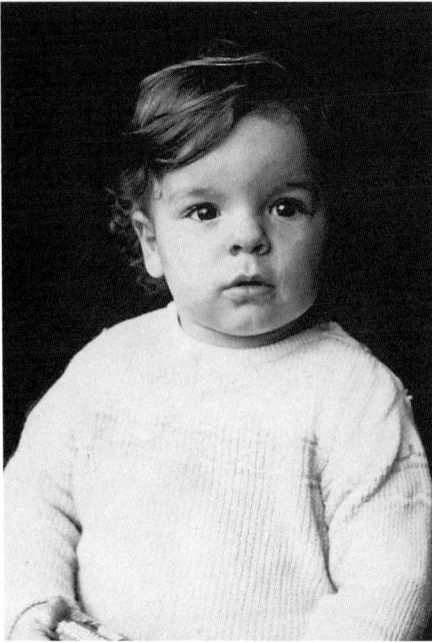

Ian at fourteen months.

Ian (left) and Paul at the Bunnerong
Hostel Christmas Party.

Beach volleyball anyone? Ian at almost
three years old.

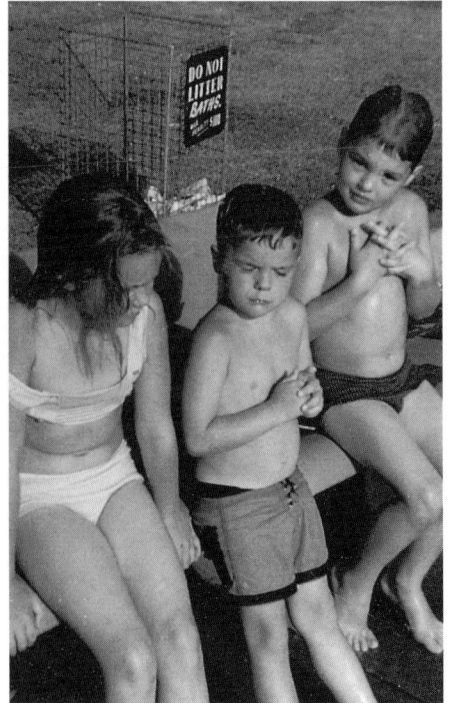

Julie, Ian (centre) and Paul down at
the beach.

The Roberts kids: Paul, Ian and Julie with Kylie at front.
Pick the clown.

Jean with the kids.

Ian with his first football trophy.

Ian at six, mustering his best smile.

An early break from the pack.

Maroubra Diggers K Grade 1974. Dave Johnson Back left, Ray Roberts far right, Ian with ball.

Maroubra Diggers H Grade 1977. Ray back left, Dave rear centre. Ian centre, middle row.

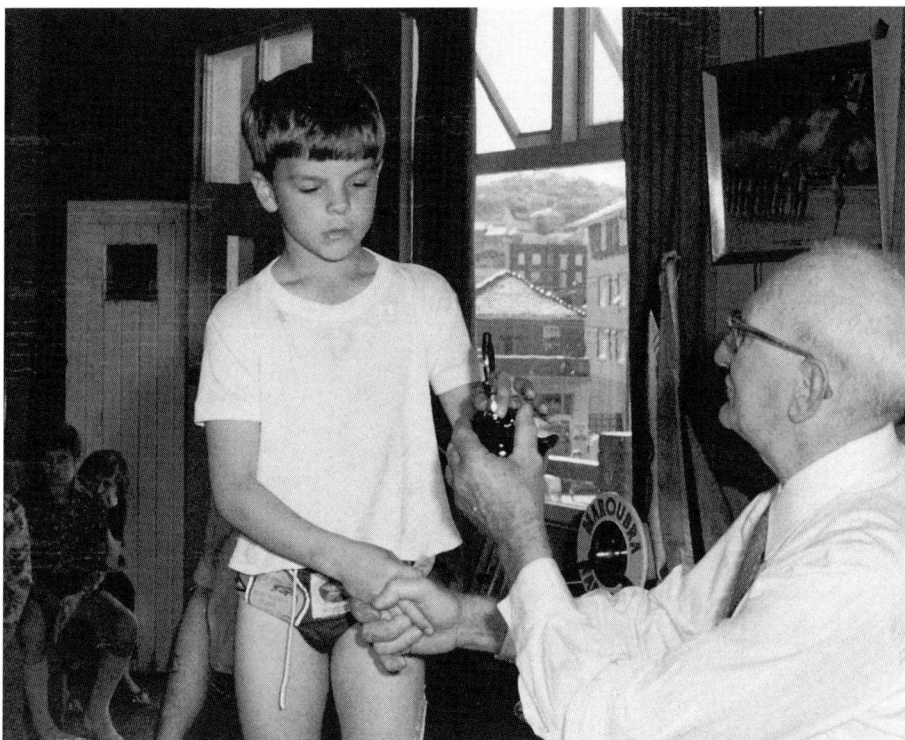

An underdressed Ian receiving his first surf club trophy at Maroubra Beach Surf Life Saving Club Presentation Day.

Ian and Kylie, the intrepid adventurers.

Ian at twelve.

Maroubra Diggers Club Champion — again.

Mascot D1 Minor Premiers and Undefeated Premiers, 1982. *Back row:* K. Wells (Manager), R. Sait (Trainer), G. Beverstock (Selector), N. Hayward (Coach), J. Lawrence (Trainer). *Middle:* N. Vasiliou, M. Viera, M. Lyons, G. Lever, I. Roberts, D. Puruto, J. Johnson, C. Sullivan, J. Thomas (Captain), M. Ingelmo, P. Smith, F. Cary, F. Rago, D. Maroon. *Front row:* M. Olsen, J. Spiteri, A. Hayward (Ball Boy), H. Beverstock (Ball Boy), G. Ferguson, B. Webb, J. Bell.

The Karate Kid at seventeen.

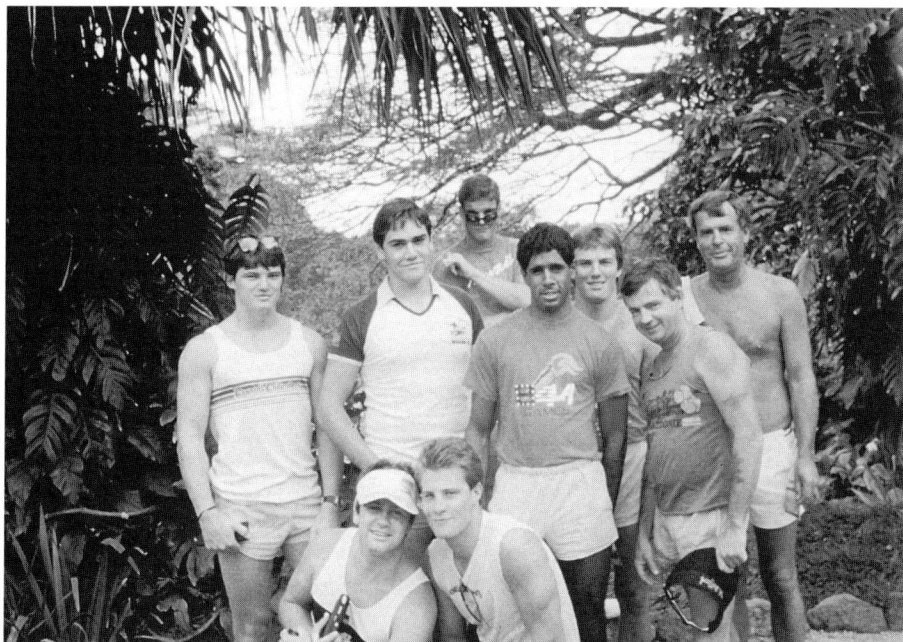

The Mascot boys in Hawaii, 1984, with Cool Shades Ian centre rear and Frank Cookson far right.

A typical Sunday night at home.

Ian flying above the pack became a common sight throughout 1986.
(*Photo:* John Elliott, *Rugby League* Week)

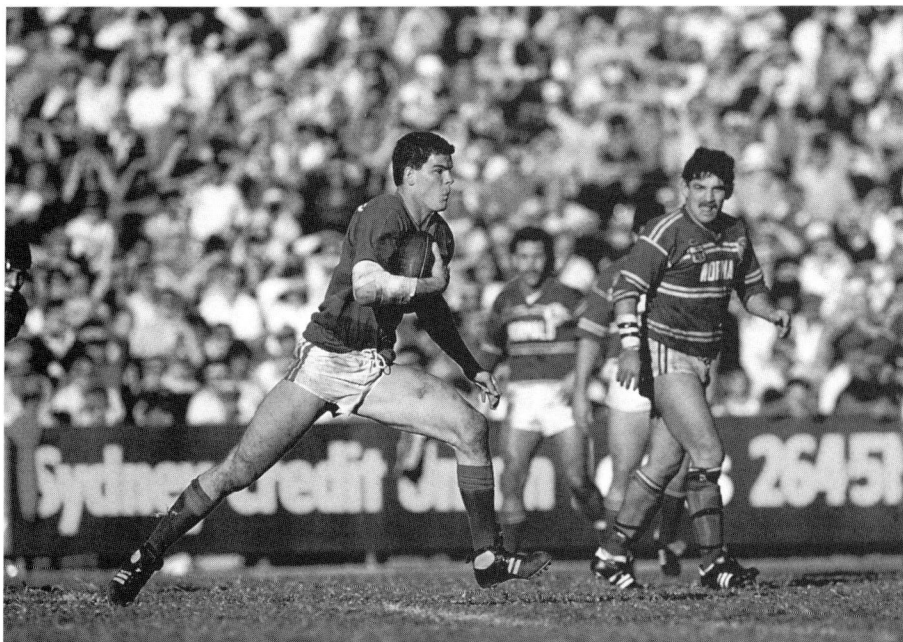

An unbeatable and powerful stride, pre injury
(*Photo:* John Elliott, *Rugby League Week*)

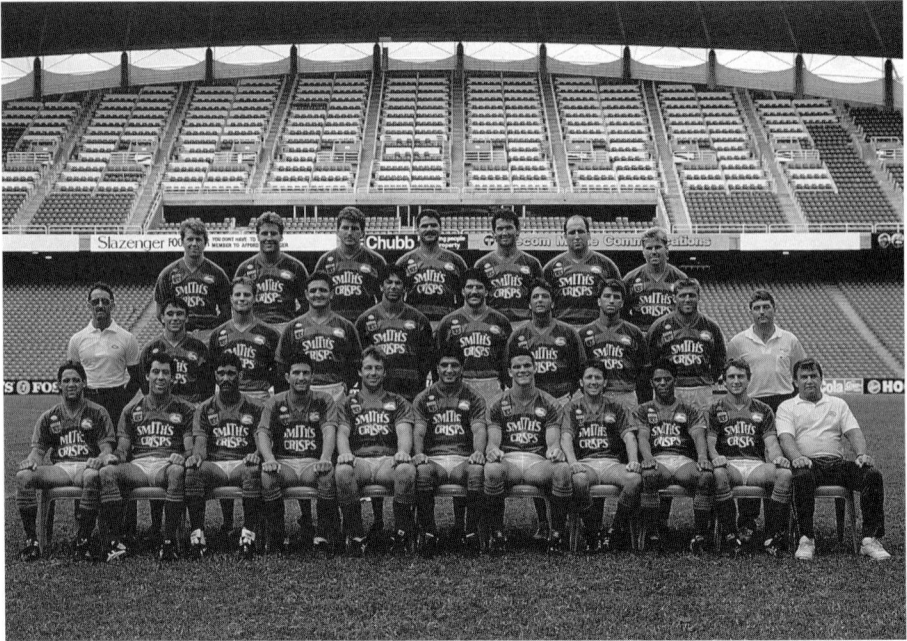

South Sydney 1st Grade Team, 1986. Ian is in the front row, seventh from the left, between Mario Fenech and Craig Coleman. George Piggins is at the far right of the front row.

Celebrating with Wigan after their Lancashire Cup win, 8 October, 1986. Ian is front right.

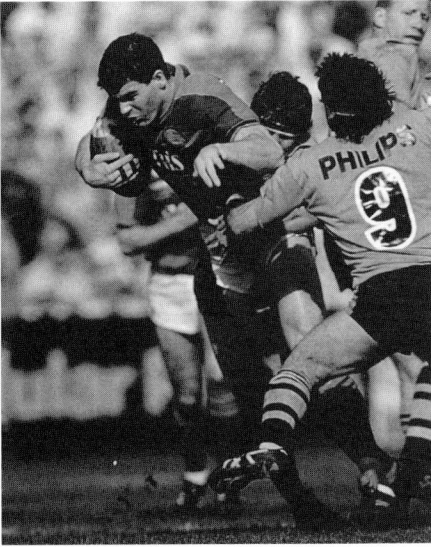

Busting the Balmain line.
(*Photo:* Action Photographics)

On-field diplomacy,
Souths style, 1986.
(*Photo:* Action Photographics)

A warm welcome to first grade from 'Blocker' Roach.
(*Photo:* Ian Collis)

Canberra's defensive line was always
hard to break.
(*Photo:* Action Photographics)

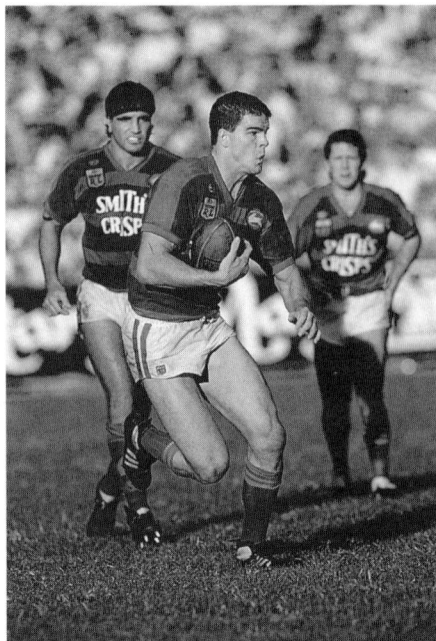

Power in motion with Mario and Craig
Coleman backing up.
(*Photo:* Action Photographics)

Ian's first Australian guernsey, August 1990.
Back row: Dave Ryan (*trainer*), Bradley Clyde, John Cartwright, Ian Roberts, Mark
Geyer, Peter Jackson, Brian Hollis (*trainer*). *Middle Row:* Shaun McRae, Willie Carne,
Laurie Daley, Andrew Ettinghausen, Craig Salvatori, Martin Bella, Chris Johns, John
Lewis. *Front row:* Official, Steve Walters, Rod Wishart, Mal Meninga (*captain*), Bob
Fulton (*coach*), David Gillespie, Des Hasler, Allan Langer, Kevin Brasch.
(*Photo:* Melba Photographics)

depraved lifestyle choice that no-one in their 'right' minds would make. The words themselves had a stigma attached to them.

It must have been bitterly amusing to Ian, as to all gays in sport, to know that the men around him who mouthed off about how they kept away from poofs were actually playing alongside one. Like anyone else, many homosexuals love and thrive on sport. Not for the perv. For the sport. For actual love of the sport! But the footy sub-culture finds it hard to accept that. And it will continue to do so as long as the culture as a whole persists with its hideous reliance on separating and defining masculinity and femininity, as if each sex should display only one possible set of traits. The world of intimate camaraderie, of closeness and affection between men both on and off the field, is not threatened or lessened by homosexuality. It is lessened by notions that don't allow intimacy to exist once it's off the field, beyond certain back-slapping limits.

To put Ian's predicament in a bit of historical context we need to go back a decade. In 1976, *The Advocate*, an American gay newspaper, was interested in finding out the number of professional gay sports-people in America. It sent out letters to sports editors and professional sports teams, and its enquiries caused great offence. Tom Nee, a public relations director for the Minnesota Twins, wrote back saying: 'The cop-out in moral lifestyle of the tragic misfits espoused by your publication has no place in organised athletics at any level. Your colossal gall in attempting to extend your perversion to an area of total manhood is just simply unthinkable.'

David Bergin, who was sports editor of the *Washington Star* at the time, then commissioned a journalist, Lyn Rossellini, to look into it. A series of anonymous interviews with closeted gay sportsmen were published, and caused quite a stir. A lot of incensed people thought these interviews must simply be fiction. Leftie Driesell, basketball coach at the University of Maryland, was one such. 'It is beyond my comprehension that a responsible sports editor could stoop to such trash when there are so many good things to write about in sports. What about the kids who read this stuff? They're easily influenced by what they read.'

David Kopay, ten-year veteran running back for football teams including the San Francisco 49ers, the Green Bay Packers and The Washington Redskins, wasn't one of the anonymous interviewees. Frustrated by the anger of the reaction, by his own closeted life, and at the end of his football career, he went public in an interview. He couldn't see how attitudes to homosexuality could get beyond the idea that it's a disease, without some of the tougher sporting gays coming out and saying, 'Look, you don't get influenced or "catch" your sexuality, and people who share a sexuality don't share any particular set of personality traits.' Kopay thought he could make it easier for sportspeople struggling against their sexuality the way that he felt he'd had to, to succeed in football.

Nothing changed quickly, or obviously. Players didn't want to deal with the possibility that there could be a homosexual in their midst. Especially one who didn't fit the picture. Kopay was at the end of his career. Younger gay players didn't want to jeopardise theirs. And sport, as an institutionalised part of society as a whole, would only be changed at the rate that society was able to be changed. That rate of change was very slow. Ian didn't hear of David Kopay until the '90s.

With a football career to think about, Ian's sexuality took on an entirely new problematic dimension. 'Before '86, when I went to the Exchange, I got to know a few regulars here and there, and it was like, "Hi, Ian." After '86, it was, "Ian Roberts! What are *you* doing here," characteristically this didn't stop him from frequenting clubs and dances where gay people went. He just made sure he hung out in an ambiguous pack of guys and girls. 'Friends like Lee were having to act as alibi for me. And say what a hetero stud I was! It was better for me to always have girls around me, too, just to avoid getting questions when I went to mixed clubs. I used to take Kylie out with me heaps, even though she didn't know about me.' Actually, Kylie did realise. 'I was the first to know in the family, even though Ern never knew I knew. I was going out with him when I was quite young. Mum and Dad used to let me go because they trusted Ian to look after me, and they trusted me. After a while I realised I was probably a good cover-up for him. Ian never put anything in front of me with regard to his sexuality because he probably didn't know how I'd react.' It didn't make any difference to Kylie what her brother was, sexually. She loved him. 'I guess I went through a period of mourning, I suppose you could call it. "Oh no, the poor guy, is he going to be happy? Is he going to miss out on having his own kids? And he loves kids," and this and that. But I wasn't uncomfortable with it. I thought, "Oh well, that's the way he is." It doesn't make any difference to me. For me, it was more a question of when is he going to tell people.'

Although a lot of the friends Ian hung out with didn't even know, Lee and a few gay friends, like Michael Gorman, did. Ian met Michael through John and Andrew, and he became part of a gang that gravitated round Ian for various reasons. 'It was a really weird experience,' Michael remembers, 'because Ian loved travelling in a pack. He was totally paranoid his sexuality would wreck his career in this blokes' sport. Anyway, basically we had this very funny routine going where we would go out in this entourage and he hadn't told some of these guys like Clem. So you just didn't talk about it. At the same time there was all this eye contact between Ian and me when we saw some guy we thought was cute.'

'There was one time early on, when just a few gay friends went to the fun park at Jamberoo, one sunny winter's day. Andrew got progressively banned from everything because he would take the rides too dangerously. He was a madman. Some of them went on these tiny one-person speedboats and Andrew went way too fast, got called off, told to stop, and an enormous wash of freezing water went right over the top of him. We were standing on the bank, pissing ourselves as he staggered up the shore, shivering, his lips blue with the cold. He turned into a complete snarling bitch, and this tough little Wollongong guy who was near turned round to him and said "Are you a fuckin' poofta, mate?" There was just this enormous tension, and you could see that Ian was thinking "Don't say yes! Don't say yes! I don't want him thinking I'm here with a poofta." He was really really tense. And then everyone just laughed. I mean, with Ian, I don't think it was any different to what makes any of us paranoid. It's just the spotlight was on him and that made it more difficult. The issue for most of us is work and parents [finding out]. The issue for him was work and parents and the fact that 100,000 people were watching him work.'

By the mid-80s the gay dance party craze was in full swing. They were the precursors of all dance parties. And the best. Ian recalls, 'John and Andrew did the music at some of the early parties. I'd just go along and have the best times, dancing all night.' It wasn't just the evolving dance music he loved. The larger venues provided a greater sense of protective numbers, and those early parties brought all sorts of people together for a good time. Sexuality wasn't an issue. It was live and let live. Maintaining sexual anonymity was a bit easier in these environments. Even so, Ian recalls that it was getting difficult to figure out who was 'interested' and who was just a bit in awe of a football player. That's him being a little modest, of course. There were lots of men and women attracted to Ian. But he was still living at home, so John and Andrew used to let Ian use their apartment to rendezvous with boyfriends.

The scrutiny part of fame made him conscious not only of himself as a footballer and as a person, but also as a body. Ian never felt deserving of the praise he received, but his physique was talked about so much that he began to fear that he wasn't living up to people's expectations when they finally saw this Ian Roberts guy. Plus he was paranoid about too much attention.

On the other hand, there was an attractive side to fame and people spoilt him wherever he went. A combination of factors saw him lose concentration on the field, and form in 1986. It had been a tumultuous year in so many ways. There was intense pressure. And excitement. Things that he had worried about in the past—discovery, pleasing everyone, competing with excellence—became infinitely greater. By the end of that first season, which had begun with so much fanfare, he was relegated to the reserves in some games, and the under 23s.

He did play in the semi clashes, against defending premiers Canterbury on 6 September, and against Balmain on 12 September. Souths lost both. And yet, only a few weeks before, on 28 July, they had scored an upset win over the Bulldogs, 17–8. In a way, the results were a reflection of Ian's lapsed form.

In the game against Balmain, Souths were accused of resorting to some of the unnecessary tactics they had worked hard all year to suppress. Ian Heads referred to the game as 'one of the most sensational semi finals of modern times' in his appraisal entitled 'The SCG Is Where the Big Men Fly'. Mario had been sent off for eye-gouging, and Ian and others had been sin-binned for an incident after a tackle of Steve Roach by Phil Gould, involving what looked a lot like a head butt by Roach. Ian scored his first and only try of the season, but there were accusations of dirty play all round, and unfair refereeing. Ian had been brought on as a replacement, and finished up unconscious. 'When you're only 21, confronting the hardest game in the world at its very toughest is going to take an extra emotional toll,' wrote Ian Heads.

Ian's consolation was that he starred in Souths' win in the under 23s grand final at the SCG, despite playing with his ribs badly bruised from the game against Balmain.

Terry Parker, Souths' club secretary, negotiated a contract for Ian to play with the English side Wigan for the five months of the Australian rugby league off-season. (Wigan's boss at that time was Maurice Lindsay, who would come to Australia in 1996, amidst controversy, as head of English Rugby League, to attempt to set up a rebel competition with Super League players.) The experience was invaluable for Ian. He got a new perspective on the game from Wigan coach Graham Lowe, who was also the New Zealand coach. Ian enjoyed the opportunity to settle down out of sight of the Australian media, and he aimed to bring home a bonus of $20,000 for his trouble.

Ian left some surprised faces in his wake when he left for England. At Souths' annual get-together, 'The Hairy Legs Folly', this seemingly shy rookie stunned people with his Mick Jagger impersonation. According to Tugger's wife Debbie, all the girls rushed up to the stage and swooned.

His first match in England was a Lancashire Cup semi-final clash against St Helens. Because of his rib injury, there had been a bit of speculation in the press as to whether he would be right to play. But he appeared on the field 72 hours after touch-down, and excelled.

IAN TRUMPS ALEX'S ACE
Sydney forward Ian Roberts was the secret weapon Wigan used to get the better of Alex Murphy and St Helens. (3/10/86)

A winning medal came his way the following week, after victory over Warrington, 18-4, when Wigan won the prestigious John Player Trophy. The British press were astounded by his fortitude. And his work rate.

59 TACKLES 'WEREN'T ENOUGH'
Ian Roberts, the 21 year old London-born forward who topped the tackle count at Warrington with a staggering 59 hits, came out of the dressing roon before training and said 'It wasn't enough. I suppose I've got this reputation for topping tackle counts because I must get there at the right time, but I thought Sunday's game was a bit of a lax effort.' (English Press, 8/10/86)

ROBERTS LICKS INJURY
Ian Roberts needed eight stitches in his lip after the [game] but that failed to stop him. Roberts received a bad gash on the lip in the first half and required emergency stitching at half time to enable him to continue. He went on to give a towering performance ... Maurice Lindsay paid tribute to Roberts' courage.

'Many players would have come off the field after an injury like that ... ' (8/10/86)

The official line was that the severe concussion and gashed face came after Ian collided with Les Boyd's head. Actually, Les Boyd's head collided with him! 'I couldn't believe it! Les Boyd headbutts me in a tackle. Wham! The guy had a head like a brick. I just reeled back, blood gushing, shocked, and tried to get on with the game. I couldn't remember anything about the game after that!' (Les Boyd was notorious for rough play, having faced many charges and received suspensions.)

BIG HITTER IAN
Graham Lowe thinks his new Australian forward must have broken some Rugby League record by making a staggering 59 tackles. 'I couldn't believe it ... I've never heard of anyone making that many tackles. Roberts' performance was just exceptional. It must be a record.' (8/10/86)

Not only that, but Ian was tackling for weeks in England with a bad shoulder he had first dislocated when he was still playing at Souths Juniors. Since then the problem recurred from time to time, especially when he had to reach for a tackle. At Wigan, the pain had become chronic, and he got by on pain-killers.

But he was the best player by a long shot, the following week, playing against the Kangaroo team he didn't make. To younger Souths' players like Terry Hill, on that Sunday October 12 Ian became a legend. 'I was sitting down with my mates, Jimmy Dymock and a couple of other blokes and going "Fuck! look at Ian Roberts!" To make that many tackles is unheard of! He was killing them! And he got Man of the Match, and everyone was going Ian Roberts, Ian Roberts, Ian Roberts, and he deserved it.' That English season Wigan went on to win the Lancashire Cup final against Oldham, Ian scored himself a second winning medal, and the overtures from the British press, trying to lure back a native son, began. Across the world, the Australian press wanted Ian back.

S.O.S. IAN ROBERTS
Outstanding young South Sydney prop Ian Roberts will jet into Sydney from England this morning to the stunning news he will have to play first grade for the Rabbitohs in less than 72 hours. (Les Muir, 24/2/87)

According to the media, first-grade football was all climax and drama. Urgency. An ongoing war. Battle wounds like the Les Boyd scar are worn like medals of valour. Each has a story, and Ian's a storyteller in the great tradition of Souths' veterans. He points to one scar from '86. 'It's quite faded now, but it was horrendous, really disfiguring. It was like there was a finger laying across the top of my eyebrow. For two years it was disgusting, gross.' 'I got a graze on my knee in the semi against Balmain before going to Wigan, and when I was playing in England I kept peeling the scab off. It turned into an ulcer. I had to have it injected with a pain-killer before all the games in England, because it was quite inflamed, and then have padding on it. (When my shoulder got bad, I was really dosed!) To get rid of this thing, which is basically a sore that never heals, they have to cut it out completely so that the area can heal over. When I got back from England, I showed it to a team doctor, and he decided he'd cut it out. I said, "Well, what do we have to do for that?" and he said, basically, that we could do it in the surgery right there. Inject it, and core it. That is, cut it out with a scalpel. Now, I'd had a previous experience with this sort of thing not long before I went to England, when my family doctor cut out warts from the bottom of my feet. At that time the doctor had said that cutting them out wouldn't be painful because the nerve endings around the warts were dead anyway. So an injection wasn't needed. Well, mate! The doctor starts cutting in around those warts and someone forgot to tell my nerves they were dead! I was in the most incredible pain. That was fine, my feet healed and I was grateful.

'When it came to cutting around the ulcer, I asked the doctor if it was the same as when the warts were cut out, because I didn't want to go through that again. He gave me a needle, which made me relieved. Then he put the scalpel to the ulcer and starts to cut, and I said, "I can feel that!" He gives me another couple of needles, and cuts deeper and deeper, and I can still feel it. The pain is maddening. And I'm sitting there, watching. And watching someone cut into your flesh is just incredible. I was quite curious. But every time he cut deep, I was out of my skin. And, you know, by now there is quite a bit of blood and I'm thinking, "What am I doing here?" and I said to him "How long is it going to take?" because I'm having second thoughts. He says "five minutes" so I go "Mate, you do it ... just do it!"'

'So he continues to cut, and I'm just crawling the walls. I'm not looking any more. I'm too busy contracting my muscles. Eventually my legs are shaking from my contractions. Five minutes later, it's out and a short while later I'm walking out into the waiting room where Lee was waiting and he says, "Shit, you look white!" I said "Yeah, I don't feel too good' and just fainted! All these people were sitting round in this medical centre at Pagewood, and I faint, sliding down the reception desk! Two weeks later he wanted to cut away some more and I said "No way! You're not touching that. It can stay an ulcer ... I like it now!" Years later I found out that people go to hospital for operations like that! If you have to cut in that deep, you go to hospital!'

Souths lost the first few games of the '87 season. But praise for the mild-mannered young hero continued unabated, as headline-hungry journos were aided and abetted by revered living legends of the game. On 25 March, *Rugby League Week* ran a two-page feature with a banner heading 'THE MERCENARY'. The subheading read 'Wanderer Roberts on the Money Go Round' after Ian dared to mention he played football for money, while fielding questions about where he wanted the game to take him. Of course all this was a mere entree to the feeding frenzy a couple of years down the track.

'The best front rower in the game.' That's Jack Gibson's shock appraisal of 21-year-old nomadic prop Ian Roberts. High praise for a youngster who has played only 22 first grade games in Sydney.

'He can do everything. His work rate's tremendous, he never stops running the ball up and can get it away and has great ability to stop the run. And he's a disciplined kid. I don't know any team he wouldn't walk straight into.'

Roberts, the quiet man in the volatile South's pack [says], 'It's just a matter of getting into the right position and being prepared to do the work. Fitness also plays a big part.' [His] commitment to Rugby League has certainly been noticed. He is in demand in two countries.

Then the article turned to Ian's ambitions in the game. *'You go where the money is. At the moment I can make more money playing in England. Naturally I would prefer to play for Australia.*

When I was nineteen I nearly gave the game away. My dad said stick it out ... I'd go back to England anytime ... the crowds really love the players and the clubs can't do enough for you. Some of our clubs could learn from them.'

In England the slower pace allowed him to fine tune his ball skills ... Roberts returned lighter than when he left ... His torture runs around the hills at Eastlakes Golf Course show he's not about to let up.

Roberts is prepared to flay his body to achieve his goals. Football is his way of setting up for the rest of his life. 'It all comes down to dollars. If it wasn't for money, no-one would be playing league.' (Darren Hadland, RLW 25/3/87)

'I KNOCKED BACK OFFER OF $100,000'

South Sydney's giant young front-rower last night revealed he almost quit South Sydney last week to join big-spending Penrith on a deal worth $100,000 for just one season.

'I seriously considered leaving Souths because of the offer. Any other footballer would have done the same ... But in the end Souths offered me a very good deal which ties me to the club until the end of the 1989 season.

I've come up from the junior ranks and I really enjoy playing football here with the rest of the blokes. It would have been hard to leave ... I'm determined now to get on with the job for Souths in the semi-finals.' (Phil Rothfield, *Telegraph*, 27/8/87)

SOUTH'S STAR IN $150,000 TUG-O'-WAR

Ian Roberts is in the middle of a $150,000 tug-o'-war between South Sydney and leading English club Wigan ... following a massive offer from Wigan.

'I've been losing a lot of sleep since Wigan offered me a lot of money. You are only in the game for a limited time and if big money is available you would be silly to knock it back. I do feel a sense of loyalty to Souths. I'm as keen as any player to represent my country, but if that isn't possible I will always try to do the best for myself financially.' (Peter Frilingos, *Mirror*, 9/4/87)

POMS BID TO PINCH ROBERTS

South's prop Ian Roberts has an open invitation to play for Great Britain next year ...

'I am flattered by the interest England are showing me, but I'm contracted to Souths for next season. I love the club and my main concern at the moment is trying to help them win the competition. I realise in the future I have to make a decision where I'm going to play. The prospect of playing for Great Britain is appealing. I am really *happy at Souths. I wouldn't play for any other Sydney club. But I enjoyed my stay with Wigan. It's a case of where my best chances lie.'*

The English offer represents a quick entry to international football—an entry which could be a lot longer coming in Australia. (Darren Hadland, *RLW*, 17/6/87)

Ian had made the grade now. The match against the Kangaroos, and his form since, confirmed him as a rising star. He was in demand, which brought out his business attitude to the game and enabled him to renegotiate his contract so that, by 1989, he would be on $60,000 a year. Satisfied for the moment, he set his sights on representative football. But selection wasn't a foregone conclusion. As Frank Cookson says, 'It's not always the best footballers play internationals. You've got club politics, and then selectors seem to pick the players from the sides on top of the competition. A good player in a poor side doesn't get the same consideration as a player of slightly less ability in a top side.'

However, Ian soared above the politics. In the last twelve months he had been romanced by the media. And he started to find himself a more willing partner, opening up from time to time. Eventually he would want to divorce himself from the press when the relationship hotted up and he was exposed to vitriol and abuse as a result. But for now, he would at least make his ambitions in football known publicly. If selectors were too hesitant, he'd go where he was wanted. Even England. Or go with the cash. He wasn't going to be anybody's fool. Time's precious when you're living anxiously.

He was a victim, in a sense, of his new found stardom. The adulation was conditional. He would learn that soon enough. He had to fulfil certain criteria. He had to always be the sweet innocent unassuming boy who charmed them off the field and astounded them on it.

GOOD ONE MR ROBERTS
The try he scored against Manly brought him a grand final reception from his team-mates. It came on the sixth tackle, after an absolutely incredible period of play. Craig Coleman searched fruitlessly for a runner on the sixth tackle, and finally picked up big 'Iron' who landed

three or four feet short in Des Hasler's tackle. Being such a big fella ... it was close enough to topple over!

'I enjoyed that,' said Roberts after the game. (RLW, 15/4/87)

IAN SET TO 'GO AGAIN' AFTER BEATING BULLDOGS
South's 50 tackle hero ... claimed he felt so good after last Saturday's defensive marathon against Canterbury that he was ready to 'go again' straight after the match. While many of his team-mates slumped exhausted in the dressing-room treating injuries, Roberts was show-ered, changed and looking 'fresh' 15 minutes after the hooter sounded victory for the Rabbitohs. He shrugged off the massive tackle count as 'just part of my job out there' but claimed a Good Friday training session had Souths keyed up. 'It started out as just a ball workout but ended up a real motivation session. George told us a few home truths. I think the boys are sick and tired of being labelled "the team that was". I kept thinking what the coach said and although I was starting to get tired, I just kept pulling out something extra—all the boys did.' (RLW, 23/4/87)

500 BONE CRUNCHERS
'Iron man' Ian Roberts is just 63 tackles shy of becoming the first Winfield Cup player to top 500 tackles this season. He will pound his 22-year-old shoulders another step closer to that tackling milestone ... Roberts, one of the most agile big men in the game, has averaged 33 tackles a game and has to be one of the best value 80-minute players in the premiership. (Ian Hanson, Telegraph, *12/6/87)*

By July Ian's shoulder problem had flared up again. It was continually painful and required surgery. Ian opted to play out the season with the pain, which would be considerable, despite pain-killers. With every tackle there was the risk of being hit at the point of injury. In June he had also torn a muscle on his neck and it hadn't healed properly.

Then, on 27 July 1987, in the game against Canterbury at Belmore Oval, Ian experienced a defining moment in terms of his self-confidence in the game. Frank had spoken to Ian two weeks earlier. 'He took me aside and sort of said, "Listen, mate, you're not playing football the way I know you can. You've got to just get out there and do what you do best. Let loose and just play football the way you can." I had become more concerned with trying to do what I was told, than just letting my instincts direct my game. Frank's reminder got me thinking.'

Before the Canterbury game, George Piggins also took Ian aside. 'George virtually said that my form had been disappointing, and this game was my last chance to pull something out of the hat, or he'd have no choice but to drop me.' Souths had lost against Manly the previous week at Redfern, but prior to that had not lost a game for eight weeks. 'I ran on the field with a little bit more adrenalin than usual. And I just went for it.' Ian's concentration on the game usually meant that the crowd noise became just a murmur, but during this game two words pierced through to distract him.

'Faggot Roberts!'

The words stung. 'Fuck! They know!' Ian felt blood rush faster for a second or two. Who knows? What would they do? The demands of the game re-focused his concentration. He went in harder. Someone was punished ... *One of his tackles in particular almost rocked the packed ground with its ferocity.* (Les Muir, 28/7/87)

'Whatever it was, I just played like I don't think I'd played before. At least that's how it felt. I just went for it. I was a like a maniac!'

The 21 year old prop was in devastating touch, either taking the ball up with unrelenting courage or tackling with the force of a bulldozer. (Les Muir, 28/7/87)

'I couldn't do enough. There was a period in the game when I was fired-up, in a heightened reality. I thought, "I really *am* good at this!" For the first time since I'd started playing, I felt invincible. I felt like no-one could stop me. That I was never ever going to *let* anyone stop me.'

That turning point at Belmore led to some of the best football Ian had played. Two weeks later, at Henson Park, he was better than brilliant.

Tugger Coleman was there. 'Easts were beating us up to half time. We came back into it a bit. Then the try that broke their back! Someone put a bomb up, and Ian just flew above them all. It's like Russell Fairfax reincarnated! There was nothing he couldn't do! He'd make 50 tackles. He'd bust a line at will. I mean, we had plays, but we were just more, like, "to 'em and thru 'em", because we had someone like him. He'd bust a line, and then he would go. He could run like an outside back then. He could run 60 yards. He was a dynamic ball-carrier. I think it was perhaps his strongest point in those days, busting a line and going. He could offload the ball—he had plenty of good ball-handling skills. *Plus* we'd put bombs up and he'd fly above them and catch them and score tries. He could jump, so we'd put the ball high and he'd love to chase 'em—he'd chase anything, mate—he'd fly above them and come down with the ball. It was just unheard of, a front rower his size so flexible and agile. If we couldn't crack a defence, we'd just go up in the air, he'd just surprise eveyone!'

Tugger had put the bomb up that day against Easts.

STRIKE UP THE BAND FOR IAN
The 'Redfern Globetrotter' earned himself the biggest contract of his life after leaving Easts wishing he had stuck to basketball as a career. Roberts was promised more dollars on his contract after Souths had won 32-18 at Henson Park ... How often does a front-row forward win man-of-the-match honours in a game that produces 50 points? Mustering all of his basketball experience, Roberts scored the most spectacular front-rower's try of the season to level the score ... Craig Coleman punted the ball what seemed to be a mile high. Wurth went for the ball but Roberts outjumped him to claim the try.

Polish up that trombone, here comes that man Roberts. A man and his ball. Magic. Music to South's ears.(Geoff Prenter, 17/8/87)

'And, I mean,' says Tugger, 'Rugby League wasn't the be-all and end-all to him. It surprised me because of the way he played. The way he played, he *loved* the game. Anyone who takes the ball up 100 times a game and makes 50-odd tackles and, you know, the pain he used to inflict on himself! They used to turn up the heat on him, he'd get smashed a bit. Sometimes you could see he wasn't all there, but pain wasn't a worry for him. You could see, he'd be like knocked out, he'd get to his feet and fall back in and two rucks later, there he'd be again ready to pick the ball up. He just had that will to win. He overcame some enormous odds a bit later. You mightn't see another Ian Roberts for another 50 years.'

'People wouldn't realise how passionate Ian can get,' says Mario Fenech. 'They see him as being quite mild-mannered. But deep down there's a lot of passion. I saw inklings of it when we were faced with dire situations at Souths, where he didn't say much, but every now and then he'd say something like "Come on fellas!" It could be at training or playing, and we'd all be surprised because *I* did a lot of talking, but Ian was just a shy sort of a bloke who deep down is simmering with passion. Where he wasn't a talker, one of his great ways of doing things was to lead by example. He'd do it, and he'd pull off a hit and shatter some bloke and it was very uplifting.'

'I was in a good position because I saw him develop [from the juniors to firsts] from a straight up and down, strong, advancing the ball, yardage man, to a bloke who had the nice long arm and he had that basketball type skill which required a lot of one-handed type thing—he has quite good sized hands—so he developed into a very good offloader, which is very important. If you can get someone to offload a good ball—they call that second phase play—which opens up different opportunities. They're worth a lot of money, players like that. Ian is renowned for his ability in this sense. In fact, the game plan when you play against him is to wrap the ball up. When you play against Ian Roberts, you must stop the ball!'

It is harder to critically analyse your own game, and the way it evolves over time. 'In the first couple of years of first grade, I played a fairly tight game,' Ian reckons. 'More like a conventional front-rower. More up and down. Well, when I say conventional I was much fitter than most. I was a lot quicker. Later in '87 I used to run a bit wider. Get more involved wider. People always tell me about my style changing. But I don't ever remember making a conscious decision about it. I think it just develops. People tell me I played my best football in those years. But I don't agree, though I know I had some really good games.'

According to Frank, 'He was the best player they had. He was leader of the pack. You could number the mistakes he made in a game on one hand. He was a non-mistake footballer. With everyone else you would say, "Oh look what he contributed today, he dropped the ball two times, missed three tackles but scored three tries." With him, he just goes through the game and does not make mistakes!' People today can still hear George talking about the greatest junior Souths ever produced. 'You could bank on one thing with Ian. Every week, he'd be your top tackle count. He made the most busts. If he done thirty tackles, ten or twelve would be real bell-ringers where they'd get up and couldn't feel themselves from their head to their toe. And with Ian he could chase you and catch you. People would have to look to see where Ian was. Ian was the sort of player that could make a tackle, and then the last-ditch tackle further down the line would be Ian again! He'd come from nowhere. The capacity was unbelievable! He was such an athletic player, there'd be often we would pack a scrum, I'd put the five-eight to lock and move Ian to five-eight because he had the speed and size to bust a line, or go up for a bomb.'

The season looked promising for Souths after that match against Easts, with Ian in tip-top form.

RABBITOHS CAN DO IT
South Sydney can win this premiership—and even from fourth spot ... Souths have the power to frustrate Manly and Balmain, and they showed they know how to handle Easts ... They rely a lot on their forwards but they have a good kicking game and a smart play-maker in Craig Coleman. (Ray Price, RLW, 19/8/87)

STOP ROBERTS He's The Player That Furner Fears Most
Lanky Ian Roberts, the Rabbitoh who reminds Don Furner of Bobby McCarthy and Ron Coote in attack, is the player most likely to deny the Raiders their first crack at the Winfield Cup semi-finals. Furner has been a firm Roberts admirer since last year's Kangaroo tour.

'If Roberts had not played so well for Wigan against the Kangaroos in the first tour game we would have won easily. But how Roberts attacks wide of the rucks reminds me of McCarthy and Coote. Easts allowed him to stand in tackles and feed his runners.'

There appears to be no limit to Roberts' ability and if Souths do go on and win their first title since 1971, his contribution will have been immeasurable. (Peter Frilingos, Telegraph, 22/8/87)

But the premiership wasn't to be that year for Souths. After narrowly winning the semi-final against Balmain, 15–12, in what was a typically heated battle, they crumbled against Canberra the following week, losing 12–46 on 12 September. Souths had lost both previous clashes with Canberra that season, but this loss was an anti-climax in a good year of football for Ian. His hopes of playing in England again had been dashed by his shoulder problem, which required treatment in the off-season, but the Dally M Prop of the Year award was a pretty good consolation for a guy who had just turned 22.

By the end of '87 you could argue that Ian had changed the image of Souths. He brought physical excellence. Then glamour and prestige. He was an '80s pin-up boy from the tough end of town, and he won his fame for playing a tough game and playing it well.

'I saw Ian Roberts at Sleaze ball. And he was dancing with a guy.'
'Bullshit, I saw him there and he had all these girls around him.'
'That doesn't mean anything!'
'He's got a girlfriend.'
'How do you know?'
'Gerard told me. He knows her.'
'That blonde one? He wouldn't go out with her!'
'I thought Gerard said Peter had been off with him.'
'Yeah, well he thinks Peter was lying.'
'I mean what he would see in Peter beats me. He's like a stick! And if he was gay, he could have whoever he wanted.'

By 1988, Ian was the stuff of gossip and speculation among 'out' homosexuals. Dinner-party conversations in some households could happily centre on whether he was or he wasn't. Most hoped he was, *and* that he would go out with them, rather than anyone else they knew. Tall, dark, handsome, a brilliant young football star with a brilliant body, he was many a guy's dream man. So it mattered what his tastes were ... who he was seeing. Everyone reflected on his predicament at some stage or another. How was he ever going to cope going out, being gay, and playing football? There were varyingly substantiated rumours about other footballers, but this was different.

Ian was not as discreet. He was seen at dance parties that were mainly gay, and on Oxford Street. Too often. Eventually, the speculation would become more politically motivated, and even a little angry. Ian's boldness would irritate some. How dare he be out, but not be 'out'.

After the decisive 'Faggot Roberts!' moment during the game against Canterbury in July, it was definitely time for increased damage control. Jean had been dropping progressively nastier comments around home about poofs, too. She was suspicious, what with his having gay friends but no real girlfriend to speak of. Was he being corrupted? Heaps of girls swooned over him, so why wasn't he jumping them, left, right and centre? It had all become awkward.

Clarise was a pretty tempestuous and headstrong girl, of Spanish extraction, who met Ian at gym. At first Ian befriended her, as he befriended lots of girls he liked. He just couldn't give them what they wanted. But Clarise was a bit more pushy than average. Beautiful and Latin, she was a personality whirlwind, bubbly and effervescent. Ian laughs. 'It was hilarious. She was this bundle of energy, like a tornado, a sexy, voluptuous tornado.' Ian didn't contrive things, but he let them happen. 'At first Clarise hung out with us. She had just broken up from a long-term relationship. I took her out a couple of times. She was pretty naive, which was good for me. But then she was horny all the time. For ages and ages I just couldn't do it. I couldn't get it up! I don't know what she thought. I think I would always make some excuse about being tired from football or something. I just wasn't that interested. Don't get me wrong, she was incredibly sexy. The first time was at John and Andrew's. I was really off my face. The situation was hilarious, really. But as a relationship, it was a bit of a disaster. I just went with it. She was fun. Then later on, it got like, "How do I finish this off?"'

They had some laughs along the way. 'One day, Clarise's mum, who spoke broken English, cleaned Clarise's room. When we got home that day she rushed over to us all concerned. "Clavees, Clavees, I find thees perfoom of yourez. I sniff. I fall down!" She held up a bottle of Stud, diluted amyl nitrate.

Jean was relieved. Not that she really knew why, but it allayed unconscious fears. 'Ian loved Clarise,' she insists now. 'I know Ian loved Clarise. He did. He used to say it … Well *she* loved *Ian*.' And of course Jean thought it was wonderful. But Ian wasn't good at lying. Clarise tagged along as part of the circus, and pretty soon she had reason to be suspicious. 'She rang up really late one night and said to me that Ian was gay,' Jean recalls. She was shocked at the outburst. And the time of night. 'We took it as sour grapes. She said, "Do you know your son is gay?" I said, "Don't be stupid!" and put the phone down.' When Jean told Ian about it, he nervously laughed it off as an over-reaction on Clarise's part because he no longer wanted to sleep with her. Ray still says, 'She was probably just mad because Ian wouldn't sleep with her.' Then he laughs.

Ian couldn't satisfy Clarise and realised he was doing the wrong thing by her. 'I felt so bad hurting her. I loved her as a friend, and I really hurt her. I just let her keep it going. I used to take her to football functions. In the end I'd led her to believe it was something more than friends. I didn't want it to turn out the way it did. After I broke up with her, I thought never again would I ever do that to a girl. I got quite upset with myself that I hurt her.'

Meanwhile, Clarise spread the word. 'She told all her friends round Maroubra that he was gay,' Michael Gorman remembers, 'because he wouldn't fuck her. There was enormous trauma about that.' Eventually Clarise calmed down and melted in to the general gang. She even moved in to Ian's flat when he bought a place at Coogee a year or so later. Ian kept new female friends at arm's length and in the dark after that fiasco. He didn't want his parents harassed. Or alerted to his sexuality by emotional and rejected girls screaming bitterly down the phone at all hours.

'But at the time Ian was seeing Clarise,' Michael recalls, 'he met another footballer, Bob, through Andrew who was playing for one of the other league teams. He was a great-looking guy, tall, muscular, with wealthy parents. Bob was more confident than Ian about his homosexuality, though still publicly closeted and gave Ian a really hard time when they first met in early '88, before he went back to the UK [where he was from]. The two clashed like anything, and were absolute sworn enemies. Bob basically said to Ian, "Drop this paranoia, it's all bullshit. Drop the girlfriends, people will accept you as you are. They will accept you as a sportsman, just get on with your life." One night they were watching TV and [another very well known footballer] came on the screen, and Bob goes, "Oh I've slept with him." Ian took huge exception to all of this. "He doesn't know what it's like. He's got no idea what I've got to go through. It could wreck my career. There's the whole sponsorship thing here. It's not just my football, it's everything else I'd be cut out of." '

Which was exactly what people were telling him. 'There was one guy who worked for the ARL, I met through Andrew, who used to tell me things like I shouldn't go to major gay events like the Mardi Gras, that I should keep a low profile. He told me *he* didn't go to those, because he was involved with the ARL, and he didn't want to give them a bad name. "Well, they employ me and I have responsibilities there," he would say. He advised me that I should remain secretive about my sexuality, too.' Ian was told he could say goodbye to any endorsements and he could forget being involved with kids in charity work or football training camps, such would be the backlash against him if it were widely known he was gay.

All this made perfect sense to an aspiring working-class boy, bred in full view of the negative status assigned to poofs. It wasn't a question for him, as for Bob, of a few mates in his team finding out he was gay. From where Ian was sitting at the very top of the football heap, it was too far back to where he started, and too many people were watching him, for him to fall. He was a cultural icon. And at 22, with the world at his feet, he wasn't about to single-handedly fight a whole culture. His experience told him that, even if individual players or coaches accepted or tolerated him, he would lose the respect of a culture. There are very few men with ambition in any field, let alone football, who want notoriety as a poof to cloud the acclaim they work for, and deserve. Many homosexuals accept it as their fate that they will never be entirely respected or honoured in their field of achievement if their sexuality is known. (Nowhere is that point made more poignantly than in the film *Priest*.) So they opt instead for respect and accolades, at a price.

For Ian, the pre-season hype of '88 brought with it comparisons to past greats of the game, especially Coote, McCarthy and O'Neill. In an article titled 'Roberts Flies High at Souths', which spoke glowingly of his 'characteristic tooth-rattling tackles and surges', George Piggins referred to Ian as 'a better and busier Norm Provan'. Photos and mentions of Ian avec Clarise started accompanying articles like this one. In fact, armed with Clarise, it was an aggresively confident Ian who spoke with reporter Ian Hanson after South's exhilarating win, in the inaugural Super Sevens tournament. He went boldly, verbally, where he had not been before:

IAN'S ULTIMATE SACRIFICE
'There will be no more beers for me until the season is over. Winning in this game is all about sacrifice and that's what cost us the chance of going all the way last season. I don't want to sound out against my team-mates but everyone in this camp has to realise they have to sacrifice things to reach the top. For me, it's going to be beer and going out. The only times I'll be going out is when I take my girl, Clarise, to dinner. This year is do or die for me with Souths and in the representative arena. I've got my sights set firmly on trying to make the NSW state-of-origin side and then the Test teams to play England and the Rest of the World.' (2/'88)

Ian finished the Sevens with 'a cut cheek, a fat lip and a badly swollen eye—a sight his new girl Clarise had never seen before. "I hope she doesn't get too much of a shock," Roberts said.' He may have been a bit heat-exhausted that scorcher of a day, after four intense Sevens games. It was a dynamic start to the season for Souths. The $50,000 prize money wasn't going to go astray at a cash-strapped Souths, either. And the win against the Raiders in the final was satisfying. Ian was right in form. 'When I read, now, what I used to say, I just cringe.' He sucks his breath in, in horror, then laughs. 'I was so concerned about living up to expectations. Being the perfect profile of a league player. Being exactly what I was supposed to be.'

One of the highlights of the Sevens series had been Ian's tackle of

St George player Brett Clark. Souths had been leading the Dragons 6–4 when Clark broke clear of the pack and raced towards the line.

There wasn't a Rabbitoh in sight, only a prop forward, but Roberts is no ordinary prop forward. As the nippy little Clark scampered towards the line, Roberts pinned his ears back and began the chase. He ran alongside Clark before bridging the gap and bundling his smaller rival over the touchline in a classic tackle. 'I thought I had no hope in hell of getting him but it looks pretty bad when you give up,' Roberts said. 'It was the biggest chase of my football career but it was worthwhile. Brett got up laughing and I was still stunned I'd caught him!' (Ian Hanson, 2/88)

George recalls that first Sevens competition, and Ian's chase. 'When we picked the Sevens, everyone said "Why did you pick so many forwards?" Well, Ian Roberts came out of a scrum, and he came from the front row and he ran down a winger! Caught him. And they were things that front-rowers didn't do. People above the average do that. That's tremendous football.'

The probability of Ian's selection for the Australia team to play the touring Great Britain side was again confidently canvassed. Especially by his biggest fan—his coach.

'He will be good enough and tough enough to throw in against the Poms and once he gets into the Test team they won't get him out,' George told one reporter. 'There is not a prop in the game who has got his work rate. He tackles all day, does a lot with the ball and is fast when he breaks through. Ian is in a rare bracket of props who has come a long way in a short space of time.'

PIGGINS TIPS TEST FUTURE FOR ROBERTS
Piggins described towering front rower Ian Roberts as the hottest property in Sydney's Rugby League after his barnstorming performance in the Rabbitohs' Sevens triumph.

'He's got to be the most valuable player in the game. The bloke trains seven days a week and there'll be no stopping him from now on. He's ready to play against the Poms.'

For a player of his giant frame Roberts showed remarkable mobility and speed. 'You can see how much he has learnt from first grade football in the past two years,' Fenech said. 'Most props don't really reach their peak until their mid-twenties and Ian's going to get much much better. I'm glad he's playing for Souths! I'd hate to be against him.' (Phil Rothfield, *Mirror*, 8/2/87)

RUGGED ROBO ALL FIRED UP
In 1986 when the Kangaroos played top English club Wigan, an Australian was the best on the field ... But he wasn't a member of the Kangaroos. Come on down, Ian Roberts. The tallest prop in the world is rapidly developing into the best. Now he is breathing fire and it will take a mighty prop to keep him out of Test Honours this year. (Geoff Prenter, *Mirror*, 2/88)

In the '88 Panasonic Cup, Souths were victorious against Canberra at Parramatta Stadium. Feeling guilty after being sin-binned, Ian provided a frenetic performance to atone. Commentators thought this should advance his prospects for selection.

ROBERTS STARS DESPITE SPELL IN SIN BIN
Just about every time he touched the ball, Souths seemed to go right on the attack. His crunching defence shattered his opponents' confidence. Only minutes into the fourth quarter, Roberts almost certainly sealed the man-of-the-match honours by setting up lock Mark Ellison for a great try.

Using his strength to classic advantage, Roberts steamrolled through the Raiders defence before offloading brilliantly for Ellison to score ... In a bid to boost his prospects this season, Roberts has concentrated on sprint training and weight work during the off-season. (Les Muir, *Mirror*, 2/88)

Everyone seemed to be rooting for Ian's selection that year, and it seemed like a fait accompli. Souths fired into the competition with a new-look home to accompany their new-look status within the game, having moved to the Sydney Stadium from Redfern Oval. It was by no means a universally popular move, but the difference in the venues reflected, metaphorically, the change that had taken place in the Rabbitohs' image within the game.

Ian was again in form in the first game of the premiership season, against Cronulla at Caltex Field.

ROBERTS MASTER OF BOMBS

South Sydney has come up with rugby league's answer to Warwick Capper ... Roberts' amazing ability to take the high ball for tries has been a feature of the Rabbitohs' early-season form.

'Ian is as good at taking high balls as any forward the game has seen,' Souths secretary Terry Parker said. 'I would hate to be a fullback with him charging down on me ... The boys put a lot of time into practising bombs with him at training.' (Tony Adams, Mirror, 8/3/88)

Up until their away game against Newcastle, on 8 May, Souths had lost only one game. It had to be against Canberra, of course, 6–34. At Seiffert oval on 19 March. 'Canberra was for us what we had been to Manly,' Mario wrote in his autobiography.

The week after the Rabbitohs' second loss of the season, against Newcastle, Ian broke two bones in his foot playing in the City Origin side. Peter Tunks, his Canterbury opposite, but his team-mate in that game, accidentally landed on it. Ian was in plaster until August, by which time Souths were out of final-five contention. Their final game, a win against Canterbury, saw Ian experience complications with his ankle, and injury once again ruled him out of a possible off-season in England. Up until that point, major injury hadn't been a problem.

Front-rowers had been dragged off the field, broken, concussed and bloody for years, often as a result of the more underhand tactics institutionalised in the game. But it was the mental, not physical, strain incurred through such constant beating which Ian Walsh thought would break some of the younger props. By 1988 there were ten front-rowers aged 22 or less, when Walsh again expressed concern that there were too many young props in first grade. He was concerned that young players didn't have the mental maturity to deal with the general bashing they would receive in tackles and scrums.

All-in brawls were few by '88. Ian had experienced a couple, in games against Canterbury and Balmain, in which it was not uncommon for players of one team to hold an opponent, so a few good bone-crunching hits could be scored. But on the whole, this had been policed out of the game. In a way, the decreasing age of front-rowers reflected the fundamental change that was taking place in the game. In *Rugby League Week*, Daniel Lane concluded: 'Maybe the game's emphasis has switched from gnarled oak trees in the front row, to finely tuned athletes.' Today, you have to look hard to find a misshapen and repeatedly broken young face in the game.

Ian seemed to be coping with all the wear and tear of front-rowing well. After initial shock at the toughness, if not the brutality, he acclimatised. As for injuries, cuts or bruises, black eyes or chronic concussion, recurring shoulder and neck problems ... nothing had kept him out of play for Souths prior to his broken foot.

He should have rested his foot properly in the '88 off-season, but Ian wanted to go on a special tour of New Guinea Souths had arranged. 'It was just the craziest experience. It was surreal, actually. We landed on some airfield where the whole place had turned out to welcome us, and I mean the whole place. These people are fanatics when it comes to league. It's their national game and they worship it and the stars of the game, literally. People travel from miles around to see their heroes. They walk for days. Players are like movie stars. They name their kids after players. There are several Mal Meningas running around New Guinea ... And thousands of Ian Roberts!' he joked.

'But the atmosphere is mad. It's like nothing you can imagine. The crowd is keyed up. They are desperate to get near the players, to touch them, anything. But you're not sure whether they want to be nice to you or rip you to shreds, and the way the security guards or police treat them, you're even less sure. They are battling to keep these people at bay, and they don't hold their punches either.'

The whole thing was a bit frightening, from the time he stepped off the plane to the time he got back on again.

SIX
RAGS TO RICHES
RABBITOH

Ray: *He was always going to be a millionaire.*

Jean: He had a paper round. Then he worked at McDonald's ... He was always doing something. For money. For money. He was crazy about money!

Ray: We never had any money, ourselves ... He always worked to get money. He was saving money when he was at school. One thing about Ian, he's never been frightened of work.

Jean: He always saved his first dollar note. Then every week he'd put a dollar note in an album.

Ray: He'd say, they'll be worth a lot of money one day. I mean, that's just the sort of thing he'd do. He had about 50 of them ... He was always very careful with his money. When he started his apprenticeship, he went to the accountant that does our tax. Ian started going to him, and Mike suggested he buy a flat and negative gear it. That's what really got him going ...

'Julian, my boss, was a Hungarian Jew, and had no concept of Rugby League when I started working for him. Back then, training was always after work hours. I couldn't do it now, work that many hours and train that many hours. Between training and playing, working, tech, and the travel, it was hectic. Before he realised the level of football I was at, Julian used to say "Look, you have to decide whether you're going to play football, or be an electrician." I was kind of, like, thinking, "You don't really know what you are saying." He soon learnt about the game and the commitment required. Then, for ages, I was his golden boy, getting all this publicity. He loved it. But I couldn't take the amount of time off work that I needed. There was a lot more promotional stuff happening, and trips away blah blah blah ... I was taking heaps of days off, and could never work back. I pretty well always hated working as a sparkie. So I left. This was midway through '88. Well, I needed a job. Football contracts weren't that lucrative then, and football didn't last forever. I didn't want to not work because I wasn't all that financial.

'I got a job as a brickie's labourer, through someone at the club. And I started to look round for a business to buy with the money I'd been saving.'

Ian had been good at scrimping and saving since his paper-round days. Since his bottle-collecting days, he knew the value of money, and was always careful not to squander it. For years he drove a beat-up car which served its purpose in getting him from A to B. He'd always been the sort of person who would think of walking somewhere, rather than automatically taking a cab, and who would sooner eat at home than a restaurant, or at a good basic restaurant than a fashionable one. He was not frivolous. It was no effort for him to be frugal because most of his pleasure in life was derived from basic physical activities, not from spoiling himself with extravagances.

But Ian's frugality was also related to a strong work ethic and a consciousness of coming from nothing. A big-picture person, he was ambitious enough to be careful and patient. He wanted to build a successful future for himself, and was prepared to be disciplined in order to reach the goal he set. It wasn't that he didn't know how to enjoy the luxuries and perks which came his way through football, he just didn't need them if they slowed his progress.

Contradicting his personal Spartan approach was an increasing tendency to make bold business investments. Perhaps prompted by a sense of infallibility which football was providing, he began to take bigger risks. After working as a labourer for a few months, he found a business he wanted to buy. 'The deli was a people business, which I liked, because I always thought I was pretty good with that sort of thing. At the time, Mum and Dad were in England for a few months, so I decided to make my own decision. My accountant at the time advised me not to buy it, but I thought the takings were pretty good.'

The shop was smack bang in the centre of Oxford Street, Darling-hurst, on the gay strip! Ian says now that it didn't cross his mind that a connection would be made between him and the location of the shop. He just took a plunge. The friends who were aware of his paranoia about his sexuality could only wonder at the move, and whether Ian wasn't again playing some subconscious game of Russian roulette with the likelihood of being 'exposed'. 'Of course, Mum and Dad came back, and I'd meanwhile bought this shop and they were like, "Oh no, what have you *done*?" They thought I was crazy!' Ray was taken aback: 'When we got back, he says casual like, "Oh, I bought a shop."' Jean was unimpressed. 'We said, "Another mad scheme!"'

While he had his head down with the deli, with barely a moment to take stock, a storm was gathering around, the likes of which rugby league had not seen for a while. And the press fed on deli metaphors, describing a League 'in a pickle' and Ian's 'carving up the opposition' as the story unfolded in 1989. Before the year was out, with some factual ingredients, some sweet eulogy, some sour speculation, and some spicy drama, football's Mr Wonderful was whipped up into a phenomenon.

By April 1989, Ian Roberts was the big story in football. Jour-nalists were frantically wielding superlatives to tie up all the angles in the big story. The elements? His superlative football, the push to see his talents take him all the way, his business mind, the end of his contract with Souths, the speculation as to where the hottest property in football would be playing in 1990, and the unwitting challenge he began to pose for the proposed league salary cap. Not to mention his private life.

Ian's injury in 1988, and the subsequent lost half season, con-firmed the tenuous nature of a career in football. Then he pulled a hamstring at training, which saw him sidelined for all the pre-season games and the first game of the competition. This strengthened his determination to maximise his opportunities before it was too late and he played the England card again.

'There's a real chance I will play in England after this year. It depends on how things go in the rep games. I am happy at Souths ... I don't think I'd play for another Sydney club. England has always been part of my thinking. I guess the time for decision is close. I'm determined to have a big season. It was frustrating missing the second half of last year after starting so well. A few English clubs have spoken to me to see my intentions. I've told them I want to see how things turn out this year first.' (Darren Hadland, *RLW*, 1/3/89)

He would assert his determination to take his career the next logical step one minute, then pledge eternal loyalty to George and Souths the next. While the passion with which Ian played the game belied his pragmatic attitude to it, his pragmatism was foiled by fact he was a soft touch when it came to people. He had already been swayed to stay at Souths once. Not because the money was better, but because he was convinced it was the right thing to do.

1989 began to look like Ian's year. And Souths'. Their loss in their first game, to Easts, 14–0, was claimed to be largely attributable to the performance of the Dragons' prop Pat Javis. Ian was back in the side by the next week, and Souths began an amazing twelve-game winning streak. Who better to start that against than Canberra, and in Canberra's home territory at Seiffert Oval? Ian was heralded in the days after the match:

BOOM RABBITOH BURSTS BACK
In the space of 11 minutes ... the Canberra players felt the full ferocity of boom South Sydney prop Ian Roberts' comeback. [He] was unleashed five minutes into the second half [and] made an immediate impact on the match charging into the rucks with gusto and rattling the Raiders with bone-jarring defence ... Piggins said: 'I rate Ian among the best front-rowers in the business and he gave us a lot more of the authority that's needed up front.' (John Blanch, *Mirror*, 27/3/89)

His performances were often fodder for print journos to feed off and you could be forgiven for thinking at times that Ian was winning single-handedly. The truth was a little more complex. Souths formed a talented combination that year. Besides the riveting forward combination, Mario wrote in his autobiography, they developed a 'great kicking game through Mark Ellison, Phil Blake and Craig Coleman.

'To complement this we had probably the fastest kick and chase team in the competition ... and could chase down a kick before it hit the ground in our opposition's half ... We dominated many teams on the strength of our ability to ruck it out of our territory, kick deep into their half and send out our chasers like bloodhounds on a scent.' The extremely fast Graham Lyons was among the stars in the game against Canberra, scoring all three tries.

Jack Gibson, the NSW coach, was in the crowd at Caltex Field the following week for the game against Cronulla. Sloshing around in a field rain had turned into a quagmire, Ian produced what Phil Rothfield touted as 'possibly the finest performance of his career'. 'I WANT ROBERTS SAYS GIBSON' cried the two inch headlines, with the subhead 'Souths Ironman a Blues Certainty', in what was just one of the raves Ian scored as a result of his performance that day. This attention from the NSW coach, though, was the most important for Ian:

South Sydney's towering young front-rower Ian Roberts almost certainly forced his way into the NSW State of Origin ... yesterday. 'Just say this,' said Gibson, choosing his words carefully, 'If he doesn't make the team we're going to have an awfully good side.'

As ever, George Piggins was on hand to give his protégé a wrap. 'If there is a better prop anywhere, I'd love to know who he is.'

Roberts threw himself through the mud to rack up 45 tackles—all of them telling blows on the Sharks' forwards. And he showed his skills with the football to send lock Michael Andrews over for the match winning try 20 minutes into the second half. Add the countless times he carted the ball up the field, and you've got a near perfect game.

The big question now is whether Souths can afford to keep the devastating prop at Redfern next season ...

With the huge wraps Gibson and Piggins have on him, Roberts will attract offers of about $130,000 for one season. Souths chief executive Terry Parker admits it's going to be difficult. 'He's a very loyal player and I believe we can come up with the right offer to keep him.' (Phil Rothfield, 2/4/89)

In the Panasonic Cup match against Canterbury on Wednesday night, 5 April, Ian emerged battered and sore from a tough game with the Man of the Match award. It was going to be hard to dissociate his name, and game, from talk of money in '89. The football he was playing ensured that. Keeping him at Souths was the concern of everyone from Terry Parker to Mario Fenech. And the media knew where to find him to chase a story.

A TYRO PROP WHO LIKES TO GET DOWN TO BUSINESS
Ian Roberts dragged his towering tortured frame past the pastrami and cabanossi and smoked ham yesterday ... Rugby League's flavour of the month could have done with a day away from his Taylor Square Deli. If he was feeling like a stuffed olive, his face more closely resembled blue-vein cheese ... his reward for starting work at 7 a.m. yesterday was to punctuate his book-keeping with interminable media interviews ... Roberts is following in the tradition of such former South's greats as Piggins, John O'Neill and Gary Stevens, self-made men who can modestly boast to being in the millionaire category. (Brian Curran, SMH, 7/4/89)

Ian floated the idea of staying with Souths in the future, in return for the deli getting catering rights to Souths Leagues Club functions. Terry Parker, who admitted that they were probably going to have to find $100,000 to keep Ian, was amused with the idea and told journalist Brian Curran: 'Catering rights for official functions? That's new. F ... me dead. Con the fruiterer. I'll have Ian the front-rower. I've never heard of it, but if it means I can keep him ... I'm happy to discuss it. He can't have the Chinese restaurant. He's not talking about that is he? I'll have to tell him to wok off!'

After a midweek win against the Bulldogs, based on a penalty count when the scores were level, George ventured, 'We're pretty hopeful of keeping him next year. We're going to have to pay the money to keep him, but he's a Souths junior and he loves the area. He'll give us the last shot at him. If we can win [the Panasonic Cup] we've got Ian Roberts and someone else on the books.' Or so he assumed. The Panasonic Cup was worth $175,000.

The next day, the *Mirror* started a relentless chipping away of Souths' hopes when it announced that at least four clubs, two local and two overseas, were already willing to offer $250,000 to lure Ian away. The bidding had opened at about $125,000 a season, big money in those days. 'Money talks,' Ian said at the time, 'So, so I'll be weighing everything up in the next few months.' Manly was one of the local clubs bidding.

No-one was working at Ian's PR more than the print journalists, and their alluring comparisons with the men of league folklore helped up the ante in the Ian Roberts stakes.

If Ian had had a moment to take it all in, he must have found it daunting. He was being taken to giddying heights by rhetoric, and shown a pretty marvellous view. But he wasn't the type to get carried away with people's superlatives. Plus he didn't have the time. 'From the day I signed the papers for the shop, I only had time to think "My God, what the hell have I done?" I felt like I was being swamped, in a permanent state of panic, you know, this twit running around trying to make himself happy, but not having a clue how. Going about it all the wrong way, last at home at night, and first out of the house in the morning. The stuff going on round me was a blur. I didn't take it in.'

Frank Cookson was worried for him, but impressed with his work ethic. 'I said, "You can't do this, training *and* this, start at five in the morning and you don't finish until ten at night. You're working seventeen- and eighteen-hour days and you have got to train in the meantime. You just can't handle it." He had to go out and do all his own buying and that sort of thing.'

The idea of investing in a business had been to enable him to work less. Now it had become a headache of major proportions. Family and friends were hauled in to work as Ian found himself over-committed and stressed out by the accounting books. 'Well,' Ray sighs, 'it got to the point where Clem was working there. Jean would go clean up, I'd be doing store work, and Lee's mum was working too. We thought, "This is bleedin' good!" He'd be earning money hand over fist and we'd spend all our spare time there working for him! Mind you, he was always prepared to work hard himself. He'd work six days a week, no worries. It's part of his life and I don't think he'll ever be short of a quid.'

It had been fun to begin with. 'I had the time of my life for a second. But it was just too many hours and even when I wasn't there, I was there, you know? All I was doing was thinking about it. It destroyed me. I'm a real worrier by nature. I used to worry that people were going to stop coming into the shop for some reason, because they all of a sudden didn't have money to spare or something. You only go into a deli like that if you have spare money. You get your basic stuff from the supermarket don't you? We opened at seven and closed at ten at night. Long hours, seven days a week. Anyway, the long hours don't make the earnings look good. But I didn't want to put a manager in. I'd only worry about that, too. When people are spending your money, you worry! It's your head on the chopping block all the time. I was only young after all. When the '89 season started, I wasn't concentrating on football enough. Even then, I was in the deli every day for at least five or six hours, often more.

'I'd have staff ringing up at 7 a.m. on a Saturday, saying they couldn't work, and Saturday was an important day for business, and I'd have a game to play! I got to the stage where I was practically living in the shop. I couldn't sleep properly if I didn't lock up at night, and I was in there opening up at the crack of dawn.'

'I got broken into a couple of times. Back door smashed down. It was incredible the damage they did, and no-one heard them! What's more, somehow the security alarm didn't go off. They turned it off both times, and you're supposed to have a code to do that. I found out about the robberies the next day when I went to open up. I thought it must have been an inside job, which was one reason I didn't get a manager in. I changed the code and that, but other people had to know it. I couldn't open every morning. One of the break-ins was just before Christmas, and they took all the Christmas hams and expensive stuff, all the big blocks of cheese. They definitely had a truck, these people. I got paranoid about security, so I felt much better being on the premises myself. As much as I could, I got people in that I knew to work, friends and family.'

Roberts runs a new delicatessen business at Taylor Square, and he has plenty of laughs doing it. 'The night of the Mardi Gras was amazing,' Roberts said. 'The people who came into the shop, and the costumes. Hilarious, and it was the best business I've ever had. We stayed open till midnight and then watched the parade.' So the big rangy forward with the phenomenal work rate is learning the short cuts with the cold meats, salamis and pickles. But as a player, no sausage meat in Roberts. Just pure fillet steak. (Tony Megahey, 'Likened to a Legend', RLW, 4/89)

'Of course, there were laughs along the way. Some of the characters that used to come in to the shop would crack me up. There was a strip joint right next door, and on the other side, a gay adult book shop. People would come in with their brown paper bags, so I used to ask to check their bags.' He laughs.

On 22 April, Souths annihilated St George 32–0. After the game Ian was going 'As long as George is happy with my form, I'm happy' to journos who, with what had become monotonous regularity, ran off headlines comparing him with football greats. It was the size of the headline that varied. This one was about a two-incher.

ROBERTS UP THERE WITH THE GREATS
'I've been in football for 25 years and seen a lot of players,' Piggins said. 'I put Roberts in the Ron Coote and Bob McCarthy category. He's a champion.'

Former Kangaroo captain, Bobby Fulton, himself a legend of the game, said Souths' effort was one of the best wet weather performances he had seen.' (Ray Chesterton, Mirror, 23/4/89)

Such has been the improvement of Ian Roberts this season that the Souths' pack has a new dimension. Roberts has been the dominating forward in almost every game he has contested this season. [He] is playing with such velocity and consistency. (Tony Megahey, RLW, 26/4/89)

ROBERTS WORTH A FORTUNE
South Sydney must win the Panasonic Cup to retain boom front-rower Ian Roberts in 1990. Roberts' early-season form has been so outstanding that he is fast outpricing himself out of the Rabbitohs' reach ... If he continues at his present form Roberts can command close to $200,000 for the next two seasons ...

    'That's why winning the cup is so vital to us,' George said. 'Apart from the prestige, it means we will be able to keep Ian Roberts. He's a tremendous player and it will be hard to keep him, but he has already promised us the last offer.' (Tony Adams, Mirror, 31/4/89)

Then, disaster struck the weekend of a brilliant win over Canterbury. The field at Belmore wasn't lucky ground for Ian. He had some bruising encounters there, confronting international forwards like Paul Dunn and Peter Tunks, who vied with him for representative honours. Not that he ever let that intimidate him. He always rose to the occasion, which is perhaps why he played some of his best and most memorable football in those encounters. He had been carted off unconscious once before, when he had clashed with Paul Dunn, and had been out cold for fifteen minutes.

    The morning of the game, 30 April, started badly enough when Ian saw a column in the *Sun-Herald* written under the pseudonym 'Harry Craven'. There was a sarcastic quip about a great footballer who had been spotted in a bar on Oxford Street, drinking with the boys. The innuendo was clear. It was the first time Ian had seen anything even approaching a comment on his sexuality in print. 'I was terrified!! I just froze when I saw it. I went to George and started babbling on, saying this guy can't do this sort of thing, and I want something done about it. George just said that I shouldn't worry about it. But I was beside myself. I was terrified that I would run out onto the field that day, and there'd be all these people who would have read it. I just didn't know what reception I'd get. Before the game, I went to sit outside and watch the reserves game for a little while, and Tugger said to me, joking like, "What about you at that gay bar?" I just saw red. I think I showed him my fist and tried to act like I was laughing the whole thing off. That day I ran on the field thinking "All these people know, and they're going to be out to get me!" I used to think about things like that in other games, when I'd always be trying to prove myself. This was worse, though.'

It was this fear and defiance that drove Ian to play some of his hardest, most relentless games. The constant barrage and beating he took would compensate for any potential revelation about himself. That game at Belmore, snide comments on field by some of the Bulldogs, lent impetus to Ian's game. He was no longer running from demons. He was chasing them now, with a vengeance, and he played like he had never played, until George thought it wiser to take him off, to stop him being a danger to himself. George remembers that game well. 'Some of the Canterbury blokes took the liberty to say a few things. I don't know what they said to him, but whatever they said, he tore them to pieces! All of a sudden they found out that they weren't dealing with any mild little faggot. I thought, "My god, they got a shock with him!" '

Ian suffered concussion early in the game. Then his nose was broken. Undeterred, he played on and made the longest solo run of the match when he broke through the Bulldog line for a 40-metre bolt. 'I remember being hit a beauty by Langers [Paul Langmack]. Ian told Ray Chesterton after the game, 'And I remember Langers standing over me saying "Please get up, Robbo, please get up." And I remember sitting in the dressing room at half time. After that it's cloudy. I'm still dazed now.' George said at the time, 'Although he wouldn't admit it, Ian was more than a bit the worse for wear. I brought him from the field because I was frightened he might blow a fuse or have a heart attack. The bloke just doesn't know when he's had enough and that's one of the reasons why this side is firing at the moment.' And the *Telegraph* ran with a back-page headline 'I THOUGHT ROBERTS WOULD BLOW A FUSE', three inches high! 'Roberts' influence on the game was immense. He is without doubt the premiership's form prop,' wrote Peter Frilingos.

During his exertions that game, Ian received a knock against his pelvis and a tackle by Jason Alchin tore his groin muscle. At first the injury seemed like a simple matter, requiring a bit of treatment and rest. If only it had been that straightforward.

Meanwhile, Ian put the deli on the market.

The next week *Rugby League Week* ran a cover photo of Ian receiving a pass from Mario, with the caption 'IAN ROBERTS: RAGS TO RICHES RABBITOH'. Inside was the story about Souths' fans' attempts to keep Ian at Souths. A bid of $150,000 had been rumoured to have come from Manly, in the escalating bidding war. Ian was Souths' home-grown prestige hero. Their star. They weren't about to let him go easily, let alone to Manly. One supporter in the crammed Belmore dressing room pledged $10,000 to keep Ian a Rabbitoh, telling him that there was more where that came from. The emotional dimension of the issue was coming to the fore and finding its way into print. Ian Roberts was not a commodity as far as the Rabbitohs' supporters were concerned. Football was a religion at Souths. It was both a way of life and a diversion from life. For players, it was a way out, one of the few ways of making something out of a life with few other opportunities. The problem was that sometimes, as was bound to happen, the bond between player and supporter was threatened when their interests diverged. Like South's heroes before him, Ian had been transformed, by the publicity machine and by the fans, into something above a mere business transaction. He had become a saviour, a young valiant knight cutting down the enemy. If he could make mincemeat of the premiers, there was no enemy he couldn't vanquish. Souths were looking, now, like serious premiership contenders.

The transfer fear was lent an edge of hysteria by the fact that Souths had lost Ian's predecesor, John O'Neill—'Lurch', mark one—to the 'silvertails' at the height of their heyday in the early '70s. 'Manly won the comp the same year they got O'Neill,' Tugger remembers. 'He was a Souths' man through and through. They were all close, he, McCarthy, Piggins. It was exactly the same as with Ian. Manly couldn't win a comp, and [Ken] Arthurson said, we need O'Neill to win the comp. He became the highest paid player in Sydney at the time. They gave him something like $10,000.' And that was the beginning of the end of that chapter in the history of Rabbitoh greatness. Surely it wasn't to be repeated.

Publicly, George was the eternal optimist. 'I can say confidently that Ian Roberts will stay with Souths. In three years I have never lost a player I wanted to keep ... Ian has promised to give us last say and he is a kid with red and green blood in his veins.' Ian responded with consideration. 'I have had several offers, but I will give Souths last crack. If they can secure my future, I'll stay. I've had some big offers and I need to give them plenty of thought, but as I have always said, I am really happy here.' (Darren Hadland and Tony Megahey, *RLW* 5/89)

Theoretically, Ian was forbidden to enter into a firm commitment with another club until after his current one was fulfilled. Clubs approaching other clubs' players, mid-season, had become a contentious issue within Rugby League, and at various times Phillip Street had threatened to take action against clubs 'tampering' with players. The settlement of a new contract for a player might pose a clash of interest for him and compromise his allegiance towards his current club. There was talk of John Quayle imposing new regulations on players, to force them to report any mid-season approaches from clubs, or agents acting for clubs. For a club like Souths, that sometimes survived on fanaticism alone, finding out about a player talking to the other side could have terrible effects on team morale and performance. It was important for Ian not to be seen to be flirting with the enemy.

Ian's earlier contracts had been negotiated with Frank Cookson acting as manager. Back in April '87, when Wigan had offered what had looked like a generous $50,000 a season for three seasons, Frank had helped Ian negotiate his more lucrative contract with Souths. Rabieh Krayem, now manager of the North Queensland Cowboys, and Johnny Lewis, Jeff Fenech's trainer, had rung Ian to offer their management services early in the '89 season, and Ian happily placed the matter in their hands. By May they were fielding offers from five local clubs as well as English clubs Wigan and Hull.

One day when Clem was working in the deli, he took a call from Darren Hadland at *Rugby League Week*. Ian recalls, 'Clem was always being crazy. He was a shit-stirrer. He told Darren that I was away in Newcastle. Poor Darren thought he was on to something "Newcastle! What's he doing in Newcastle?" "Oh, negotiating a big deal with the Knights!" says Clem, all casual like. All crap. Then

Clem hints at some outrageous sum, way more than Manly had offered at that stage.

'When Darren eventually got in touch with me to confirm his "information", I couldn't just straight out deny it. I would've felt like an idiot saying "Oh, my mate was just making it up as a shit stir. He always does that!"'

Rugby League Week ran the story, 'KNIGHTS CHARGE', on 24 May and quoted a pretty ambiguous Ian: 'I am really flattered by the money being mentioned. At the moment I am not close to signing with anyone.' Newcastle naturally denied the story, leaving mud on poor Darren's face.

However, high-profile football personalities watched aghast as the bidding continued. Lewis and Krayem were asking for an unheard of $250,000 for a season, even as Ian's groin injury was proving a frustrating impediment to his rep game chances. No-one could believe that a footballer was worth the money being offered, especially with the salary cap becoming effective in 1989. The *Daily Mirror* headline on 17 May screamed, 'ROBERTS WANTS $500,000', and Peter Frilingos claimed at least eight clubs were still interested, despite the fact that Lewis and Krayem had specified to clubs, in writing, the amount being sought. The press were wetting themselves over this story.

What made the bidding story so spectacular was that it was being played out against the proposal by the league heirarchy in Phillip Street to impose a ceiling on what clubs could spend on putting a team together. This was an attempt to ensure that poorer clubs would remain competitive against clubs flush with funds. If a ceiling of $1,500,000 was imposed, as was being proposed, clubs would have to be wary of spending too much on any one player. John Quayle, the ARL's general manager, issued a warning to clubs. 'The League's salary cap committee will immediately inquire into the financial affairs of the club that signs Roberts, no matter what the fee. To say the least, the asking price for Roberts, which includes provisions for unheard of benefits, is staggering.' The league was obviously concerned that, in the stampede for Ian, clubs would flaunt the new ceiling rules. It would be impossible both to field a team and pay what was being asked for Ian without breaching the rule. There was only one league player in the world whose contract could enable him to earn more, and that was Ellery Hanley, who was on $13,000 a game with Wests.

The ARL saw the salary cap as 'the only way some clubs will survive', and John Quayle explained the League's somewhat spurious argument. 'Our aim is not to bring the top sides down to the stragglers, but to give the battlers a chance to close the gap and still remain financially viable. And we will do that for them, despite themselves.' This patronising approach involved clubs being invited to participate in the League on the condition that they agree to the new salary rules. The League would then make its evaluation of each player's worth. This would be the amount the League would use when adding up and assessing the total salary that each club could spend on its players. Transfer fees received for players exiting clubs would not be deducted from the cap, and would give clubs extra funds. Business deals with clubs, such as Ian's suggestion of catering rights at Souths, would be scrutinised closely, taken into account as salary and deducted from the 'cap'. There were still grey areas, as with Ellery Hanley, whose salary was paid by a sponsor. The League would still assess his worth and deduct this from the cap total. This seemed to mean that players could be paid huge amounts if their clubs had good sponsors paying players direct. The League would review 'ceiling caps' each year, and would lift them as a club's ability to pay improved.

To encourage the local bids, Ian had earlier kept alive the option of playing in England, where there weren't any salary restrictions. 'If I got the right offer from England, I'd sell up my business right now and be over there in a flash,' he told *Rugby League Week* in April. 'I like the way they play the game, the people, the fans and the fact it's only an hour to Europe—great way for a young guy to see the world.'

Souths' salary cap for the 1990 season was assessed at $800,000. They couldn't afford Ian at the price being asked.

In this scenario of salary caps and bidding, George Piggins emerged as the media's anointed underdog when he was elected president of Souths. George was credited with conducting a one-man revolution to save Souths, which, while it led the competition, had the smallest budget of any club. Souths had floundered since mismanagement in the early '70s and they were in dire financial straits. George had challenged the administration who were attempting to sell off one of its few assets, part of the League Club building, because he thought the price being asked was way too low. The move to the Football Stadium had affected business at the club in Redfern, and George wanted to rectify this by upgrading facilities at Redfern Oval and moving back. He wanted to re-involve Souths' Juniors, who had become alienated from the senior club when the ARL had forced Souths to move, and had dropped their much needed $130,000 sponsorship to the Senior club. Souths lost $200,000 in 1988. George's dream was to amalgamate the two clubs.

A true believer in the spirit of Souths, George had been generous with his money after retiring from his truck business at forty. He had even used it at times to help retain players like Mario and Ian, while coaching for a pittance. It was easy to sympathise with this former great and his undying loyalty to his troubled club while Ian, one of the Rabbitohs' new greats, was being lured away by dollars.

George's election was symbolic, but the battler ethos that surrounded him and the club provided a neat moral backdrop to what was emerging as the Ian Roberts scandal. George was torn. He wanted what was best for Ian, and that didn't necessarily mean having him staying put. But whatever he felt personally, his canonisation by the public was making Ian look more like a pariah to the fans.

The question of club loyalty, apart from contractual obligations, has arisen time and time again in rugby league. A football career is only about ten years long, provided a player stays uninjured, and it is sensible to maximise pay opportunities while they are there. Players in the past had been lulled into a sense of false security by club rhetoric which encouraged them to stay put rather than seek more money elsewhere. Sometimes it's done with a 'We'll always do the right thing by you, don't you worry' approach, or 'There'll always be a place for you here'. The fact is, neither the League nor the clubs were willing to admit to players, at the outset, that the game is a business. They were too busy trying to interfere with, and control, the market forces driving the game, at the same time as they encouraged them. The game benefits by bums on seats, and by sponsorship. If a club is doing well, it attracts both consumers and advertising dollars. It is smart business to respect the customers. Club and media rhetoric glorifies their role. They become the treasured and revered loyalists of the game. Players, in turn, are encouraged to revere the fans, to think about them when they make their decisions.

At many times in the past players have allowed considerations such as not disappointing the fans to sway their better judgment. They allowed their passion for the game to cloud their perception. They often stayed at a club for less money than they could get elsewhere because they were convinced it was their obligation. However, most players who have been on the receiving end of an involuntary farewell from a club will contend that club loyalty is a one-way deal. The clubs expect you to be loyal to them, until they they have finished with you.

Over at Manly, team captain Paul Vautin, a loyal Sea Eagle for nearly a decade, was about to be neatly shoved out the door to make room for new purchases. Vautin was to be offered a drastically and embarrassingly reduced fee for the '90 season only a year after being paid the highest amount for any forward at the club. He was to be told that, due to the financial situation at the club, and based on his form, the offer made was the best available. Then Manly put a $50,000 transfer fee on his head to help cover the costs of their buying spree. Vautin, whose team had suffered a bad season in '89, was not exactly ready to be put out to pasture, but he was at loggerheads with the club admin over the replacement of coach Alan Thompson. The way Manly ditched him didn't flatter him, or allow him to enter the open market with a great deal of bargaining power. And the Manly administrators obviously didn't consider the wrath of the loyal supporters when it was aimed at them, instead of at a player. (Ironically, years later, Vautin would be a diehard supporter of Manly and the ARL when Manly were telling players that their pay was determined by a scale system based on their value to the club, and were awarding some young inexperienced players much larger salaries than players like Des Hasler or Cliff Lyons!)

While the game pretends to honour a more socialist tradition, and the administration would like the clubs and players to honour a feudal tradition, rugby league is actually a series of franchises operating according to partially interfered with market forces. Roy Slaven, from

Radio JJJ, never one to mince words, said at the time: 'If Robbo can get $500,000 for two years, well good on him. Look what television is making out of it. When you've got Moose [Rex Mossop] and Trout [Graham Hughes] on salaries of hundreds of thousands a year and they're merely the hangers-on. If it wasn't for the mercurial and beautiful handywork of people like Robbo, the dollars wouldn't come in.' The times, they were a'changing, but slowly. Market forces wouldn't break free until competition was introduced into league football years down the line.

Meanwhile, Terry Parker, among others, blamed the greed of the player rather than the willingness of clubs to pay. 'I think there is no doubt the player's profile is increasing and the money they want is increasing with it. There are more teams playing and more teams bidding for the same amount of players. This is what has increased the rate.' And some players blamed the greed of players. Mario Fenech didn't for a second expect that Ian would knock back lucrative offers. 'With me, I love the game. But for Ian, it's different. It's a game. I've heard Ian say that to me. But he's clever, because he saw it as an opportunity for him to get out. And it catapults him, through his great physical qualities, and he sees that as his opportunity. I was never born with natural ability. I was born with dedication. Ian was born with both. I can remember quite vividly a conversation, and me being sort of a bit pissed off at his business approach to the game. He knew that he wanted to do this and he wanted to do that, and this was his vehicle to getting there.'

Frank Cookson placed a bet each way. On each side of his divided loyalties. 'It's like all walks of life. The football career is a very short-span thing. Tomorrow you could break your leg and be out of the game forever. Or even be a paraplegic or something. You get what you can, I reckon. I am a person loyal to Mascot and Souths. I wouldn't go anywhere else. I wouldn't even go to watch other teams play, if they weren't playing Souths. But that's different. I'm not getting money out of it. I mean, Ian should have been in a situation where he set himself up for life out of football.'

In years of football, players can suffer a great many privations apart from injuries. They can be harassed and generally have their privacy shot to pieces. They are scrutinised and are expected to be role models for their generation. Of course the perks can also be great. They are the rewards for long years of dedication and discipline, and, in a free enterprise system, they are the returns for their investment.

It didn't matter what Ian said in respect of wanting to stay, or of giving Souths last option. Some fans began to express their disdain for the whole business. Inevitably, it was Ian who bore the brunt of this. It was bound to happen. He was accused of being disloyal to a club that had supported him over the years. And he was phoned and visited at the deli by people who just wanted to give him a piece of their mind.

While Ian wanted to utilise all the opportunities he had earned through football, he had a genuine attachment to some aspects of the club, not to mention George. And he felt the wrath of the fans deeply. He didn't know what to do, except try to direct a bit of the heat elsewhere. 'Supporters don't understand the pressures players are under,' Ian said at the time. 'We see these big carrots before us and I'm not talking tens of thousands, I'm talking a lot more. I didn't set the price. Supporters don't seem to realise that it's not up to the player. My manager, Johnny Lewis, does that. I just go out there and play my best. I would play for $5 a game if I had to!' Hmmm.

The next chapter in the saga started when Ian tested his healed groin in a reserves match against Balmain on 17 June. After six weeks out, he was keen to get his game form back, but within ten minutes he was limping from Leichhardt Oval after a tackle. In the short space of time it took to make a crash tackle, his hopes for the most successful year of his life crashed. Exasperation can hurt more than pain. It seemed inconceivable that, for the second season in a row, he could be sidelined by a serious injury only a short way into the competition ... that an injury could cost him his 'dead cert' place in rep football. He simply had to be playing, to be considered for selection, only a short time away. And he had to be playing in order to justify the fuss about his worth. Having played only fifteen games in two years was enough to play infuriatingly on anyone's insecurities.

Wrenched groin muscles have a reputation for being as stubborn as they are painful. Paul Sironen, who had a groin tear in '87, advised a long rest as the only cure. A long rest was out of the question.

RAGS TO RICHES RABBITOH

ROBERTS IN DOUBT FOR REST OF YEAR
Roberts could miss the rest of the season after he ripped his groin muscle in the first minute. [He] was confident he had overcome the problem. Roberts' asking price for a season is in the vicinity of $200,000, but after yesterday's recurrence, his price may well have tumbled. (Alan Clarkson, Sun-Herald, 18/6/89)

Darren Hadland jumped on the doom and gloom bandwagon in *Rugby League Week* a little while later with the 'SALE PRICE ROBERTS' story. 'My value hasn't dropped … it's gone!' Ian was quoted as saying. 'As yet no-one is sure what the problem is.' Anxious to restore at least some sympathy for himself, Ian was stoking the story out of proportion, and Hadland willingly dramatised his predicament:

Roberts' worth has plummetted more quickly over the past two months than stocks in a Wall Street crash.

Two months ago the 23-year-old prop was the most wanted man in Sydney. His signature was worth $250,000 by some reports. Big spenders Manly were prepared to pay Roberts plenty. Now they may not be so keen. He is branded a liability … a terrific player when fit, but injury prone. It's a tag which hurts, yet all Roberts can do is smile at the cruel cards dealt him. The string of sensational performances at the start of Souths' winning run are all but forgotten. And suddenly the critics have surfaced … As Souths finds new limits to their heart and spirit, it is easy for their star prop to get left behind. (Darren Hadland, RLW, 28/6/89)

But poor Darren had been led away from the scoop again. By the time his story went to press, the most trumpeted signing in years had taken place. While, up in Queensland, five men were facing gaol sentences of up to fourteen years after being charged with having consenting gay sex in private, and one of the men had been held in custody for two weeks before being charged, in Sydney, at the rear of a less than salubrious little Lebanese cafe in Newtown, Ian had been ushered unceremoniously into a murky backroom by Rabieh Krayem, to meet with Doug Daley and place his signature on the richest contract in world rugby league history.

FINDING OUT

The *Mirror* had sniffed it out and they ran with a story—contrary to Hadland's—on the same day. The sensational revelation, by Ian Hanson, Tony Adams and Jack Darmody, hit the stands and scooped Hadland to smithereens with a story that threatened to plough a schism a mile wide, not only between Souths and Ian generally, but between George and Ian personally.

SEVEN
THE OUTCAST

'ROBERTS: MY ANGUISH', splashed the *Mirror*'s three-inch back page headline, followed by claims that Ian had in fact already signed with Manly for a record $250,000 a year. Then it went on to allege via George Piggins that Ian was helping to negotiate with other Souths players on Manly's behalf. George talked of sacking Ian from the side for the rest of the season.

Ian was contacted before the story went to press, and was told that George had said: 'I asked him if he had signed elsewhere and he said emphatically "yes". And I believe 100 per cent that elsewhere is Manly.' Ian said George had 'got his words mixed up. George knows what I told him and those were not the words I used.' Ian denied having signed with Manly. 'That's not true. No way! That's not true.'

Ian says now, 'When George called me and asked me whether I had signed, I said "George, mate, I've got to keep it really quiet. I don't want it to get out". He asked me again, and I said, "Let me put it this way, George, you'd better start looking for a front-rower for next season." I had to do the right thing by him and let him know so that he could make plans for the following year. George was like a father to me. He didn't begrudge me doing the best for myself. But he hadn't mentioned the poaching matter to me. He must've got off the phone and rung the papers almost straight away, but he hadn't asked me about it. I guess he just assumed it was true.'

In response to the allegations he was helping poach other players,

Ian said at the time, 'They're bleeding lies—I've been made a scape-goat. I can't believe it.' In response to the threatened sacking he told the *Mirror*, 'It's the biggest slap in the face I've ever received—all I have ever tried to do is the right thing by Souths and now this happens.'

Hooker Jim Serdaris had asked Ian's advice on contracts, as he was due to sign a new one with Souths. Ian had advised Jim to contact John Lewis if he wanted contract advice. Serdaris hadn't done this, nor had he turned up to to sign his new contract, as scheduled, on Tuesday, 27 June. George heard that Ian had been seen talking with Serdaris at training, and he also had sources which confirmed Manly were inter-ested in players other than Ian. George defended his actions to the *Mirror*.

'There were rumours among the players yesterday that Ian had signed with Manly but I didn't believe it because he told me Souths would have final shot at him.

'We offered him as much as we possibly could but we couldn't match the offer from Manly.

'But what stirred up the kettle were reports that other players were also ready to follow Roberts. I had to nip the situation in the bud to save the club. To lose three or four players could destroy our future.

'The decision to recommend we cut him has been among the most painful I've ever had to make, but I have to do what's in the best interests of the team. I can't really blame him for going to the highest bidder, and Manly have got themselves one heck of a footballer.'

A meeting of the Souths football club committee was scheduled for Thursday, 29 June, and would hear George's recommendation for sacking.

A spokesman for Ian told reporters Ian hadn't even received an offer from Souths, and implied the signing hadn't taken place. 'We can only assume from all of this that Souths are trying to shame Ian into signing. They are hoping to bluff and embarrass him into signing the same way they did with Mario Fenech, Craig Coleman and Phil Blake last year. It's just scare tactics and it's sad to see this happen because Ian Roberts is 100 per cent South Sydney.' The year before, Fenech, Coleman and Blake had been banned from playing the end of season games until they signed contracts for the following season. Mario claimed in his autobiography: 'George was the real force behind the sacking because he said he needed an answer about our future. I thought the course of action they chose was a disgrace. This gun to the head tactic didn't gel too well with the supporters either, but George was very stubborn about the whole issue.' Terry Parker had given the three 24 hours to sign or take a pay cut. All three wanted time to consider other offers but buckled after the ultimatum.

However, George wasn't trying to shame Ian into signing. He knew Ian was lost to Souths, who could not compete with the offers Ian was getting as early as June. 'Players only ever left Souths for one reason, we never had a player leave because he didn't like the place.' He was using the media to save his club, he explains. 'It was a tactic to cut Manly off and stop them getting Serdaris too. Here you are, you've got the Australian coach, the chairman of the ARL, all in for Manly, and here we are poor old Souths being devastated by Manly, and the thing was, we were trying to use the media hype to more or less get them to say, "Look, we've fed off Souths enough. If we try to get the other player, we're all going to look like bastards." We used those tactics to save our bacon. You got dirty on the fact you were losing these kids you gave a start to. You've only got to look at the ex-Souths players in the grand finals for Manly in '95 and '96.

'No-one at Manly has a mortgage on knowing a good player over the years. We knew Ian was good, just as we later knew Serdaris was good, and Hill, and Dymock, and Carroll. The fact is you can't blame players for accepting to go anywhere for better money. It's only a matter of time before your players go to greener pastures. You can't get offered the sort of money Ian was offered, and knock it back. I said to Ian at the time, "If you were my own son, I'd drive you over the bridge to get it." I mean, look, Manly have to be commended that they have the money to do things like that in rugby league. They've run a very profitable leagues club, and they've been able to afford players. We haven't been as professional at running our leagues clubs.

They're not entitled to be punished because they've been successful. Which is not to say I haven't been disappointed to lose players. I was terribly disappointed to lose Ian.'

Ian was sacked by Souths. That is, Souths gave other clubs, or more specifically Manly, the opportunity to buy out his contract for the rest of the year, before the League's transfer cut-off date of June 30, the next day! It was unlikely a club, even if they had been negotiating with Ian's agent, could or would take up the offer, given Ian's groin. And no club would want to be seen as contributing to a contract dispute between a player and his current club. The buy-out deadline came and went as expected. A stalemate existed.

The confrontation brought out Ian's obstinacy. He was injured by the implication that he was involved in poaching, and by George's public announcement of the signing, which Ian was under strict instructions to keep quiet. But he was reluctant to criticise George personally. In shock that the matter could have escalated so violently, and following the advice of his management, he prepared a statement for the *Mirror* which threatened legal action as a means of clearing his name. That statement also maintained that his football future had been jeopardised by Souths' allegations. Looking back on the whole episode now, guys like Frank felt Ian over-reacted a bit to George's manoeuvres.

'ROBERTS: I'LL SUE SOUTHS' by Tony Adams, appeared in the *Mirror* on Friday, 30 June, and the press relished the in-house battle between the legendary figures of two generations.

'These allegations from Souths have done untold damage to my reputation and now I'm led to believe one of the clubs my managers have been negotiating with have lost interest because they think I'm a ratbag. As far as I'm concerned, club loyalty has gone out the window and I want all my fellow players to know just how far loyalty goes in a club's eyes. Two years ago, I recieved a two year offer to go to Wigan worth more than $100,000 a season but turned it down because Souths begged me to give them priority. I did the right thing by them but all that has been forgotten. Business is business and we are obviously having a major disagreement along those lines ... But next to my

family, I'd say George Piggins is the closest man in the world to me. I grew up with all these blokes and coach George Piggins is still one of the nicest blokes I've met.'

That night George phoned Ian and advised him he would still be considered for selection when his groin was better. Ian had already spoken to the *Sun-Herald*, and on 2 July another prepared statement appeared in its 'Zorba and Hollywood' column. It spoke of Johnny Lewis and George, pitted against each other over this matter and quoted Ian at length:

'These are great men, honest as the day is long, and I am sorry they have been embroiled in this whole issue.

'But for Souths and George, in particular, to openly suggest that I have embarked against the club by way of poaching young players for monetary gain is untrue, hurtful and defamatory. Three years ago I walked into Souths' boardroom and feel I got taken for a ride.

'I vowed it wouldn't happen to me again, and when team-mates approached me about people who could ensure that the club did the right thing when contracts were discussed, I told them honestly that I could recommend the people who are looking after my interests.

'That was the end of my involvement. To suggest otherwise is a downright lie.

'My dealings with John Lewis have been with a handshake and he hasn't recieved or sought a cent—the tainting of his name has upset me more than what Souths have done to me.

'He has built his life around helping young people, not destroying their future.

'I can't believe Souths would think I would undermine them— players have phoned me this week to let me know they don't believe what has been said.

'They have even told George I haven't been involved but he obviously doesn't want to listen.'

That same day the *Sunday Telegraph* had the more recent information, under the headline 'GEORGE WILL PLAY ROBERTS'. George qualified the 'sacking' when he spoke to Phil Rothfield: 'We gave him permission to negotiate with any other club but it's past the deadline now and he's a Souths player for the rest of the season. When I suggested [Ian] should be released, I was thinking only of South Sydney. But I still think he's a terrific kid and he's got something to offer us for the rest of the year. He says he'll give it 100 percent and that's good enough for me.'

The very public spat had ended in mutual respect and reconciliation. George told Brian Curran at the *Sydney Morning Herald* the following week:

I felt sorry for Ian being tangled up in it, but once I believed that he was gone, my main objective was to save what other players we had, for the club.

And to think that Doug Daley [Manly's chief executive] and his team of poachers weren't trying to poach more than Ian out of the place, well that was ridiculous. They definitely were.

They were trying to get onto Jimmy Serdaris, you know. There was also rumour about Darren Schott. But they come after the main prize and they got it, Ian Roberts. They didn't just probably get one of the top footballers in the Sydney competition, they also got a tremendous person.

Ian's one of those types of kids that the people of Mascot who brought him through the juniors and all that are proud of. For them and for us to have lost someone like Ian Roberts is a great blow to this district and to this club. But I don't hold any animosity towards him looking after himself because, if it was my son, and the amount of money difference I believe it to be, I would have been advising him to take the money. You come down life once. You've got to enjoy it the best way you can. (5/9/89)

George had impressed Ian with those same words once before, and Ian now had a job to complete at Souths. Ian wanted no mumblings about clashes of interest in the lead-up to the finals that year, and despite going to the highest bidder, he wasn't disloyal to Souths. He recalls now there were times when he baulked. 'It was touch and go there at times. At home, Mum was saying "Sign with Souths". She couldn't bear all the trouble caused. Mum and Dad had already been subjected to abuse from fans and that, so I had them to consider. I started to ask myself whether it was worth it. Then I thought, "Well, I've passed up money to stay with Souths before", and Dad agreed with me that I had fulfilled my obligations.'

While Ian's relationship with George may have emerged relatively unscathed, his image with Souths fans was tainted forever. The week after threatening to sue Souths, Ian was at the Stadium to watch the game against Penrith. There he experienced the animosity that some supporters felt towards him when he was heckled and abused as a traitor. One woman was so overwhelmed by the emotion generated by the whole affair that she burst into tears in front of this departing son of Souths. Following what looked like Ian's whingeing about being hard done by in the past, another fan sent him a cheque in the mail for one dollar, a sarcastic jibe at what was perceived as Ian's money hunger. 'He sent me a two-page essay with it', Ian told reporters at the time. 'The bloke should be patted on the back, he spent that much time wording it. He just bagged me unbelievably. In the end he said something like "I've come to the conclusion that after all your financial difficulties, you could do with this donation". He said he would like to make up for the money I'd missed out on at other clubs by deciding to stay with Souths for years. People like that don't really know my situation. For a few weeks it got pretty heavy. People were ringing me up and really abusing me.' (Tony Durkin, *RLW* 8/89 and Phil Roth-field, *Telegraph* 8/89)

Ian amused himself by banking the cheque. He wasn't the first to leave Souths to better himself, and he certainly wasn't going to be the last. He was following in the footsteps of other greats, like O'Neill, not to mention Peter Tunks, Jimmy Morgan, Ron Coote, Ray Branighan, Jimmy Morgan, Ian Moir, Tom Mooney and Bob Moses. The media had built this particular conflict, the climax of which had elements begging for sensationalism. It didn't help that Ian was injured. To some it looked as if he had been directed by Manly to stay off the field.

In a futile attempt at damage control, Ian maintained he hadn't signed, and even suggested he might yet go to England and play for two years. 'Everyone thinks that I've signed with Manly but it's only speculation. I honestly haven't come to terms with anyone yet. I've never denied negotiating with anyone, but the rest is pure bullshit.' He then alluded to talks with Wigan. 'I haven't signed yet—we've been negotiating—but there's a few things they won't come to terms over. If they don't, there's no way in the world I'll be signing with Souths after all the shit I've copped through the speculation.' (David Rowlands, *Sun-Herald,* 18/7/89)

Maurice Lindsay refuted Ian's story, saying they hadn't heard from Ian for a while. 'We began negotiating with Ian back in February and our interest was at its greatest in May, but we haven't heard from him since, so we can only assume that he's changed his mind.'

Ian continued to voice his frustration with the sometimes cruel criticism. After all, he had spent so much time and energy in the past ensuring that he was liked, and doing the 'right thing'. In an interview with Phil Rothfield which appeared in the *Sun-Herald* on 22 August, he said: 'I haven't signed [with Manly] but after what happened at Souths through the year when they virtually asked me to leave, do you think any other player would stay? You know what I mean.' He qualified his previous statement when pressed. 'All I'm trying to do is look after myself. If I'd signed, there would only be a few people who would know about it. All this talk is really frustrating.' He went on to vent his anger at an ungrateful Souths, flailing out at his detractors: 'Twelve months ago I'd go out of my way to help people and kids and things like that. But it just makes you realise you're just a piece of merchandise. They want to know you when things are going well but when things are going bad people just brush you. You should see some of the hate mail I've received. I've been there [at Souths] four years now and I'm not getting ahead enough financially. Who's going to know me in six or seven years?'

When asked why he had stayed at Souths despite being offered double his money to go to Penrith two years previously, he answered: 'I suppose I was a bit younger and wanted to stay around at Souths with all my mates. I don't want to sound ungrateful but I've been playing for five years now and I haven't got much out of the game. Like I drive a beat-up Datsun. It's a real broken down box. It's ten years old and I've never had the money to go out and buy anything else. People just don't believe me ... I probably would have bought one [a new car] a couple of months ago after I sold the shop, but people would have got the wrong idea. They'd be saying "Look at this bloke in his flash car—it's all the bloody money he's getting from Manly for next year'. Addressing the accusations that he wasn't playing because Manly didn't want him to, he said: 'They've made me into a real ratbag. I'll just say if I hadn't come back against Balmain I'd be fine now. There was huge pressure at the time. I just wish I'd waited a bit longer.'

Ian was desperate and distressed by the mass outrage directed against him. After three years of raves and adulation, it was inconceivable and horrific to him that he could have been seen as such a hero one minute, and the biggest bastard in the world the next. He defended himself from every angle.

Rothfield complimented Ian for being a clean and disciplined player, especially for a front-rower. 'Yeah, not like some of the blokes running around. It's just me. I never even think I've tried to belt someone on the field. I think the only time I've got angry is over things like eye-gouging and that's only ever happened to me once. That was in a game against Canterbury. It might have been accidental, but I hit the bloke. But I've never been sent off, and I've only been sin-binned for professional fouls.' Ian desperately tried to convey the perception that he was the better man in all of this. 'Paul Roberts and Wayne Chisholm were the first two to see me at training They shook hands and said "Look after yourself, brother". The average player knows the situation. They realised it wasn't me going asking for all the money. I didn't go chasing anything. I don't think any player's worth that much ... I play League because I like playing it. Mate, I'd play for $10,000 or $20,000, I just like playing. But if someone offers you a lot more you've got to listen to them.'

Mario was disappointed with Ian, but not angry. 'It was a funny thing that we had there, and Ian will relate to this, we were all Souths blokes. We were Mascot people, we grew in the area. All we wanted to do was play for Souths ... We were very, very filthy that we had one of our great born and bred players poached from us, but we couldn't blame Ian.'

*

All Ian could do now was to somehow get back on the field to regain his honour. 'I'm doing everything I possibly can to get onto the field,' he told Phil Rothfield. 'I'm up at 6 a.m. seven days a week to work in the gym and have physio for a couple of hours. Then I go through the same routine at night. I had a CAT scan and it revealed that a ligament actually pulled the bone off my pelvis. I've had everything done trying to get it right. It's a lot stronger now I've been going through this special routine for the last three or four weeks. But they still say I'll have to have an operation to get it completely right ... George has told me he'd start me if I was fit. But I'll have to tackle blokes at training first to make sure it's OK. If he's going to give me the chance, I've got to be 100 per cent sure that I can get the job done. I just get dirty hearing people say that I'm an injury-prone player. I've been playing since I was four and I've only had two injuries ... I've obviously lost a lot of conditioning, but I've worked very hard in the gym and done a lot of swimming.'

Commenting on the media pressure, he said, 'It's probably been hardest on my family more than anything else, particularly my mum. I mean, what can I do about it? People are always going to say that I'm faking but I know it's legit. People don't realise what I've missed out on this year. All the City games, the State games and possibly even the Australian team. I would have given anything to play this year. I'd just love to play for Australia ... At the moment my mind is just set on possibly playing again for Souths this year. I think we can win the comp and I'd love to be part of it.'

Souths won the minor premiership by a mile and looked a strong possibility to take out its first premiership in eighteen years. George always said that a comp is won by the side with the best forward pack. He was hooker in that last premiership, surrounded by internationals. John O'Neill and John Sattler were his props, Bob McCarthy and Gary Stevens were behind, with Ron Coote as lock. In '89 Souths had arguably the best pack, with enough good forwards in reserve. However, Les Davidson was the only international, and Balmain, who Souths faced in the first semi, had five! Balmain would go into the game favorites.

A comeback for Ian wasn't looking likely. His injury needed time to heal and it seemed that he had played his last game for Souths.

Nathan Gibbs advised the *Sunday Telegraph*'s Steve Gillis that such injuries usually took from six to twelve months to mend, but Ian threw himself into anything that would speed his recovery.

Ian Roberts has tried everything but black magic this year to try to get himself back on the football field. He's had massage, acupuncture, chiropractic manipulation and naturopathic treatment. He's had cortisone needles, physiotherapy, hip manipulation, and undertaken courses of strengthening exercises and stretching exercises. None of it has solved the problem of football's most perplexing injury—severe abdomen-groin strain.

The big fellow has for weeks been pushing a car ... and also using the vehicle as a tool in an advanced form of sit-ups. 'I came up with the idea of pushing the car as a means of strengthening the damaged muscles. I've been doing it for ten weeks, three times a week, pushing as hard as I can in a series of 100m runs for 30 or 40 minutes a session. The sit-ups were Nigel Websdale's idea. He's had a lot of success treating the sporting injuries of people like Pat Cash ... I couldn't run far and I was trying to think of something slow and strenuous that would help the muscles.' (Greg Prichard, 'Roberts Semis Rev-Up', Mirror, 8/8/89)

RABBITOH PROP DISCOVERS LIFE'S HELL OFF THE FOOT-BALL FIELD
The prop's problem has been pinned down to a combination of three factors—instability of the symphysis (pubic) bone, bursitis in a hip, and a referred lower back problem, 'the most difficult of all sporting injuries to diagnose and treat,' according to Gibbs. (Ian Heads, SMH, 7/9/89)

Meanwhile, Ian had met Neil Halpin. 'Neil was the first doctor who I thought made sense of my injury. People had been treating my hips, my knees, my stomach. He was the first to say the pain is actually coming from your groin. Neil was like a saviour, no kidding. And the thing was, a lot of doctors didn't like him. They didn't want me to go and see him. "We can fix you. We can fix you!" I don't know what it is but doctors are quite bitchy to one another. Competitive. Neil had me under anaesthetic and stretched me out in order to release the scar tissue that had built up around the muscle tear I had—there was a 10 per cent chance that he could have snapped the muscle entirely, but it was the only way I could possibly relieve the area enough to get on the field. I felt so good I was out running around two days later. When you're young you feel invincible. It was Neil's opinion that I would have to have an operation, eventually, but that in the meantime I couldn't do any more serious damage than I had already done, apart from tearing the muscle more, if I played in the semi.'

By early September, the news was that Ian could be a starter in the Souths team for the all-important semi against Balmain. The many sports writers, in practically as many ways, rallied again for what would be the final chapter of the Ian Roberts saga for 1989.

ROBERTS—SOUTHS GAMBLE
Piggins' hopes were boosted when [Ian] came through four rugged training sessions during the week. With Roberts fit, Boyle in excellent form and Les Davidson recovered from injury, Souths will field a super pack of forwards. (Sun-Herald, 3/9/89)

ROBERTS ON THE RAMPAGE
South Sydney's 'tower of power' front rower was today declared a certain starter for Sunday's major semi-final against Balmain. (Peter Frilingos, Mirror, 4/9/89)

ROBERTS A STARTER FOR SOUTHS IF HE'S FIT
The forward hasn't played for three months, but it has hardly affected his reputation. His absence has only served to make his reputation stronger. (John MacDonald, SMH, 5/9/89)

BLOCKER: 'ROBERTS DOESN'T WORRY US'
'He's a good player. No doubt about it. But his inclusion won't worry us,' Roach said. 'I know he's a very good player but he hasn't played for 16 weeks. And Souths have won all those games. They've proved they can win without him', Sironen said. (Ray Chesterton, Telegraph, 5/9/89)

THE OUTCAST

IRON ROBERTS PACKS A WALLOP
In this sportswriting caper they drum into you that the pen is mightier
than the sword. Whoever coined that ancient phrase obviously never
saw Souths' prop Ian Roberts in action in boxing gloves ... At training
this week the only stomachs in danger of injury were those of the
unlucky souls thrust into the purgatory of holding the punching bags
for Roberts to hit. Roberts hits hard and often, driving his fists deep
into the punching bags with concentrated power from fists made of
steel. (Ray Chesterton, Telegraph, 6/9/89)

IT'S TRENCH WARFARE
Serdaris was forced to make way for experience, big match firepower
and the long-awaited comeback of Ian Roberts. 'Only a fool would
not play a champion. Ian Roberts says he will be right and that's good
enough for me,' Piggins said. 'He has trained the place down and we
have to go with him.' (Tony Megahey, RLW, 6/9/89)

George knew the difference that Ian made to his side's chances of the
premiership, both psychologically and physically. But Ian wasn't as
ready as the hype made out. 'On the day of the semi, I hobbled into
the ground. I couldn't even walk properly. I couldn't even get out of
bed! Mum and Dad had to give me a hand to get out of bed. Neil
stuck me full of needles and on I went.'

Mario, who has now gotten over the disappointment of Ian's defec-
tion, was grateful for his effort. 'Ian, being very unselfish, played in the
semi. Mind you, he was on one leg. The courage he showed! He played
the whole thing! Honestly, I rate it as one of the toughest and greatest
exhibitions of courage I've ever seen, and I've seen some beauties. He was
on one leg and he was hurting really badly and they tried to give him
curry. You know, you had Blocker Roach who was quite an aggressive
bloke and they really went for him, because there was a bit of publicity
about Roberts playing and that he was the great white hope for us. And
they pounded him. But he kept going and going. And in the finish, I'll
never forget coming off and Ian was basically on the floor in excruciating
pain and basically had fucked himself up really badly ... it was hospital
style. It looked like he'd have to be carted off in an ambulance.'

145

At 10–all, and with the play inside Balmain's quarter, it looked like a tired Balmain would succumb. However, a Mark Ellison kick was charged down by Benny Elias and regathered. The ball was quickly passed wide, resulting in a try by Andy Currier. This psyched the Balmain team up for what turned into a 10–20 loss for Souths. Ian was too gone practically to notice. 'I know I played terrible. What did I expect—no training apart from a run around a few times.' Mario, like George, reckons 'If Ian was 100 per cent I'd have a Grand Final trophy under my arm. As it was we lost valiantly.' Jeff Fenech drove Ian back to the club. 'I couldn't fucking walk! Jeff was worried when he saw me because I was like a spastic. All the way I was in agony.'

Football once again ended on a disappointing note. At least it was in keeping with the general tone of the year which, for all its remarkable highlights, was filled with stress and tension, heartache and physical pain. The season wasn't over for Souths, who had another crack at a final berth the following week, against Canberra, but football was a long way off for Ian. He spent the next weeks in pain and on crutches. Without him, Souths lost their one last shot at a premiership.

Rugby League Week ran a feature on Ian in November, questioning his worth to Manly, who had paid huge bucks for a player who seemed prone to injury and who had never played for Australia, or even State of Origin. Ian stuck to his 'two injuries ever' guns, and the fact that, no, he wasn't worth $250,000—but no-one was.

The post-mortems continued on what could have been, for Souths, if Ian had been fit through the season, or whether he had been foolhardy to play in the semi. Manly had a clause enabling them to terminate the contract if medical evidence proved he was not fit to play. Ian, not one to publicly dwell on the negatives, ended on an optimistic note. The game against Balmain was 'a risk worth taking. All I really needed with the injury was six months off, and whatever the outcome after the Balmain game, I was going to get it. I wasn't pressured to play.' As for the future? 'I have never been more determined before the start of a season. I really feel I have something to prove to myself ... not anyone else.' (*RLW, 11/89*)

But privately, and in the years to come, Ian would lament his decision to play. By April the next year he told Mike Colman of the

Sunday Telegraph: 'I played for all the wrong reasons. I played to show Souths supporters I hadn't walked away from them and when it was all over, it didn't matter one bit. The whole thing has shown me there are some people you'll never satisfy, and those people don't matter. They'll be against you no matter what.' In 1993, he told Danny Weidler: 'I didn't want supporters thinking I was this prick who was just out for the big money. I wanted to leave with the supporters thinking maybe I wasn't such a bad bloke. It was the most stupid thing I've done. I was young and stupid. It just fucked me up for the next season. I don't want to sound like I'm out to bag Souths, but I never got a phone call from them. They saw how I left that stadium. Not a phone call.'

EIGHT
MONEY MATTERS

After he sold the deli, Ian bought an apartment at Coogee, and began looking for a new job. This was during all the furore about his Manly contract, and his groin injury. A chance overhearing of a conversation at the club led to Ian becoming embroiled in what looked, at first, like a simple insurance job. Phil Blake was being offered a job as a life insurance salesman, and turned it down. Ian thought that he might be good at that, and offered his services to the guy, who was introduced to him as John Wiseman.

Wiseman was working out of an office in Bondi Junction, selling insurance policies, and had enlisted other high profile players in sales. He was second in charge. Ian recalls, 'The brokerage seemed to like to use footballers to encourage sales. John would go and set all these meetings up and we'd go along to them, and people would sign up with us. We'd get paid our commission and that was it. It was all so easy. We made good money out of it. Everyone seemed happy. I would only pop into the office at Bondi Junction once or twice a week, just to go to these appointments he'd set up for us.'

At the end of the year Frank, George, Ian and four others, including Jack Gibson, formed a syndicate to buy the Charing Cross Hotel. George and Jack already shared ownership of an Eastlakes nursery and a sports store in Maroubra Junction, and George had become a millionaire by selling his fleet of semitrailers and the patent on a pallet-loading system to the TNT transport group in 1985. The hotel purchase was Frank's idea. That Ian was invited to be part of the deal showed there were no hard feelings from the people closest to him in the Souths hierarchy. The opportunity was perfect for Ian. He'd be part owner of a business, with mentors he loved and trusted. Work hours would be tailored to suit. He dived enthusiastically into a hotel management course.

The syndicate paid $1,800,000 for the pub. The deal went through in December. Ian paid his share of the deposit, with the balance of $135,000, for his share, due in February, when they would take over the running.

He had continued working in insurance in the off-season and during this time he got to know Wiseman. 'John and I became friends. We spent a lot of time together socially, and when I went down to the kids' hospitals, he used to sometimes come down with me and give the kids presents as well. I got to know his family, his wife and kids. And he was a smart guy, incredibly intelligent too.'

Wiseman struck Ian as a man of many talents, especially when it came to business and investment. Ian was impressed and a little envious when John spoke continually of his successes investing in Futures. 'He was dealing in foreign currencies, buying and selling different currencies at different times. He'd tell me of a deal he was about to do, then, a week or so later, show me the figures he was banking, the profit from the deal. Every now and then he would show me his bank books at the office or somewhere, and he'd have an extra $20,000 in his book, because one of his deals had come off. He was a friend by this stage, a friend letting me in on his business successes. He seemed to get quite excited when a deal came in. He would buy presents for everyone. Really throw money around. He was easy with his money. Was always generous. Paid for dinners and all that. He was a real high flyer, always had a really nice car. He was obviously making good money.'

Wiseman was charming and urbane and that impressed Ian, whose experience with businessmen had been limited to a cruder version of self-made, working class ex-footy players and such.

Ian recalls: 'Over a period of time there were quite a few deals that he told me about. Then he began to say to me, "Why don't you invest some money?. You could make some good returns." It was only pretty small amounts, to begin with, like five or six thousand dollars. The first amount was only a few thousand. But the guy was doing me a favour including me in the deal. Plus he had done me the favour of getting the insurance work, and that had paid off well. The deal was I'd give him the amount, and get that, plus a percentage back about a week or two later. So, if I put in $2,000, I was going to get $3,000 back. Then he would re-invest the money in another deal. It was great.'

Ian would see the paperwork indicating the returns he was getting for his money, before re-investing. Other projects, more lucrative deals, began to come up and encourage Ian to leave his money in, and allow Wiseman to manage it for him.

'I was much more confident by now,' Ian recalls. Before he knew it, Ian found himself helping to raise hundreds of thousands of dollars for a transaction that would bring in millions. 'John actually approached me and some of the other guys at the insurance office for money for a deal he had in mind with Russian Roubles. He came to me and said "Look, I'm doing this big deal ..." and it was to our mutual benefit if we went in with him.'

Wiseman had been a generous friend to date, which had made an impression on Ian. 'At one stage he shouted me and a friend an all expenses paid trip to Cairns, scuba diving for two weeks. He wanted to do something for me, and knew I loved diving. Business was booming, and he spared no expense, I can tell you. The place I stayed was plush, and he footed the bills for all the diving gear.

'Other times, he flew me up to the Gold Coast when he was up there on business. Once he flew both myself and Clem up to stay with him at Jupiters [hotel casino]. We had a bit of a flutter. John didn't seem that interested in gambling much. But everyone there seemed to treat him like a king. Everything was on his tab, and he spent like it was going out of fashion. One particular trip to the Coast, he was tipping everyone like crazy. He was throwing money everywhere. I remember he was really happy, he was over the moon, like he had pulled some big deal or another off. He was that high. This was a man on top of the world. When we checked out, the bill was thousands!

'We drove back to Sydney that time. I can't remember why. Oh yeah, John was pertrified of flying, for some reason, so Clem and I drove back with him. We had a great trip back. It was hilarious. I don't think John knew quite what to make of Clem though. He's got a kind of weird humour, which cracks me up, but which John didn't really relate to. Clem was riding in the back of the car, and at one stage we turned around and he just sitting there, all relaxed, and totally naked! Like he had stripped without us knowing, and was all matter of fact about it. He kept saying on the trip that he was going to get out of the car naked, and onto the roof. Now John was a pretty anal guy, all spick and span. Ordered. So Clem knew the idea of it unsettled him. Anyway, the next thing, I look around. He's gone! He's disappeared from the back seat and John freaked thinking that he's riding along on the roof of the car, naked! He pulled the car up all anxious, and got out but Clem had gone. It turned out he had crawled into the boot of the car via a folding back seat, without us knowing! I just cracked up but John didn't think it was funny at all.'

Ian roused the interest of some of his friends in the rouble deal Wiseman was working on. 'By this time I was saying, "This guy is a champion!"' A few of the other footballers who had become aquainted with John through the insurance business had invested money with him too. The big lure the quick returns they were assured. Some of the older men were a little more wary. George Piggins recalls that Wiseman and some business colleagues had approached him during '89 with a fund-raising scheme to help save Souths from poachers. After a meeting with the men in his home, George hadn't pursued the idea. The next he knew of the man was through Ian and Frank. Frank recalls he had decided to invest money in John's rouble speculation, once his fears were allayed by Ian's assurances that his own investments with Wiseman had all paid off. George Piggins recalls, 'Ian came to me at one stage, and I said, "I'll lend you $40,000 to go into that deal, but it's just a loan. I'm not going in." I didn't have enough on this guy.' Ian put George's scepticism down to lack of the sophisticated acumen which Wiseman displayed.

Ian felt he had come a long way from Botany, to be in Wiseman's orbit. After all, the man had associates who were men of stature. Murray Farquahar, one of his colleagues, was the retired Chief

Stipendary Magistrate of NSW, and from time to time, Ian was privy to some big money talk. These men were high level movers and shakers.

Meanwhile, Neil Halpin had been attending to Ian's groin injury since the match at the Football Stadium. Surgery seemed to have the problem in check. Then he damaged his abductor tendon at training in February. Neil advised Ian that he should have surgery as a preventative measure against further damage, even though this meant missing the start of the season. Neil wasn't certain, either, that the groin would repair. 'I think the groin was the worst injury Ian had. I think it was an injury that could've finished him off.' He didn't say that to Ian at the time. This would be more pressure. The Sea Eagles had a lot riding on Ian, big money, and he knew it. They'd had a bad season in '89, and ditching Paul Vautin proved a very unpopular move with the fans. The only way Ian could prove himself, and get paid, was by playing. Still, there was grumbling that he was an expensive dud, because he had made only eighteen appearances on field out of a possible 46 in the previous two seasons. After three operations and sporadic weight work, Ian was a shadow of his former self, down to 102 kilos from 111 a year before.

Graham Lowe was appointed coach of Manly in '90. He had coached Ian at Wigan, and Ian had lived for a couple of months with Graham and his girlfriend. He was defensive of Ian's form at the time. 'The injury was a result of Ian doing too much work to get in form. By pushing too hard too soon. I cannot recall any player I have ever coached who is as determined as this bloke to do the right thing. Ian's contract is determined by his appearances on the field. It's a straight-forward case of no play, no pay.'

Happy for any port in a storm, Ian responded enthusiastically, eagerly christening Graham his new mentor. 'I don't want to sound big-headed,' he told the *Sunday Telegraph*, 'but something I learned from Graham Lowe is that to really succeed you have to believe in yourself. If I don't believe I'm better than the other guy, if I don't think I'm worth more than he is, I'll never beat him ... the fact is I don't get paid if I don't get on the field. Even if I could I wouldn't take the money without playing. I just wouldn't.'

MONEY MATTERS

The only surgeon Neil Halpin trusted to perform the operation Ian required was Fraser Young, who had just retired from St Vincents Hospital in Sydney, and moved to Queenstown, a small mining town on the west coast of Tasmania. Ian flew with Neil to Tasmania for a relatively new type of operation. 'I was a bit of a guinea pig, so the op got quite a bit of interest and publicity. The whole thing was weird, though. I caught a bus from Hobart to this obscene place, which looked like the surface of Mars!' To anyone who hasn't been there, Queenstown is like something out of a science fiction movie. The bleak architecture of a hastily built mining town is surrounded by a stark and barren hilly landscape, its flora destroyed by pollutants released in the mining process.

The payment of the balance on the Charing Cross Hotel was due when Ian was in Queenstown. 'My available funds at the time were tied up in investments and I was going to be away when the hotel money was due, but John assured me he would get the money, and give it to Frank in time. Meanwhile, I'm at the end of the earth. I was stuck in this hole of a place for what was evidently a revolutionary groin operation! I was frantic the whole time. I was making calls left right and centre, to John, to Frank, back to John, to try to co-ordinate things and get the money to Frank in time to meet my end of the deal for the hotel. The final date was getting closer, and I'm freaking out because I'm not there to sort everything, and John's going, "She'll be right", and Frank's getting understandably panicky. So am I.'

In the end, Frank was unhappy when the money didn't turn up at the designated time. In effect, Ian had defaulted. 'He [Ian] couldn't come up with the money. Had me running round town like a fool supposed to meet some bloke with the money. Meanwhile the bank is waiting. We had to pay by 11 o'clock on this particular morning. Ever tried to arrange a loan for $135,000 in ten minutes? George and Jack had put their company up as collateral. It was a very precarious situation. I didn't have any money at that stage. I had a unit at Maroubra that I owned, and which I didn't want to get rid of. You always like to have something to go to, your home and contents. Well, I had to put that on the market to cover the pub- had to take unders for that of course. And interest at that particular time was 21%. I was paying

$6,000 interest on a bank loan while I was waiting to sell the unit. I was in a very tight situation. But that is life.'

When Ian got back from Tasmania, he found his money was still tied up with Wiseman's venture. Frank's rouble investment was still tied up too. But though Ian had to renig on the hotel deal, Souths blood is thicker than water. 'The guys involved in the hotel didn't kick me out [of the deal.] They were really good to me', Ian recalls. 'They wanted me to borrow money and stay in. Frank was especially considerate. He's always been good to me.' But Ian couldn't extend himself any more.

He worked at the hotel, though. This meant Ray didn't have to find out what had happened, for a while. 'He was here for a few months, I suppose', Frank recalls. 'He always worked Friday nights in the back bar. And that back bar was never open prior to that. He used to work it by himself. He was taking $600 or $700! People would come in and want to talk with him. Sit around the place. He was very good with people. I think, had he stayed in the pub, we woulda made a motza. Ian's dry humour, and his joking around kept the customers coming, and he was obviously in his element. He was good for business.'

Meanwhile, none of the speculators in the Wiseman's rouble scheme had seen any returns. They had been told the turnaround time would be two weeks, but weeks had now turned into months. Anxious enquiries received smooth assurances from John. Sometimes, it seemed, you had to be patient. The calls started getting more urgent as people who had sunk in tens of thousands of dollars, began to panic.

For Ian, that was when the real trouble started. For some of his friends who had sunk money in, he was their only contact with Wiseman. So he got the irate calls and was getting understandably anxious. Unbeknowns to Ian, and to other investors, so was Wiseman. But he didn't let on.

At least the Queenstown operation looked successful. Finally, Ian was fit and ready for football. The big comeback was 8 April, 1990. Manly v. Brisbane. Short of match practice, and running on 75 per cent power, he played a strong 80 minutes. But that was all anyone needed to see. A couple of days later, Jack Gibson, metropolitan selector, and City and NSW coach, was planning his City Origin side around Ian.

Graham Lowe switched Ian to the second row, where he would basically remain, in the game against Norths the following week, in order to take some of the pressure off his groin. On Anzac Day, in the City v. Country clash, he played himself brilliantly into state of origin selection. In magical form, he entranced the critics and the spectators with his graceful unloading of the ball, on the fall, to runners. It was a brilliantly timed reminder to everyone of what the fuss was all about when it came to Ian Roberts. Unperturbed by two or three players at a time trying to disarm and topple him, he seemed to calmly assess the play and, at a moment of his choosing, flick the ball exactly where it had to go.

Now he was touted as the man who could save the Blues, who had been humiliated two years running by Queensland. Provided he beat Paul Dunn, David Gillespie, Glen Lazarus, Mark Sargent, Craig Salvatori, Peter Tunks and the like to front-row honours alongside a likely Steve Roach. The worst they were saying was that he hadn't played enough lately to be judged. The best, that, yes, he *was* the best forward in the world. He made the side, and was pitted against fellow Manly front-row import, Martin Bella, in the first Origin game of his career. The two were dubbed the odd couple because of their different styles. Martin was a head down, hard-yarder in attack, while Ian ran wide of the ruck. In defence, no-one matched Ian's tackle rate. Their clash in the first Origin game on 9 May, at the Sydney Football Stadium, was ferocious. But NSW won 8–0. Roberts and Bella were now Manly's buys of the year!

With a grateful sigh of relief, Ian was back somewhere he could feel comfortable, proving himself, and playing the reluctant star for a rapturous media again. After the furore of the year before, the journos were gently healing Ian's public image. Once again Ian was sounding like a good down home boy, full of humility.

He was quoted by Steve Crawley of the *Mirror*, on 30 May, 'You know, I never followed football. To be honest, I don't really like foot-ball. I wouldn't go to football on weekends if I wasn't playing. Mum and Dad used to take me to games when I was a kid, and I'd always drift up the back of the hill and play. Now I play because there is always something else, you can always go higher, better yourself. Football brings out the character in people. I'm happy at Manly. Now all I worry about are the kids. Kids are the best thing about football. Kids are honest.'

Crawley reported Paul Broughton, a NSWRL official, telling how Ian had stayed behind at the Prince of Wales Children's Hospital at Randwick when the State players had visited. He then reported back to head office that he'd promised nine kids footballs, and that he wanted to deliver them personally. 'Every endorsement, promotional or advertising fee he earns is now donated to the hospital. He would not like a big deal made of that. In fact he is not one for big deals at all.'

Wiseman could always placate Ian with viable explanations as to the delay in the big currency deal. In the confusion of legalities, paperwork and contracts that big business seemed to be, it was easier for Ian to leave complex details to Wiseman. His understanding of finance was extensive and he seemed to maintain a grip on a multiplicity of deals simultaneously, and he worked so frenetically, it was impossible to keep up. In this business, the timing of one move or another was determined according to a complex business logic that, as yet, escaped Ian. He could only watch, learn, and hopefully profit.

Not everyone else was content to be patient while Wiseman worked his entrepreneurial magic, and Ian's life behind the footy facade was getting uncomfortable for him. 'My parents' place was the only place I really felt safe at this stage. Everyone was ringing me everywhere, and saying "Where's John Wiseman? Where is he? Come on, you know where he is! You're fucking running with him!" Every day people would ring up. It was a nightmare. It was terrifying for me.' The calls inevitably got more threatening as people started to realise that there might be something wrong, and their money might be in trouble. 'One day, one footballer investor who was owed $60,000 rang up and said, "I want this f..n money. If I don't get it I'm going to the police." And he said "You're the f..n one who got me into this thing. You're the one who f..n told me how f..n good it was going to be, and that you'd put all this money in yourself!" I don't blame people for getting upset. At the time, I just didn't really know what was happening. About an hour after this guy's call, when I was at Mum's place, another guy who was owed $80,000 rang and was pretty heated. Mum's number was the only one he had, and he was lucky he caught me there. Unlucky for me. I was pretty shaken after that call. I used to go to Mum and Dad's thinking I'd be safe from harrassment there. Everywhere else I would jump every time I heard a phone. To Dad and Mum I think it just looked like business was booming for me. I was making and getting calls left right and centre, and as far as they knew, I had just invested my money.

'I felt like I was harrassing John every day, going, "Look, we've *got* to get these people their money!!", and he'd say "It's coming." He'd say he was busy working on some new deal or setting up a new company. He'd say stuff like "The bills are being put together. There is a lot more infrastructure in setting up a company and this that and the other to get it all into place, and you've just got to be patient for 6 months" ... "Six months!? John, you told me they'd have their money within two weeks!!" These people weren't concerned with the new companies or deals he was working on. They were told they were part of a certain deal which would take a couple of weeks!'

As time went on, Ian became more desperate to see some returns. By this time, he was party to a number of business investments through Wiseman, all of which required ongoing financing.

John secured a property development deal with a sometime Queensland associate that enabled Ian to capitalise on his Manly contract. Wiseman saw it partly as doing Ian a favour. He says, 'Under the deal that Manly did, there was no way that $200,000 of Ian's money could be released in cash. He could only get it invested into an income-producing investment, i.e. a property trust.' Ian, inundated with more paperwork, plush brochures and prospecti, was more cautious, but, having accompanied Wiseman to see some of the developer's projects, felt reassured. 'Manly released funds on the strength of a letter from the developer,' says Wiseman, and $130,000 of Ian's Manly contract money was transferred into the property deal. As Ian explains, 'By this stage I thought it was the only sure way I could save my financial arse. I wasn't worried about making a massive profit anymore.' He just wanted to see some reassuring returns.

So did Wiseman. And he and some associates had meanwhile formulated *another* plan, to pull off the motherlode of all deals.

One of the other football players who had got to know Wiseman through the insurance business, and who became involved in this new project, recalls its origin as May 28, 1990, when Wiseman introduced him to one 'Rocky' Cartwright, at the Excelsior Hotel in Surry Hills. There he was invited to invest in a fantastic business venture along with Murray Farquhar and a few others, including another footballer. Like Ian, the other footballers had become cautious, and baulked at raising the $150,000 that was required for this new scheme, but two of them decided to raise a part of the funds for this new venture.

The scheme was straightforward really. The plan was to employ an ex-Australian Navy minesweeper armed with exocet missiles and a squad of mercenary commandos to remove 500 tonnes of gold from the Central Bank of Manila, supposed to have been stashed there by the deposed President Ferdinand Marcos under false names. The removal of the gold was to be coordinated with a coup against Corazon Aquino, the then president, which was evidently scheduled to take place. The gold was to be taken from The Philippines to a hiding place probably in Dubai, where Murray Farquhar had business interests and contacts, and then presumably delivered to its owner upon payment of a commission, on the reported $5 billion of gold! The feasability of the plan, and the sheer scale of the logistics involved, didn't seem to get in the way of people's anticipation of the phenomenal returns, and so financing the enterprise was seen as the main headache.

Despite the rumours and statements, Ian is adamant that he was not an active participant in the gold plot. He says now, 'The whole thing sounded like a fairy tale to me, and I had no money available in any case, even if I'd wanted to go in on it.' But he definitely had a vested interest in seeing the deal pulled off.

On June 8, he went with a woman he had met through the other gold investors into the city to the Registry of Births, Deaths and Marriages, in order to obtain an extract of the birth certificate of the woman's de-facto husband. Ian says that at the time he felt he was simply doing a favour for Wiseman, who, with a couple of others, was going off to The Philippines that day and so was busy with preparations.

Ian went to the airport that afternoon. Wiseman and few of the other businessmen were off to Manila to check out arrangements for the execution of their plan. They were curious to see first hand what they were getting involved in. In Manila, they realised something was amiss. Nothing seemed particularly organised and the sheer futility of the venture became dauntingly apparent. Meanwhile, they drove around in limos and stayed in luxury accommodation, which one unwitting businessman somehow ended up paying for with his Amex Gold Card! Effectively, this trip marked the end of the men's hope of obtaining the gold.

Back at Charing Cross, Frank and a couple of the others, who hadn't had much to do with Wiseman on a personal level, had decided to do a bit of poking around about the bloke. They had long since become fed up with the run-around they felt he was giving them with his over-complicated money rhetoric, and they wanted to get to the bottom of what had happened with the rouble deal.

They were shocked by what they found out. Frank's sources revealed that Wiseman was regularly at Jupiter's Casino, in Sothern Queensland. He confronted Ian, who shudders when he recalls the encounter. 'Frank said he had someone follow John, who found out that John was supposedly punting big money at Jupiters Casino! I refused to believe it. I said, "No, Frank, you're wrong, I know this guy! I've been at Jupiters with the guy. He hates gambling. He hates it when he loses $5!!" '

'My disappointment in the whole thing,' Frank says now, 'was that even when I told Ian, he didn't believe us. I put things on him that were happening, and he was, like, "Oh no, that wouldn't be John. I have got as much respect for him as I have for you and George." I said, "Well, maybe you have, Ian, but you have known us for a lot of years, and you've only known this bloke five seconds." Ian was naive. He kept on falling for the guy. I gave him dates, names and places, everything. Ian said, "Frank, I have stayed up at the casino with him, when we met this one and that one up there. He hates gambling!" I

said, "Ian, he is gambling! He is gambling on the race horses, on. ...'"
"No, he doesn't gamble." "I'm telling you, he bloody does, you
know!?" Christ!'

Frank was basically asking Ian to accept that most of their
invested money had been punted at the casino! That his business deals
with Wiseman had been elaborate shams. 'I told Ian what Wiseman's
nickname was at Jupiters,' Frank continues, 'and what he was doing
up there and who he was associated with, and I gave him a run down
of people. I had a bloody investigation done, because there were people
I knew who knew who he was, knew where he lived. The first bloke
he got mixed up with in business there went broke. I spoke to other
people about it. I got a host of phone calls, later, from people who he
had been in business with, who said they had lost money.'

Even the insurance operation, it was murmured, had to close
operations because too many customers were defaulting on policy payments after the first one or two payments. Frank thinks Wiseman lost
his home because the insurance company held the mortgage on it, 'and
bloody well took it'.

For years now, John Wiseman has heard all sorts of stories allud-
ing to his less than successful business record, and while nothing being
spread surprises him—'People don't let the facts get in the way of a
good story!'—he vehemently defends himself on every aspersion cast
on his name and character. 'Everyone claims to have information from
private detectives. As far as I know only one private detective has ever
been hired to follow me.' He was hired by one woman who had had
her own unfortunate business relationship with Wiseman, and who
was extremely bitter. 'He spoke to some guy in security at Jupiters,'
Wiseman continues, 'who said that I'd been seen there gambling. Big
deal. During my time there, I did gamble. No question. But I did not
lose whatever amount people claim I did. Who knows? Who was there
with me? Who can say John Wiseman lost a million dollars, or John
Wiseman lost $100,000 and who can say it was my money? No-one!
I think the most I lost was about $3,000! And the whole business going
round of me supposedly taking people's personal cheques and cashing
them at the casino is just ridiculous. If anyone bothered to check,
they'd know that the law prohibits the passing of personal cheques

through casinos. I mean, the whole thing is a joke. I've been painted as some con man by people who are simply not aquainted with the facts of the matter.'

The facts as he sees them, Wiseman concedes, are almost as embarrassing and pitiful as the rumours of his conning people and gambling away their money. 'Simply put, it was me who was had. I was conned—by someone else! An accountant I knew had put me onto someone, when I was up in northern Queensland, and I was offered an opportunity to make a lot of money purchasing Russian roubles.' This deal allegedly had some colorful characters straight out of James Bond films, including the KGB. 'I even saw the roubles that were being dealt at one stage, a whole huge suitcase of them, though I suppose I only saw the top layer. There could have been toilet paper underneath for all I know. Anyway, it looked like a massive once-in-a-lifetime opportunity, and yes I was greedy, and I thought, well, I haven't got the money for this, but if I can raise it, I can make everyone, including myself, a big return. Looking back on it, I'm the first to admit I was stupid.

'The [accountant contact] guy did the runner on me. He took off with everyone's money, and to this day I do not know where he is. He disappeared along with any hope of getting our money back. Everyone lost their money, and no-one was more hurt by that than me. That was a turning point in my life.

'Up until that point in time, I was as normal as the rest of them. I'd never been involved in anything wrong, never done anything bad. All of a sudden I got offered this fantastic opportunity to make a fortune and I thought it was easy money. I was naive, that's for sure. That was the end of my business life effectively. And all the accusations and all the rumours since then, about me being some lowlife scumbag, have only made things worse.'

Wiseman says the reason he has never pursued legal channels in order to redress the defamation and slander he suffered in the stories going round about him, is the simple fact that he genuinely felt remorse that he had been the cause of people's losses and he had no desire to aggravate their feelings of loss, and their embarrassment. Or his own.

Ian was stunned when he was first aquainted with the information that Frank and the others thougth they had about Wiseman, 'I just didn't believe it! I couldn't believe all that of John. I knew the guy! There was no way I could accept that I had been had. All the business deals. All the paper work all the meetings! And John had explanations for everything. He was just too intelligent.'

Ian was in shock, too. He wasn't ready to accept what Wiseman was accused of. It wasn't just about making money. It was about pride, and trust, and about Ian's ambition to better himself, to make something of himself. To prove himself to others, particularly his Souths mates. He was an impressionable kid from a blue-collar background. To him, John Wiseman with all his highbrow white-collar ways should have been the infallible one, and Frank and George the ones stuck in the rut of working class cynicism. Ian was going to lead his mates on to a sophisticated business future.

Frank wasn't about to shake Ian out of that dream easily. Not with that much money involved. 'I think at the time Ian resented me saying these things about John Wiseman, because I am probably the opposite to Ian. I am very outgoing. I say what has to be said. Sometimes I have got to chew my tongue off, but I would rather have it out and done with.'

'Ian was fed a bit of burley to get him in, and get others in,' George Piggins explains. 'Murray Farquhar was part of it. Retired judge, and there was not scandal around at that stage, a man high up in society. To a young man, if someone introduces you to a judge, and you thought you were dealing with such people as that, you wouldn't think they'd be associated with something risky. So when one deal went bad, he probably stuck it because the guy said he'll get it back the next deal. I just don't think he knew how to cut himself off.'

'I don't know how much Ian lost in investments with John,' Frank shakes his head, 'but he kept on going back in and going back in. I mean, the money I had invested wasn't my worry by this stage. Admittedly, Ian had given me the wrong story on a couple of things in the first place that would have stopped me from going in. And there was a bit of greed that come into it, too, don't worry about that. But I had asked Ian whether he had literally got the money back from his investments. He said he had. He hadn't. It was always shipped off into some

other investment. It was later *on* that he said that Wiseman had transferred his money over to this prawn business in Dubai. And then, when
Farquhar came back from Dubai, I happened to be there at the pub.'

Murray Farquhar was a regular at the Charing Cross Hotel.
Frank used to have a yarn with him. 'I never used to mind Murray
Farquhar. I got on all right with him, but, I mean, he used to make
up all these stories. He said, "Ian, you were never in the Dubai business. I was running the business over there myself, the prawnery", what
did he call it, "the co-op". He said if we decided it was big enough
later on, and we decided we wanted to buy our own ship or something,
you could come into it. I told you that, to start, if we went good you
could invest in it." ' Someone had obviously confused the issue which
in turn led to this contradiction. As Frank says, 'It just gets more and
more involved. I only knew the outside. I only knew what they told
me.'

Murray Farquhar was certainly doing some sort of business in
Dubai, apart from arranging somewhere to stash the Manila gold. John
Wiseman had discussed investment in Dubai with Ian at some stage,
and Frank felt Ian believed some of his money was invested there, until
Murray came along and blurted out that it wasn't.

In the end, if you believed Farquhar, it was just as well, 'because
Farquhar,' as Frank recalls, 'came along later with a story about how
his lady friend in Dubai had bought a shipment of prawns, while he
was back here in Australia, and prawns fetched so much a kilo in the
States. This may have been fair dinkum, this part. Who would know.
I never ever queried it. Anyway, it was going to cost $27,000 to insure
the load. She didn't insure it. And when they got out to sea, the refrig-
eration broke down on the ship and they lost the whole lot.
$250,000—this is what Farquhar told me. That is how he said he did
his money over in Dubai. He told me himself. I don't know whether
that part is true or not.'

Whatever the facts were in the more fantastic business ventures,
John Wiseman remained within the orbit of the people who lost money
in them. He even seemed to struggle to make amends, in his panic over
what he assured everyone was his temporary loss of good fortune. And
this confirmed for Ian that John at least had good intentions all along.

Frank received a couple of cheques from Wiseman, as part repayment of his loss. But the cheques bounced and George, for one, looking out for his mates, didn't accept for a second that the repayment attempt was sincere. George attended a meeting that Frank arranged with Wiseman at the hotel. George recalls he let Wiseman know what he thought of him, 'and Wiseman had brought that Farquhar along and Farquhar said something, and I said "Look, I don't know why he brought you here." I don't know whether Murray was supposed to be the stand-over man, but he would drop gangsters' names all the time. I don't know whether it was meant to frighten you or what!'

More than anything else, the involvement of these men from Souths in the business dealings of Wiseman led to the parting of the ways for some hitherto close friends. In the end George and Frank left Ian to his own devices, to sort out his financial mess in his own way, even though it appeared extremely odd to them that Ian continued to trust and associate with Wiseman.

NINE

SOUTHS' LEGACY

Graham Lowe led Manly's re-marketing of 'Roberts' Kangaroo Tour Destiny', after NSW lost the last game of the Origin series, 10–14, at Lang Park on 13 June. France's tour of Australia was pending. 'To me he has always had "international" written all over him,' but Ian was not named in the Australian side to play the touring French team in Parkes. ARL Chairman, Ken Arthurson, tried to assuage the strong feelings Ian's exclusion aroused: 'I rate Roberts an absolute certainty to play Test football. He's a terrific player and he'll be a Test player before he's very much older.'

Some of the 28 players selected for the Kangaroo tour of Britain and France at the end of the year might end up playing in provincial games only, and not the Tests. Since he wasn't selected to play in the team against France in Parkes, even if he was named in the squad for the tour, as seemed likely, what were the chances of him playing in a Test match? At the time, some players talked of not making themselves available for the tour. Ian was determined to play in a Test match. 'My goal is to play for Australia, not the Emus.' He said his piece. The Australian coach, Bob Fulton, played diplomat. He couldn't make guarantees to anyone. 'The biggest thing when the team goes away is that there are six games before the first Test. Whoever has the form gets the start.'

His position is made more interesting because he is also eligible to play for Britain. Roberts said he 'came within a whisker' of deciding to play for Britain in 1986 and recently rejected the chance to play for the British on their current New Zealand tour. (John Macdonald, *SMH, 22/6/90*)

Maurice Lindsay had called Ian from New Zealand. 'I appreciate the offer very much but Australia is my country and I want to wear the green and gold,' Ian patriotically told *Big League* magazine. Different day. Different mood. Different reporter. Different tack. 'I have had a desire since I was a kid to play for Australia and that's still my aim. Naturally I'm disappointed at not being in the Test side to play France but that is something I've got to live with ... I'm no more disappointed than my team-mate Martin Bella.' Graham Lowe went into bat. 'Australia's lucky he's so fiercely loyal. I'm stunned he's not in the Australian side. His form this season demanded he be in the pack somewhere.'

At this stage, Ian had yet to survive his first clash with Souths, since leaving. And that was sure to be a friendly reception. Souths had tumbled to the bottom of the ladder in 1990 and Ian's home town were out for blood. Manly was their historic foe, and Ian was the turncoat helping to improve their fortunes. George Piggins himself, bearing no personal animosity towards Ian, could only grieve over the effect of Ian's departure. 'You only have to see what happened when we went from '89 to '90 to see the impact losing Ian had on us. We went from minor premiers to running last and a lot of that was due to Ian. He just made that much difference to us, it wasn't funny. Of course, his groin injury affected his game at Manly. His covering game probably suffered, and he played a tighter game at Manly than he did at Souths, but he was still a heck of a player. But that's why he got a lot of criticism off the fans. They would've been thinking, "If you'd stayed with us, we would've bloody still been a good side." To them it didn't matter that what we were paying him compared to Manly was chalk and cheese!'

June 24 will go down in infamy ... Well, it won't. But Souths lost 20–26, and might have won if they'd concentrated on the game earlier, instead of vengeance on Ian. When the severely bashed, dazed and bleeding Souths expatriate was carried out of the game after 34 minutes, Souths were down 4–16. 'The first game when I played against Souths was the most brutal game that I have experienced. I don't think I was scared, exactly, but I knew what they were like, what I was in for.' Terry Hill concedes, 'That day Ian got targeted and targeted real heavy. Mark Carroll deliberately cut out of the line and crushed him twice. Shoulder charged him, not so much deliberately. But he was targeted to be put out of action. He got carried off on a stretcher.'

'It was a set play and I knew he was going to get the ball,' Carroll said at the time. 'I just lined him up and hit him with my shoulder. I don't like to put guys out like that. I hope he wasn't hurt.' Carroll hadn't played with Ian the year before. 'I didn't know what all the fuss was about when they were talking about Roberts [before the game], but that's George, I suppose.'

'Ian probably copped a bit of a hiding,' Mario recalls as he relates Ian's pain to his own. 'I copped it too, brother [when I left Souths]. That's how life works. I'll never forget about the first time I went back, my first game with Norths. Mate, it's a nightmare. They drive you mad. I was shitting myself. They give you a bit extra. I played against Ian that game and I'd be a liar if I said we didn't put a bit extra in. A former mate playing for the opposition. You can't help it.'

The final ignominy for Ian was the Souths supporters cheering when he was taken off injured.

'I knew I'd be in for extra attention,' he told journo David Middleton almost jovially, 'but if they went after me, then they were leaving holes for others. But I'm not dirty on them. It's just the way things go.' Now he is more honest. 'They butchered me. Every time I took the ball, Mark or Mario, whoever, I didn't know where I was. I cracked my jaw, fractured my cheekbone, pinched a nerve in my neck. I just got hammered.'

Courtesy of the Souths front row of Fenech, Carroll and Davidson, Ian escaped with a triple fracture of the cheek, two below the eye and one above, and a fractured jaw, which looked like sidelining him for up to five weeks. Once again he would miss out on an Australian jumper, as due to player injuries, he had been set to be called into the squad to play France at Parkes. Manly officials were furious. They intended scrutinising video of the game. 'I accept that it was a tough game, but I have a duty to protect my players. This could even cost him [Ian] a Test jumper this year,' Lowe told Ray Chesterton who himself seemed pretty incensed at 'the injuries to the well-performed and fair-playing Roberts'.

The mauling Ian got in the game may have been the epilogue to the story of Ian's farewell to Souths as far as the players were concerned. But the overall legacy of his departure, courtesy of the hype which helped stir up the Souths supporters in '89, was the homophobia he began to experience from 1989 onwards. The week after the game David Middleton wrote in *Rugby League Week* that the 'bitterness among the Souths players ... even led to hurtful rumours being spread about Roberts' private life'.

It's hard to trace the path and the growth of the bitterness against Ian, as the simple truth about his identity left the quiet whispers of the players' change room and found its way into a louder and more disrespectful public domain. Tugger Colman, for example, didn't spread 'hurtful rumours'. He just chatted with less discretion now, about what he pretty well knew to be true. That's how Terry Hill found out about Ian, the minute he started playing firsts in '90. 'Craig Colman used to run around admitting to everyone that Ian was a fucking poofta, because it didn't worry Tugger and he said so. Tugger loves Ian, and saw him all the time socially. I didn't know Ian that well at Souths, and obviously I was a bit surprised when I first found out, when I was seventeen or so. And I said, "Fair dinkum? Don't think so!" Well, that's what *you* think. This was years ago. There was this really macho image. They were really hard. That's just the way it was back then.' Back then in 1990.

Club loyalty didn't extend to Ian any more. Homophobic Souths people didn't have to curb their prejudice any longer. It was all part of the unwritten book of behavioural ethics called 'Cop It Sweet' or 'Redfern Rough Justice'. Nothing unusual. The negative comments were spread by people who didn't know Ian personally, but to whom he represented something worth despising. He was a traitor now—plus he was a filthy faggot—so it was good riddance. The result for Ian was that the homophobic taunts, abuse and confrontations began to proliferate.

Some sports journalists were able to get an overview of what was happening. They saw and heard of some of the nastier insults dealt out to Ian. Maybe it was guilt that they had played a small part in creating this nightmare for him by hyping up the greed versus loyalty stories the previous year, and getting the Souths fans worked up. Or maybe it was just that they liked him as a person, but in the years to come he certainly got fair treatment from the sporting media. As if they were on side.

Frank Cookson witnessed a kind of rough humour and grudging tolerance in the confines of the pub. 'There were always rumours about Ian by the time he was working in the pub here, and I remember one night overhearing this bloke saying such and such about Ian, and I said to him, "He's over there, why don't you ask him?"' Frank also witnessed Ian's various reactions to the jokes and innuendo. 'Here on another night [at the pub], when we first come here, I heard all the stories, some used to say he carried a photo round in his wallet. And I used to just gee him up, you know, and I said, "Have you got a photo of Joe Lydon [Ian's teammate at Wigan] in your wallet?" He said "No. Why?" I said "Oh, a couple of Souths' blokes said you're carrying a photo of Joe Lydon round in your wallet." "No way," he said. Anyway, there were a couple of blokes in here and he copped it sweet. He laughed. I laughed. One night here he got serious. A couple of blokes said "Is Ian Roberts going to wear gloves when he's serving beer here?" I told Ian. Well, he got the shits. He poked me in the chest, knocked me back about three feet! I said, "Don't tell me, tell them". I thought it was a joke. Five minutes later there's no worries with him. He only got the shits at that particular moment, over that particular thing, you know? Some things he takes to heart, some things he laughs off. A bloke called Robert Sait, played with Mascot. He had a go at Ian one night. And Ian copped it sweet, and let it blow over his shoulder because he had a bit of respect for the bloke. He could have pulled him apart if he'd wanted to, you know? Overall, as far as fighting's concerned, he'd just as soon avoid it.

'He went downtown one day, down George Street, near the Queen Victoria Building. This would have been not long after we took over the pub. A few young blokes give him a blast, six or seven years ago now, "Oh, you big queen", blah, blah, blah, and one of the blokes came over to him, and abused him. So he knocked the bloke out and put his foot on his throat and he said to the other guys, "Come on!" And the other blokes shit 'emselves. But to him that he knocked out, he said, "If anyone asks you how you got bashed tell them a faggot did it!"'

Just the month before this incident, a group of eight youths had lured and bashed to death a gay man in Alexandria Park, in inner Sydney. 1990 was a bumper year for poofta bashing generally, with five murders resulting from countless vigilante bashings. These are hate crimes, pure and simple. Unprovoked, they are not crimes of passion or of greed, just unfettered hatred for another human being.

Theo Lianos, who became a friend of Ian's around this time, and later a flatmate, witnessed a lot of prejudice directed towards Ian, as well as the effect it had on him. Verbal abuse started to get commonplace. 'After a game, we would wait outside the change rooms, and you would always hear stories about him. During the games too, you would always hear abuse being yelled out to him, like "You fuckin' fairy, go back to the Mardi Gras!" and much worse.' Grant Windred, another friend of Ian's, worked for a television station. 'I don't remember any particular game or incident. You just remember the general words used. We used to televise the games, and Nicole, who I worked with, used to hear stuff over the speakers all the time. Ian being called a poofta and a faggot and all that sort of stuff.'

Theo worked on building sites in the city at the time, for Schindler's Lifts. 'There was usually a big lunch room where all the different contractors would have lunch and morning tea together. You'd get to know them all after a while. Ian would make it into the papers, and there was always that "fucking good football player, but did you know he's a fucking fag?" and at the time, no-one "knew", and you would hear mixed reactions like, "No he's not, I met his girlfriend" or "My missus knows his girlfriend". And then, "No, I am telling you, a mate of mine reckons he's seen him walking down the beach, holding hands!" And stuff like that. At the beginning, I was a little embarrassed, and I thought, "Oh no, they're going to find out I live with him, and they're going to think I'm a poof!" And the idea of that freaked me out at that stage. After a while, I didn't care what people thought. I was proud of knowing him. When they started going on and on, and these were Manly supporters too, some of them, I would say "I know Ian Roberts". Some wouldn't say anything, and some would say, "Oh, he's a fag, isn't he?" I always used to say "No, he's not. He's got a girlfriend." And they'd say "How would you know?" "I just happen to live with him and I know what's going on." I used to lie about it. That was the thing to do. I had heaps and heaps of arguments at work because of that, and because they would say bad things about him. Half the time, I think they were scared because there was this fairy or poof, playing at *their* game. They couldn't do what he was doing, and they were supposed to be real men, you know.

'Occasionally, someone would say something positive. One bloke said to me, "Do you know Ian Roberts?" I said "Yeah, he's my flatmate." He goes "Oh, he is gay." I said "No, he's not." He goes "With all respect to you, you're sticking up for him, but I know for a fact that he is gay, because my flatmate is gay, and his best friend used to go out with him." And he mentioned his name and I told Ian what happened when I got home. He said "Really? Oh, shit. What did you say? ... What did they say?" It really used to worry him, yeah. Some things hurt him. He hides things. He doesn't let people know. He takes it out on the football field probably, or on the people closest to him, sometimes. Or he keeps it in himself. He just gets so frustrated.'

Ian was still extremely cautious about who found out about his sexuality. When he had first met Theo, it wasn't discussed, though Theo—gay himself, and closeted and paranoid in his work environment—had heard rumours. Eventually he became one of Ian's faithful companions and, like Lee, was forever employed in putting people off the scent. He used to field a lot of questions from interested parties, from guys and girls. 'So many girls were madly in love with him', during the football season at least. 'I was forever being questioned about Ian's movements. "Where was Ian last night?" "What was he doing?" "Where did you guys go?"' The whole time Theo had to think quickly ... camouflage their movements into acceptable hetero-speak.

Souths stalwarts like Dave Johnson, who remained loyal to Ian, also felt protective when they heard derogatory comments about him. 'He was like a son as far as I was concerned. I'd say to people, "Look, if you want to say something [like that] about Ian Roberts, don't say it in front of me!"'

Late in June the police contacted Ian about the failed Manila gold scheme. 'They called and asked me to go in to see them at Surry Hills to help them with their enquiries. When I got in there, they had a statement already prepared for me to sign, saying that Murray Farquhar had wanted me to obtain someone else's birth certificate, which wasn't correct. It had been Cartwright who'd wanted it.'

It was reported that phone conversations and meetings in which the Manila gold was discussed were being taped from the outset, and supplied to the police by Cartwright and another guy involved in the plot, Anthony Evans, who, it emerged, were most likely the originators of the scheme, and who were both former policemen.

Cartwright and Evans, it was claimed, controlled the funds raised for the venture, which allegedly went into a bank account operated by the Fraud Squad. At least one investor wasn't even aware he was investing in the gold plot until the Fraud Squad paid a visit. It was rumoured that the man had been contacted by two of the men involved in the scheme and asked to invest in the purchase of a hotel. He gave them in the vicinity of $20,000, and was stunned when with the Fraud Squad showed up with questions about his dealings in the gold plot! His complete ignorance of the operation became quickly apparent, and he received a cheque from the fraud squad for the full $20,000 'hotel' investment. The footballers who put money into the scheme weren't as lucky. Kogoy reported in the *Sun-Herald* (29/8/93) that three footballers invested $71,000, or about $25,000 each, and, despite some attempts to trace their money, never saw it again.

It seems likely that some of the funds invested in the gold operation, financed part of a clandestine police operation. Certainly, a lot of fraud squad detectives were kept busy tracking the operation, which they nicknamed 'Farquhar's Folly'. In fact it was everyone's folly, because, in the end, the only charge that could be laid against anyone involved was one of conspiring to obtain false Australian passports.

For Ian, being implicated in something that resulted in any sort of charge, was disgraceful. But several people involved were charged in July. Murray Farquhar pleaded not guilty to a charge of conspiring to commit an offence under the Passport Act between April 10 and June 15, 1990.

John Wiseman, who was also charged but never convicted of a passport offence, says he felt like a fool, in that he had been had a second time around, and claims 'the same connection was involved both times, [in the rouble deal and the gold deal] in steering [the organisers] towards me. They knew we were desperate and they knew I could get access to money through the footballers.'

Looking back on that period of his life Wiseman says, 'I was stupid. I was trying to be as rich as the footballers. I saw a way I could have a great life without having to work hard for it. I went headlong for it and closed my eyes to the truth. Probably in all reality these deals couldn't have come off, but I pursued them because it wasn't my money. It was a risk I could afford to take if something went wrong.'

Despite this admission, he considers that he did the footballers a favour 'by taking the fall for them' in relation to the gold scheme: 'I mean, it wasn't actually me who went into the records department to obtain someone else's birth certificate, was it?' he now says. But, as one of the footballers was reported as saying, 'If the three of us [footballers] are guilty of any wrongdoing, then we are guilty of being naive. We were duped ... I've got nothing to hide, but I still find it embarrassing talking about it, even two years after the event. This whole business has made us look silly.' (Peter Kogoy, *Sun-Herald*, 29/8/93).

Ian, of course, thought nothing of running an errand for a business colleague and is now extremely embarrassed, not just by the gold scheme, but by the memory of all his dealings with Wiseman. He is reluctant to talk in detail about this period of his life. And at least one source says she knows how Ian feels. 'It's only with hindsight that you are surprised about how far you were prepared to go, because John was such a good salesperson! I can understand how people like Ian could continue to be involved with him over a period of time, because I persisted too, for a fair while.'

Initially though, from where they stood, people like Frank and George felt that Ian was 'running with the guy[Wiseman]', simply by virtue of his continued association with Wiseman. In their minds, Ian was looking more like the side-kick. Ian simply felt he was too deeply enmeshed, financially, to be able to extricate himself, let alone to simply cut his losses and walk away.

In the nightmare that his life had become, he couldn't face Frank. He hadn't worked at the pub for some months, but he would run into Frank occasionally, and nervously chatter about the latest deal John was working on, and how Frank would be paid back his losses at any time. Frank didn't want to hear it. Ian had always had trouble expressing how he really felt. He would remain silent even when his relationships with other people induced conflicting emotions. Hate, love, anger, pain. The more he felt the swell of strong feelings inside, the more he felt it imperative to appear in control. A bit like the Souths breed around him, who wore emotional and physical toil on prematurely wizened faces.

Frank recalls the last time he spoke to Ian. 'He avoided me. I said "Ian, I have rung you five times. You've never got in touch with me." This is going back five years now. He said, "I will be around at your place tomorrow morning. I have got things to show you. I will be around there at 9 o'clock." I said, "I hope you are hanging by the neck until you come here, Ian." I will never ring the bastard again. Mind you, I have got a lot of respect for Ian. I never lost any respect for him at all over the thing. I don't hold Ian responsible [for my loss] and I still don't.'

George is a bit incredulous that Ian has never vented any real anger. 'He worked hard to get that money. And for someone to just swoop in and take advantage of him! I'm surprised Wiseman didn't have someone take something out of his hide.' Frank says he filed a statement years ago with the police. And every twelve months he sends John Wiseman a card, and gets a return call. 'He's a bankrupt now and he says, "The receiver said I can pick out any creditor to pay debts to first, and Ian says you should be the one who gets paid off first." I just go, "That'll be nice, John."'

The property deal was Ian's one last ray of hope. Ian, increasingly uncertain about any aspect of his affairs, decided to set up a meeting on his own with the developer. He jumped on a flight to Queensland. He is flippant about it now, but at the time, 'I was panic-stricken. You have no idea. Almost my last hope was pinned on this investment.

'So I'm sitting in this incredibly plush office a bit later, and I'm being told basically that my money is not in a building project! I was told that when the money had been transferred, it went straight to Queensland, and was cashed, and only $20,000 was left and placed into a property trust.'

What he thought was meant to be a property investment of $130,000, had been somehow explained down to one of $20,000, and he was never to recover the balance, despite eventually proceeding with civil action, with John Wiseman's co-operation, and being awarded $100,000.

Whatever the details of the case, this was another financial dead-end as far as Ian was concerned. The meeting in Queensland was a lot shorter than had expected. He had time to kill before his flight back home. 'I was in a bit of a daze after I left the office. I went to the movies, looked around the shops at what I could've bought, and then, when I still had a couple of hours, I went to gym to work off some stuff. While I was there, can you believe it, my fucking bag got stolen from the locker I had put it in! I don't know if I did the lock up right, or whatever, but when I came back from my workout, my bag, my money, my clothes, my plane ticket, were gone! So I'm thinking, "What am I going to do?" I didn't have any money except for 80 cents change down my sock, from a drink I had bought in the gym. And I'm standing in my shorts and a skimpy singlet. I reported it. The gym didn't take any responsibility. There was a girl I knew in Brisbane who worked at a pub, so I went there on the off chance she was working. The pub was miles away. I ran there. It was now getting close to my flight. By some good fortune she was there, and I told her what had happened, standing there in my shorts, and a singlet, and she gave me $10 to get a cab to the airport. I thought I'd just get to the airport and it'd be sweet. But, as I was pulling in to the terminal in the taxi, I was watching the bastard plane taxi out! So I go to the desk and ask this woman if I can get a ticket for another flight. I explained what had happened and it was only because someone recognised me that they knew I wasn't bullshitting. She said, "Well, you've missed the last flight tonight. The next one is tomorrow." I'm thinking, "My God, I've got about a dollar in my hand now. What am I going to do? Help!" So I'm going, "Oh fuck, fuck, fuck!" I decided I'd just have to spend the night at the airport. Then they tell me they're closing the airport for security reasons. I was booked on the first flight out in the morning. I rang Dad and hardly had enough time to say, "Dad, I'm stuck here. What can I do?" before I heard that BEEP and we were cut off. I ended up sitting and lying on a bench a couple of hundred yards up the road from the terminal. I'm just lucky it was a warm night and not raining. I was under this lamp on this bench, waiting all night. I couldn't sleep. And I was petrified of missing my flight.

'In the end I just thought it was funny. I was sitting there thinking "No-one is going to believe that Ian Roberts who plays for Australia and who everyone thinks is well off, has had all these things happen to him, and is spending the night on a bench like a bum, in a bit of skimpy clothing and a gym towel." I suppose there was a thousand things I could've done to get out of it, but I wasn't bothered anyway by this stage. I thought it was quite novel, like a little adventure. It's funny you know, but through everything, I never lost a sense of humour.

'You just get to a stage where you're too drained to even get angry. Despair is not the word for it. It's like there is no way out. I've destroyed my life and I've destroyed everyone around me. Everyone I've touched has been brought down. I had failed in life. I was twenty-four and I'd failed. I'd caused so many problems for people it was catastrophic. I just couldn't believe that I had destroyed that many people. That's how I was thinking. In actual fact it wasn't me, but if it hadn't been for me, they wouldn't be in the situation they were in.

'Mum and Dad had found out by this stage. They had started to suspect something when I was getting stressed out by all the abusive calls I was getting. They were used to me being quiet and that, but I know during this period Dad sensed something. He'd try and corner me and say things like, "Look, I know something is wrong! What's the matter? You're too quiet." Most of the time I had this incredible feeling of despair. It makes me sick in the stomach even now. There were many nights at that time, when I just tossed and turned staring at the ceiling. It's hard to describe the torment. Anyway, one particular day, after a call from someone who had lost money, I went into my room. My Dad came in and found me sitting there kind of shaking. "What's the matter with you? What have you done?" Because of how I looked I think he thought I'd killed someone or done something really bad. He said, "What have you *done*, boy?" I was trying to face this and I said to Dad, "I can't tell you, it's impossible to tell you." I was just too embarrassed and ashamed to admit anything.'

Eventually Ian broke down and everything spewed out. He felt a combination of stupidity, gullibility and shame. 'Mum hit the roof. She hadn't liked John from the first day she met him. She couldn't believe I'd been so stupid and so took a long time before she let up on me knowing that. Dad was more like, "Well, boy, it's happened now, you can't change it, you've got to get on with your life. Just play football. Play the best way you know how, because it's the only way you'll get yourself out of trouble." He said, "Sure, that money would've been great to have, but unfortunately it's not there anymore and you're not going to see it again, so get on with your life and make a life of it. You've dug your hole, boy, you've got to dig yourself out of it." '

'I told John Wiseman I'd break his arms,' Ray recalls, 'when it got to where Ian had put his money in. I said to him "Look, if you do Ian on this, I'll break your legs so you can never run away!" For ages we never knew there was a problem—Ian told us he had the money invested. Then he told me the truth.' Jean says one day when John came around to their house Ray had to hold her back. 'I just wanted to hit him. He was just standing there, not saying a word, and I was screaming and yelling at him and trying to hit him.' Strong maternal instincts got the better of her on that occasion. 'I mean, Ian's just a big kid. A big, soft, loving child. I think he'll always give people the benefit of the doubt. Always.'

'I look back on that time now,' Ian says, ' and I truly think that if I hadn't told my Dad and Mum there and then I probably would have killed myself. I probably would have ended up doing myself in.'

The three of them sat at the kitchen table at Botany, where they had thrashed out so many family problems and differences. A tough but simple solution emerged. The only avenue open to Ian was to pay the people back the money they had invested. Out of his own pocket. That, of course, meant saying goodbye to basically all his earnings for the next year or two. It meant starting from scratch in a couple of years. Ian bit the bullet.

Ray took Ian up to the Charing Cross Hotel. Ian couldn't bring himself to face Frank by himself. Ray did all the talking. Ian in his humbled state must have looked like the errant son. Just months before he was the ebullient harbinger of good fortune. Now this. 'When Ray came in to see me,' Frank says, 'I said, "I don't hold Ian responsible. I don't expect my money back." He should have checked anyone else's money was going into a sound investment, if he wanted to put anyone in that situation, but as far as I was concerned the money was gone.'

Ian hasn't been able to face Frank since. 'I've been a coward, that's what it is. I've been afraid to go and see him. He had so much trust in me. I fucking hurt the guy and I hate knowing that I've done it. As soon as I see him, I just cringe. I know he is really disappointed in me. And the thing is that, even now, Frank probably thinks I'm working with John, that I'm still associated with him, because I think he's amazed I haven't been more aggressive about my losses.'

The other of Ian's connections who had invested with John in the rouble deal weren't as lenient as Frank. They wanted their money back, and they wanted it now. Wiseman sympathised with Ian's predicament. 'They all knew what they were getting into, they knew the risk, they were all over twenty-one, but when they lost their money they screamed blue murder. They were going to double their money or get a third of their money on top [in the rouble deal] and next they're saying Ian Roberts has come along and done the wrong thing by them, and they get paid back by the goodness of Ian.'

Ray and Jean were getting calls from people like Noeline Piggins, George's wife, who wanted repayment of their loan as quickly as possible. Noeline, it was said, had some cause to be angered by all the goings-on, as she was related to the man who had inadvertently invested money in the gold plot. 'Ian's dad came over home one night,' George recalls, 'when he found out Ian owed me the money and said, "Look, I'll sell my house to pay you." I said no. As far as I was concerned I wasn't taking money from someone who never borrowed it. I would rather wait. Anyway, Ian showed up here one day, and gave me the money back.'

Ian sold his first unit in Mascot to raise money to start repaying people's losses. Later he would sell his house in Coogee to complete repayment.

It took two operations, but Ian recovered quickly from the injuries sustained in the match against Souths, and was selected to play against Newcastle in a crunch match on 21 July. He had proved he could handle big pressure, even after long injury stints, and Manly's turn-around in fortunes in 1990 were being attributed in part to his class and influence.

Soon after that he was picked for the Test side to face New Zealand on 19 August, at Athletic Park in Wellington. Finally, he was to have his chance to prove himself wearing green and gold, and cement his place in the team for the Kangaroo tour of England and France at the end of the year. Bob Fulton congratulated the selectors, describing the side as superb. Steve Roach said, 'It's great to see Ian Roberts in the side. He deserves it—probably more than anyone.' Ian was surprised, thinking the selectors would stick with the Parkes team.

'I was over at my girl's place when the team was announced on the TV,' Ian told *Rugby League Week*. 'We went out and celebrated until about five o'clock. I haven't had any sleep.'

My girl's place? 'The "girl" was David, a guy I had been seeing for a few months.' You get good at substituting girl for guy in your mind so you can spew out the required response without even thinking.

Ian flew to Wellington for what was the highlight of an otherwise dismal twelve months and his thoughts escaped his prison of doom for precious minutes at a time. 'It was a relief to get away, and I was happy for my dad that I had earned an Australian blazer, but it was just a charade for the press when I said things like, "This is the proudest moment of my life," because, really, I was just exhausted from financial woes.' Australia won the match 24–6.

Then Manly suffered a loss to Newcastle, followed by a bad loss to Penrith at Brookvale. But they won all their matches in August and faced Balmain in the first semi final on 1 September. This was only Ian's second appearance at the Football Stadium for the year, the first being the game against Souths, and it was his first match against Balmain since the disastrous semi he had played for Souths the year before. This time, playing in a different side, he helped crush the Tigers, 16–0. And he was in position, for the first time in his career, for a decent stab at the premiership, followed by a tour representing Australia.

Then, a week later: 'Could Dr Neil Halpin make his way to the Manly dressing room . . . urgently!' The call came over the public address system at the Stadium. Ian had just been stretchered off in the semi against Brisbane. It was his groin! Again! During the game, Ian tore his groin muscle from the bone, busting a tackle. As he came crashing down, he had just started to realise the excruciating pain when Gene Miles came rocketing in and knocked him senseless with a high tackle. 'Miles got a lot of shit put on him for that tackle. But I was glad he hit me. He saved me a lot of extra pain. I was squashed under him. I couldn't get up. When I came to, I didn't know where I was. I felt the pain then. I thought "Uh-Oh, it's gone!" The other side this time. And this time it was worse.' Darren Hadland captured the drama:

In a deathly silent Manly dressing room Roberts was still on the stretcher, his arm shielding his eyes from the television cameras and the horde of journalists desperate for news of his condition. But for the 25-year-old international they could have been a world away. Instead of a Kangaroo tour, the big Manly forward was left to ponder yet another summer of rehabilitation, agony and anxiety. Disappointment was carved all over his face. His words were soft as he steeled himself to fight a war he thought he had won earlier in the season. On a television interview Manly coach Graham Lowe said Roberts would come back a stronger and better player. He also asked why do things like this always happen to the really good blokes. Hear, hear. (RLW, 12/9/90)

George Piggins, angry for his friends over their monetary losses, didn't hesitate to talk to the media in order to get some satisfaction and alert people as to what went on.

'LEAGUE STARS LOSE $1M' cried the front page banner head-line of the *Sun-Herald* on October 14, 1990. The story beneath talked about a man claiming to be a dealer on the Sydney Futures Exchange, who had obtained up to a million dollars from at least 15 Winfield Cup stars. Ian was named in the story, but George was the only man quoted, and he had a lot to say.

Meanwhile, Ian had his sixth groin op. But who's counting? 'I started to question why I was punishing myself so much. I'm just not the right build for this game, I thought. But then, somewhere along the line I'd get determined again. When I realised that I had nothing else, I had to beat it and fulfil my potential properly. Neil did the first operation just after the semi. He hadn't done many. He didn't fix all the problems. It was quite funny. At one stage during the operation I sat up and saw Neil. "Hey Neil. How are you going?" I was really happy, and really drowsy. He said, "Good mate. Why don't you just lie back down now." Afterwards I thought it was a dream. There were incredibly bright lights. Neil was in a funny mask with that blue thing on his head. Evidently it happens every so often. The doses they give you while you're under aren't enough. You don't feel pain when you wake. That is something like the last sense to return. So they just increase your dose and keep going.'

I just can't wait for the new season to start. I want to prove at Manly just what I am capable of doing, but I keep having a nagging doubt in the back of my mind ... The doctors tell me my progress since the operation has been perfect and I should have no further problems with the injury. I just hope they are right. It was a tremendous blow to me being ruled out of contention for the Kangaroo tour. (Geoff Wilson, Sunday Telegraph, 23/12/90)

'I had to go back to Queenstown to get it fixed up. Neil came with me. When I think of the number of times that guy went out of his way to get my football career back on track!! There aren't many doctors who would travel to Queenstown with you, for an operation with another surgeon! Neil and I have been good friends ever since, and I love him dearly for being such a supportive friend over the years.'

Another result of the trip? A hole in Ian's upper inside leg, where a muscle once was.

TEN
STATE OF SHOCK

'It dawned on me at this time that there was always going to be something traumatic happening in my life.'

Ian met Jake, a big league fan, at the New Year's Eve Rat Party in 1990. The two had a lot of eye contact on the dance floor. For Ian it was 'love at first sight'. Like a lot of the guys Ian found attractive at that time, Jake was cheeky, streetwise, a bit rough and blokey, physically lean and sinewy. He was nineteen, and was a bit in awe of the brilliant footballer, and still confused about his attraction for men. Ian recalls, 'We were just good friends for ages and ages, and he stayed over a few times. Then one night we ended up having the most incredible ... experience. Calling it sex makes it sound too common. It was more than that for me. Jake had only ever had sex with one other guy, but we had become incredibly close. We just ended up consummating the special connection we had. After that we had a pretty intense and wonderful time together for the next six months. He was really passionate, and responsive. Affection-wise, it was the best relationship I'd had, at that stage.

'We didn't go out much. We mostly hung round my place at Coogee. Jake always had to make sure people didn't know we were together in any way other than as friends. All his friends were straight at that stage. No-one was allowed to know.'

Michael Gorman, who has observed Ian's relationships over the years, saw his choices as reflecting a slow progression from fear about his sexuality being made public, and the embarrassment that would cause people, and from very low self-esteem to a grudging self-respect. Ian always knew what he was, and accepted it as part of himself. But the society, in which he was raised ensured that he was uncomfortable, not only about his sexuality, but a combination of things.

'At the time he met Jake,' Michael thinks, 'he was still very much hung up about the image of the poofta. I think he really loathed the idea of sex with a real "nancy". He wanted guys that passed as straight. Some of them were borderline straight, like Jake. Ian seemed to hate all the bullshit, the queeniness, everything the Albury [a full-on gay pub] stood for, bleached hair, artifice, everyone going on about material possessions. There's a lot of the poor Botany kid in Ian. He is very, very insecure about his background, about his looks, things that people would not think he'd be insecure about. It's not like a chip on his shoulder. It's something deeper than that. It's like "My folks had it really tough, and I just don't understand you guys who didn't."'

This inferiority complex helps to explain in part Ian's excessive efforts to prove himself physically and to better himself financially. It explains what led him to very real and disastrous problems in his life. It also determined the quality of his relationships. 'You could see in the boyfriends,' Michael continues, 'that none of the things that made him insecure were going to be there, threatening to him in any way. He was very defensive. He was attracted to guys who weren't going to overpower him.' Mentally or physically. Yet Michael and other friends watched Ian take a beating from Jake.

While Jake outwardly fitted the usual criteria of Ian's boyfriends, friends watched him accidently lock onto the masochist in Ian. The type of homosexual relationships Ian grew up on were based on being allowed to get only so close to someone, often in fairly secretive snatches, here and there. His capacity for love was constantly frustrated by the secrecy accorded these taboo relationships. Now, even as an adult, the choices he made were restrictive. Like so many young gays, Ian had become masochistic in a sense, desperately wanting and needing closeness with a lover, but somehow believing that that need should not, or would not, be fulfilled. His love gushed out in torrents in areas where it was socially acceptable. That is, in a platonic sense, whenever someone was weak or sick in some way, and needed him. His friendships from early childhood were often based on his protective nature. Everyone comments on how he looked out for the underdog.

His friendship with Lee was like that. Lee, who is compact for his age, can recall countless incidents where Ian leapt to his defence over-protectively. 'One night we had left Jamieson Street [the night club] and I was driving. Ian liked to sink down low in the passenger seat, so anyone driving past would hardly see that he was there. This night I pulled up at a traffic light and these guys in the car alongside started giving me heaps. Ian was nearly asleep next to me, but he must've half heard what was going on, and he snapped up, getting all angry, going "What did that fuckwit say to you? What did you just say, mate?" The guy yelled some abuse and threatened him, and then I reckon he must've been shitting himself when Ian got out of the car and walked over to his window, and he saw the size of Ian. Ian was crazy mad. He just can't stand it when he sees someone get picked on when they're outnumbered or just a little guy. The loudmouth in the car was frantically winding his window up. They weren't so tough now, and Ian asks him to wind it down so he can talk to them. He likes to say his piece and then he calms down, but the guys were giving him heaps and telling him to fuck off. So he just smashed his fist through the car window! Glass and shit were flying everywhere. It was mad! The guy driving the car just floored it and they sped off, freaking!'

Ian was vulnerable to someone else's suffering almost as though he was responding to his own ... to the child he tried to keep hidden within.

In attractions that were sexual as well as emotional, he responded to people who were physically weaker than himself. He found it attractive when someone appeared to be in need of protection which he knew he could offer. As long as he could establish that co-dependency, he also felt there was less risk of being hurt or humiliated.

Jake was the worst person for Ian to be seeing, because he was sorting himself out sexually, and holding Ian at arm's length in his confusion. So for Ian it represented the unfulfilment he was used to, the rejection that he feared. This rejection was slow and agonising, painfully consolidating long-nurtured feelings of uselessness and unworthiness, perpetuating an ugly cycle. 'After a while,' Ian recalls, 'I couldn't handle it. I used to get really upset. I went from thinking he was the best thing that happened to me, to the worst. He just slowly turned, and then we had a really horrible time for another six months after that!'

People with low self-esteem can be too comfortable with someone treating them badly. They can let the hurt go on for ages because they have grown up feeling unworthy of love and—like many homosexuals, subconsciously disliking themselves because of what they are constantly told is their affliction—they don't know any better. Even well into adulthood, they can be suspicious of, or reject, someone who claims to offer them unconditional love.

Not that a lot of us in this society don't suffer from this to some degree. We are either insecure and possessive too early on in a relationship, expecting to be dumped at any minute and sometimes provoking it, or pursuing a relationship vigorously with someone who is sending out strong signals of apathy. If anyone reaches adulthood undamaged these days, they must've struck it lucky with perfect role models all the way, and lived in a cocoon.

Ian's experience, though mild in comparison to that of many gays, still meant he was a damaged traveller, meeting damaged travellers. His affair with David, a guy he saw for a while before Jake, had ended because David was too needy. 'I was freaking out because David was incredibly possessive. It got to the stage where I couldn't go anywhere without him knowing exactly where I was and how long I would be. He would get all emotional and upset, even threatening, and that was the last thing I wanted to deal with. I used to imagine he would go crazy and just blab to everyone about me, or get hysterical in public.' After squeezing gently out of that predicament, he started chasing Jake's affection. After months of beating his head against a brick wall there, he was eventually left flattened and exhausted.

At the same time, other aspects of Ian's life were stirring public interest.

His agent had marketed, among other things, an *Ian Roberts*

Total Energy poster book—a series of glamourous body shots, perv material, complete with mandatory 'girlfriend' in the background. The 'girlfriend' was little sister, Kylie!

'They were telling me they wanted me to have a girlfriend, and this, that and the other. Like all the agents I had, they said if you are known to be gay, we can't do anything for you. They actually ended up asking me if I was, and I just thought, finally, 'Fuck this! I'm not going to lie to them. It's better that they know, because I don't feel comfortable with the girlfriend thing.' So I told them. We just sort of drifted apart after that. I didn't get another agent for years.' It caused discomfort for him to deal with people who wanted to scrutinise his life.

Ian's association with the Manila gold plot hit the papers on March 22 and 23, 1991. His name came up in a hearing at the Downing Centre Local Court. Robert Bisset, an employee at the Registry of Births, Deaths and Marriages, testified that on June 8, 1990, Ian and another person were trying to obtain the birth certificate of William Leslie Robertson, the de-facto husband of one of the people involved, and Detective Sergeant Anthony Scott testified that he saw Ian farewelling Farquhar and three other defendants, and one of the footballers, at Sydney International Airport on the same day.

When questioned by the media, Ian continually denied involvement in the gold plot, or any other rumour concerning him losing a fortune. But by the time he finished paying people back, he had lost nearly half a million dollars.

Because of his continued association with Wiseman, he was pursued by other people who had been involved in business with him, and had lost money. And there seemed to be no shortage of those. 'I started warning a lot of people off John, and when I met people through him, I was cautious with them. I'd even warn them about John if I thought they didn't know him properly. I met a guy, Bob, who is now a business colleague and friend, when John was running a food outlet for someone. I'd met this guy a couple of times before I said to him "Look, I know John well, and if you give him any money . . . just don't give him any money." John had been trying to interest this guy in a nightclub. There were that many schemes I just didn't bother listening anymore. I didn't trust Bob at first. Eventually, he offered to give me a hand with some charity things, and eventually I relaxed. But, it's not like I was in touch with John all the time. I just kept tabs on what was going on. I had to for my own peace of mind.

At one stage, a woman tried to enlist Ian's assistance in redressing her grievances against Wiseman. She was incredulous at first that Ian was not prepared to assist her in any way that would bring his name to the public's attention. 'At the time, I couldn't understand his attitude,' she says now. 'I thought he was just protecting John. But a couple of years later when my name was made public in relation to the matter, and I got a lot of attention, it dawned on me what Ian had meant and I often felt I should apologise to him for expecting him to come forward with me. I have a greater appreciation now of what it must be like for a well-known person to get any media attention, the way things get twisted and sensationalised. But at the time I was angry.'

Calls for help affected Ian deeply though ... As usual, he found the anguish of others the most unsettling. 'John's wife rang me one day, screaming because their situation was so bad. She was upset because she said they couldn't pay their rent, and I could hear the kids crying in the background. I felt for those kids and what they must've gone through with John's problems, and I had gotten quite close to them over a period of time.' Ian gave the family money as late as 1992. John and his wife took the kids to Disneyland, and away from the stress of failed business ventures, if only for a short time.

Ian still wavers between extremes of emotion when he contemplates what he calls 'the money thing'. He only talks about it in snippets and then not without choking back tears and retreating into silence to brood. He looks back in anguish. He's still confused by his belief in the basic goodness of human nature. Then he hates himself. Or he feels sorry for himself. He feels sorry for everyone else too, including John Wiseman. 'The guy has probably had the most impact on me of any person I've ever met in my life. My dealings with him nearly destroyed me. That, with all the other things in my life. When I think of all the nights that I lay in bed, not crying, but like, "What have you *done*, Ian? You've lost everything!" It literally went on for years. I mean, I'm still not out of it now. I don't feel like I am. I'm getting on with it, but I'll never be out of it. Never. Never ... 'I was a wreck for months. I wasn't able to face people. I can't believe I was playing footy at this stage! I used to somehow get out and play. In a way it was probably the only time my mind left my problems.'

One night in hospital at the end of 1995, the author left Ian with a tape recorder to privately convey any thoughts he had after talking about this chapter in his life. 'My biggest problem in life is that I've trusted people too much, and I've always given people the benefit of the doubt. Well, maybe not trusted—it was more like a continual hope that everyone was wrong, and that I hadn't been that gullible. Frank and all that would disagree with me here, but I don't believe John set out to rip anyone off. He just got himself into a problem. Then he went bankrupt and tried to get out of it. Because he wasn't a bad person. He just unfortunately does things and he doesn't mean to hurt anyone but he does ... He has certainly played a crucial role in some people's lives.'

The confusion of thoughts, the torment, and the compassion that Ian still feels about the loss of hundreds of thousands of dollars is part of the larger emotional legacy of his early life.

On 30 March, 1991, after the game against Wests at Campbelltown, Ian recalls, 'We were walking out of the change rooms, and you have to walk through their clubhouse to get out to the bus. One bloke was saying, as we walked past, "He's a fucking faggot, that Roberts!" just loud enough so I could hear, and he knew I could hear. He didn't think I was going to say anything. I turned round and there were a group of guys, and there was this older guy who'd said it, and I said to him, "Oh mate, don't fucking backstab me! It's more fun plunging the knife through the chest!" He didn't know what I meant. "What?" "Are you going to say it to my face now, you fucking coward? You and I can go and sort it out, just between the two of us! Here's this faggot calling you a piece of shit! So you can tell all your friends that a faggot called you a piece of shit." His son or whatever was there came up to me and sort of apologised for his father, saying he was drunk and was just mouthing off and didn't mean any harm by it. Sometimes it just got to me.'

It tended to get to Ian more and more during '91 and '92.

By April 1991, after four matches, Ian still couldn't sprint properly. He had only started running the week before the first round, against Brisbane.

'The doctors have just told me I can play again, but I wanted to come back at the start of the season ... Because I haven't been able to hit the line at top pace, I have really taken a belting.' (Darren Hadland, RLW, 10/4/91)

He was good enough for the rep football selectors, representing City in their win against Country on 25 April, and NSW in the first two Origin clashes.

The first Origin match was at Lang Park on 8 May and the Blues lost, 4–6. The match was memorable, for Ian, because of the aftermath. 'I got hit after the game, but I never caught the guy. I was coming out of the change room after the game and signing autographs. I had my head down, signing, and I copped a smash on the back of my head. 'FAGGOT!' I looked up and saw the guy charging through the crowd. Don't get me wrong. Ninety-nine per cent of people are cool, and people can say what they want, I'm not bothered, but once someone lays a hand on you it's a different matter. There was nothing I could do. I was just left with a stinging head and feeling like a bit of an idiot, although I think the kids and that standing around were more embarrassed. For me probably.'

The second Origin clash was at the Football Stadium three weeks later. Ian suffered an injury in the first half of the game, which looked at first like it was a broken neck, but which was in fact a pinched nerve. NSW salvaged the game 14–12, and Ian almost looked like pulling off another recovery in time to play the series decider. But he didn't.

Roberts is probably the most enigmatic figure in the Sydney premiership. Roberts' ability to remain competitive in the toughest Rugby League premiership in the world on such a skimpy preparation, silently enduring the uncertainty of his groin problem, is an astonishing performance. Even more so when you consider he has emerged as a strong Test candidate ...

Although outwardly Roberts looks as if he is carved from granite, his strength and endurance have dropped ... the pain has been considerable. (Ray Chesterton, *Mirror*, 29/5/91)

Apart from putting his body on the line all the time, and continually aggravating injuries, Ian was paying another price on the field. And he paid it again and again. The old concussion. It was probably not surprising, given the way he played. 'You just get to the stage where your pain threshold must be higher than the average person's. You learn to live with pain that would generally disable someone else. I'm not saying I'm any better than any other person. But, for example, when I worked as a sparkie, guys would whinge and carry on if they gashed their hand or whatever. I would just wrap it in a bit of tape and get on with it.'

Sometimes getting on with it was more difficult. Theo Lianos remembers: 'There were so many times when I would be at a game and go to wait outside the dressing rooms and someone would come out and get me or another friend to go in and help Ian get home. You'd go in and Ian would be standing under the shower or something. He would see you and recognise you and go, "Hi. How are you?" and be pleased to see you. And he'd come out of the shower and try and dry himself, and you could tell he was still in Disneyland. He didn't know what he was doing. You'd have to lead him to his clothes and tell him he had to get dressed. And, you know, like, "Put your undies on first, Ian, then your pants ... then your shirt!" If he couldn't get his shirt on you'd have to button it for him. He'd have a throbbing headache, and you'd drive him home, and he just went into his bedroom and slept. And slept. It happened like that so many times!'

By mid-June his neck was right and he was back on the field. But he was by no means in the mood for a week of headlines surrounding another controversy of his own making.

Dave Johnson, and plenty of others, will tell you, 'Ian is a guy who is very, very gentle. It takes a lot to goad him. He will take a lot of insult and stuff like that, and he just won't budge, particularly if it is against him. Against him, he doesn't seem to jump. But if it is against his family, or a friend, or someone who is defenceless, he will fight staight away. And it is swift. And it is harsh.'

It was at the Manly v. Balmain game at Leichhardt Oval on 23 June, shortly after the half-time siren had sounded, that a scuffle broke out. Balmain fullback Garry Jack emerged from it, his face bloodied and disfigured. The referee, Graeme West, witnessed the whole thing. He simply gave both Garry Jack and Ian ten minutes in the sin bin, Jack for starting it and Ian for retaliating.

Following the game there were outbursts from Balmain coach Alan Jones, and from Jack, who had two ugly gashes on his face held in check by fourteen stitches. They lodged a complaint with the NSW Rugby League and wanted the perpetrator of Jack's injuries cited and brought before the judiciary. The League dismissed the complaint, saying it would take no action. This decision followed close on the heels of another unpopular decision after an incident involving Mal Meninga and Michael O'Connor in the last State of Origin game. O'Connor emerged with a broken nose, and Mal was let off.

A furious Jack publicly named Ian as the perpetrator of his face rearrangement, claiming he received eight quick uppercuts of the type for which Ian was quietly famous. He also claimed he was held by one or two Manly players while Ian bashed him. League headquarters was inundated with angry calls and NSWRL general manager John Quayle was forced to call a special news conference at which he restated the League's position: when a referee sees an incident and takes what he thinks is appropriate action, they are loath to overrule him. That would undermine the authority of the ref. He defended the decision by West.

A lot of people had been calling for the League to make drastic changes to its citing process. (Quayle, alone, decided which cases went to the League judiciary, and a lot of people thought he was lenient towards Test players.) They wanted an independent tribunal to decide which matters went to the judiciary.

Jack threatened to sue Ian. The cuts to his face were infected and it was thought he would have to have plastic surgery to correct ugly scarring. Meanwhile, a profusion of stories on the matter seem to start with 'Battered Balmain fullback Garry Jack ...' because it sounded good.

Jack was quoted extensively. 'Roberts came in and grabbed me and while another Manly player held me he just punched the tripe out of me like a punching bag.' 'No-one should be bashed the way I was. One on one I wouldn't complain. But not what happened to me.' 'It seems there's two rules, one for Test players and one for the rest ...'

John Quayle was quoted. 'During the fight there were a number of players being held and unfortunately Jack was one of them. Probably the player wouldn't have gotten 14 stitches if he didn't do what he did. They've got short memories, some of our players. Especially Garry Jack.'

Ian was quoted. 'Everyone knows my style of play. What's been written in the papers, it's just a fictional story for the public.'

On 28 June, Jack filed a staggering $100,000 law suit against Ian through his solicitor, Chris Murphy, in the NSW Supreme Court. It was claimed that Ian Roberts 'wrongfully and intentionally' punched Jack 'repeatedly in the face' while other Manly players held Jack, and that Ian had acted out of 'malevolence or spite' and had intended and succeeded in humiliating him before the public, his team-mates and officials. The previous December a former Cronulla player, Steve Rogers, had sued a former Canterbury player, Mark Budgen, and was awarded $68,000 when Justice Lee found that Budgen had unlawfully assaulted Rogers during a match in 1985 which had resulted in a broken jaw for Rogers. Les Boyd, with whose head Ian was acquainted, was also sued over a 1983 State of Origin incident which resulted in an out-of-court settlement.

Video footage told the current story a bit differently from Garry Jack, and so did the Manly players. Balmain's Brian Smith had put a bomb up just seconds before half-time. It was taken by Matthew Ridge as Balmain players were stampeding towards him. The siren had sounded when Ridge got punched by Jack in the confusion of players. Jack never denied swinging the first punch; he just said it never connected. Ridge said not only did it connect, but he was held by other players when Jack hit him. Ian saw this and, without thinking twice, he retaliated on Ridge's behalf. Ridge said at the time that Jack 'copped what he deserved' and 'got his just rewards'. According to Terry Hill, who was still at Souths, 'The story was going around that Ian had bashed him because Jack called him a fuckin' poofta and all that. But he was helping his teammate. Don't worry about helping blokes, he's one of the most loyal and staunch blokes. He'll stick by you all day. Which is good, fair. But if *you*'re not fair, you can't expect him to be. And then he whinged about it, poor Garry Jack, in the paper!'

Then Jim Comans puts in his two cents' worth. The man partly responsible for clearing the thuggery out of league during his time as the League's judiciary chairman, he was in a sense one of the men responsible for the clean-cut and fresh-looking athletes you see in the game today. Even though Ian was a pioneer of the new-look game, Comans said, had the matter gone before the judiciary, 'If it could be shown that Ian Roberts was guilty, he would have received nothing less than twelve weeks.' But that was a big 'if'. 'To see the battered face of Garry Jack on television this week made me feel quite ill,' Comans added. 'You don't see boxers looking that bad. At least in the ring they wear gloves. The bare-knuckle days were supposed to have gone out over a century ago.' He also said the fact that Jack started the fight was not relevant. 'The game of rugby league is in trouble when players feel they have the right to be judge and jury in incidents like this one. That was always pointed out when players tried to come down to a judiciary hearing and tell me they were only retaliating. Any incident when a player is bashed the way Jack was does nothing for the image of the game. The quicker it is obliterated the better.' His comments didn't help his close friend Quayle, or Ian. But Comans had been getting impatient with what he saw as the inconsistent way the judiciary was handling matters since his departure. Steve Roach got four weeks for patting a ref on the head! 'That wasn't thuggery! You [should] never lose your sense of humour.'

'Player's Don't Have Right to be Avengers' pronounced Phil Rothfield in his column in the *Sunday Telegraph* on 30 June. 'League's image suffered a worse battering than Garry Jack's face from Quayle's non-action on one of the most brutal and sickening incidents for years.' He went on to speculate on the concern all the mums and dads would now have about their kids playing the game. What would the kids be told at coaching clinics to explain away the incident? Oddly enough, Phil ran an 'exclusive' in the same paper, starting, 'Ian Roberts has been hurting as much as Garry Jack since last Sunday's controversial brawl'. Who knew who was feeding the controversy? Ian had a big say in the same 'exclusive'.

What really upsets me is that I've been painted as a coward and a thug.

People who know me realise it couldn't be further from the truth ...

It takes a lot for me to blow my cool.

I just wish people would have a closer look at the video. Didn't they see what happened to my team-mate Matthew Ridge?

He was being held by two Balmain players, when Garry Jack punched him. OK, Matthew's head wasn't split open so there hasn't been any fuss about it.

There were three Balmain blokes on one Manly player, after the whistle mind you, so I reacted ...

Look, I really regret doing what I did. Ninety-nine times out of a hundred I wouldn't have done it.

But in the heat of the moment you've got a split second to react.

You don't have time to think, 'Gee, I just saw Matthew get hit and I lost my temper'.

I'm very sorry it happened. You don't get a kick out of hitting blokes. It's not in my make-up ... I've got nothing against Jimmy Jack personally. I actually like the guy.

We worked together [with Gerry Carroll]. But on the field he's just another opponent.

Some of his accusations this week like calling me a thug and describing it [as] a cowardly attack have really hit home and hurt.

It's been said I'm three stone heavier than him ... How big's Matthew Ridge? He didn't have much of a chance.

Seeing Garry Jack on the television news and in the papers is bad for Rugby League. I'm very sorry it happened ... it's not good for the image of the game. Of course I'm concerned what the young kids would think.

I've always prided myself on setting the right example both on and off the field. Every player has a responsibility in that area ...

Walking down the street or driving round in my car people have been yelling out 'you thug' or 'you coward' and that sort of rubbish.

I've heard a lot of people ringing up on the talk-back radio and having a shot at me ...

Why's it Ian Roberts' fault?

Rothfield covered all bases. Another story in the same paper gave the referee's angle. 'Jack got involved after I'd blown the whistle for half-time,' West was quoted as saying. 'There were two Balmain players driving Matthew Ridge back in a tackle and Jack came in to strike the player. I put Jack in the sin bin as the first instigator. Ian Roberts went in as well for carrying on with it. I don't think the brawl was any worse than you see at other games.'

For all-male contact team sports, brawls have always been a head-ache for administrators. The AFL had fun introducing its brawling rule in '96. Emotions on the field are all pointed towards team play and team loyalty. If a player is psyched and witnesses something happening to a team member on the field, outside the rules, you'd have a hard time convincing them it's an individual matter for that other player to sort out.

Ian is embarrassed talking about the Garry Jack incident, or any injuries he inflicts in fighting. Fighting connects him with an uglier part of his roots. But he's animated when talking about injuries he has received. It becomes a joke then, at his own expense.

In June, Ian was again selected to play for Australia against New Zealand. On 3 July, Australia lost the first Test at Olympic Park, 8–24. When Manly played Brisbane on 14 July, Ian injured his leg and was taken off early in the game. But he was right for the second match against New Zealand in Sydney. Ray and Jean were at the Sydney Stadium on 24 July to watch their son assist Australia in its crushing defeat of the Kiwis, 44–0.

Theo felt sorry for Ian's parents as they sat in the crowd that day. 'At the Stadium, Mr Roberts, Mrs Roberts, and Paul, us four sitting there, and all the people, when Ian came running out, were like "Ah ya fuckin' faggot, Roberts!" I just wanted the ground to swallow me up. I wasn't embarrassed for me, or for Ian. We're used to it. I was embarrassed for them. They just sat there through it ... At one stage they got up and clapped something Ian did, and we four were the only ones clapping. I mean even the Australian people were saying things about him. Some of it was kind of good, like "Ah, he's a fucking fag, but he's a good football player" ... And Mrs Roberts had pieces of cake and tea, and sandwiches for us, which she busied herself with while all this was going on. As if she didn't even hear it.'

Ian never discussed how those taunts affected his parents. 'I remember Graham Lowe said to Dad, the first time he met him, "You must be very proud of your son." And Dad said, "I am, but I'm equally as proud of all my kids." Dad wouldn't have cared if I was a street sweeper. As long as I was happy cleaning the streets, then he would be proud of me.

'When I ran out on the field for Manly, I was starting to cop heaps, every game. Every game. From the crowd. The guys at Manly got used to it, so it didn't bother them. Sometimes, I copped it from other players. Once, when I got cut, a Norths player was yelling, "Don't let that bastard fucking bleed on us!" We were packing for a scrum. But, you know, it's a Catch-22 situation, because I know guys say things like that when they are geed up for a game or frustrated. When you see them off the field socially, they're fine. But for them to have said it means it must be a problem for them. I've been called "poof" and "faggot" that many times on the field. It's part of the game, abuse.'

Ray and Jean got to hear a hell of a lot of yelling about Ian's homosexuality, from anonymous 'admirers'. They could hardly avoid it if they wanted to watch their son play football. 'Rumours started when he was playing with Souths. I didn't cope very well,' says Jean. 'She had so much pain, they both did, which was caused through Ian,' Theo recalls. 'It must have been really hard. She is such a nice lady, Ian's mum. They're the type of people that mind their own business. They're just really hard-working people that have just stayed within their family all their lives and worked hard to get the best for their family. But they are both basically really really shy, private people, and they like to keep it that way. They have always been like a second family to me. I don't have much family and they will always call up and ask me to join them for Christmas or something. It hurts to know what they've been through.

'First there were the threatening phone calls when Ian left Souths, like "We're going to put a bomb under your house" and "You're the parents that gave birth to this bastard". Then came the "Your son's a fucking faggot" type. It was especially hard on Mrs Roberts. She's still not used to it. She still has a hard time coping.'

Jean got it the worst. 'I used to get it at Qantas. Comments about poofters and football, all the time.' One day she remembers cleaning the toilets on a plane. 'One fella actually got out of one of the trucks, and came onto the aircraft to where I was cleaning ... it upset me to think about it even now,' she says, her voice thin and faltering. She concentrates for a moment to control her tears. Ray gently chastises her to bring her back. 'I can't help it, it upsets me!' she snaps. 'That's why I don't like to think about it ... Anyway, he grabbed my wrists, quite hard, and shook them, like, you know, to make out that they were limp. To see if I had limp wrists, or to say I had a limp-wristed son. It still upsets me, to think that someone would make a point of doing something like that.' At the lunch room at work one day, 'One fella said, "Ian Roberts is a poofta." ' The guy then related a fictitious story about Ian publicly sucking someone's dick at Taylor Square. 'He didn't know who I was at the time. I said, "You don't even know him" and I told him who I was. I said, "You don't even know what he is or who he is!" ' Jean left work distraught and went home.

Ian didn't hear of the Qantas episodes, or others, until years later. 'They wouldn't tell me about episodes like that, because they knew it would upset me. And it would have. It would be unbearable, them being hurt and me not being there to fight back. That would be the worst!'

But they confronted Ian about his sexuality a couple of times, which wasn't an easy thing to do. Homosexuality, they knew, was a fact of life. But it was a fact of life you didn't want too close to you. Certainly not in one of your children. It was something that could be dealt with from a distance. You didn't celebrate Uncle Charlie's

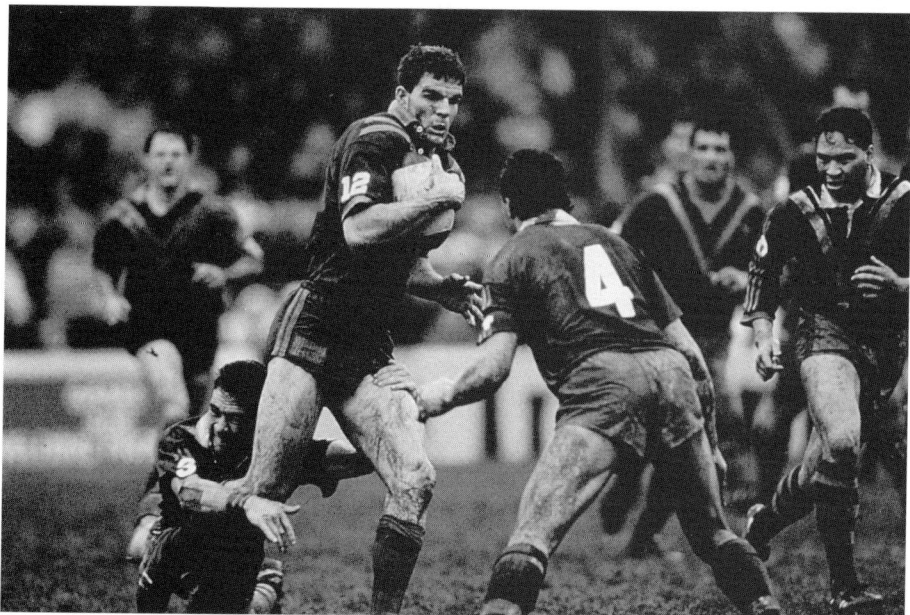

In action against New Zealand. (*Photo:* Action Photographics)

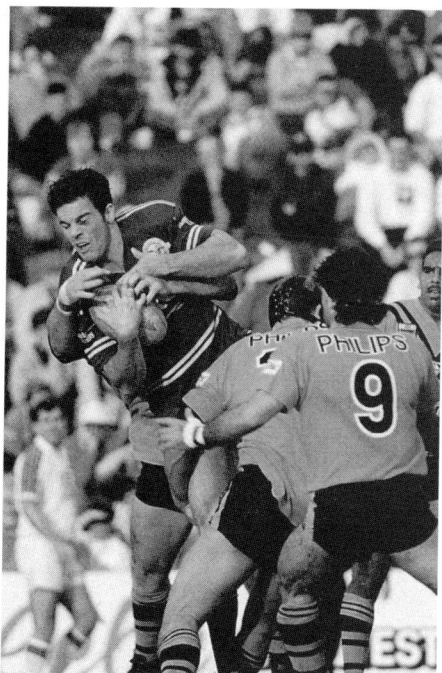

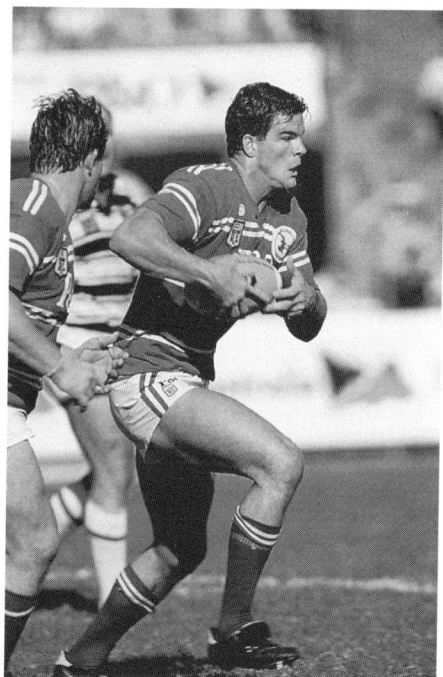

Power surges by a determined Sea Eagle.
(*Photos: Left* – Clifford White; *Right* – Action Photographics)

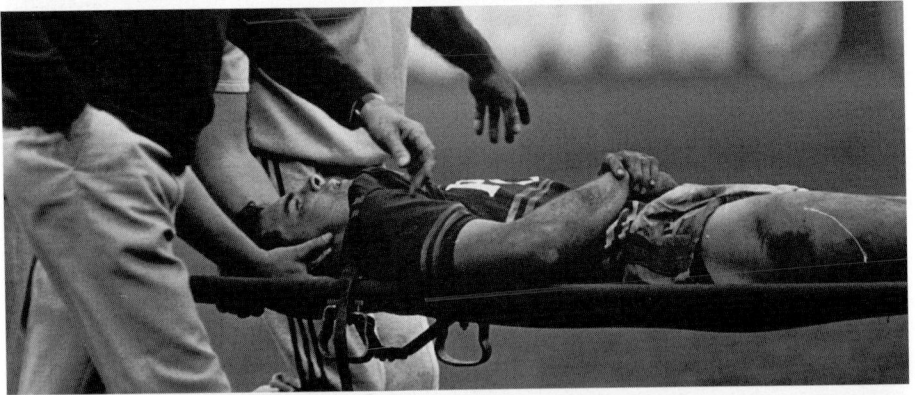

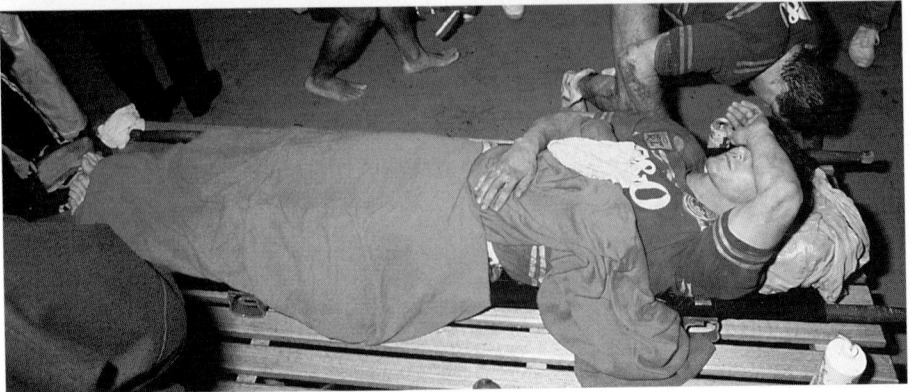

The horizontal part of the game is something Ian became all too familiar with
over the years.
(*Photo:* Action Photographics)

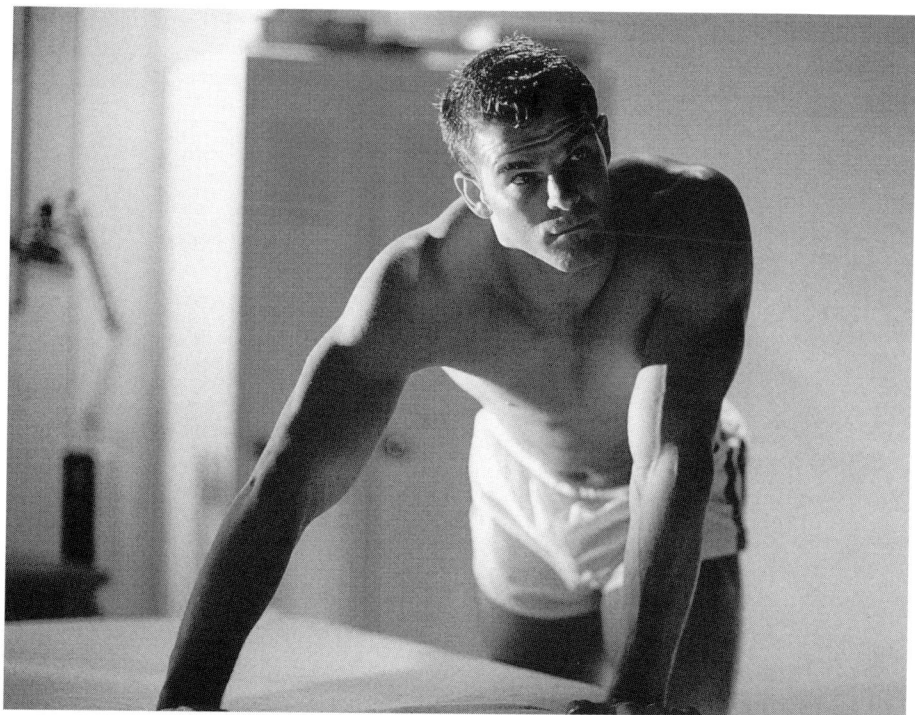

This page and overleaf: Promotional stills for an early ARL publicity campaign.
(*Photos:* Action Photographics)

Below: In front of the cameras for the Men of League Calendar (*Photo:* John Elliott, *Rugby League Week*).

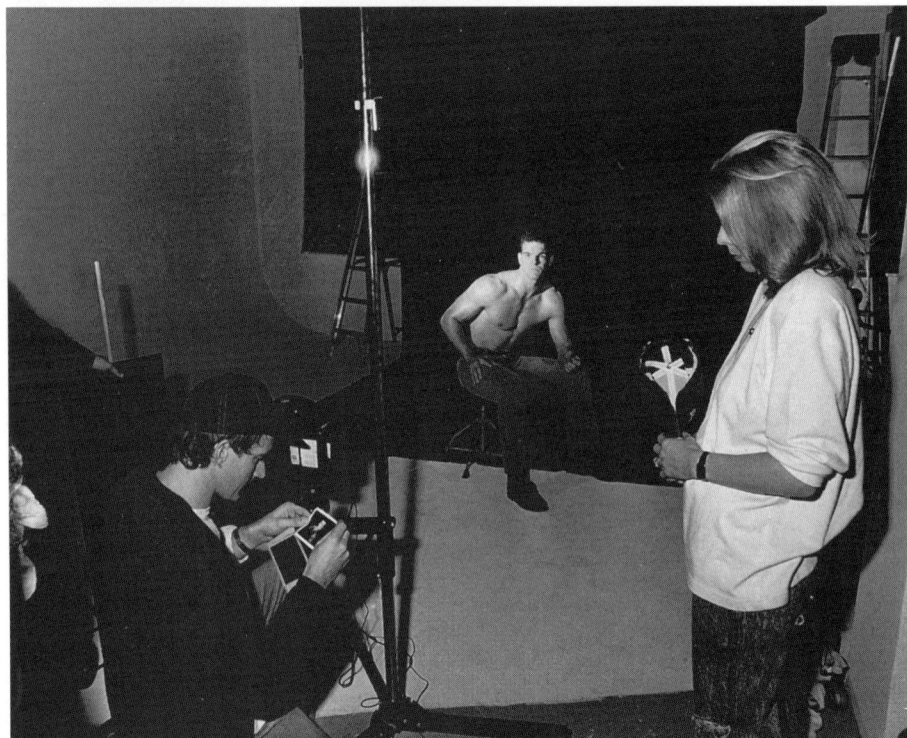

Marketing the Total Fitness Body with a glimpse of the compulsory
female accompaniment. *(Photo:* Tony Lyon)

Lee, Ian and Theo at a dance party, early 90s.

Another dance party.

Blake.

Ian with Blake.

Ian visiting Dawn and Blake in hospital.

Ian with friends Eve van Grafhorst and Troy Lovegrove, late 1991.

Anger erupts against St George. Later featured in a Puma campaign.
(*Photo*: Craig Golding, *Sydney Morning Herald*)

Unless unconscious, injury was never a deterrent. Mangled, repaired and off again.
(*Photos: Above* – Action Photographics; *Left* – Clifford White; *Right* – Chris Elfes)

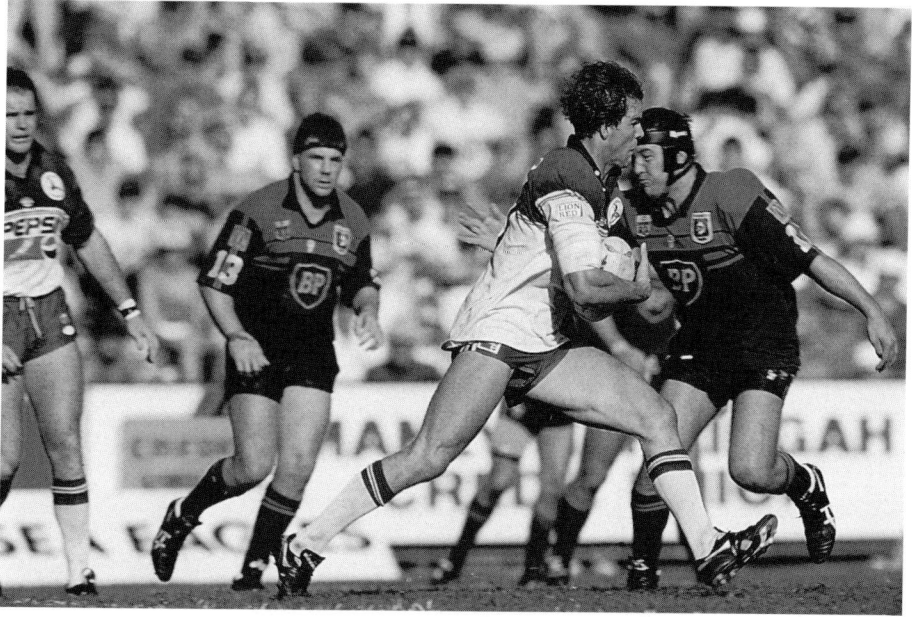

(*Photos:* Clifford White)

(*Photo:* Action Photographics)

(*Photo:* Action Photographics)

Sometimes not even Mal Meninga could stop the momentum
(*Photo:* Clifford White)

The marked man. (*Photo:* Action Photographics)

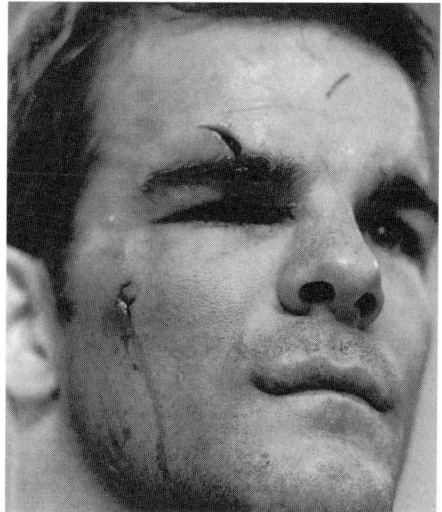

Left: A panicked Laurie Daley calls for help as Ian fears for his eye after an incident in the Test against Great Britain. *Right:* Some more scars for life.

1994 Kangaroos. *Back row*: Brian Hollis (*Trainer*), Tim Brasher, Laurie Daley, David Furner, Michael Hancock, Dave Ryan (*Trainer*) *Third row*: Terry Hill, Paul Harragon, David Fairleigh, Ian Roberts, Paul Sironen, Brett Mullins, Steven Menzies, Paul McGregor, Bradley Clyde, Wendell Sailor *Second row*: Mark Beaven (*physiotherapist*), Frank Ponissi (*Trainer/Statistician*), Steve Walters, Allan Langer, Nathan Gibbs (*Medical Officer*), Shaun McRae (*Skills and Strength Coordinator*) *Front row:* Geoff Carr (*Manager*), Andrew Ettingshausen, Jason Smith, Dean Pay, Bob Fulton (*Coach*), Mal Meninga (*Captain*), Glenn Lazarus, Steve Renouf, Brad Fittler, Ron Wilkinson (*Manager*). (*Photo:* Action Photographics)

Terry Hill gets a dance class for the London club scene.

relationship the way you celebrated someone's wedding anniversary or anything. You didn't talk about it. The only people they heard talk about homosexuality were those mouthing off or preaching against it. Ian reassured his parents. It seemed easier on them. Better all round. It was what they were hoping to hear, and Ian wasn't ready to risk finding out that their love was conditional. And he didn't have the energy or the know-how to help them through anything.

People Ian didn't know seemed to get satisfaction from reminding him he was a 'failure' by publicly sensationalising, and being disgusted by, his rumoured homosexuality. It was a social habit to hate 'pooftas'. It was a desire to inflict pain. A need to punish Ian, or his family. By brandishing some ancient dogmas and calling them morality, people think they have a licence to practise inhumanity. And it is more often the ignorant, or those with an axe to grind, who wield the axe; people who themselves feel victimised or insecure are the first to want to bring someone else down. With homosexuality, it is sometimes those with sexual insecurities, who repress or are embarrassed or angered by their own homosexual tendencies, who will lash out. Or it is just kids, quoting from their parents' catalogue of insecurities, phobias or fanaticism. It is always chilling, for example, to see children who haven't yet had time to discover their own sexual identity, spitting venom about God's hatred of homosexuals or how disgusting homosexuality is. You have to wonder where the rights of that child end and the rights of the parents to indoctrinate start.

Ray and Jean are over-dismissive, now, of what must have been hideous experiences for which they were totally unprepared. 'We used to hear a lot of nasty things. I didn't care one way or the other,' says Ray, who is as stoic as his son. 'But Ian was the one who copped it,' Jean adds, 'He used to get it at the games, but no-one knew who *we* were.'

'There's one good thing about Jean and I,' Ray continues. 'No-one knows us in football. Ian's the one that plays football. We've never tried to get in any of his glory. In all the years he's been playing, we've met quite a few people, but we don't go round making out we're anything. Most of the time we would go to the game on our own ... About the only time when we felt we knew what it was like [to hear abuse yelled at a son] I think we were playing South Sydney. Cliffy Lyons' mother and wife were sitting in front of us. People were abusing Cliff. It was the worst racism I've ever heard at the football, that day. You could see that his mother was really hurt. South Sydney supporters can be shocking. I said to his mum, "Don't worry, love. They're not even worth the worry!" '

'It never stopped us going to football,' Jean insists, and then rethinks her position. 'Sometimes we'd miss a game. I'd think, "I don't really fancy going." '

Ian played in the deciding match against New Zealand, on 31 July at Lang Park. Australia won 40–12. His form had deteriorated somewhat by this stage in the season. His work rate was still high. But his lack of strength in attack was noted, not least by Ian. 'I don't feel I have the leg drive. Perhaps that's the problem with my attack,' he told *Rugby League Week*. This lack of explosive force was partly due to his weight still being down around 100 kg, and the long-term effects of the groin problem.

At half-time in the game against St George, on 11 August, 'A guy just leaned over the barrier as we were leaving the field and punched me on the side of the head. I can't remember what he looked like, but I can remember wanting to rip his throat out. He tried to duck back into the crowd, but I was over the barrier and had grabbed him before he got away. It's all a bit of a blur. I know he was shitting himself. The people around were cheering. One woman was screaming at me to leave him alone. She was swearing and carrying on like I was some bastard. The police were there pretty quickly, and they were saying, "Don't hit him, Robbo, don't hit him!" They ended up charging him with assault. I was in a bit of shock. It's not something you expect. I was thinking about the game.

'In the second half, one of the players kept going "Faggot!" I whacked him in a tackle. The ref pulled me aside and I said, "If he calls me a faggot one more time I'm going to rip his throat out." I'd had enough. Every other time, I just let it go as part of the game. I mean, it's not like there's a code of chivalry or anything out there. That's why you can't let it get to you. And usually I don't. But occasionally, you can't help it.'

There is a famous photo, taken at that game, of Ian, standing defiant and victorious, fist clenched and yelling, over a St George player he has just deposited on the ground. Puma use the photo in one of their ad campaigns. More than anything else, it captures the anger and frustration Ian felt at that stage in his life.

Ian feels that 1991 was the year he played some of his best football. Many disagree. But he did use football as a release for a lot of pent-up anger and frustration that year. 'I had an enthusiasm for the game around that time that I had never had before and I have never had since. It was a feeling of indestructibility about myself, and a craving to win, win, win.'

That didn't necessarily translate into what others thought was his best football.

'It is that year that I started to do all these big hits in the game. I made a conscious decision to try to cut people in half. There was a huge buzz from that which would just uplift the whole team. I discovered that at the game where the spectator hit me. I got knocked out in that game. In backplay. I was KO'd when I was getting up. I was just running back into play and their fullback made a break and I remember thinking, "I'm going to fucking kill this bloke!"

'I just felt this intense hatred when I was playing. A feeling that I wanted to hurt someone. In that year there were some tackles that I look back on now and I think, "How did I do that?"

'It was pure hatred!

'I'm not like that now and I don't think I'd like to be like that again.

'All the week leading up to a game, I was just on edge. Wanting to cut someone in half. I was incredibly angry. My life outside the game felt like it was going to be in deep shit for years to come.

'My reputation for being a big hitter started that year, I think. I used to get so pumped on the Friday or Saturday night before a game. After the final training session, when it was just the players having a talk with each other, I'd be geeing everyone up, going, "We're going to kill someone." It was a running joke for years after. Tooves [Geoff Toovey] would always stir me, "Hey Robbo, are you going to kill some bastard?" But that's how I used to be. I used to get real vocal. "We've got to believe in ourselves!" I had this incredible feeling. Even with the ball I'd be thinking "These bastards aren't going to stop me."

'That's when *I* think I was playing my best football.

'I don't say as much now. I concentrate more on basics now. "Watch your hands. Let's do the simple things right and we'll win." Back then, I was thinking "Fucking kill them! Let's *give* them the ball, then we'll chop them in half."

'You know, at Souths they used to be like that and I used to be bloody scared! Now I felt like I understood where that can come from. I know, because I've been there.

'I'd do anything to win now, but not that. That was just a phase.'

At the end of his two-year contract, Manly offered Ian a new one on a sharply reduced salary, citing pay cap restrictions as the reason. Manly's chief executive, Doug Daley was quoted as saying, 'We outlined the position to Ian, the ball was in his court and he accepted the terms because he said the club had looked after him.'

In the game against Canberra at Brookvale on 18 August, Ian felt an exhilarating resurgence in form. At which point he tore a ligament in his *knee*! He didn't know it then, but he wasn't going back on the field for Manly in '91.

E L E V E N
B L A K E

Ian was the only footballer to appear in the Men Of League calendar for both 1991 and 1992. 'Popular demand dictated he make a return,' said producer Narelle Hughes. 'He's called "the body" so he could hardly be left out.' The Prince of Wales Hospital had been contacted to send some kids to the launch of the 1992 calendar. At the launch, Ian immediately noticed Blake. 'There were a lot of kids there who were talking and laughing with the players, and then there was this frail little kid, alone, who you could tell was really sick. He had a couple of nurses with him who were kind of talking to each other, and ignoring him.' So Ian bowled straight over, sat down and gently lifted the fragile seven-year-old boy onto his knee, where he remained for the rest of the event.

Ian went to visit him in hospital the next day, and started going in every day after that.

'About the third day,' Dawn Stenning, Blake's mother, recalls, 'I went out of the ward with Ian and said, "Look, you can't keep coming in because Blake will start to expect it, and you're a busy person, and when you can't make it he'll be disappointed". "No," he said, "that's fine. I won't disappoint him". I said, "Apart from that, Ian, you have to realise that my son is HIV positive." Ian just said that he had wondered whether that might be the case. He said he had met one of the other children in the same situation. I said, "Look, Blake will not live much longer. He will die, and I'd rather you knew it now. I don't want him to get used to you, and then get disappointed, in the time he has left." '

At this stage, Blake was in and out of hospital often. 'His gall bladder was shot,' says Dawn. 'A lot of the time he was in incredible pain. He would walk around like the Hunchback of Notre Dame. He had some difficult operations that had never been done on such a small child before.'

Dawn, a single mother, had prematurely given birth to a tiny, frail child, who had received an infected blood transfusion. When she met Ian she was going though a lot of trauma dealing with the hospital administration in what was one of the earliest cases of a child with AIDS-related illnesses. She was a battler, though, fiercely protective of Blake's right to live as happy a life as possible in the time he had, and it seemed to her that the bureaucracy didn't always share her concerns. She is a strong-willed woman though, with a bawdy and cheeky humour which maintained her through hard times.

Team-mates and coaches all say that, although Ian was pretty introverted around adults, he was outgoing when it came to the charity side of being a celebrity. 'I don't have to tell you about the amount of work he has done,' Mario Fenech observes. 'At Souths we'd often go to the Prince of Wales Hospital and the Children's Hospital [at Camperdown] and Ian built up a great relationship with the kids. He does things that people wouldn't even know about. I was club captain for about seven years and involved in a lot of the profile stuff, and way back then, Ian was very sensitive, and felt sorry for people that were hard done by, and that's a lovely quality. A lot of people believe that because they're good at football they're better than others, which is not the case. One of the great positives of my career is that I've always been very humble and I'm very grateful for anything that I've got. I respect other people. And Ian is very similar too.'

As with his protection of the little guy, the underdog, he gravitates to those who seem ignored or disregarded and feels their adversity. He is easily moved to tears over someone else's predicament, but rarely over his own. Ironically, the many people he has helped over the years could have no idea that their hero felt so vulnerable and isolated himself.

When he was in hospital with epilepsy, a visit by football players made a lasting impression on him. 'They went round the ward. I was so impressed. I looked up to footballers so much. When I started playing first grade, I was getting some fan mail from kids in hospital, so I started going to see them, to talk or take them a football or something. I guess I just kept going back after that. The first couple of times you go to see new kids, you really are the football player to them, but after that you're not. You're just their friend. And they're no longer impressed with who you are.'

Penny Douglas runs Ronald McDonald House, which is attached to the Prince of Wales Hospital in Randwick. It is a house where children can stay with their families while they recuperate from operations or illnesses. She met Ian in 1991 and has had a lot to do with him since then, both on a personal and a professional level. Recognising a vulnerability in him, she has always felt somewhat protective. 'When my boys were ten and eight Ian took them to Wonderland one day when I was working. A couple of days later, I was speaking to someone at the Australian Rugby League with regard to something at the hospital. Ian's name came up and I mentioned he had taken the kids out. And this man said, "How could you possibly allow someone like that to take your kids?" And I said, "I'm not sure where you're coming from." He said, "Well, you know he's gay?" I said, "I have known he was gay from the minute I met him, but it doesn't change anything. In fact, I think it would be good if he announced it to the world!" I was quite taken aback by the attitude, I have to say.'

Penny learned of Ian's visits to the hospital when she worked in the children's ward of the hospital. One of her tasks had been to prepare State of Origin players for tours of the ward. 'Often when you take people around a hospital you need to explain to them that the children are not going to look very well. Some of the kids will become more distressed by such visits, while some are happy to see you. People have to be prepared. They are often shocked when confronted with sick children.

'Ian was in the tour for 1990. I really got to know him, though, when I moved to the House in April 1991. He would make visits or drop in to take kids to football training, or up to McDonald's or Pizza

Hut or wherever. At times he said to me to let him know if we need any equipment for the House. At one stage we needed a Nintendo machine, for example. He would organise for those things to be bought. Then he won about $1200 as part of an award, or something, and he just sent me the money and said to buy something for the House.' He donated the money from the Ken Shine Award, given by the Australian Rugby League.

Penny continues, 'Ian was one of those people I could ring up at any time and say, "Look, there's a kid here who would really like to meet you, who's been watching you play football for years, and could you drop in and say 'g'day'?" And he does. He would arrive, and he just sits down and has a talk with them. Keeps in touch with them. Rings them up. Brings them a cap or something with football autographs. Rings up later to see how their treatment has gone. At no time has he ever said no, he can't do it. He might say "just give me a couple of days to organise my time." But if you asked some of those other guys, it'd be, "Well, OK, how much do I get for my signature?"

'Yet he is very shy, too. I have often seen him walk into rooms of large numbers of people, and everybody knows who he is, but he doesn't ever go out of his way to let anybody know. He doesn't ever talk about what he has been successful at. He always talks to people and asks them what *they've* been doing, or in the case of patients, about their illness. Some people start attacking him about whether he's played well or not ... and he finds that very difficult.

'He never wanted any attention. Some people, before they visit here, say, "Oh, is there going to be a camera there? Or television?" I always try to say no, because these sort of visits need to be private. It would never occur to Ian to ask about press coverage, I am sure, at *any* time. It would be his preference to visit privately.'

There is no ulterior motive on Ian's part. 'I get quite angry sometimes when I see how charity is so easily used as a photo opportunity for one thing or another ...'

It was apparent that Ian found some refuge in the company of children. 'He could talk to kids,' Penny noticed. 'He found it easy. They don't care if he doesn't say a word. He's Ian Roberts. He is so famous, such a good footballer, they just want him to be there. No brush-off. The kids are in awe of him. But he still manages, "How are you going, mate? Gee, what happened to your leg?" He makes those sort of comments when a lot of people just can't. He has gotten used to kids here with no hair, one leg, one arm or whatever, and he is just always asking "When is your next treatment?"'

Among the hundreds of children he saw over the years, it was inevitable that he would get especially close to some of them. Penny saw how easily affected he was by the suffering he was powerless to stop. 'There was one girl here who had the most enormous crush on Ian. She always wanted him to go and visit. He got to know her pretty well, took her to the football, and they had a good time when they were together. When she was dying in Dubbo Hospital, her mother rang Ian and said, "Alex is dying and she really wants to see you." He went there. Got on a plane and went to Dubbo for the day. He didn't think twice about it.'

Ben was probably Ian's initiation to emotional involvement with children who were unwell. 'One day one of the trainers at Souths said there was a little kid in hospital and he supports Souths. I went in to see him, then I started going in all the time. Ben was five or six, and had this form of gangrene which was very rare, and they thought he was going to lose a leg. I struck up a really good relationship with him, and his family, who were from Canberra. I went and saw him every day, and took him toys and things. When he left hospital that first time, we kept in touch. He was in and out of hospital quite a bit, too. I recently went and watched Ben—he's fourteen now—compete in a swimming carnival for physically challenged people.'

Through knowing Blake, Ian would be forced to confront a lot of his own emotional baggage and, though it would plunge his life into more chaos for a time, he would eventually re-emerge, and start to own his whole life for the first time.

Dawn had made a decision not to tell Blake everything about his illness. She wanted him to live as normal a life as possible, with the hopes of any child. She gave the decision a great deal of thought, but she had witnessed the trauma of terminally-ill children screaming "I don't want to die" and didn't want her son going through that. Ian respected her wishes and started sharing with Blake, as much as possible, normal childhood adventures. He became, in fact, Blake's surrogate father.

Ian and a couple of friends, like Theo and Chris, another flatmate of Ian's at the time, would take Blake and some of the other kids to football training. Blake felt a camaraderie he had never known. 'I was lucky to be allowed by the men to go to the semi,' Dawn remembers. 'Ian sat in the players' area. He had said, "When you get to your seats send word and I'll come up." And then Ian comes up through the stands, everyone is saying hello to him, and he picks up Blake. Then my son disappears with him and I didn't see him till the end of the game. Oh, he was all right! Didn't give a damn about his mum!' she says with characteristic good humour. 'He was right up in the top near the commentators' box.' Dawn has a video of Blake at the game, sitting on Ian's knee. The camera panned in for a close-up at one stage, and the commentator, who had been at the calendar launch, introduced Blake to the crowd on the PA system.

Dawn has all Blake's special events on video. He was little but used to the spotlight. He had gone off to see the Queen, and when US First Lady Barbara Bush was out here, they sent Blake to meet her because they didn't have enough leukemia children! Mrs Bush never knew she was chatting to a child with AIDS, whose father happened to be an American Serviceman who didn't want to know about his child! One newspaper reported that Blake fluttered his eyelashes 'flirtatiously' when Mrs Bush complimented him on them. 'He was seven years old. How does a seven year old flirt?' Dawn wants to know.

Ian took Blake to the 1991 Grand Final. Dawn was incredulous at the change Ian had provoked in her son. 'Goes off to the final, and he wouldn't even kiss me goodbye when Ian comes to collect him. Off he goes, and the nurses all looked at me as if to say "Is that Blake?"'

'I wasn't allowed to go to the final. Blake didn't want me to. It was the same when they went to the movies. Blake didn't want me going. I used to say "Why?", and he'd say "Because it's boys only!" Well, it was like going out with his dad. It was boys, you know. It was fine by me. I guess I should have been as jealous as hell. When

Ian was around, I didn't exist! The two of them used to gang up on me, and rib me and that!

'Before the final, Blake had just had one of his operations and was on medication, and I thought, "No, it's not fair to Ian, because of the pain and things", and one of the doctors who rang up to check on Blake's progress said, "Tell his mother he's going! Ian wants to take him and Ian's aware of his condition. There are some things that medicine can't give him. There are thousands of other kids who'd love to watch a bloomin' grand final with a football star!"'

So off they went, Ian laden with medication, and care instructions.

'It got around the hospital that Ian was coming in every day,' Dawn continues. 'It got to the point where he had to come in the back way, to sneak in, because as soon as he came in the front everyone would be at him. "Would you come and see this little boy?" "Would you do this?" "Would you do that?" But he was coming to see Blake. If Blake was well enough, he and Blake would go round the other wards.' It was a good distraction from the pain. Dawn recalls one of Blake's bad days. 'I was walking around the ward with Blake and he was clinging to me, sobbing in pain, and Ian walks in, and he has Wayne Pearce with him, and Blake just breaks from me and throws himself at Ian, crying out, "Oh Ian, please help me!" And Ian grabs him and lifts him and says, "Look, matey, I've brought a friend to meet you" and poor Wayne is going, "Don't worry, I'll come back another day, I'll come back another day." Blake was in pain, and it broke Ian's heart. Other people couldn't put up with it.'

Like others who became friends with Ian over these years, Dawn wasn't told he was gay. Ian protected people from their own prejudices that way. And himself. That way it wasn't awkward. 'Everyone kept saying to me that Ian was gay,' Dawn remembers. 'I said, "Well, I haven't heard it." My brother said, "Don't be silly, Dawn. He would get shit and hell, in league, if people knew." It seemed like everyone knew, or everyone said. But Ian had never. At this point he used to talk about a girlfriend who he had a four-year relationship with, and he was trying to get her back. I mean, it didn't worry me. I used to say, "So what if he is?" "But Blake's with him," one of the mothers

said one day at the hospital. Ian had just walked out with Blake. Blake
and I had a lot of gay friends. Gay people will move among people
who have HIV straight people, once they know what's wrong with
you, often won't. That's why we didn't make it common knowledge
about Blake. I was asked early on, when Blake was diagnosed, and
everyone was documenting everything, did I hate gays, because gays
were supposed to have spread AIDS? I used to say that gay people
were people, and like all kinds of people there were good and bad.
Mind you, I'd never met a bad gay person. The Bobby Goldsmith
foundation [a gay organisation] had lent us a microwave, and clothes
dryer and video. And one of the gay guys gave us a dog, a cocker
spaniel. To me a person's sex life is their sex life. It would only affect
me if I wanted to go to bed with him, and I was hardly in the running
for that.

'For my forty-fourth birthday, Ian had a party for me, at Sizzler's.
It was for Blake, of course. Halfway through he comes back with this
great big Lego medieval castle! I said to Blake, "I wonder what I'll get
on *your* birthday?"'

Ian took Blake to see John Farnham in concert. Blake had met
John the previous year at a fund-raiser. Because of Ian, Dawn recalls,
the three of them received VIP treatment the whole evening. 'Blake was
sitting on Ian's knee at the concert, and Ian's sitting there just patting
Blake's head. Blake had really shiny hair, and only three people were
allowed to stroke it, me, mum and Ian. And you had to see the look
on Ian's face when he was nursing Blake and Blake wasn't watching.
It was total contentment. That's why everyone thought Ian was Blake's
dad. He *did* love him. I mean, they didn't have to talk. Blake would
just lean on him, as long as Ian was there.'

Ian's knee was tolerable enough for him to tour Papua New
Guinea, but he was reluctant to depart for the tour, on 26 September,
in case Blake died while he was away. Blake got upset if ever Ian
couldn't make it in to see him. On the night of a party Ian was to
attend with Blake and Dawn, he was called to training and rang Dawn
to cancel. 'He could hear Blake crying in the background. He said,
"Look, don't worry, I'll be there." 'No! You have to expect to have
to do things,' Dawn replied. 'Even if you were Blake's father, you'd

have to work.' But Ian got Penny to ring Graham Lowe at training and explain. Ian was fined $1000 for non-attendance. 'Lowey never took the money,' Ian recalls. 'Graham was great during this period.' Once when Manly was playing away, Graham arranged a flight for Ian a day later than everyone else so he could be at the hospital for one of Blake's operations.

Blake went to the airport for the farewell. He was crying on Ian's shoulder and Dawn saw that Ian was distraught. 'He was saying "Don't worry, darling. Your mate won't be away that long." Oh, it was just so touching, you know?'

On the tour, Ian again witnessed hysterical support from the New Guinea fans, some of whom suffered more injuries than players. 'Although several players pulled out of the team because they didn't want to tour New Guinea, it turned out to be the best time. Not the games. At the games, the fans were beaten into submission. Continually. In front of the players. At one game, one over enthusiastic fan got on the wrong side of the police and received a few good blows of the baton. Then he was ejected by being passed over the heads of the crowd and through a barbed wire fence. He landed on the other side all gashed and bleeding. Then, for good measure, they set the dogs on him to savage the poor guy for a while. All this right in front of us! I'll never forget it. Forget the game. It was insignificant in comparison.' Ian got some scuba diving in around Rabaul harbour, exploring the ships sunk during World War II. He also received a special award from the Papua New Guinea government for the work he did with the local children.

He scored a try in his first match against New Guinea on 6 October, which Australia won 58–2. And they won 40–6 on 13 October. Despite the scores, the wins weren't easy. Ian came back severely cut and grazed from the hard playing surfaces and doctors had advised him not to see Blake until he was healed.

'Blake was at the airport to meet me,' he recalls. 'After that I didn't visit and it wasn't because of the sores. They healed in a few days. I just *couldn't* go.' Jake had started dating girls at this time, and Ian was racked with jealousy and confusion. He didn't know how to compete with a woman, but he found it difficult to walk away from the situation, which only maximised his pain. He felt so drained and vulnerable for a time that he had nothing to give Blake. 'It's not that I didn't want to see Blake, but it was everything and everyone that went with it. I stayed in love with Jake for what seemed like ages. He used to pop around and see me every so often. That just dragged the agony on a bit, I think. Eventually, he went on to live with another girl. (Then *she* left *him* for another girl!) He still sees guys occasionally, but he's always taking out girls. He's bisexual, I guess. He's a classic bisexual. He really is.'

Ian's sense of loss was of course compounded by his financial situation. Something was drastically wrong. Ian realises now that it was probably the worst time to become involved with a terminally-ill child. 'There were too many other things going on in my life, is what I'm saying. I was overflowing with grief, what with one thing and another. I just wanted to close up shop. Your body just gets to a point where it says "fuck you". I didn't really understand Blake's disease itself, either.'

People were looking up to him, yet again, and had great expectations again, that he would do the 'right' thing. That's how Ian felt at this point. 'For Blake, it wasn't so much that *I* wasn't seeing him, when I stayed away. But if I didn't go and see him, it seemed to me nobody did. My friends seemed to take my lead. Because of me, all the friends he had made seemed to vanish. And Dawn had noticed that more relatives and their kids seemed to visit Blake when I was around. I mean, I'm not big-noting myself. I'm just explaining my guilt.' Penny saw that. 'Through Ian, Blake became part of something. He was accepted into the world of mates, really. Blake had spent so much of his time just with his mother, or in a hospital ward with nurses looking after him, he really enjoyed being part of a gang, and Ian would arrive, often with a group of friends, who would just sort of hang around with Blake, tell jokes, muck around, and go away again. They wouldn't even really talk to Blake all that much. It was quite funny. Blake just felt happy he was a part of the group. It was a really important part of his life, that group.'

In the end, Ian rallied himself and resumed his commitment. 'I think Blake punished me from then on. He held back, at first, as if to say, "Well, if you had nothing to do with me, I'm going to have nothing to do with you! You shouldn't have done that and you're going to live to regret that forever." I know that sounds like a stupid thing to say, that a kid could do that. But I felt that. Like I'd been a failure, again. I'd let someone down, *again*.'

Ian couldn't explain any of this to anyone, let alone Dawn, who saw that Ian and her son were alike in that respect. 'When either of them is troubled about something, and you say "What's worrying you?" they just say "Nothing", but you see a facial expression telling you otherwise. But you couldn't get them to talk until they were ready. You could not get Blake to talk, and Ian is a lot the same. He is a very private person. They can both be very stern and tough on the outside, but they are sort of marshmallow inside, right?

'People always thought that because they had such similar temperaments and they had similar facial features, Ian was Blake's dad. The kids would say, "We know you're Blake's dad, but aren't you a famous footballer?" Ian would say, 'Well, I am a footballer, but I'm not his dad, though I wish I was!" Blake would emulate Ian's likes and dislikes after a while, too. He didn't like beer in a can. He didn't like butter. I used to say, "Hey, mate, I want my son to fatten up, not get any leaner!" '

Penny thinks Blake knew he was going to die. 'If you are in a hospital bed for that length of time, you hear lots of people talking about you. They think you are asleep or whatever. There are issues terminal kids have to work out like why their parents are crying every time they are near your bed, or why people you haven't heard from for months send you flowers and pay you a lot of attention when you have a relapse. I think with Blake, Ian was important, because he felt that his mother had someone to look after her when he went. Kids need to know that everything is going to be all right, when they're gone, that the fish will be fed, that Mum won't be too unhappy. Blake was somebody who felt that *he* looked after *Dawn*.'

Ian stayed with Blake until 3 a.m. the night he died. Earlier that April evening, they had all been to the first birthday party of Ronald McDonald House. 'They were all playing computer games and Ian's like Blake,' Dawn recalls. 'If he hasn't played a game before, he likes to sit back and just observe, before he participates. Neither of them like making fools of themselves. Then, when he's ready, he'll join in, when he knows he'll do alright.' Blake was weak and in pain at the party. He was given heavy doses of morphine later that night. They should have helped him pass away quickly, but he was in and out of consciousness until he died at 8.45.

Ian was rung shortly after. He was in shock. 'Even the night before he died, I just thought he was sick again. I was upset for him, but I wasn't concerned he was going to die. He was in and out of hospital and sick all the time. But when the phone rang that morning, somehow I knew what it was. I went to have a shower, and I was just stunned! I turned the radio on and that Madonna song about an angel was playing. It was like Blake was singing it to me. Everything the song said was just perfect.'

Penny knows that Ian had conversations with Blake about his illness. 'He would say things like "You've got to keep on battling, mate", and things like that. And, for all we know, Blake probably lived a bit longer than he was supposed to, with Ian's visits.' But, despite the fact that he had always known Blake's death was imminent, it hit Ian like a ton of bricks when it came. He was simply not prepared for the effect it would have on him. 'He didn't ever think that Blake was going to die,' Penny says, 'even though Blake had a feed tube in, and oxygen, and all sorts of things, towards the end. I still don't think that he had accepted that Blake was actually going to die. And that may be wrong, but he was *so* distraught. I was there when Blake died, and Ian arrived. It was hard for him to go through that. He wasn't able to express how he was feeling easily. He said that he just felt terribly sad, and that he didn't think it was going to be as painful as it was. The first time some-body important in your life dies, I think you suffer physical pain. There is a physical pain in your heart. And Ian was visibly in pain.'

'He just came in and threw himself across Blake on the bed, sobbing,' Dawn recalls.

'The closest I was, with Ian, was when Blake was buried,' Penny continues. 'He was very supportive of Dawn, despite his own trauma. He was there for her at the funeral. He almost took the father role in both the service and the wake. He was wonderful to Dawn, he really was. She didn't have anyone else there who was as supportive. But then, I think he realised that he had to gradually withdraw from that too. I think that whole period of his life must have been a steep learning curve for Ian.'

Penny sees less of Ian these days. 'Since Blake died, Ian has withdrawn his total commitment to kids, and I think for very good reasons. When Blake was dying, I said to him that I thought he should be very careful with his contact with the children. I felt he was going to find it increasingly difficult to maintain that sort of relationship. He was really giving 100 per cent and coming to visit them regularly, and being very much involved in whether they were getting better, or responding to treatment. And I said to him that most of the children that come here will survive, but every now and then a child that you come in contact with will get under your skin, and then you will find it very difficult if they don't survive.

'We spent a lot of time talking about how you need to be very protective of your emotions when someone is sick, when you first meet them. A while after Blake's death, Ian was seeing other children. Alexandra died too, and he began to withdraw more. I think this was important for him because he was just becoming too upset when these children weren't surviving their treatment. Now he comes to a Christmas party or birthday party, and he sees children he has known before, who have survived, and that is good for him to do. But I don't think it was good for him to continue to go through the trauma of watching children not survive.'

Reminiscing over photos of Blake, one day, Dawn chattered endlessly, with joyful relief almost, about what Ian meant to Blake and her. 'I've got photos of Blake from age one right through, and he's smiling in them, but in those ones with Ian, he's happy. It's like there's a light inside him, and he was in pain the whole time!' She jokes about the ribbing that Blake and Ian gave her, but she is still flattered when she relates the fuss Ian made of her on her birthday, and when he tried to have the hospital provide her a bed in Blake's room.

'This is one taken at half-time.' Dawn carefully passes a photo, a sacred momento. 'He's in the jumper that Ian gave him. He loved that jumper. He wouldn't wear it until Ian went on the field. Then he put his jumper on. And he would take it off at the end of the game ... I think it was the night after he died, I looked up and there was a jumper there and I said "That's not Blake's jumper." It was Ian's. And he had written verses on it in texta. The last line, I remember, said, "I wish I was with you to hold your hand." We buried Blake in that jumper, and in the coffin he had a football which Ian brought him back from New Guinea, with a few other things.'

As he jogged, Ian thought of the words he had written on the football jumper they had buried Blake in. 'I wish I was with you to hold your hand.' He thought about that Madonna song, and how he had heard it that morning that Blake died. It was as if he could hear Blake singing it to him. He could hear the words as his feet directed him along a path he had run a thousand times before.

He was running. Still.

He had always run. He had worn his own path from running.

Along the dismal meandering road, skirting the black silhouettes of Botany industry, around the bleak and unwelcoming shores of Botany Bay. The periphery. He knew that best. It used to feel safe. But this night there was pain. Not of a physical kind. And different to the anguish he had felt a lot over the last twelve months. More threatening. And it was all through him, feeding at his core. He feels raw and uncomfortable. Exposed. To himself.

He reached a point on the sandy foreshore, and he couldn't go any further. He is too heavy with something. Something is wrong.

Before he knew it, he has buckled under this strange weight. Crazy in this agony, his big hands gestured erratically. Anywhere. Like insect antennae flailing the air for a movement enemy they sense nearby. He glued them hard on his face. Then something wrenched him as it exploded deep inside and surged out of control. In heavier and heavier waves it smashed against his wearied mind and rushed past his hands into the night air.

Ian then heard a strange inhuman guttural cry. It was coming from within him. Then a torrent of tears, released by the sound, escaped down his face and dropped onto the sand below. His whole body shuddered with the release, but his mind couldn't escape an infuriating frustration. Hammering him down.

He was oblivious to everything but this frightening catharsis.

There was a pressure on his shoulder pushing gently. He was startled. He looked up through his fingers. There was a concerned face peering through. He quickly bundled the escaping emotion.

Someone had come over to help. Had recognised him. 'He knows me, Ian thought. 'He doesn't know me. He knows photos and sound bites. He's speaking. Say something!'

"Yeah, I'm right, mate ... A mate just passed away ... Thanks."

He didn't feel the embarrassment he usually feels. He wasn't ready. He was never ready. But this night he didn't give a fuck.

Something about this night, something about him was chaos. Shaken, he moved on, hoping to find peace in another place.

This was a cry for peace. He had never known it.

'All the attention I had been getting since 1986 never made me excited or big-headed. It was flattering, but it also made me paranoid. It made me focus on myself, my looks and my physique. I used to think that people were going to see me and be disappointed because of all the hype about me. I didn't feel I could live up to it. Whenever I saw video footage of myself playing football, all I could see was this ugly, scrawny bastard. When I looked in the mirror, I thought I was too fat! I really thought I was fat! At this stage my diet habits got crazy. I was always pretty strict with myself, but at this stage I wasn't exactly bulimic, but I was obsessive, and no matter what I did I wasn't able to fix my faults. There were times when I would go and throw up because I had eaten some fat, because it made me feel disgusting. I was always counting calories. I had done the Men of League calendar, and lots of promotional stuff, and apart from that, got lots of comments and attention about my body in the media, out, wherever. I was so self-critical. I'm my own worst critic, always. I just thought I was a fraud or something. I'd look at blokes like Des Hasler [a Manly footballer], and set them up as ideals.

'I felt more and more uncomfortble whenever I was in a public place. Because of my height, too. I felt eyes scrutinising me all the time, watching for me to slip-up or something, or saying, "Oh there's Ian Roberts, what's the fuss about his body?" Or "God, he's an ugly bastard." Because I *am* ugly. You feel like you don't want to let people's expectations down. I know I was paranoid.'

But he didn't know how to feel another way. And fame only increased his fear of exposure as a fraud.

He was a chameleon. Theo noticed. 'He would be, and still is, a different person with different people. He is never the same person. He is a different person with business people, with friends, a different person with sports associates, with the gay public, everyone.' In all his relationships he tried to meet what he thought were expectations of him. This was the expectation he had of himself. And he never questioned anyone else's right to demand things of him.

It was disastrous. He lost a half million dollars trying to be a financial messiah to everyone. He wanted to be the father Blake should have had, to protect and save him from pain and death. He wanted to be the kind of partner that Jake would never want to leave. He wanted to be the perfect football hero, the perfect son, the perfect friend. The perfect good guy. But he couldn't be without failing himself, and without failing.

'I always had this feeling that I was letting people down.'

He set himself up as a centrifugal force in a sometimes disparate and disenchanted circus of friends. 'Lee came to me one day, frustrated,' Dawn remembers, 'and said, "What's Ian got that I haven't got?" I think Lee was quite jealous of Ian, and competitive. I told Ian and he couldn't understand it. It started off as a sort of a hero worship, and then Lee thinks, "I'm older, and I can do just as good as you, and I can get the girls." Because the girls fawned all over Ian! Girls would go to any lengths. It wasn't unusual for a girl to turn up at his bedroom window, at all hours of the morning. And Lee was probably envious of all that. But Ian just really couldn't understand it. "But why?" he'd say.'

Juggling friends around his sexuality definitely didn't help matters. It alienated some of the people who were best placed to help him. Good friends, and family who knew, felt distanced by him. 'Julie and I used to compare notes,' says Kylie, who used to work in the same building as her sister. ' "What have you heard today?" It wasn't up to us to say, "Yes, he is gay" when people asked us, when we thought he obviously didn't want people to know.' They had taken his silence as a sign that he didn't wish to discuss that aspect of his life.

Ian had introduced Dawn to the MacDonald family in Queensland, who he had become close to over the years, through football. 'They had become like a second family to me, and they were kind enough to invite Dawn to stay with them after the funeral,' Ian recalls. 'When I was there,' says Dawn, 'Glenys said, "Is Ian gay?" And I said, "Well, I've had no evidence of it." Not that they cared, either, but they heard things, you know. And her son Trent had asked Ian outright, "Are you gay?" And Ian said, "No, son, I'm not. I've got a lot of friends that are gay. But I admire you for asking me. I know a lot of people haven't got the guts to ask me that."'

At the same time, Ian would dedicate himself to people who were almost complete strangers. Theo saw it happen. 'I used to say to him, "You've got no idea about people!" He would say things like, "Well, they're very nice to *me*." I'd say, "Of course they're nice to you." I'm sure he realises that people have different motives, but he doesn't like to admit it because after all he's a normal human being, and no-one likes to be told that people hang around because of who you are, not because of what you're like. It's like an insult. But I used to get the shits with him, and tell him because he'd leave himself open all the time.

'You've got no idea what it was like. Whenever I was out with him, he didn't have much privacy. People always dragged him this way and that.' And if they were polite then Ian was always obliging. 'He realised, and always learned the hard way, that people were befriending him for different reasons. That's why over the years, Ian has had that many aquaintances, but he's always saying he doesn't have that many friends. Because it's true. He doesn't.'

Ian sort of knew the score. 'I think I always felt alone, in a way. I just filled up my life with things, so that I could tell myself I wasn't, but deep down, I was on my own. I felt that I didn't fit in *anywhere*. I guess I was always like that, but now I was *realising* that I felt that way. And the feeling was much stronger. No matter where I was. I would go out with people somewhere. I'd get to one place, and feel uncomfortable and want to leave. It didn't matter where it was or what group of people it was. I just felt awkward and out of place. I preferred to be at home.

'I got a bit panicked. What if I was going to always feel that way? I got to the stage where I questioned whether I even knew what "relaxed" felt like, it was so unfamiliar to me. Had I *ever* been comfortable?'

'He tries to keep everyone happy,' Theo continues, 'and he gets so frustrated that he can't, that he ends up turning on the people he loves the most, I think, and that's where he got his nastiest. He would be nastiest to you when you were close to him.'

Ian's friendship with Clem ended in bitterness that year over little scuffles about the 'money thing' and about Ian himself. Ian isn't inclined to recall much of the detail except that their split was acrimonious. 'We had all these arguments and a lot of nasty things were said. Clem had lent John Wiseman money to invest, and I paid it back to him.' A combination of issues came to a head. 'Clem's side of the story,' Theo thinks, 'is that he was deeply hurt because he didn't know Ian was gay and Ian used him. They'd go to clubs and Clem's friends would tell him Ian was gay, and Clem would say with confidence, "No he's not. No he's not." In the end he felt he'd been made a fool of, because Ian hadn't trusted him enough.'

John and Andrew became alienated during the frenzied period when Ian was dealing with Wiseman, and Andrew wouldn't talk to Ian for some time because he saw a side of Ian's personality he didn't like, and he didn't trust Wiseman.

'He cheats if he's losing,' says Chris Smith, one of Roberts' many non-league friends. 'Or if we're playing cards and he's losing, he'll say it's too boring and want to quit. If he loses he's grumpy, and if he wins he rants and raves about it all night. (Amanda Olson, Telegraph Mirror, 3/9/93)

Ian took out frustration on Jean, who was after all one of the main reasons for his striving to be something he wasn't. 'I was round at Mum and Dad's one day. I was in the middle of paying back people the money they'd lost, and Mum was going on about something to do with the money and my head felt like it was going to burst. "Just shut up, will you! Shut up about it! I feel bad enough. I know I'm a fuckwit! What do you want me to do, wear a sign on my forehead saying 'Dickhead. Please kick me!' I don't need to be reminded, you know! They copped a lot of shit at that time, but those couple of years were the worst of my life.'

Ian was struggling with a paradox. He would deny who he really was to people close to him, yet instinctively defend his right to be who he was to anybody on the street who challenged him in any way! 1992 was not a good year to goad him. 'He would go through stages,' Theo remembers. 'There was one time when he wouldn't put up with *any* shit from people. One night he said, "From now on, if anyone says *anything* to me, I will just give it to them!" He would turn around if he heard something said behind his back. "Did you say something?" He would get out of his car and walk back to someone who yelled out something! Once, at a dance party, a bloke made some smartarse comment, and there were a whole bunch of "wogs" sitting there [Theo is a "wog"] and he turned round and said, "Did you call me a faggot?" and they all shit themselves. They really did. And one of them said, "He said it! He said it!" pointing to one of his mates. Ian said, "If you have got a fucking problem, you know, tell me to my face." "Oh no, you are a fucking good hooker! You are the best!"'

Things were tense around the house at Coogee. Theo laughs about it now. 'I have never met anyone so easy-going, and yet so difficult to live with. He used to get the shits that year! Like, you'd wake up and you'd be, "Where's Ian?" and you go down and he'd be scrubbing the kitchen, you know. *Scrubbing* it! "*What* are you doing?" "Oh, it's fucking dirty. You don't fucking clean up! You don't! Look at the fucking mess!" And he'd pull *e-e-e-every*thing out and clean everything, you know. Everything out! It'd be like "Oh-Oh! Time to go!"

'There was a point where I wasn't working, and he was genuinely concerned, I think, about me. All I was doing was going out, and getting out of it, partying. I didn't give a fuck about anything else. I'd only see him for about an hour. I'd wake up, and he'd just tell me off. I'd get up and have a shower. Get dressed. He'd still be telling me off.

I'd be walking out the door. He'd still be telling me off. I'd just go out. Meet friends. Get home in the morning. He'd just be waking up. Get up. Be really loud. Come in and kick me and stuff. "Wake up. Why don't you get up and get a fucking job?" I just remember seeing him standing over me, telling me off all the time, you know!'

Ian became impatient when friends talked about their day-to-day problems. He thought them trivial. 'And I was angry at friends like Theo and Chris who also became close to Blake, because they seemed to walk away from his death *with* something. They each seemed to have something special they got from Blake which made them feel kind of serene, and I was just this seething mass of hatred and guilt. I mean, Theo had stayed [at the hospital] the night he died. Theo saw him die, was with him, when he died. And afterwards he would talk about it all the time. At the time I had a really hard time coping with Theo and Chris and everyone that had been around him. I was even angry at Dawn, because I thought she should have been truthful with Blake about the fact he was going to die. Because he sensed it. I'm sure he knew. Then I'd think she did the right thing.'

Theo stood his ground, and earned grudging respect. 'Ian preferred to have lots of people around him when Blake died. To distract him. That was how he dealt with the situation. I couldn't stand it. I stormed out one day and we had a huge fight in the garage. We didn't really speak after that for a while. I was going overseas. He came to me and said, "Look, mate, I know we haven't been getting on but I just wanted to say I hope you have a good holiday." I didn't see him for ages after that. He went to Perth for some reason. But when I was at the airport to go overseas, Lee handed me an envelope from Ian. Inside was a card and a cheque for my holiday ... He will forgive and forget. I could have the biggest fight with him, and the next day he would ring and say, "Do you want to go to the beach?"'

'Every now and again he'd relax and slip back and become the person he really is inside. A big kid. When he doesn't concentrate, he forgets, and he will say a stupid joke out of the blue, and think it's really funny, and laugh and laugh. That's Ian when he's off-guard. You laugh at him laughing! When Ian is really relaxed, he's a real practical joker. And he loves it when you play jokes on him. He loves it. And his laugh!' Theo mimics a long loud guffaw. 'He was always mucking around on the phone. He's forever pretending to be Constable such and such. I was always being arrested ... He's a real big softy. The real Ian is just a kid.'

While the real Ian was often tucked behind the moods caused by internalising the many things that affected him, he fronted life with a bravado. And there were relaxed moments when he would be taken unawares. His off-beat humour sustained him. He adores Monty Python, and Benny Hill. He could easily explode into uproarious laughter at the ridiculous, and surprise people. In his memory banks were stored an extensive repertoire of quips and retorts which he could access in an instant. And which made him chuckle whenever he uses them. If you greet Ian with 'What do you know', a string of retorts fly out almost unconsciously, 'You can't nail jelly to a wall, eggs don't bounce, steam-rollers don't roll steam, paperboys aren't made of paper ...' One of his favourite Benny Hill moments is a scene where one of Hill's shapely, gorgeous, blonde bimbos is stategically concealed behind a flimsy short shower door, with her much older, more debonair lover. She seems to be looking down at her lover's crotch region when, in a coarse Cockney voice, she exclaims, "What's this thing called, love?" From off camera, a French director storms on, and we realise the shower scene is part of a film shoot. The director is frustratedly shaking his head at the actress, 'No! No! No! The line is, "What ees this *theeng* called *Luurve*?"' You can remind Ian of that scene any time and his amusement will jolt him out of whatever mood he is in.

Football suffered pretty badly as everything caught up with Ian in '92. 'I was lucky to be in firsts that year.' His mind wasn't on it. He was lacklustre. He played in 19 games that season; 9 wins, 8 losses and 2 draws. He did not make the selection for rep football and it was a very average season for Manly. 'I know I played terribly. I had no interest in it whatsoever. I didn't care what was going on. It was all happening inside my head.' The big hits were still in his game, but there wasn't the focus.

'When I was running along the beach at Botany the day I collapsed, everything seemed to just catch up with me. It just took me over, and I know it sounds tacky and graphic, but I fell on my knees and just put my head in my hands and cried, thinking, "Fuck, what have I done with my life? Why is this happening to *me*?" Blake hadn't died that long before, and I *had* been thinking about him, along with everything. I was sobbing. It must have been building up for months and months ... no, not months, years! I think I was scared. I remember thinking, "Stop this. Get a fucking hold of yourself! You have to go on."

'It was such a personal thing, a feeling of not knowing where to go or who to turn to. It cripples you, it fucking cripples you. I never had the energy to do anything, to bother with anything. I just didn't have the energy to live. To get on and do things ...

'I know how close I got to killing myself and I can understand how people who aren't lucky enough to have supportive families like mine, can just give up. I know Mum and Dad were worried about me for a while there because I had just lost it. I just wanted everything to stop and I didn't know any other way of making it ... Well, I never thought seriously about suicide. It would pass my mind, but then I'd always say, "No, fuck, you're only 26. Whatever happens, something positive must come out of all this!"

'That year I got into drugs quite badly. I had never taken much prior to that. I didn't ever like the effect that alcohol had on me, and the couple of times I'd gotten stoned, on grass, I just seemed to feel asleep, or get zombied. I didn't enjoy that much. Actually, one day, Dad was funny. I came home stoned. I was about twenty, I suppose, and he opened the front door and sniffed the air and said, "You bloody stink. You're stoned!" I walked inside and crashed on the lounge room floor watching TV, and when everyone was going off to bed, Dad just said, "Leave him there! Don't touch him! He's *stoned*! He can sleep it off there!"'

Ian chuckles at what he sees now as his dad's sensible response to the situation. 'When ecstasy was the big new drug to take at dance parties around '85 and '86, I had it occasionally, but during the foot-ball season I was usually too concerned about my form to party much. In '92, though, I used drugs as an escape, a way of not having to think too much. A way of not dealing with anything. That's why so many young confused and troubled people use them. And everyone freaks out going, "What's causing these problems in our young kids today?" like they haven't a clue. For many, it's a way to forget. I wouldn't say I had a drug *problem*, because I don't think I've got an addictive personality. But I took things too often. Around me, I just thought that day-to-day living had become too hard. It was time out.'

At 26 Ian was entering a crisis of identity that he should have had in adolescence. It's a phase which for many gays is delayed because their emotional adolescence can only begin when they have the freedom to live it.

'Slowly, I guess, as I mulled over things in my head, and the effect of Blake on my life sunk in and I started to get angry that I lived the way I did. It dawned on me that being a good person was the only thing that mattered in life. Why should I be a coward, and live feeling uncomfortable with myself, ashamed. I was a good person. So I started to think, if anyone has a problem with my sexuality, why should I take it on as my problem, like I had all my life? It was *their* problem. I didn't have a problem with it. I never had. I had been through the biggest learning curve of my life. Being gay becomes like nothing when you face things which are really difficult. Being sick is a problem. Losing half a million dollars is a problem. Just being who I am, me, is not and should not be a problem. For anyone.

'Blake actually set me free to sort my anger out, which was about *my* life, not about his or anyone else's. When I think of all the energy and time I spent worrying about making myself acceptable to others, and of all the other people out there, in my field doing the same thing, I felt cheated. Like, "What have I been doing it for?" There are more important things to get on with." He started to embrace a saying he had heard, 'It is better to live a short life standing up, than a long one on your knees.'

TWELVE
RAY AND JEAN FIND
OUT

'**A**bout the middle of '92,' says Michael Gorman, 'I got a call from a friend saying Ian Roberts was at the Albury. Which was absolutely inconceivable, that he would go there, because we had been going through this charade of fake girlfriends and so on, and all of a sudden he turns up at the Albury Hotel and everyone goes, "Thank Christ!" He just said, "Yup! I don't care anymore. I've just decided *Fuck it!*"

'Very soon after that he started going out with Shane Goodwin, which I thought was very sad, because he finally started to be comfortable being gay, and then entered a relationship in which, once again he was trying to take care of someone else.' Although there were friends that felt Ian needed to address certain aspects of his own predicament first, in the end most would concede that Shane provided Ian with a new perspective on his life as a gay man.

Ian remembers the time well. 'I met Shane on June 14. I wasn't looking for any sort of relationship, that's for sure.' In fact Ian tried to dissuade Shane from coming around to his house all the time. 'He was so helpless when I met him, in the end I felt I had to look after him. Me, at that stage! But he used to side with me in everything I said and did, even if he didn't believe me. He never questioned me, which is probably not the best thing. But at the time it was soothing,

I suppose. He was always saying "You've got to get on with your life now." A bit like Dad.

'Shane had come from a pretty rough time at home, himself. He ended up staying at the Coogee house. He wouldn't go back home. When I had to sell up and move out of Coogee, I was actually intending to go back to Mum and Dad's, where I stayed a lot anyway. I didn't have the money to do anything else. Shane went and rented a little one-room thing, in Coogee, above a shop there, with a share bathroom, and I ended up moving in there with him and we stayed there for nearly a year!'

'Ian needed someone to protect,' Michael continues. 'We went through this thing in in '92 when we'd all still go out in this huge gang, like to the movies, and of course if someone said something to Shane, he'd snarl back and Ian would have to come in and calm it all down. That meant Ian had to confront, publicly, the sexuality issue and all the whispering behind his back and it was a really nasty period.

'In a way, I suppose, he matured through Shane and became more comfortable with the gay thing. It had been the gay stereotype, not the actual people, he'd been uncomfortable with. But we all thought it was the oddest thing. He went from being practically homophobic to going out with Shane. It was like he wanted to be busted, finally, about being gay. He was spelling it out.'

Ian was going through a personal rebirth. Being in a stable relationship was like some kind of recuperation, too. For the first time he had a full-on mental and sexual relationship with a man. Theo's larrikin of old started reappearing more often. Shane got Ian to do things he never dreamed of doing, in public. He recalls convincing Ian to go on one of the rides at the Royal Easter Show in '93.

'Ian would never go on rides if we went to Luna Park or somewhere, mainly because of his size and I think he was always self-conscious about making an idiot of himself. You could tell he wanted to, though, and this year I just bought him a ticket and said, "Come on, you're coming on this time" and dragged him with me.

'He was trying to be all cool about it, and this ride lifts you up high and just drops you down suddenly, this sheer drop. And I'll tell you now, I was sitting next to him and he laughed like I've never seen anyone laugh in my life. And from him laughing, I just started to cry from laughing, I couldn't cope. And he just kept laughing. Constantly. And you know how he laughs. After a while, it was hurting me and I was like, "Will you shut up!" Even when the ride stopped he couldn't stop. Everyone else on the ride was silent, or screaming, they'd be looking at him like he was mad. For ages after he couldn't stop talking about how much he laughed. We got him on another one at Australia's Wonderland, not long after, where they take your photo as the ride drops you down, and we've got this picture of four of us, and you should see our faces!

'We laughed a lot that year. Ian and I started playing in a mixed indoor netball comp! Ian played centre, and our team made it to the grand final that year. The whole thing got really bitchy when the team that was used to being on top used to get shitty with us. The guys in all the teams used to play pretty rough. I used to get creamed all the time! One night one of the girls from the other top team starts really having a go at Ian. She was abusing him, and started accusing him of being a filthy faggot and that. So Ian just says, "Yes, I am!" and he grabs me and kisses me right in front of her! We pissed ourselves afterwards. The whole thing was funny, Ian running around, big as he is, with a fuckin' short netball thing on that says "C" for centre!' Shane cracks up at the memory.

'The thing about it, too, was that Ian gave the netball everything he had. And seeing this giant, as solid as him, trying to be as flexible as he could . . . he'd overstep sometimes and just knock someone over. He was so tall, you could just throw that ball and he'd jump above everyone and catch it. And he'd be so excited to win!'

In the midst of it all, Ian was probably oblivious to the fact that he was free, and not ashamed to say who he was to people closer to home. He had taken the first step in making sure that his sexuality could no longer be a problem for him, or anyone else close to him.

Now it was time for the next step. Ian didn't make a conscious decision to tell his parents about his sexuality. He just became more careless about their requirements, more careful of his own. In the past when Ray and Jean had confronted him, he'd protected them. After all, in every other aspect of his life they had been his main support, his source of strength. His mum had always been sensitive to him doing the 'right thing'. In 1989, rattled by bomb threats and abusive calls, she had wanted him to re-sign with Souths, just to restore the peace. She feared for Ian, for her family, for herself. And it was Jean who encouraged his charity work. Her son was a well brought up boy giving something back, repaying a debt. He came to resent just how extensive this 'debt' was. Jean had heard enough and seen enough to have fears about her son's sexuality. She tried to guide him and she dropped reminders. 'She was always making nasty comments about poofs as I got older.' Jean was also concerned about who he was hanging with and how it appeared. 'I never made it easy for her. "I pick my friends, Mum, not you!" I'd always been staunch like that. But, things they said of course would rattle me. I wanted to protect them. I loved my family so much. They were everything to me.'

For Jean, family was an interdependent support network. They stuck together. For Ray, it was important for family to provide his kids with the strength that they needed to go out into the world. To dare. Ian grew up imbued with a strong allegiance to both ideals, confusing as that became for him.

One fateful day, Ray and Jean phoned Ian. 'I rang him up and said we wanted to speak with him.' Jean laughs. 'He always knows when I'm angry with him because I ring him up and say I want to talk to him. He knows not to come round!' Yet again they had experienced an incident involving Ian's sexuality. Jean was upset, and they determined to confront Ian with it. Again. Dread was what they felt as they waited, although Ray was calmer. 'We just wanted to *know*. I mean, we had an idea, after all this time.' But what they really wanted to know was that their suspicions were not founded. That they would have peace of mind.

'I came home after training and my mum's sitting there. Mum and Dad were *really* upset. You can tell with my parents. My Dad said, "You've got to sit down and talk to us, boy."'

The kitchen table. The TV on. Ray got to the point. What they wanted to talk about was awkward enough without dilly dallying around.

'Dad came straight out with it. He said, "Are you gay?"'

Ian's initial reaction was involuntary. His body sounded panic stations. There was a ringing in his ears, a silent siren which sent his heart racing. He felt faint, in an instant realising that this time he was going to confront it.

'I looked somewhere else and just said, "Yes, I am."'

'My Dad had said to me a few times before, "If you're gay, it doesn't bother us. You can tell us."' He had said that when they confronted him after one of Jean's uglier scenes at Qantas. 'But I knew I would have been disapointing them.' The words 'You can tell us' are an inducement to lie. What they really mean is, 'You can tell us the *good* news.'

This time round, Ian took them at their word, and Ray and Jean had their fears confirmed. And yes, it *did* disappoint them. The fact he was a tough football player was always Ray and Jean's hope against hope. They were banking on those old stereotypes despite their experience with Uncle Charlie. 'My Mum went off the handle. She was saying, "I didn't bring you up funny!" "I didn't put you in dresses!" And then, "You're not a poof, son!"'

'My Dad just said, "I can't believe that!"'

Ray had been gushing with adrenalin when he heard himself ask. Now he just slumped. 'We had said we wanted to know, because we were sick of the rumours. We'd rather know one way or the other. When he said "yes", I just went "uuuuuggghhhh", like that.' He makes a physical gesture representing defeat, sinking into his seat at the kitchen table, right where it had happened. 'I was deflated. I'm not going to pretend I wasn't. I said, "All right boy, if you are, you are. You're still our boy."'

Jean gently reminds him. 'Well, we didn't take it *quite* that well!'

In those first horrendous minutes that seemed like they would never pass, Ray and Jean probably spewed forth what, for gays, have become parents' cliched responses to *the* news.

'WHY?'

'Why do this to us?'

'Why do this to yourself?'

'Why do you want to be gay?'

'Where did we go wrong?'

The world over, courageous men, feeling not so courageous, reply with the truth as best they can. 'Why would I want to be gay, and go through this?'

Ian was trapped in a tornado of emotion he had finally unleashed. He had never been good at fronting outbursts. But he was trapped, and he didn't feel all that sustained by the most important fact: He had truth on his side. At last. And truth, as they say, will 'out'!

Parents often get angry first. Anger at their naughty child. Anger after the years of blinkered thinking, of suspecting, thinking 'maybe'. Anger, before the 'why us?' stage. Ian tried to let the torrent wash over him, but the tears streamed down his face. 'I was crying, and all I could do really was just sit there and cop all this abuse.' He stared past his parents. He couldn't look them in the eye. The TV sat by uselessly, blankly blinking at him. He blankly looked back, wanting to be swallowed by it. Into *that* world, out of this. 'Mum said some horrible things. Then she would go quiet for a bit. Then she'd be like "Get out of this house!" Dad would go "Shut up, Jean!" Then she would get quiet again. Then start again. "I don't want to ever see you again!"'

When they were able to think clearly, things began to fall into place.

'Things made sense to them. About my friend Lee. Because I told them Lee wasn't gay, but he knew I was, the whole time. Then they could understand the bond I had with him and why I was so close to him. "No, Mum, he *doesn't* mind that I'm gay. He doesn't care." And I didn't have any other close friends who knew I was gay, apart from guys who were gay themselves.'

'So *we're* the last to know?'

'No, mum, I haven't gotten round to telling *anyone*!'

Looking back on the moment of truth, his parents skirted round the things that really bothered them when they found out. Ray says, 'The biggest worry we had was AIDS. We said "That's what your mother and I are terrified of."' Jean recalls most vividly her fears for Ian. 'And we thought someone would use it to bring him down or ruin him.'

Ray: We didn't want that to happen.

Jean: When it comes down to it, it isn't anyone's business really, is it?

Ray: We said, 'For goodness sake, keep it quiet then, until after you've finished your career.'

That was probably the worst thing poor Ray could have said. 'I think we might have stirred something up by saying keep it quiet!'

Ian agrees. 'When Dad said that, I just thought "NO!" It got my back up, finally. "I'm not pretending for *any*one! I'm sick of pretending, of being something that I'm not just to make people happy." Everyone wanted me to be this and that, and I was at that stage where I didn't care any more if I revealed myself and people were disappointed. I just didn't give a fuck ... Yes I did. I was disappointed Dad said that. I said to Dad that after all the things that had happened to me, that just don't happen to other people, after all the hurt I had caused them, I just had to get it into the open, with them at least, or I would go insane. And I said if no-one likes it, then that's the way it's got to be.

'After a couple of hours it settled down and Dad said, "Well, I don't like it, obviously, but you're my son and I love you, and I'll always love you."'

In some ways, Ray had an easier time accepting the truth than Jean. He hadn't endured the same privations that Jean had. Hadn't been affected by life's challenges in the same way. 'No-one had given me any trouble about it. It was never brought up to my face. Most people think that I'm an aggressive sort of bloke, which I'm not. Only one bloke, recently, a young bloke, said, "Cor blimey, Ian's treading on glass!" when it appeared in the papers. Whether they were frightened of upsetting me over the years, I don't know.'

Or frightened of telling a father his son's a poof. Telling a man his sperm is 'weak'. That the end of the genetic line has been reached.

Through his Uncle Charlie, whether he was aware of it or not, Ray had come to accept differences in people. To respect them, not feel threatened by them. Ray had encouraged that quality in Ian, too. 'Dad had always said, "As long as you're a good man, that's all that counts." It's been a big learning curve for Dad. All those kinds of things he said to me, when I was young, it's not like they backfired, it's like "Oh no, all those things he was listening to, they affected him, but not in the way I thought they were going to." But they still affected me in the right way. For him, it was like "I didn't think it was going to come out like this, but all my teaching has affected him." Dad has watched me handle a lot of things over the years, and I think he thinks, "Well, he's had all adversities and he's struggled through, so maybe I've done a good job".'

Ray and Jean are not accustomed to having to talk to strangers about their son's sexuality. At first Ray is uncomfortable and defensive when asked about his reaction to finding out. 'What was I supposed to do? What did people expect of me? To pretend I only ever had one son and not two? And be miserable? I'm proud of him! He's my son, and I love him!'

Jean went to bed that first night, after Ian had confessed, and thrashed around, torturing herself. Planning. Ian had crashed in his old room, exhausted.

'Mum came to me in the middle of the night. I don't know whether it was the first night or the night after. She woke me up and hugged me and said, "I'm *so* sorry. I love you."

'But then, a few days later she'd lose it again. "I'll have to put you in *dresses*," she screamed one day.

'I got that angry with her at times. Impatient. "You're not worried about *my* life." And every so often she'd snap out of it and apologise. Then she'd say, "I don't understand. I don't know why you want to be like that."

'I'd repeat again and again, "Mum, I don't have a *choice*! Ask yourself, why were you attracted to Dad?" 'She said, "Well, because he's a man."

'It's like when you ask a straight guy why they're attracted to women. "Because they're women." "No, forget that they're women, what is it that makes you attracted to them?" They can't define it, exactly. And I say, "Well, it's the same with me and men!"'

It demands a new way of thinking when you tell a mother that you are as attracted to men as she is, and as attracted to women as she is. Everyone sits down and tries to define why they have their sexuality. Big-picture questions. Uncomfortable when you are a grand-parent already, and you thought the big picture you had had for all those years was standard issue.

Ian was harder on Jean than on Ray. Less patient. 'I got the impression Mum was worried because she was embarrassed by me. It didn't seem to be embarrassing for Dad.' Ian felt Jean held him at arm's length. 'She would say, "I don't want to talk about it. If that's what you are then good, but I don't want to talk about it. I don't want you bringing it around here." And I would say, "Well, good, *I* won't *come* around here!" I love my mum so much. And she had been through some terrible things. And I know her reaction was no different than a lot of mothers' reactions. "Mum, that's who I *am*," I said again and again. "If you want to be a family then you talk about that. I am part of the family." It has helped her a lot to see how the rest of the family is, and how close we all are. I would say to her when she would go on about how hard it was for her, "Look, I've lost all that money and Blake has died, and I put up with shit about being gay, and I'm still willing to talk about it to anyone. That's how I got over it. What you are going through is nothing! You know all the shit I put up with in my life. You know how close I was to an absolute breakdown at 26 and killing myself! Don't tell me what you've been through. You've been through nothing!" And there was always another barrier. Another excuse.'

The frustration that Ian built up, and the anger, during different episodes of his life often came back to haunt Jean. Secrets he bottled up because he had to. The resentment is something all gay children have to resolve with their parents at some stage if they are ever going to have fulfilling lives and honest relationships, without some sort of chip on their shoulder. For gays, who have carried the secret of their sexuality alone, who have protected parents, who have burdened them-selves with guilt, blamed themselves for their sexuality, felt shame, felt undeserving of success, to finally confront their parents and say, 'This is honestly who I am. This is who you brought into this world,' there is a sense of a weight being lifted. Even if the reaction of the parents is negative, there is a sense of liberation. Of a new beginning through which the scars of the repressed life can start to heal. Whenever people promote repression as a better alternative for a gay person, and resistance rather than acceptance by the people around, they, in effect, promote a deviate society, full of people who are not acting according to their natural state, and who are therefore to some extent mentally and physically ill.

The fear that differences in people are somehow threatening is the basis of so much prejudice. Including parents'. Jean did try hard in those first months, but she was sensitive to her society's conservative demands. And she had already experienced, through Ian, what happens when you rock the boat. She had dealt with the crank callers. Men at work grabbing her, chiding her about her son. She obeyed the rules to keep the peace, because she feared for her family. Feared for Ian. She was sorting through the double dilemma of her socially conditioned revulsion to homosexuality, and then her fears for what her son might encounter in the face of everyone else's repulsion. She was more comfortable with Ray's gay uncle and his lover because 'No-one voiced what they were.' Ray found that easier too. 'They didn't put on "antics" when we were there. To us they were quite normal.' Ray and Jean were concerned to maintain a 'normal' environment for their grandchildren. 'You don't want kids growing up too quickly. They grow up quick enough, without help.' For Jean, 'if the grandchildren accepted Ian and Shane the way they are, it doesn't matter about their sexuality, does it? It's just Ian and Shane. It doesn't really matter.'

Parents often find it comforting if they can disguise homosexuality, keep it looking 'normal', so that no-one is embarrassed about it and the children are 'protected' from it. Which of course is how gay children get isolated in the first place, often believing they are alone and that their society offers them no happy future. If the signals they receive about their sexuality are negative, they can only feel shame and guilt, and become secretive. And maybe try to lead a 'normal' life, because they sense that is the condition upon which their parents' love is based. At 27, Ian was exhausted with meeting this condition. He was ready to risk the rejection of his parents in order to escape the limbo in which he'd been living. Ray said 'keep it to yourself', not realising the price Ian had paid doing exactly that for all those years.

Ray and Jean decided to confide in Kylie. 'They told me, and I said, "I know", and they were like, "Well why didn't you tell us?" I said I didn't think that it was my business to.' She was protecting them too, because even though she knew they had been 'exposed' to gay friends of Ian's, she also knew they would be disappointed to find out their son was gay. 'I think it actually hurt Dad a lot, even though he didn't let on as much as Mum.'

Shane knew that he wasn't popular with either of Ian's parents. 'I overheard his dad one day saying to Ian about me, "He's a queer and I don't like him. I'll never like him." Ian would get upset and say, "Well you better get used to it, because it's not going to change! You can keep on thinking that it will, but it won't." And I wouldn't tell Ian I'd overheard. Because it's his dad and that. I think in the end Ray realised and was able to help Jean a lot.'

Ray's personal philosophy returned to haunt him, thinks Ian. 'He was the one who had always said that anyone I loved was good enough for him. He always said he didn't care who I brought home. And that had always really meant something to me, Dad saying that. That was where I got my values from, which were important to me.'

It might not have even been the fact that Ian was gay that entirely bothered Ray. Like most parents, they had an idea of the type of partner that their son should have. In time, Jean would sometimes meet a gay guy she really liked and thought was a suitable son-in-law, and go 'Why can't you go out with a guy like that?' 'Because he's not my type, Mum.' Shane was the meat in the sandwich for those first couple of years of his relationship with Ian. He was part of the package deal Ian was foisting on Ray and Jean.

Shane recalls that first Christmas at the Roberts'. He wasn't invited but Ian insisted he come. 'Ian would say to them, "Why can't he come around? He's coming!" The whole thing was pretty awkward. The other Roberts kids have always been great. Kylie, for example, has always been incredibly sweet to me.'

Ian is always saying stuff like, 'I lived with my sexuality twenty-seven years before I could admit it to my mum and dad, so I don't expect someone else to get used to it overnight.' But he expected to find a fast-forward button on his parents. 'Some of the things Mum did would really hurt me. And she wouldn't even know. Like when I brought Shane that Christmas, and some of the family were there, like my auntie, she would say, "I don't want them to see him. He's your partner but I don't want them to see him." Because it embarrassed her. She just could not get her head around it, so I began not caring. Then she would say, "How can you not care what people think?" I would say "Mum, I'm doing nothing wrong!"'

'Mum and Dad know that Ian is happier now,' says Kylie two years later, 'and Mum has said, since finding out, that Ian has done so much good in this world already, and he is such a good person that it doesn't make any difference to them. It just doesn't matter.'

Ian's friendship with Ray is as strong as ever. 'I think Dad realises, now, that being gay has nothing to do with masculinity, and is no threat to masculinity. It was he that taught me that being masculine wasn't about being tough or insensitive. It was about having a certain independence in the way you thought. Not just being led by a pack. And it was about being brave enough to find the right set of principles to live by. "Being a man is being responsible for yourself and your actions," he always said.'

Ray and Ian had a relationship based on shared experience, football primarily, which had bonded them. 'I've always been close to my dad, and I realise a strong father/son relationship makes things easier. Nowadays, if Dad doesn't like me being gay, it's because of society's reaction to it. I know my dad thinks, "As long as my boy is happy. As long as all my kids are happy doing what they're doing, I don't care what they do. I don't care who they're with. As long as they love the people they're with, I don't care."'

Revealing the truth about himself to the people who gave him life empowered Ian. Not straight away. But later on he'd say, 'The thing is that people don't have to respect me, but they have to respect that it's my life and they don't get a say in it. That goes for parents as well. I will listen to my parents, but everything I've learned and all the mistakes I've made, *I've* made.'

Graham Lowe had been forced into retirement because of illness, and Bob Fulton returned to Manly to coach in '93. There was an influx of young blood into the team, and 'Bozo' Fulton began playing Ian in front row again.

'At a pre-season game over in New Zealand,' Ian recalls, 'we were playing a bunch of tough islanders who were just interested in killing us. I didn't want to play. I hate pre-season games because of the chance of injuries, especially in those kinds of games.' That game Ian tore the posterior cruciate in his knee, but that didn't affect his form immediately. 'Most people can get up and play with that sort of problem for five or six years before the knee gets sloppy.'

'The game plans over the past couple of years didn't really suit my style. It's good being back in the front row. But it is also tremendous having so many young players in the side—their enthusiasm and will to win really rubs off on you.'(Dean Ritchie, *Telegraph Mirror,* 3/5/93)

LETHAL AGAIN
'It is as if I'm starting over again. Bobby Fulton is a remarkable coach, incredibly astute. He does not go in and say we should have scored here or we should have done that. He looks at the whole picture and the players are the ones who benefit.' (Alan Clarkson, *Sun-Herald* 16/5/93)

Ian credits Fulton with giving him a new perspective on the game. His coaching techniques were more exact. He was specific in his game analysis. Terry Hill reckons, 'Bob is the kind of bloke where he'll talk to you about your game, look at areas where you've got to improve from the team's point of view. And what the team's got to do. He's just a complete coach. George Piggins would never pull me aside and say, "Son, I think you'd better be doing this a bit more and doing that." He was a forwards man and rarely got involved with the back-line. To the forwards it was, "Put the ball under your arm and go forward." At Manly I do whatever comes naturally. Under Bozo, I know what plays are going on. I'm involved in plays. You get to work out what you're doing and where you've got to be at certain times, who you're going to be with, and who's going to get the ball. And before a game we'd have a stretch and workout, and then a video session for half an hour or so.'

Ian agrees. 'Graham Lowe was the great motivator. He wasn't so much into tactical things. He was more into hyping a guy up and getting him pumped, and then just letting him motor through it, without necessarily thinking. Just keep going and going. Persistent. Phil Gould had been more, "You step back. You take a look. Take a breath, see where to go. And do it!" Phil was basically our coach first year at Souths, but I had him in Origin as well. I had had Tim Sheens in Origin football and he was more or less the same. Study the videos. See where their weaknesses are and hit them. Tactics and that. But I really started to reap the benefits of that when I was under Bozo. Because he was really good like that. He was a perfectionist. Tactically he is the best coach I have had.

'He be like, "If you're good at something, don't be scared to use it. Take a chance." Bozo was like "If the opportunity is there, and it's a 50/50 split, go for it! Back yourself. Whatever *you* think. Back your instinct."

'George had got a bit lost in the coaching. He didn't know too much, technically speaking. But you gained from George because he was so positive and committed to it, even though he was lacking. You drew off George because he was so committed to the club, to Souths, that it was a buzz to play under him. He really got you into the spirit of the game. Frank Cookson had been more of a step man. It was like, "All right. We'll have two forwards up. We'll have a backs move. Then we'll have a forwards move. Then we'll have another backs move." Everything was a bit mechanical. The game plan didn't allow too much for personal or individual flair.

'I think I played my best football at Manly. I played more intelligent football at Manly, but that's only experience. It's not until you start to get older, and you have experience, that you realise you have time to think. Everything is not a rushed moment. And when you practise moves over and over, and sidesteps, and hitting the bags and spinning and all that, it becomes inbuilt. And your reflex actions are helped to be more precise, more correct. And it's not a conscious decision. You don't even make a decision on the field. You just react. It's more of a reflex. People ask you, "Why didn't you do this?" and "Why didn't you do that?" or "Why don't you do this any more?" You can't answer because you don't know why your reactions have become the way they have.'

Publicly, Ian skimmed over his private agony of the previous couple of years with some white lies: 'I'd been making some good money in the insurance game, he told Danny Weidler, early in the '93 season, 'and that started to dominate my life. I wasn't thinking about football. I'd work all week and wake up Sunday and think "I've got a game on today". How could I have been so stupid? I was playing terrible football. This is a tough tough game and I'd hardly been giving it the attention it deserved. This season I've been thinking football. Winning has helped, too … It's a lot nicer being stopped by people in the street and them talking about how well the side is playing and how well you are going, rather than explaining what's wrong.'

Once again, he is THE man. 'All this attention … it's really the team who should be geting the wraps. You know, it's the kids here. I'm really enjoying playing in their team. I really feel it's my responsibility to show them the way. I've got the experience but I've got to use it.' (Danny Weidler, *Big League*, 4/93)

Roberts also paid tribute to another mate—however this friend watches every match from the grandstand. The giant forward and girl-friend Amanda Roberts have been virtually inseparable during the past six months. (Dean Ritchie, Telegraph Mirror, *3/5/93)*

Ian was actually paying tribute to *Shane*'s attendance. Amanda, a friend of Ian's, had agreed to pose as his girlfriend for the article. 'Amanda regretted doing that for me, and I regretted using her, too. Basically, I did it for Mum. Mum was like, "Oh, you don't want people to know! You don't want people to know. It's bad, bad, bad." You know, of course you're affected by that. Inside, I felt like rebelling, and just going "stuff it" for years. But you're always careful about not embarrassing or hurting the people around you. So I did this, thinking I was helping my Mum out. But then she was like, "Well, what did you do that for? That was a silly thing to do. You don't have to lie. You just don't want people to know!"'

What has been the biggest thrill of your life? 'Attending the premiere of the film Milo And Otis. *But the girl I took wasn't too impressed.' Who is the toughest opponent you have faced? 'Denise. She was my first girlfriend.' Is there any sporting dream you would have liked to achieve in another sport? 'I wouldn't mind getting into jelly wrestling with some of those girls'. (Star File,* Telegraph Mirror, *31/3/93)*

As their relationship progressed that year, Ian started taking Shane to games and to training with him. 'At first I'd just go along to training and sit as far away as possible out of the way,' Shane says. 'That was the way Ian preferred it at that stage, and that was fine by me. I think I felt pretty embarrassed to be there. Right from the start though, the players knew who I was, I think. And right from the start they were always really nice to me. All of them were just so friendly. There was probably only one player who ever had a problem with it, and his mother is gay. So maybe that has something to do with it.' Within a year, he would be more acquainted with the players, and would be running out on the field with the team. Dressed as Manly's mascot, the Sea Eagle!

Ian was selected for the NSW Origin side, after captaining the City Origin side. He was the league's form front-rower again. NSW won the first game, on 3 May, at Lang Park, 14–10. Ian impressed observers at one point when he saved the game by diving on a loose ball after Allan Langer had made a big break and Andrew Ettingshausen and Rod Wishart had tackled him close to their line. The ball wandered out of the tackle like a live grenade.

His great chase to be in position to dive on the loose ball probably saved the match. The fact that Roberts was there emphasised his marvellous athleticism. Ian Roberts is back—and how! (Alan Clarkson)

NSW went on to win the second game at the Football Stadium on 17 May, 16–12, and clinched the series. Ian was in good rep form again.

FINDING OUT

While it was generally recognised he didn't have the same tackle-breaking power he had in the past, his fitness and his incredible offloading ability were unsurpassed. He could remain standing with three or four opposition players clawing at him. In the first Origin match there were times when NSW didn't capitalise on some of his miracle passes simply because no-one thought he could get one away at times when he was covered by maroon jumpers. And still standing. 'I think he's the best in the game at it,' Bob Fulton said later that year. That ability, his voracious appetite for taking the ball up as first receiver, and his tireless tackling, were the hallmarks of Ian's game.

Australian selectors like boss Don Furner kept a close eye on player performance during the Origin series. Ian was considered in with a good Test prop chance, alongside dead certainty Glen Lazarus. He was selected, and played in the 20 June Test at Carlaw Park, Auckland, in what was a 14-all draw. Ten days later, Australia beat New Zealand at Lang Park, 16–4.

Rugby League had its own peculiar coming of age during that match, and embraced Ian's homosexuality, when, amidst the usual sophisticated tactical insults players levelled at their opponents to throw their game—things like 'wogbastard' or 'Your wife's a lousy lay'—Ian got 'Everyone says Shane's a good root!', to which he replied, 'Yeah, you probably know!'

With his resurgence in the game, and his comeback from a lousy previous year, there was renewed interest in Ian personally. The media ran stories that year of his denial of involvement in the gold scam, his denial of any money loss, his football form, and softer and prying ones on the man behind the footy star. Ian's sexuality was by now widely discussed in football circles, even though no journo would broach it and Ian was still planting decoys. Ian got a little more frank, a little more honest, when Alan Clarkson did a full-page feature, 'LETHAL AGAIN', which spoke sympathetically of 'the horrific experience that shattered the young prop'—the hospital vigil and the death of a family friend which wrecked his football year (*Sun-Herald* 16/5/93).

Then Danny Weidler researched his feature for the July issue of *Inside Sport*. Ian led Danny on a wild goose chase. 'It took him two weeks and all these interviews, and I knew the only question he wanted

242

to ask me was about my sexuality. He could never get to it. The first few days we got along well, went and had a few beers, and I was friendly, you know, social. But after that, I felt like he'd be intruding if he asked me the question. I've spoken to him since and he said to me "Yes, the only question I wanted to ask you was that, and I just couldn't get round to it." ' The article danced around the issue.

As he squeezes out of his Mazda MX6 he looks like he has money ... and he has. Pop earrings into the two vacant holes in his left ear lobe and you complete the picture ... 'Any footballer who says he doesn't like the attention is a liar. Still I'm a pretty private person. People get the wrong idea about me because I don't seek attention.'

He'll talk to anyone, but he won't initiate a conversation—not because he's aloof, but because he's shy. He's a background person ... 'I don't try and be trendy. It's just the way I am. I can't help liking the music I do, or liking going to DCM or dance parties. It's what my friends do.'

'It turned out to be another bullshit story,' Ian laughs. 'A fantasy life that didn't exist. The hilarious thing was that just a short time before, I was living in that one-bedroom hole above the shop in Coogee, with a bed as the only piece of furniture, and our clothes stacked in piles on the floor. Driving a borrowed car!'

There was always an uncertainty as to whether 'it' was anyone's concern, or everyone's. In an ideal world, it wouldn't need to be. But in a world where hatred against people because of their sexuality leads to anger, violence, death and suicide, and where these people are portrayed continually as 'different' from everyone else, a gay footballer wasn't only gossip and scandal of scoop proportions, but could be publicised to make a real and historic difference to people's lives. While gay journos were clamouring for Ian to make a stand, some mainstream journalists were offering positive encouragement in a way, by focusing on the whole package of Ian as a person, and almost celebrating his difference from another stereotype—that of the football player. And it wasn't necessarily done in a sensationalist or gossipy way, in order to establish Ian as a news story.

'Ian Roberts is readily recognisable as a rugby league powerhouse yet is something of an enigma off the field,' Lisa Olson discovered when she did her feature for the *Telegraph Mirror*, on 4 September. Coming to the fore was respect for Ian's difference, though of course no journo ever stated what that was. It's just a shame that, in trying to disarm one stereotype, she relied on another.

Despite those chiselled looks, Roberts is no pretty boy bimbo, nor is he one of those assembly-line boofheads that every code of football seems to turn out these days, the kind that do impressive macho stuff like smashing beer cans on their foreheads while simultaneously burping the team's fight song. In fact Roberts hates talking about Rugby League ... [He] shuns the macho lifestyle, preferring to hang out with his non-football playing mates.

Olson quoted Matthew Ridge's testimony to Ian's work with kids and the fact he flew to England to visit a child he had met when at Wigan, and who was now dying. 'If a lot of players had done that, the media would have been all over it because it's a great story, but [he] didn't want the publicity.' It was a Clayton's outing, one of several during this period in the guise of the usual ARL PR player profile. Matthew went on, 'He takes a lot of heat because he chooses to lead a lifestyle that's different to a lot of players, and that really bothers me ... I knew straight away he was different. He doesn't go down to the pub with the boys and he doesn't judge people by the cover. He looks much deeper than that. To me, people who bag him for what he does off the field are the lowest form of life. If they took the time to know Ian, they'd know he's easily one of the best human beings around.'

A story hit the news in August that the Auckland Warriors were after Ian and Greg Alexander. Ian had had informal talks with the club, but diplomatically stated that he wouldn't settle anything until his current contract expired in 1994. That got Frank Stanton, chief executive at Manly, negotiating. Ian's current contract was signed when he was in no bargaining position at the end of '91. He was firing on all cylinders now. He had played in only four losses in the comp that year right up to the semi against Brisbane, and was starring back in representative football. Stanton confirmed that Ian was Manly's player of the year, their prized possession, and not only because of his play. Image was important at this high-profile club and Ian's general all-round likeability, his affability and interaction with the fans, especially the kids, gave him a big tick in this box. Then he won the Dally M Prop Of The Year and he was runner-up in the Dally M Player Of The Year award, missing out by just a point, even though he missed several club games because of representative commitments. Manly pre-empted negotiations elsewhere by agreeing to renegotiate Ian's remaining year at the club, provided he sign for a further three years, to 1997. At this time there was still the salary cap and players' salaries were limited, so what Manly offered could not be bettered by much, elsewhere. Ian was happy to re-sign.

On 4 September, Manly lost the semi against Brisbane, 4-16, and for another season, another year, a premiership eluded Ian. But his new contract enabled him to complete his crawl back from financial oblivion. He was able to put a deposit on an apartment in a new complex in Camperdown, and he and Shane moved into a place, not only with its own bathroom, but with access to a rooftop swimming pool, tennis courts and gym!

The day after the semi-final loss, the 'INSANE GOLD SCAM' story hit the papers as Murray Farquhar went to trial on the passport charges. Ian denied involvement. 'It's all wrong,' he told the *Sun-Herald*. 'I did not put any money into those schemes, and that is what I am filthy about. I have had a gutful of the rumours. It's not right. I spoke to my solicitor during the week and we are working out what action we should take.' The whole mess was still too close for Ian, as he recalls now. 'Word had got around that I'd lost a lot of money but no-one seemed to know exactly how or why. I just used to deny it rather than talk about it.' Rumours started that Ian and Greg Alexander were behind a bid for Rogues, a trendy East Sydney nightclub. This was a proposal to use the guys as a front for investors, for which they were going to receive 10 per cent of profits. Nothing came of it, though.

In December 1993, in court during Farquhar's trial, the Crown prosecutor, John Agius, likened the gold plot to a *Dad's Army* folly.

Agius told the jurors that it wasn't their role to determine if the men had legal title to the gold, whether it existed, or whether a coup was going to occur, but to address the issues in respect of the charges only. For all the effort that went into the operation, these seemed quite measly in the end.

The police produced a taped conversation between Farquhar and Evans, made on 1 May, 1991, in which the men use the codenames of 'Brushie' and 'Bullwinkle' for each other. Farquhar, who was in Dubai at this stage, hadn't decided whether they would stash the gold at the airport or at Customs. The police also produced transcripts of meetings. One had Kron advising Evans that he had a 'girl in place in the Central Bank of Manila' and an influential contact codenamed 'Orlando' set up.

Mid-trial, Murray Farquhar died and the charges against Wiseman did not proceed.

Some gay journalists and activists, insensitive to Ian's personal predicament, publicly, even ruthlessly, demanded he stand up for the gay cause. For them, at last, here was an Aussie hero type who was gay and out, in the sense of frequenting gay nightclubs and events. He didn't lead as secretive a double life as most other high-profile and celebrity gays in homophobic professions. Even though he was 'out' to this extent, they wanted him to stand up on a soap box and shout that he was 'out' to the world. His privacy was expendable in the name of a cause.

The prospect of being a spokesman for a cause was terrifying for Ian then. It was a role for which his life and his personality had not prepared him. He preferred the background. The political game was one he hadn't played. It was uncharted waters. His whole life had been about mastering something until he was sure of winning.

In February 1994, the Gay and Lesbian Rights Lobby conducted a public debate to discuss the pros and cons of outing known gay celebrities as a way of furthering the gay cause. That's cause, not agenda! So long as there was so much violence against homosexuals, and they didn't have equal legal rights to heterosexuals, young gays were still growing up isolated, guilty, and feeling hopeless about the future. The rate of teen gay suicide was practically ignored, and the lack of positive gay role models still meant that gay children felt alienated from their families and communities. Resentment had grown that so many people in so-called respectable or powerful positions were gay but closeted which read gay and ashamed or scared of losing their position. The AIDs epidemic had raised the prejudice bar higher. It was coined a gay disease, despite the fact that, worldwide, 70 per cent of adult HIV infections came through heterosexual sex, while only 5–10 per cent came from homosexual sex! It was now dirtier to be homosexual. Even if you didn't see AIDS as some sort of wrath of God, homosexuality was somehow tainted.

Young gay men were forced to leave their families with a more pessimistic view of their future than ever. Even if safe-sex campaigns had reached them, a general malaise blurred their thinking. These were the people most in need of gay role models. Lives could be saved by adult gay men in important positions saying, 'You can be gay, and have a career, a future, be happy and fulfilled. It's not the end of the world, despite the messages you have been getting so far in your life.'

For too many kids, it was. It is no coincidence that the suicide rate among young men aged 15–29 has increased in the last 25 years from 5.8 per 100,000 to 17.8. For nearly all other categories there has been a decline over this period, but suicide is the leading cause of death among 15–19-year-old males. And for every successful suicide attempt, there are, purportedly, 30 that fail. The irony of all this is that the number of suicides resulting from the victim's poor view of his sexuality is concealed from statistics, because the coroners and the victims' relatives do not record such information. If they know it. Many suicides are not going to reveal the source of their shame, even when they are escaping it. Part of their purpose in the first place is to spare their families. One in four gays and lesbians have admitted, in studies, to attempting suicide, while US studies show that homosexual youth are two and three times more likely to suicide.

A father of a gay suicide was quoted in 1996 as saying he was proud of his son for making the right decision, for having the courage to spare his family and himself the humiliation of living his life in an unchristian way. *His* child obviously never had a chance. Being born into some of the more extreme Christian groups is an added handicap. During the debate on legalising homosexuality in Tasmania, which sometimes raged in the early- to mid-'90s, some Christian parents had their children at the forefront, carrying placards, 'Gays Means AIDS', or appeared on national television debates proudly expounding, with venom in their voices, their God's hatred of homosexuals. What hope would a gay child in any of those families have for self-esteem? The ongoing struggle, within the pioneering Uniting Church, for acceptance of homosexuals is a miracle of goodness on earth when seen in the light of what was happening elsewhere. The Pope, the Roman Catholic God's representative on Earth, predictably continued to denounce homosexuality as evil.

The issue of gays and families always elicits hysteria in the lay public, as if the two things are mutually exclusive. In 1996 when a gay group applied to have a float in a community parade in Holroyd, Sydney, certain assumptions underlined the reaction against it: That float would be some kind of debauched display which families and kiddies had to be protected from. And that gays somehow infiltrated these communities, rather than being brought up within them. Holroyd was no exception. A gay teenager in that community, where councillors who supported the float out of fear of a discrimination law suit received death threats, could hardly be expected to develop a positive life-affirming self-image.

The debate on outing in 1994 exemplified how diverse homosexuality is. There was bitterness and enmity in Hanover's Cafe on Oxford Street that night. And disagreement. Most felt anger, and not much sympathy for the closeted gays in government, and in the churches and in the media, who led secretive homosexual sex lives, while publicly endorsing conservative stances. Some of them even publicly condemned homosexuality. But others were reasonable enough to recognise that a person outed against his will was not going to be a positive or cooperative role model for gays. The then recent and incorrect 'outing' of Jason Donovan in England was a contentious issue. Gays in favour of outing seemed to expect Donovan, who had been sympathetic to the plight of gay people all his life, to accept it with equanimity. Any protest on his part made it look as if he was ashamed that people might think he was gay. The principle of the matter was not important to the radicals, and Donovan was 'punished' by a pretty successful publicity campaign against him. Gays ended up looking extremist, vindictive and vengeful. The campaign of outing being conducted in England was obviously terrifying for people who had worked hard to ingratiate themselves within the status quo, to separate themselves from the gay sterotype, and to achieve something in their lives. But many thought there was a greater good at hand, and if a few individuals' careers were hurt, then that was the price of acceptance for others down the line. If a life could be saved by people accepting the wider truth about homosexuality, then that was worth it. And it was a matter of life or death. In that spirit, one of the speakers, Stephen Dunne, read a list of names, including Ian's, of well-known closeted gays.

There was disagreement, however, as to how to break a vicious circle. Whenever people, incendiary news articles, or groups deliver bad publicity, closet gays of all ages cringe, while 'out' gays on the street bear the brunt of a self-perpetuating hatred. It is self-perpetuating because few gays of any profile act as a buffer to discourage the misinformation that is spread. Society doesn't warm to the brave radicals who are out there, fighting. Their extremism causes discomfort and hostile reaction, as does any movement for change. It never takes long for the talkback radio maestros to conduct a chorus of disapproval—'I just don't see why they've got to shove it in our faces' or 'Why should these people receive special treatment that the average Australian doesn't get?'

The changes that have been wrought by activists have not established equality, let alone equal quality of life. The media will often assume a tolerance and equality for gays which does not exist in the real world. And the same media reinforces prejudice by sensationalising and beating up stories and ramming only the gay stereotypes in people's faces. Like a ravenous pack, they descend upon what looks like a story, whipping it up into a frenzy that has nothing to do with the public interest or lifting the collective consciousness through education, and everything to do with selling sensation, and selling papers. During the Holroyd parade farce, the *Telegraph Mirror* ran with the very deceptive headline 'Gays Ruin Family Parade', just because they wanted to participate! Only the gay media desperately continue to expose this.

During the 1980s, reported casual street violence against gay men reached its highest levels, though much more went unreported because of fear and embarrassment amongst victims, many of whom were still reluctant to trust the police handling of such matters. Many gays come to accept violence as a part of their existence, and it wouldn't even occur to them to report it, though good changes have been implemented in the police handling of such matters.

Still, 20 per cent of all non-domestic murders were of gay men, and the percentage would have been much higher had more of the thousands of barbarous beatings resulted in death.

But there was an outcry when the NSW Parliament passed anti-vilification laws to protect gays. This was seen by some as reverse discrimination. Censorship. It was thanks to people like Ted Pickering, a Liberal government ex-minister, crossing the floor of parliament to vote with Labor, that the legislation got passed. Despite an ill Fred Nile attending parliament in pyjamas to stall the vote. Ted Pickering, as police minister, said he had witnessed too much of the inhumanity to let it continue, and a small but pulsating crowd of relieved gays outside parliament house gave him a heroes' reception for his defiance of his party.

The press had a field day in 1994 when a gay bar tried to protect gay patrons. Many gay bars were popular with a new breed of liberal-minded straight youth who enjoyed the freedom and friendliness of gay dance parties and clubs in the '80s and '90s. The trouble was, by the early '90s the reputation of these clubs as being havens for fun and gorgeous single women, attracted a larger homophobic element who, for whatever reason, felt threatened by the presence of gay men. Gay bashings were actually occurring *inside* gay venues and dance parties! The Flinders Hotel moved to stop the violence in the only way it could, by banning heterosexuals. Well, the feigned outrage, particularly from the ignorant right-wing supermarket media was colossal. 'Reverse dis-crimination!' they cried again in their columns and talkback shows. The attitude was: 'How dare gays do this! We gave them everything they wanted and now they turn on us.' The whole thing was blown out of proportion, and the actual problem of violence was totally ignored by most of the mainstream media. For conservatives, it was a chance to score cheap ratings points, using gays, and the first to tear down the veneer of acceptance were those who had the least interest in it in the first place.

In the '90s, some of the loudest self-appointed 'authorities' on gay matters have been the most ill-informed. They spread disinformation and generalisations about gay 'lifestyles' without, it seems, the least experience of them. The *Sydney Morning Herald* ran one article that perpetuated the myth that people become gay because it is trendy, the journalist substantiating his claims with tenuous evidence of the experience at one university in America!

It's enough to make you wonder if gay people are often too sensitive to the need to be fair. They know what it feels like to be treated as less than human. Every gay person walks down the street just a little self-consciously. You know that, as a gay person, if you hold your head up a little too high, with a little too much pride, someone will want to knock it down again. The Mardi Gras Committee conducted argumentative meetings to try to decide what to do with the big dance parties. Gay people were being knifed and bashed at events meant to celebrate their acceptance. But the issue was a divisive one. Many gays feared a backlash against them, just as in the '80s AIDS was often used to discredit them. Most, too, aimed to be able to enjoy their lives in a shared environment, away from the ghetto mentality that separated them from loved ones, friends and workmates throughout the wider community.

Gay celebrities were vulnerable in a different way to gays on the street. If they were outed, they would be sitting ducks. Open targets for violence and hatred, they stood to lose careers and lives they had carefully built. Sports stars like Martina Navratilova lost millions of dollars of endorsements when her sexuality was made public. And it is not uncommon for prominent gay conservatives in churches or politics to suicide rather than face the disgrace of being outed.

Difficult and complex issues face gay people when they try to discern how they can live their lives with a degree of pride, and how they can command the respect that is given to any other person who is a good or talented human being without having to pretend to be someone else. Though probably more than half the people at the debate on outing on that balmy February Mardi Gras Festival night were not in favour of it, Stephen Dunne's speech in favour got the most publicity. It was extremist. Besides mentioning names, it virtually demanded that these people assist the gay cause and stand up or be stood up.

Ian resented being lumped in with closet gays who worked in the media and publicly harmed the gay cause with their conservative banter. 'It's easy for people who have nothing to lose to make accusations. But what does Dunne know of my life, or what I've been through, as a gay man? Nothing!' And what does 'out' mean? For someone in the public eye it means telling millions of people that you don't know, and who don't know you, or care about you, intimate details about yourself. For someone not in the public eye, which included nearly all of Dunne's audience, it presumably means telling your family, friends and work colleagues. But being prepared to tell anyone? An approaching gang of poofta bashers? No-one expects you to be that out, but that's how out Ian would be. After calling Ian a closet homosexual, Dunne wondered on behalf of the audience what that must be like. Ian felt his decision to make a spectacle of his sexuality could only be his decision, when and if he was prepared. Obviously, that decision was going to affect the way he lived his life. And how his family lived theirs. If anything, the demands made Ian more obstinate.

Meanwhile, back at the front, that same month at Tamarama beach, egg-throwing was becoming an almost institutionalised part of the Mardi Gras Festival. A gang of teenage boys yelled homophobic taunts above the beach as they pelted eggs at people from the cliffs. This occurred over a few years during Mardi Gras thousands of gay tourists flock to Sydney, and a lot find their way to Tamarama to catch the sun, away from the Northern winter.

Ian recalls, 'An American guy got eggshell stuck in his eye. He was hit in the face. Then Jamie, the seven-year-old kid of a friend of mine, was hit in the back. Can you imagine how terrified he was? This thing from out of nowhere hit him. He had a welt the size of a cricket ball. These bastards were throwing these eggs, laughing their heads off. I had my leg in a plaster. My knee had been operated on, and one of these kids is only twenty metres from me, he's got a towel wrapped around his head and he's screaming, "Roberts, you fucking faggot." Laughing his head off, thinking he was so cool with his sunglasses and towel. He was pelting eggs and kept missing. I kept ducking. They all went off and I thought, "Right! I'm going to find them." I was that angry. They had hit all these people just minding their own business.

'There was about twenty of them so I thought they'd stand out. Shane and I drove the car round for ages. We waited for them to come back to the beach rearmed, and then run up this back lane about two hours later. We were pretty patient. Shane had a couple of eggs that hadn't busted. Anyway, we drove after them and they had slowed from a run to a walk and sat on a wall, laughing and carrying on. We pulled up and got out of the car and they shit themselves. I limped out, but Shane was quicker and hit one of the guys with an egg, right in the middle of the chest. And I was running round trying to get them. They ran into about four houses in between Bondi and Tamarama and a couple of their fathers came out and told us to fuck off. I said, "I know where you live and I'm going to put a brick through your window every day for a week." One guy said, "We know you. We know who you are!" I said, "Yes, good! You will always know who I am, and every time you see me it will annoy the fuck out of you! Why don't you control your kids? Do you even know what those bastards do?" '

THIRTEEN
TERRY, THE TOUR AND
BLUE

Terry Hill's transfer to Manly in 1994 was a bonus for Ian. Terry was from home territory, and could be relied upon to be tactless enough to call a spade a spade. 'I think I got on straight away with Ian because I related better to him. The clean-cut kids used to think "what's going on here?" the way I carried on. It wasn't so much the swearing but the bagging them, like. Ian knew how to take it, because he was from Souths. At Souths, you've got to remember, if you played under Craig Coleman and Mario—I mean, Tugger used to cut Mario's underpants every training session! This is unheard of at Manly. No-one played tricks on each other. You go there, you sit there, you train, then you hop in your car and go home. That's it!'

Terry was a few years behind Ian at Mascot. He's a happy-go-lucky, cheeky guy from a tough Souths working-class family, eternally grateful to have found his pot of gold through football. Ian welcomed his forthrightness, and his loyalty. Terry was in awe of Ian, not only as a hero on the field, but as a star who took the time to give him advice when Terry was first being graded at Souths. 'It was 1988, and I went to South Sydney grade training and, I don't know why he done it or said it, but he came over to me and said, "Mate, you see them blokes over there", and he pointed to the blokes I was training with, "they're all good blokes, don't get me wrong, but you don't want to be training with them, you want to be training with blokes like him, David Boyle and that." Then, all of a sudden, shit, I was up the front. I was running with Ian Roberts!'

In 1994, Ian found himself discussing his sexuality with another football player! Terry made light of it, too. 'I come from Erskineville and Newtown, like it's really tough. It's a really hard town. Ian always thought that *I* thought he was a fucking poof and that I hated poofs. That's the perception he got from me. And he was totally wrong! He said to me at Manly, "Mate, I didn't think you liked me." And I said, "Don't be ridiculous, mate. I love you!" And he said, "I always thought the guys from Souths didn't like me because they knew I was gay." Terry set the record straight and years of quiet paranoia melted away in a grateful big sigh of relief. Terry treated Shane as he would any of the players' partners. Shane says, 'I was always treated with respect, I think, because they all liked and respected Ian as a person and as a player.'

1994 saw a continuation of Ian's form on the field. After an uncertain start to the season, with seven points after seven rounds, Manly's solid defence helped produce a series of wins to secure a top-three spot. Ian was crucial in defence. When he won Man of the Match after Manly's 11–8 win over North Sydney on 13 May, he deferred to the young and brilliant Steve Menzies. 'He's the best young kid I've ever had anything to do with. He just takes so much pressure off me.'

That game saw examples of Ian's famous knockout hits which were perfectly timed to drive through players and knock them for six. They lacked the hatred he felt a few years before, but had the effect of lifting the entire team with their passion and ferocity. Ian was leading by example. He found he was not only respected, he was revered by some of the young players, whose teenage years were the late '80s and early '90s. They were a new slick breed of professional athletes. Ian was an inspiration to them.

In his own way, at his own pace, Ian was starting to change football's perception of homosexuality. The fact that, within football, he found a supportive attitude to his sexuality from guys like Terry was a huge help. In fact a lot of players had got used to it over the years. Or they'd be 'Well, he's gay, but he's all right. He's not the normal gay. He's different.' Ian was starting not to give a stuff about the people who didn't like the idea.

He was 28 now and had never played in a grand final. He had become one of the Mr Nice Guy elder statesmen of league, who had battled great odds to be playing, let alone playing with the passion he did. A lot of the sports journos had come to like Ian. They always gave him a break.

Witness his recent appearance on the Sports Show. He was almost turning away from the camera as questions were being asked of him. Also, his arms were crossed. Signs that he was shy and intimidated ...

Quite simply, he prefers to be a background man. Except when it comes to performing on the football field. (Danny Weidler, State of Origin souvenir, 5/94)

He doesn't hide the fact that winning the premiership has become a personal obsession. He believes his time is running out. (Ray Gatt, Australian, 16/6/94)

NSW lost the first Origin game on 23 May, at the Stadium, 12–16. Ian injured his hamstring in the first five minutes but played until half-time before coming off.

He elected not to play in the second game in Melbourne and jeopardise the rest of the season by aggravating the injury. NSW won. Glen Lazarus injured his knee so Ian got to play in the decider at Suncorp Stadium.

If the Blues won it would be a record three series in a row, and the first time they had won a series decider at Lang Park.

A few minutes into the game, Ian's head connected with the head of Jason Smith in an off-the-ball accident. He was going in to tackle Smith, who was making his Origin debut, convinced that Smith was about to receive a crucial pass from Maroons' halfback Alfie Langer, metres out from the Blues' line. Ian tried, too late, to pull out of the charge, but only managed to get his arms out of the way before his head crashed sickeningly hard against Smith's, in what many saw as a deliberate attempt by Ian to put his opponent out of the game.

Smith was stretchered from the field. He was taken to hospital for inspection by a neurosurgeon, where X-rays revealed a hairline fracture of the cheekbone. Darren Smith, who replaced his brother on the field, said he hoped Ian was suspended for the rest of the year, as Queensland manager Dick Turner vowed to cite him for the incident.

If it had been a deliberate hit, which the commentators of the game very much doubted, it was foolhardy. Ian was badly concussed and was taken off as well, to have eight stitches inserted in a deep eye gash, before he insisted he was well enough to go back on the field. He eventually had to stay off when the bleeding could not be stopped. NSW went on to win the decider 27–12, but there was no celebration for Ian.

The Queensland Rugby League lodged a complaint and by a two to one decision of an ARL committee comprised of John Quayle, ARL deputy chairman John McDonald and Queensland Rugby League general manager Ross Livermore, Ian was cited to appear before an ARL judiciary on 22 June. John Quayle voted against the citing.

Ian became only the third NSW player in Origin history, after Peter Kelly and Mark Geyer, to appear before the judiciary. They had been suspended for three and six weeks. Ian didn't like the blemish on his record. 'I'm just not the sort of player who would do something like that deliberately,' he pleaded. At the judiciary he said, 'It's really embarrassing to even be here. In the ten years that I've played it's been a bit of personal pride that I've never had to front down here ... I can't believe it got to this stage. I'm still in a state of disbelief that I'm here. There was no malice and no intention there to hurt anyone.'

Frank Stanton, who spoke as Ian's representative, went through the video footage of the incident frame by frame. 'If you are going to take a man out of the play, gentlemen, you don't do it with your head or face,' he said.

Ian was acquitted. Officials at Canterbury, Jason Smith's club, were furious. Coach Chris Anderson took the incident right out of context when he said, 'The verdict gives anyone the licence to take a bloke out and get away with it. It's been a sickening affair and I really feel for Jason.'

Dave Johnson, who had become President of the Special

Olympics, East Sydney, hosted his daughter Natalie's eighteenth birthday party shortly after the incident. 'We were having a party here and there was a little fellow, a Down's syndrome bloke, and actually his father is one of the top heart specialists at St Vincent's, and this little kid—has been in 'A Country Practice' and 'GP' also—is looking at Ian all the time. Every time I would go round, he is staring at Ian, and I said, "What's the matter, Saxon?" He said, "I want him!" and he disapppeared for a while. One of the kiddies came up to me and said, "Go and see Saxon. He is upset." And I went down. He was at the gate and I said, "What's the matter?" "Oh, Roberts," he said, "He hit this bloke in Queensland," and all that. "I want him. Just him and me." He wanted to fight Ian, and was going "You and me, Roberts, just you and me!" And I asked Ian if he would mind going to have a talk with Saxon, as he was upset. And he was down there a couple of minutes and the next minute they came back up the stairs. They have got their arms wrapped round each other, best of friends. And you couldn't break Saxon away from Ian after that. I don't know what he said! ... At the end of the night I was telling his father, and his dad said, "Oh, Christ, I just bought him a North Sydney jumper. Now he's going to want a Manly one!"'

By early August, Ian's knee wear and tear, which he had been containing all season, caught up with him. Or, rather, stretched away from him. He missed two games and came off after 23 minutes in his comeback in the crucial game against Canberra on 28 August.

'He's our forward leader and we can't get through unless he lasts a whole game,' said [Cliff] Lyons. 'Our pack has gone well this season and we've got other good players. But Robbo's just that important to us with his unbelievable workload and experience ... [he's] a player many claim has proved himself to be the best ball-playing forward in the world this season.' (Neil Cadogan, RLW, 31/8/94)

The injury was a cruel blow to Ian. It was still bothering him, and he was loaded with pain-killers when he played in the first semi against Brisbane on 4 September. They lost 4–16. Ian now feared for his selection in the Kangaroo tour of England and France, which he had already missed out on before, because of injury. 'I had an arthroscope straight after the Brisbane game. Then I got picked in the Kangaroo side. I had to have an injection in my knee before the medical so I could get through it OK. Neil Halpin knew that I would be fine by the time of the tour.'

By this time, Ian and the author had talked at gym and over coffee, over months, about gay issues, and about his unique situation as a somewhat defiant and independent-minded football player, honed by years of stubborn resistance to niggling challenges and subtle demands for his conformity. He often said that his hard yards were nothing compared with those of other gays he encountered. He was always grateful for, and in fact often defensive of, the homophobic behaviour he had been subjected to. And in a way, his selection for the tour supported his contention that a lot of the rugby league establishment was fair. By '94 there wouldn't have been a selector who didn't know he was gay. The people he respected in the game were good men, egalitarian in the true league spirit. Even though they may have found it difficult at times to understand him, they did not allow that to get in the way of their professionalism. That, and the acceptance of Shane at Manly, provided Ian with a vital security.

With that grew a boldness, and a desire to make a difference for others going through the pain of growing up gay, those whose breaks hadn't been as good as his, whose families hadn't been as loving, whose experiences had been more wrenching. It became apparent to Ian that he was in a position to lend a hand, to make a difference. And for the first time since Blake's death, he felt ready again to look out for the little guy. The difference, this time, was that his own life was more resolved. He was stronger, and willing to share his experiences, but whatever he did, it had to be on his terms, at his pace.

Circumstances provided *Blue*. As a photographer, the author dealt with the editor at Studio Magazines. She had seen a previous shoot I had done with Ian. 'Would Ian do nudes, for *Black + White*?' she wondered. 'Maybe.' 'KJ' played her cards deftly, like a pro. '*Actually*, we are doing a new magazine, same quality, directed more specifically to the gay and lesbian market.' (Everyone was talking about that market, wherever it was.) 'Hmmm. All right,' we thought, 'a first issue gay magazine, with a cool, hip, but *not* an outing article, to run with the shots. Something tongue in cheek. Stir people along. Make them think. Suggestive and supportive to gays. No big statement. Toe in the water type stuff.'

We decided Ian should do it. Studio Magazines, who produced *Black + White*, had chic. If you were wanting to make a bold and classy statement, they were the people to do it with. Heaps of celebs had stripped and caused a splash in their arty glossy pages. And for a gay footballer who had limited his options in the straight advertising world, there were possibilities of picking up a bit of work in niche markets that thrived on liberalism and controversy.

We shot a dozen films on two occasions, trying to capture Ian's sensitivity as well as the athlete in him. Of course his knee was shaved from the recent operation and he was severely handicapped at the time, stiffly shuffling around the locations. He was pleased with the shots, though he didn't care for the ones chosen by the magazine when he was overseas. The interview for *Blue* was the day before he left for the Kangaroo tour. The questions focused broadly on Ian as a person.

Ian's knee was still uncomfortable when the time came for the tour medical. He couldn't move it without pain, let alone run, tackle and be tackled. 'Neil knew it would be right by the time of the tour. It just hadn't settled down from the previous operation which had been to clean the knee out and shave back the knee cap. So I had a painkiller injection to get through.'

At the Holiday Inn in Coogee, where the team was staying before departure, Ian's naturalisation ceremony took place as part of the publicity for the tour. He was finally an Australian citizen.

Terry Hill roomed with Ian in England. 'We were on the plane, and he'd said, "Mate, I want to have a good talk with you." I said "Good as gold!" So when we get to the hotel, we unpacked all the gear and we had a talk. Basically, he just wanted me to know about everything. Not about being gay. He knew I was cool with that. But he wanted to *explain* it. Ian would probably laugh when I say this. He said, "Mate, I was doing things with a neighbour when I was *five*!"

He said, "I can't turn around now and say, 'Oh, I don't want to be gay now! I was born that fucking way. I can't help it. That's just the way it is.'" Which was cool with me. He explained it all to me and everything was sweet … It wasn't long before he was pointing at a bloke and saying to me, "He's not bad", and I'd say, "What about her!" about a girl.'

Ian says, 'I wanted to let Terry know the score with me, and that I wasn't going to go to great lengths, like I had in the past, to hide everything. And he was cool with that.'

In the first Test of the Ashes series at Wembley Stadium on 22 October, in a very tight match, Australia went down 4–8. The second match was at Old Trafford in Manchester on 5 November. In the twenty-first minute, Denis Betts' boot accidentally came crunching down on the right side of Ian's face, when he was down, right over his eye. Ian couldn't see and when the trainer arrived his first anxious question was 'Is my eye still there?' He was bleeding profusely and hardly conscious. He had three separate gashes around his eye, which required fifteen stitches. Australia went on to win the Match 38–8.

During the tour, it was leaked to the media that Studio Magazines had scored *the* Ian Roberts coup. That he was outing himself. Australian team officials started fielding calls for him from Australia, while the contingent of journalists on tour swarmed around the hotel in Leeds, where the team was staying.

The first draft of the Peter S. James article, which was to accompany Ian's photos in *Blue*, *was* an outing. Somewhere in the middle it read, 'Ian Roberts is gay, and proud of it.'

Ian would have freaked if he had read that he was proud of being homosexual. He *is* homosexual. No choice. Maybe he would agree he is proud that he is not ashamed of it, or that he tries to be a good person in total. But that was beside the point. The magazine had allowed us the opportunity to alter the article, and Ian had yet to sign off his approval of the magazine's use of the nude shots of him. The 'proud' statement was slashed and references to his 'lifestyle' rearranged so they read ambiguously, but were constructive. Ian saw the second draft, and doesn't know how close he came to being outed then. Not that the changes made it any easier for him over in England, where he was beseiged by reporters who had been leaked juicy bits of information.

Terry was surprised by the homophobia within the team when they got a whiff of what the commotion was about. 'I think that people who knew Ian got to accept it more easily. Like at Manly. But on the tour, where the people didn't really know him, and all of a sudden he was out. Honest to God, I reckon he wouldn't have had any back left, there were so many knives in it. No-one would do anything to his face, because they were all too scared. But to me, they were saying "Ian Roberts is a fucking poof?" "Yeah, well so fucking what? Is it hurting you? It's got nothing to do with you." I'd be at a party and someone would say something, and I would react, and they'd go, "You're just sticking up for him because he's your mate, blah, blah." I said, "Hang on a minute. What has he done to you, for you to turn round and say, 'He's a fucking poof!' What's he done to you?" There's no comeback! For Ian, away from Manly, it's very tough. There was always that "Is he or isn't he?" Then they find out he is!'

'When Shane arrived over there [in England] everyone started asking questions, "What's going on?" and they kept saying to me, "What's happening?" And I'd just say, "Nothing. Why? It's none of your business." '

'They'd ask, "Have they done anything in front of you? Are they *kissing*? Have you *caught* him?" '

'I'd just say, "Don't be so ridiculous. It's none of your business." Ian kept it to himself, what he'd done, and everyone appreciated that. But on the tour he was really open about himself, and didn't care what people thought. I thought it showed a lot of courage. He didn't know how everyone was going to take him, but then he just got to the stage where he thought "Fuck them!" Some players said some pretty bad things about him. A couple of blokes were like "Oh, it's disgusting!" I was like "Okay, you've had your little say. That's enough. He's my mate." I don't have to name those blokes because they're going to know who they are, but I've never told Ian.'

There is nothing to be gained from naming names of poofta bashers or of closeted poofs. They are simply conformists to a quietly

Before and after, Mardi Gras, 1995.

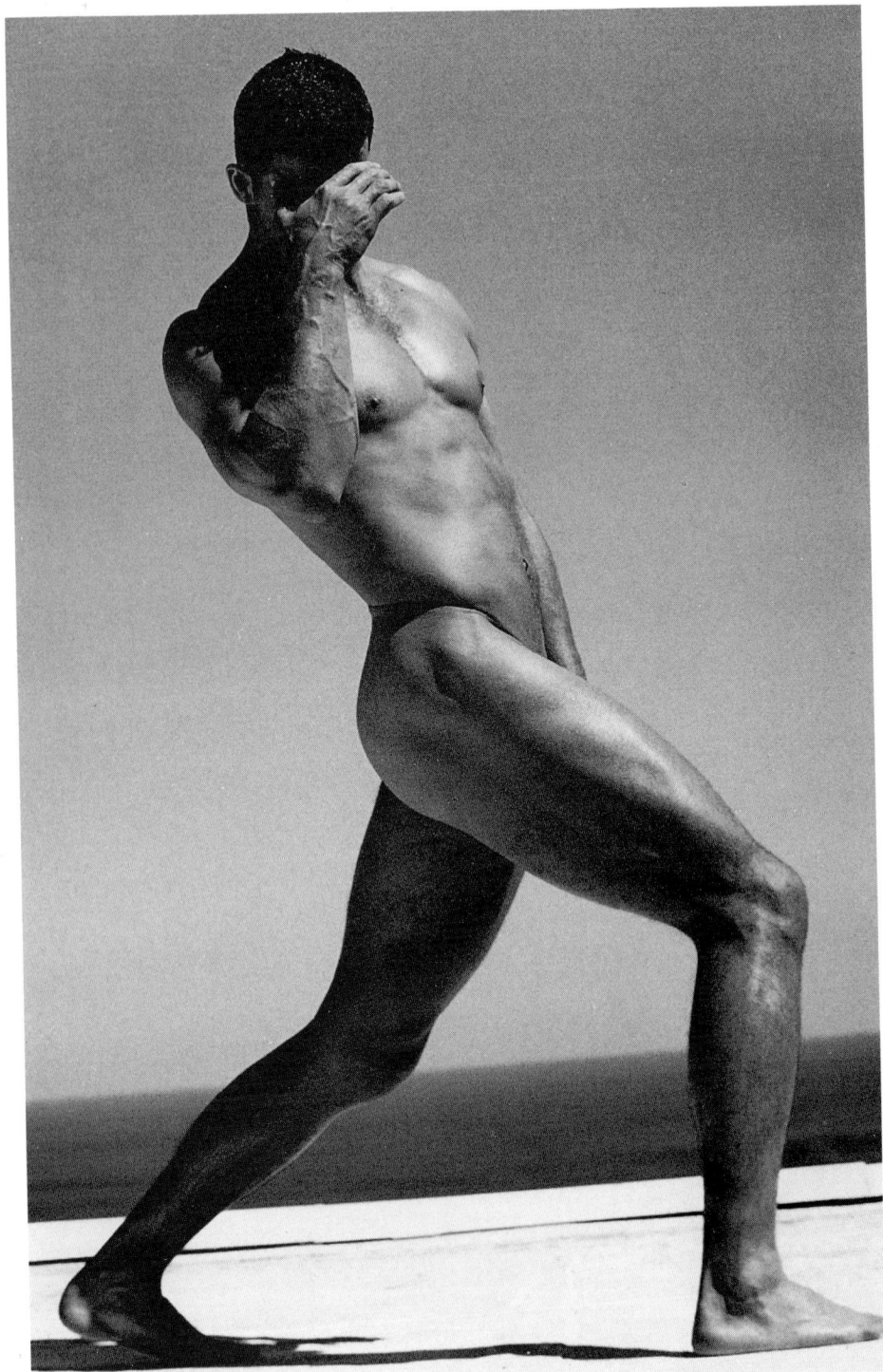

From the *Blue* shoot, courtesy *Blue* magazine.
(Photos: Paul Freeman)

In the spotlight: two paintings from a series by Ross Watson inspired by Ian's new status.

An Oxford Street shop window, Mardi Gras 1995.
(*Photo:* Shaney Balcombe)

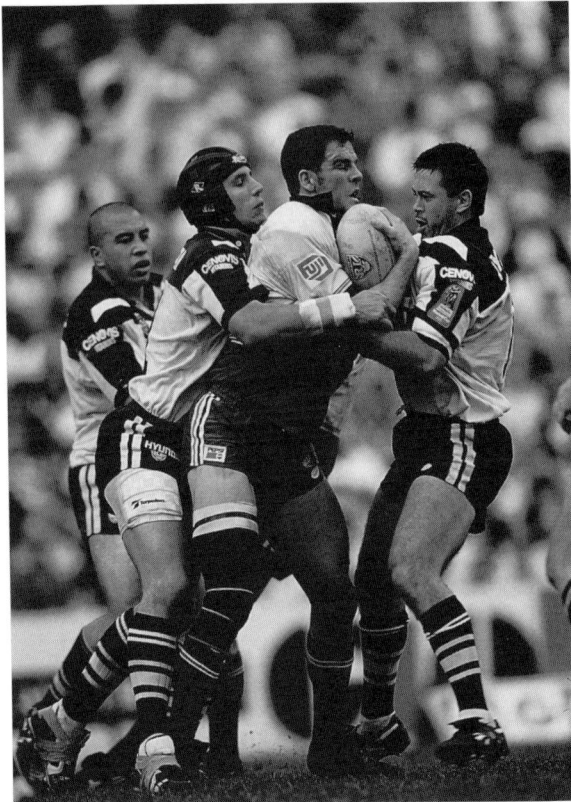

Stubborn persistence in
the '95 Grand Final.
(*Photo:* Clifford White)

Ian with friends at his farewell party, close to the completion of the book.
Author Paul Freeman is lolling at the front.

Ian basking in sunshine on his balcony in Townsville.
(*Photo:* Paul Freeman)

condoned part of their culture. It is the people who break out of that, who think for themselves, who are noteworthy.

Terry continues. 'We were on the Australian bus at one stage. There were a few players sitting behind us. I was sitting with Ian, and one of the players said, with a lot of aggression, looking out the window, "Look at the fucking poofs! Doesn't it make you feel sick? They're holding hands! Fuckin' pooftas." Ian just ignored it and when we got back to the room, he just said, "He's a fuckwit, that bloke. He just lost me forever." The guy is barred for life, for Ian . . . I think a lot of players are jealous of Ian. He's a good-looking bloke, big bloke, tough, great player. You know, anything to bring him down and they feel better.'

'One of the players on the tour' Ian recalls, laughing, 'was telling me and Terry how he was out at a club and two "faggots" tried to pick him up. He didn't know about me at this stage. And Terry and I just glanced at each other and cracked up, because the guy is as ugly as sin! He was saying "Fucking faggots" and he picked the worst two people to tell. I was cracking up thinking, "Mate, *that* is the biggest compliment you are *ever* going to get." But we doubted that any gay guys would have such bad taste!'

Terry recalls a fun day held for the team. 'I think it must have been hard for Ian. We went out to this pub, in the country, it was about 40 degrees, real hot. Everyone had a great day getting on the piss and socialising. And I think Ian spent nearly the whole day in the bus, by himself. He said he was feeling a bit crook and wanted to lay down. But he said to me before, "Oh mate, it's not my scene sitting around here getting on the piss."

'I think that Bob [Fulton] was sensational the way he handled the situation on tour. Bob was great. One day, he rang our room and said he wanted to have a talk with me. I think Ian had just had a bit of a blue with one of the officials about Shane eating at the breakfast table. Ian was all worked up. Bob said, "What's happening? What's going on down there?"

'I said, "Nothing."

' "Is Shane staying there?"

' "Mate, he called in for one day."

' "Is it bothering you?"

'I said, "No, it's not like Ian does anything in front of me."

' "Mate, fine, not a problem."

'Bob asked to see Ian. I told Ian Bob had been as good as gold. He said, "Mate, don't just tell me that to cover for him. If he was dirty, tell me." "Mate, he was as good as gold!" Ian went to see him, then.'

Ian remembers, 'He was pacing about the room, when I got there, and I could sense there was a real air of uncertainty or uneasiness, and he sat down and said, "Mate, Shane I don't have a problem with. But he can't stay in the hotel." Which for him was probably a really hard thing to say. But it was really cool, because he was so professional with it. I told him Shane wasn't staying there. He said, "Mate, I have no problems whatsoever, what you do is what you do. You play football well, and that's all that matters to me." '

'After that, I got all emotional. I was moved because that was quite a big step in my life.'

Terry recalls: 'He came back, "Fuck, I respect Boze. I can't believe it. I sat and had a talk with him and he was fantastic!" '

'Bob's the first to stick up for Ian. I've seen him jump to his defence that quick it isn't funny! And he's in a difficult position, especially with his mates from the hard school who are all probably going, "Fuck, he's a poof!" '

Furthermore, Ian was amazed at how some of the guys on the tour were so cool. 'It's funny because the public have no idea what these guys are like as people. They only get to see the tough footballer side, but not the humanity in them. Real pros like Glen Lazarus, Steve Renouf and Michael Hancock, but particularly Kevin Walters and Alfie [Langer], went out of their way to make me feel comfortable. It just didn't seem to bother them at all. Like it was the last thing on their minds whenever we spoke. Sometimes I'd be having coffee or something to eat at the hotel with one of my English gay friends and they would always make them feel welcome. Always genuinely polite to them, like "How are you, mate? Is Ian feeding you OK? You being looked after?" I know it sounds stupid but it really meant a lot to me. When I think of the number of times I've been called a slimy faggot on the field, I realise that half the time the guys really couldn't give a fuck whether I was gay, black, Jewish or whatever. That's just on the field and off there's some really good cool people.'

Even some of the less cool people amused Ian with their paranoia. 'On the tour I got sick with the flu on two separate occasions, and one of the medicos on the tour came to me and went, "Mate, what's wrong?" in a *very* concerned voice. I'd had a flu at home just before we left and I never get crook. In the past ten years I'd probably only been sick twice.

'He said, "What's wrong. You keep getting these *flus* ... Have you had an AIDS test?"'

'I said, "It's not a problem, mate."'

'All of a sudden I've got a flue, I've got AIDS!'

Back in Australia, the ruling in the civil court case, which awarded Ian $100,000, made the news, and was another embarrassment for Ian on tour. 'I am preparing for an important Test match. I do not want to talk about my business affairs,' he told reporters. One report estimated that Ian had lost $250,000 of his own money in failed business ventures. Meanwhile, Wiseman continued trying to broker deals.

And Rupert Murdoch's $500 million proposal to create a super league was announced.

Since entering the television arena in a big way, Murdoch had invested a lot of time and money in sport. Televised popular sport equals ratings.

He'd already been involved in setting up Premier League soccer in England in 1992 for his BSkyB channel, and he had made the historic purchase of TV rights for the National Football League in the US for $1.7 billion, pushing out the CBS network which had held the rights for 30 years.

In Australia, where he was entering the new pay TV market with Fox TV, and where he had 14.9 per cent of Channel Seven, he was attempting to shore up the TV rights for rugby league, which is the most TV-friendly football in Australia. He had already become a sponsor and part owner of the Brisbane Broncos and Canberra Raiders through the Queensland Newspapers group and Ansett. And, with a view to establishing a world-wide league, he had taken steps to set up teams in South Africa, and expand the competition with league in Britain. The competition would be beamed into Asia on Star TV, and into Britain on BSkyB.

The plan was to take over and modernise the existing competition. He wanted to ensure the high standard and quality of the game by reducing the number of clubs participating in the competition to between ten and twelve. These clubs would receive a guaranteed income of $2 million plus whatever local sponsorship they gained. The revamped league was also prepared to nut out a deal which gave clubs a percentage share of any marketing profits the league as a whole earned. With fewer teams, there would be more corporate dollars to go around and ensure that the clubs could afford the highest quality players. In other words, a leaner, meaner league.

Ken Arthurson, chairman of the ARL, returned home from the Kangaroo tour to deal with his challenger. 'We owe it to the pioneers who set up the original league to ensure it isn't plundered,' he told the *Sun-Herald's* Alex Mitchell. 'One thing I do know, however, is that in this world everything is negotiable. If we have to negotiate to maintain control of the game, then we will.'

There was a big hitch. Even if Murdoch nutted out a deal with the ARL, there was still Kerry Packer to deal with. And with the existing TV rights for the league held by his Channel Nine, and his interest in clubs like Easts, Souths, Wests and Manly, the League was bound to witness some pretty heavy moves and counter-moves.

Another hurdle was the fact that existing clubs faced extinction or mergers if they wanted to survive. The ARL had skirted around the problem for years. It recognised the need for culling, but was unwilling to face the flak from the old-boys and traditionalists who the League had encouraged through years of their own marketing of club rivalry and competition. In some ways, having their hand forced by the new initiative would mean the ARL wouldn't have to bear the criticism for dismantling the monster (turned dinosaur) they had created. Murdoch could. Problem solved. Clubs like Easts would be forced to merge with Souths into an Eastern Sydney side, and St George with Illawarra into a Southern Sydney team. Regions for each club would expand, giving them room to move and obtain sponsorship and a bigger pool of young players.

Despite the obstacles, contact had been made with clubs and players to drum up support. Needless to say, the whole idea was the subject of excited speculation among the salary-starved stars of football feeling salary starved. Disquiet had been growing in the years that league attempted to market itself into the '90s. League was beginning to realise its marketing potential, through daring campaigns like the Tina Turner series of ads, but players weren't benefiting from any increase in status. They remained subject to the dictates of both the League and the club contracts that were standard at the time.

There would be no salary cap in the new league. The market would determine wages, not the amount that the poorest club could afford, and the players could look forward to lucrative contracts. Not only that, but the new league promised to provide additional perks for players and involve them in other aspects of the game. They intended to butter the players up with long-term employment guarantees and contract conditions they had only dreamt of.

Initially, players and clubs were keen for Super League, thinking that the ARL would want to to be a part of it to remain as the game's administrators.

Despite his mangled face, Ian made sure he was available for the deciding Test at Elland Road on 20 November. This was his first and perhaps his only Ashes series and he wanted to be part of an Australian win. But at practically the same point in the game as at Old Trafford, he was hit high again. And again he was led off, hardly conscious, blood streaming down his nose from cuts to his forehead. He spent the next 30 minutes pleading to go back on and when Bozo finally gave him the OK he raced on with a turban of bandages wrapped around his head. In a total of 50 minutes on the field, he topped the tackle count, assisting Australia to a 23–4 victory and a two-one win to secure the Ashes.

Then Ian took Terry out on *his* town, after the Ashes victory. He introduced him to places where no-one batted an eyelid at anybody else's get-up, race, creed, colour, or body-piercing, and everyone had harmless fun.

'I was a bit spun out myself by the gay clubs in London,' Ian recalls. 'London is such a city of extremes. Terry and I got lost.' In the extremes? 'No, we got lost in one of the clubs. It was a maze, and every time we tried to leave, something distracted us, and then we couldn't find our way out!'

Terry remembers at a club called Trade, 'I was shitting myself when this big burly guy approached me, and Ian wasn't around. I thought, "What do I do?" I said, "I'm here with a friend, mate. I'm straight. Sorry!" I don't know what I thought was going to happen. You say "no thanks", and that's cool. In the end, I relaxed and started chatting to people more. By this time I wasn't saying "I'm straight". I was saying, "That's my boyfriend over there."'

'And all the time players were going to me, "Fuck, how do you put up with it? I can't *believe*!" or 'How did you do it? How did you put up with him for three months." And I turned around and said, "Mate, it's the best fucking three months I ever had in my life!"'

Terry made things easy for Ian. 'Terry has been amazing through everything. He's so cool. For a guy who's got that real ocker image, he's amazing. Fantastic. In London, he was telling guys that I was taking him to all these clubs and it was crazy and mad. He couldn't care less what people thought. He just told it like it was.'

'I think, prior to the tour, Bozo probably always thought I was embarrassed by my sexuality. Whenever he heard stuff or people made digs at training or whatever, he would just let it go by. He wouldn't say anything, thinking that I would be offended. But he could tell by the end of the tour that I wasn't, because Terry was telling him all about going to gay clubs and that. Making light of it. And bringing me out of myself a bit more.'

The gay footballer, Bob, who had harrassed Ian years before, for being too closeted, looked Ian up, that trip, and the two partied a bit together. Ian had met him in '87 when Bob played a season in the ARL Competition. Tugger Coleman had kept in touch with Bob, too.

'I always knew Bob was gay,' says Tugger. 'He'd be up-front about it. You doubted he was too because he was a tough bastard. Played in the front row. He used to give it to blokes, mate. He never told me about Ian until '93, when I stayed with him in London.'

TERRY, THE TOUR AND BLUE

Like Ian, Bob still wasn't officially 'out' in football circles, and Ian felt he had grown so much since the days when he was chided by Bob for being too paranoid.

The provincial games, in France, were easy wins, if you were lucky enough to survive them. The French are famous for their interesting tactics in these games. In Perpignan on 27 November, against Catalan Selection, Ian retaliated against some foul play. 'Dean Pay was exhausted. Everyone had been partying a bit the night before and Boz took him off and just sort of told me, "Go out there, Robbo, and give it to them. Just give it to them!" We were playing a bunch of animals!' The famous Roberts machine-gun uppercut was captured on video for the first time in close-up, and played over and over in the news reports in Australia, much to Ian's eventual embarrassment. Terry stirred Ian about the incident. 'We were just talking one day in our room during the tour and Ian said, "Mate, you know I don't like violence. I don't like fighting, and what I did to Garry Jack. I don't like seeing people get hurt." He said, "It hurts me if I see someone get bashed up. I feel sorry for that person." And I thought, "Okay." And he was playing that day and he punched the fucking shit out of this guy. But, I mean, they deserved it. Honestly, they threw bottles, they threw everything on the field, the spectators. They played that dirty. When we came off the field the first thing I said to him was, "Jesus you're a nasty person. What about that poor guy you went off at." Just geeing him up!'

Australia then gave France a world-record thrashing, 74–0, in Bezier on 4 December. It was Mal Meninga's farewell as Kangaroo skipper and the Kangaroos played with an edge to make sure he went out on a good note. Ian got replaced at half-time, but was rapt to have been part of this match. He played with distinction the whole tour and was the only front-rower to earn four Test jumpers. He told journalist David Mason, 'One thing [this tour] has done is made me filthy that I missed the 1990 tour through injury, because I've now realised what I missed out on!'

After the tour Shane and Ian went on a mad two-week jaunt round Europe via Eurail. They bickered their way from city to city, arguing over who would lug a ginormous trunk of a bag which they would have been more sensible to check into a locker in Paris, where they started. Shane was treated to Europe the Ian Roberts way. 'We lived on bread rolls and bananas. Nothing else. Ian would not eat anything else. And it became so pathetic that the gums in our mouth were cut and sore from eating bread rolls! Hard, crunchy bread rolls. And that's all he would eat! All the food he reckoned was fatty and oily and disgusting. Wherever you went he had to have bananas and bread rolls, cheap, easy and good for you.'

FOURTEEN
EVERYBODY FINDS OUT

An actor for so long in someone else's script of his life, Ian could easily be genuinely surprised at the consequences of his own actions. 1995 was to unfold as a kind of grand finale of him being the unwitting cause of far-reaching effects.

Blue came out, and by a hair's breadth, Ian didn't. Things went roughly according to the plan. The positive message of the article was received clearly by those for whom it was intended. There was a kind of bemused applause from the print media, and a few wisecracks about the irritatingly ambiguous article. Ian's street cred shot up, since he wasn't paid for the spread, and of course he expressed his habitual surprise at the reaction he got, despite being secretly pleased.

But though he willingly waded in up to his waist on this, he was about to be pulled in deeper. *60 Minutes* had been onto the Ian Roberts story when he was still in England. 'Richard Mortlock, a producer on the show, rang me and said, "Look, we believe you are going to come out." Richard was really supportive.'

Do it on our show! was the general gist of the calls early in '95. Only we will do the story right by you. Everyone else will fuck you over. We'll be sensitive to the issue.

Journalist/presenter Neil Mercer talked with Ian after he got back from Europe in February, and wanted to do a sensitive piece for the current affairs show *Real Life*, but pulled out when he realised he couldn't get Ian on the show without a scripted interview that ensured he wasn't outed. Mercer then tried the softly softly approach and assigned the story to Tracey Hutchinson, a recruit on the show to gently coax some sort of admission of Ian's homosexuality from someone. Hutchinson was obviously uncomfortable ethically with her directive, whatever it was, and the story was canned. She resigned her job with the program shortly after.

Protective and concerned friends warned Ian of the consequences of an exposé. Ian laughs at it now. '"What have you done, mate?" one guy who worked in publicity for the ARL said. "There'll be no more football and you won't get any advertising work."

'In the end, I said, "I'm doing it because that's the way I am."

'"Well, as long as you're prepared for it."

'This guy was actually quite supportive later on. I think he felt it his duty to warn me about what he saw as the repercussions. Then, after I made my point that I didn't regret any consequences, I think he admired my stand. I'd started to feel I was responsible to the larger community, not just to myself. We get so hung up on being successful that in the end we lose sight of what is actually important.'

A promotional company was loosely representing Ian at that point, loosely to the extent that, when *Blue* came out, they played down any business association with him, and in a peculiar fashion according to one journalist, who had asserted in print that the company managed Ian. They wrote a letter to the journalist saying their company didn't represent Ian, but that he was represented by another company that happened to have a very similar name. The journalist then revealed in print that the two business names were registered to two people who, in fact, worked for the one promotional company!

The reaction to *Blue* among many gays was warm. And, as 1995 was to prove to Ian, there are many types of homosexual, other than those identifying with the term 'gay'. (That peculiar and inappropriate word has taken on connotations which are unpalatable to lots of homosexuals, including those who, for one reason or another, are secretive or in denial about their sexuality, and the many who don't identify with the gay stereotypes often portrayed by society. Yet the word 'homosexual' is clumsy too.)

Of course, a lot of 'out' gays had known of Ian's sexuality for years. Even if they lived quiet lives, they heard through friends. There was a grapevine. But few ever expect high-profile homosexuals to 'out' themselves nor would they dream of outing them, and subjecting them to large scale homophobia. It was understood that those gay with the most to lose would be the most reluctant to understand their sexuality. In the '80s and '90s too, the gay press was filled with examples of hate-related violence towards gays of lesser profile, of police discrimination in their treatment of gays, of anti-gay vilification by everyone from so-called moral authorities within churches downwards, and of the law pursuing gays. So when the *Blue* hit the stands, there was surprise that Ian *had* taken such a bold public step. A sharp intake of breath, en masse.

The gays who didn't demand anything from Ian were to be his mainstay throughout '95. And the thousands of people who rang, or wrote or approached him to say, 'Good on you, mate'. They buoyed Ian's sense of right, and he was satisfied that, come what may, he had done something good. People came up to him to tell him all the time. 'Thank you for what you have done.' 'You made me tell my parents.' 'You made me not feel shame.' 'You made me tell my friends.' 'You made my friends accept me.' 'You helped me try to understand my child.' 'You helped my child understand me!' 'You helped make the world safer for my child.'

At the ABC's Mardi Gras viewing room overlooking Oxford Street, in March, just weeks after *Blue* appeared, Ian was received like royalty. That night David Hill took him aside and told him that what he had done was truly courageous and commendable. And in the Super League camp, he was a hero too. He must have felt like he had dismantled a barrier, allowing people to flow through and express acceptance without prejudice. Lachlan Murdoch and some of *his* associates, who were young, aggressive career men, proved themselves to be cool and hip and accepting. The irony was that some of these educated young people were cogs in a mammoth media works whose tabloids would often churn out the most sensationalist and stereotyping stuff about gays. But Lachlan gave many cause to hope that issues like homosexuality would gradually get a more consistent break. When the much-scrutinised young Murdoch became head of News Limited in April 1997, Tony Sarno, an editor with Fairfax, who had worked under Lachlan some years before told the *Sydney Morning Herald*'s Paul Sheehan, 'One morning Zeb (Rice, one of Lachlan's right-hand men and a good friend) and Lachlan came to work with exactly the same crewcuts, and you realised just how young the generals at News really were. It makes News an interesting place. It's the young progressives who are now running the show, and conservatism is lower down in the corporation. Normally, it's the other way 'round.' (*SMH*, 19/4/97)

Back at training for Manly, Terry Hill made light of the *Blue* situation, which helped everyone relax more. With disarming frankness, he was able to bridge communication gaps that it wasn't in Ian's nature to attempt. He was a bold and cheeky ambassador for Ian's right to be himself, bringing disinterested humour to Ian's predicament.

For the first time in Ian's life, his separate lives were converging, and he felt exhilarated to be relaxed at last. Himself. Not that that entailed any obvious change in his behaviour. The relief was internal.

'The last couple of years of football have been the most enjoyable for me. For the first time in my life, I realised, I was happy. And I was happy with, and loved, football.' At last. He even started laughing at himself.

'He started to have a regular joke with Boze,' says Terry. 'And me. I mean, I would not deliberately embarrass Ian. And at first the other players were like, "Did you see what Terry did to Ian? He went up and got this pair of socks and when Ian was getting a rub down on the table he went up to him and held the socks at his crutch and shoved it in Ian's face and said 'Oh, you'd love to suck that, wouldn't ya'. And Ian just laughs at him!"

'OK, maybe someone else wouldn't get away with it. And if you said, "Get this in your mouth, ya fuckin' faggot" he'd punch the shit out of you because you deserved it. I mean I talk with a lisp and they always gig me about that. And you've got to cop as good as you give.

'With Ian everyone was a bit curious. But no-one would ever say, "Hey Ian, are you gay?" I'd walk in and everyone'd be sitting around, and I'd stick my head in my locker and yell, "Hey, Ian, are you ready to come out of this fucking closet yet?" That's just the way I am. If it helps everyone relate better, well, fantastic. I'm happy because Ian's a mate of mine and I want him to be happy too.

'At Manly they know he's a great bloke and nearly everyone loves him. He's cool. He can really get you going, too. Has a laugh. He's a loveable bloke. Like, my dad's one of the staunchest blokes, and he said to me, "Ian sat down and talked to me for hours!" Some people you only have to talk to for a minute and know they're a nice bloke.

'When I stir him, Ian laughs. He knows there's no spite whatsoever.'

Nonetheless there were still players who revealed some spite that lurked beneath a veneer of civility. Whether that came from homophobia or just competitiveness is sometimes debatable. Because things would occasionally get heated at training, what with players ribbing one another, and not everyone could dish it out and take it like Terry. 'Terry and I had a good relationship,' says Ian. 'But we'd always bag each other. He'd bag me about being a poof and Ridgey and I would often have a go at him about his lisp. Terry and I would bag Ridgey about being a wog or whatever.

'One night when we were at training, Terry and I were joking around with one of the players. I said he looked like that character in *Mask*. We were just shit-stirring each other. Nothing unusual. It was during a ball session and this guy just snapped. Then he went right over the edge.

"What about *you*, you fucking faggot? At least I don't suck knobs like you, you faggot! All you want to do is go and suck Shane's knob and fucking take it up the arse!"

'And this was in front of everyone. The whole team. And everyone was embarrassed. For me. He's tried to make me uncomfortable but he made everyone else uncomfortable in the process.

'My first impulse was to bash him. Knock him senseless. I fronted him off the field a bit later. I said, "If you ever do anything like that again, if you ever try to make me or anyone else uncomfortable like that I'll cut loose." He just went "Oh fuck off", sort of dismissing it. He apologised before a game a bit later on. Tried to make light of it. "You shouldn't be embarrassed about being a poof, mate." That was his way of laughing it off. I said, "You made all those young guys uncomfortable. That was the thing that affected me the most."

'A couple of weeks later he spat the dummy again. He did almost the same thing!

'There were a couple of other times when I overheard players mouthing off about me being a faggot. I confronted one bloke getting himself all worked up about how disgusting it was. He hadn't realised I was in the change rooms. I reacted on that occasion, but you can't do much about that sort of backstabbing. I think sometimes people just don't realise what their comments say about themselves.'

'I get along with nearly everyone at Manly and I've got a good rapport with most. A lot of guys who might be disrespectful of someone else who is gay, may not be with me, because they know me.

'It's like saying "Well, Ian might be gay, but *he's* all right." He's an exception to a rule. Which is a kind of warped sense of what I'm about. I'm not saying one type of homosexual is better. And this is what some people think. I think concepts of manliness and femininity are warped. There are strengths of character and weaknesses. Why is femininity such a dirty word anyway? All men have qualities you could call feminine. It's a pity a lot more guys aren't allowed to be in touch with that side of themselves. The world would be a better place. And I'm not talking about men doing womanly things. I'm talking about understanding, sensitivity, gentleness. Not being so emotionally stiff.'

Mike Gibson is just one who stumbled over his eulogising of Ian and into his homophobic subtext later in the year, when he wrote, 'By his courage, by his belief in himself and the manner in which he chooses to live, by the matter-of-fact dignity with which he has spoken out, Ian Roberts has done considerably more for his cause than those fairies who flap around Oxford Street in their lipstick and tights.' Despite good intentions, this was selective poofta bashing, a refusal to relinquish the old stereotypes. And Gibson had jumped on the 'reverse-discrimination' bandwagon when the Flinders Hotel and Mardi Gras tried to prevent gay people from being bashed at gay venues.

Focusing on gay people when they are in party mode, particularly around Mardi Gras time, and basing an image of gays on that is like taking a straight bloke in a party context—drunk for example, brown-eyeing passers by out of a bus window or maybe stripped naked, covered in shaving cream and chained to a pole after a bucks' party—and saying, 'look at that heterosexual!' Mardi Gras is gay people at their most celebratory. So instead of seeking vengeance for all the shit they have been through in their lives, instead of forming vengeful vigilante groups, they party a bit, and people complain! They ignore the fact that, like Ian, who is a football player, gays perform other functions in their lives and careers for the other 99 per cent of the time.

Fortunately, for every exponent of a conservative or reactionary right wing view, there is a Peter Fitzsimons, a Debbie Spillane, a Roy and HG, a Lisbeth Gorr (aka Elle McFeast), to name but a few. Fitzsimons, in an article entitled 'The "Mature" Country Still Looking For Pioneers', egged Ian on. 'Where are the open gays in Australian sport? ... It's absolutely no-one's business but their own of course, but it will be interesting to see when Australia's first gay sports pioneer turns up.' Spillane joined his call for a role model to move sport into a new era of enlightenment and true egalitarianism.

Selective poofta bashing is not solely the domain of ocker journalists. Often gays themselves run for cover to avoid association with the gay stereotype. Especially if they have football associations. And they assume Ian is their ally. 'One gay guy from a big football family—I won't say his name, his brother was a high profile Souths player who started at Souths—came up to me in Gilligan's, a gay bar, and starting going on to me about "feminine gays".

'"Doesn't it piss you off the way all these queens carry on, and wear their tight little lycra tops? It gets the rest of us gays a bad name. My dad's bad enough about it as it is, and then he sees all these poofs, and he just can't understand why I want to be like them. No wonder so many guys just keep away!" He just went on about it, and I said, "Look, mate, I'm the wrong person to talk to. I have a lot of friends of all types, and I respect a lot of qualities in lots of people. I don't judge people. Everyone is different, and everyone is human, and I'm sorry you have a problem with that."

'I don't know why he was picking me to mouth off to. I don't have those insecurities that make me want to say that some people are worth more than others. I mean, my boyfriends, the men I have loved, haven't always been what you'd call macho. But at least they are being true to who they are, they're man enough to be in touch with their feminine side!'

More and more, mere statistics on things like gay victimisation, low self-esteem and suicide, came to life for Ian, as lonely and desperate people called him for assistance and advice. 'I came to realise how lucky I was with my family. I might whinge or get impatient about my parents, but I have been able to front them and talk about things because the bottom line was, in the end, they loved me and wanted what was best for me, even if that was painful for them.' Ian started to get nervous calls and letters from people he had known over 26 years of football. 'Lots of people I've grown up with, or their relatives or friends, have contacted me. One kid, Sean Ryan, rang me one day. I had played football against his brothers at Mascot. He was the youngest of about three boys and four girls—Catholic family. He wanted some advice.

'He said, "I'm like you. I like guys." The kid was literally shaking through the phone.

'"What do you mean?"

'"You know, I'm like you. I have sex with guys. And I play football."

'The conversation went like that. I knew what he meant. I was just trying to get him to say it. "What, you mean you're gay?"

'"No, not gay! Like you. I play football."

'"Mate, you mean you're gay."

'"No! I play *football*! I'm like *you*!"

'"Mate, I don't think you understand. I'm gay. I'm as gay as they get. Gayer! They don't come any queerer than me. Women do nothing for me. Sexually, on a scale of one to ten, they're a zero."

'I shocked him. Then I had a talk with him. The poor kid was so fucked-up. One of his brothers had been really hassling him. He'd said some really nasty things. He had apparently just told his parents about himself. He was getting desperate. And this is how stuffed it all is, that brother I ran into recently—it was really late and he was in a drunken stupor at a gay hotel! When he saw me he muttered something about how he had stumbled across the hotel but doesn't know how he got there! Yeah, right! The thing was, he was closeted and was bullying this younger brother, trying to talk *him* into living life the same pathetically sad way *he* was!

'I don't know if I helped Sean at all. I saw him a couple of weeks later, near Taylor Square. I was at a cafe. When I yelled out to him, and he acted like he'd been sprung. He looked all guilty and embarrassed. It was pissing down with rain, and he only had a T-shirt on. It was like he had run out of the house on impulse. It turns out he had been to a gay sauna nearby.

'I said, "Oh, you've been to the sauna, have you? Mate, I don't care, it's cool, as long as you're enjoying yourself and you're safe!"

'We gave him a lift home and I said to him, "Any time you want to speak to me or you have a problem, give us a buzz. You shouldn't have to be running around ducking and hiding like you were terrified."

'He didn't have any friends of his own age who were gay, and he wasn't comfortable with gay bars. He was paranoid and didn't know you could actually make friends there. He only mixed with the football crowd and went to straight places. And saunas.

'I told him, "If you ever want me to speak to your parents I'll help you out, if they don't understand it." Because his mum and dad are lovely people. But the things his brother said . . . I'd wipe my family if they didn't accept me. I told him that.'

'Sean rang me the other day.

' "Should I get a girlfriend and try that?"

' "What are you speaking to me for? I'm not into that pretending shit. I've made those mistakes and I've moved on."

'He's just lonely. I think he just said that because he doesn't know how to have a normal conversation with a gay person. A lot of guys have no concept that gays talk about everything! He just needs to make some gay friends who are in his situation.

'We both knew one of the older guys from Mascot, who is a closet gay, and I said to him, "Mate, you don't want to end up like so and so, and be sixty and lonely, living a tormented life, with no-one!"

'There are so many guys like that. I get calls from guys like Sean all the time.'

For Ian, the occasional breakthrough made everything worth it. 'One of our trainers at Manly—his nickname is Jed—actually said to me, "I don't like fucking poofs. Most guys don't like poofs. But even I've started to change the way I think. What you've done is incredible, just amazing."

'People who hated you before, actually have a bit of respect for you. "Well, at least he's got balls" type of thing. Blokes have said that to me. "I never liked poofs but I have to admit you've got balls." I guess in a roundabout kind of way that's supposed to be some sort of compliment.'

Mario Fenech admires Ian's courage. 'I don't know if I would have had the courage to come out. You don't realise what the football fraternity is like. And it's an institution that we grew up in from a very young age. But times change. The wheel of life goes on. This will hopefully broaden their horizons. We're all born equal. I'm fortunate I was raised the way I was. I look after myself and while no-one interferes in what I do, I respect people whether they're black, green, whatever. What he carried for years would be like carrying a brick in your chest.'

The Kangaroo tour had knocked Ian's knee about a bit. He gave his all, as usual, and paid for it afterwards. He needed a rest when he returned to Australia after the tour, but played the first of the pre-season games, even though he views them as unnecessary risks before the season proper commences. In that game, in Auckland, against Canterbury, Ian got booted in his bad knee. He was almost right by the second premiership game against Souths.

By Round 5 against the Gold Coast at Brookvale, on 2 April, it had become apparent that Super League and the ARL were not going to be working out a compromise for revamping the game. The powers that be, who benefited from the status quo, obviously didn't like what they perceived as a threat to their business interests. Rather than talk about that, they threw around persuasive and emotive phrases like 'club loyalty' and 'obligation to the supporters', over the next several months, as part of their own PR exercise to obtain support. But behind all the rhetoric, on all sides, were simple business considerations. Super League were just more upfront about theirs and more willing to cut the players in on the bottom line.

'There were all these bits and pieces in the paper and on the news the night before the game about Murdoch signing up all the top players,' Ian remembers. 'At the ground, before the game, Boz was talking to all the players, individually, and saying to me that "If we do this right you'll be able to pick up an extra $100,000" and that if I'm going to end my career it would be a good way to go out. Even then it started going through my mind. "Hang on, there's got to be more to it that that." Because the quality of the players Murdoch had signed up made me realise that he had a pretty high percentage of the best players. There had to be more to it. Then Ken Arthurson spoke to us and said that if anyone signed with the new Super League they would never play for Australia again. And all the Manly guys would be looked after!

'I went into the ARL later that week. We were all to go in to sign something, and I was just waiting to see what it was first.' The ARL had held out a carrot in order to get players to sign a five-year loyalty agreement, but had backed up the offer with a threat. And there's nothing like a threat to get Ian Roberts' back up. 'I got in to the ARL and there were about a hundred blokes there and none of them knew what was going on. Which made me really suspicious. And no-one had time to talk about it. So I left. But I only left because I couldn't be bothered waiting. That afternoon, I just fronted up at the Super League offices on my own, because it just made good sense, to me, to hear both sides of the story. John Ribot came out and met me and took me into his office. Lachlan Murdoch was already in there. And I just listened while they told me their plans, and explained their vision for the game. I wasn't so young and naive. I knew football was a business. And you have to look after number one, because no-one else will. In ten years nobody is going to give a stuff what Ian Roberts is doing. You've got to make the most of it while they do.'

'When John Ribot was talking about what Super League wanted to do with the game, you didn't need to be Einstein to work out that it was because of Foxtel and cable TV. But what they were planning and the incentives they were offering! At the ARL you are just a commodity. Super League made you feel like an asset. You play this long, then finally the ARL offers you a golden handshake, $100,000 and "good on you". And you ask yourself, why are they getting this money *now*? Why wasn't the money about before? I remember being told at Manly that everything was put on a scale. Nobody could tell me what other players got but it was being worked out on a scale system. According to your worth and seniority, etc.

'You have to realise that, for me, this Super League thing was like the goose that laid the golden egg. I'm facing the last few years of my career, and along comes a chance to make some good money. It was a dream come true for someone who hadn't had a lot of luck financially. I would have been mad not to investigate the opportunity. Anyone would be!'

Ian had initially made comments on TV, maintaining his loyalty to the ARL, but he started to have second thoughts.

MANLY STAR RE-THINKS ARL DEAL
'I regret saying what I did ... I had not spoken to representatives of News Limited. I hadn't given the Super League concept much thought ... Sure the money is great, but what News Limited is plan-ning for the future is mind-boggling ... I won't be deciding my future today.

'I have never been worried about public perceptions of me. I do what I do because I weigh everything up carefully before making what I consider to be the right moves.' (Tim Prentice, *Telegraph Mirror*, 6/4/95)

This from the man who had spent nearly his whole professional life worrying about public perceptions! Ian was threatening to upset the proverbial apple-cart for the second time in his career. Manly was blue-ribbon ARL, too. Ken Arthurson, who ran Manly for years, was at the helm of the ARL, and Bob Fulton, who was a friend of the Packers, was totally committed to the status quo. Both knew which side of *their* bread was buttered.

'My dad was saying, "Go with the money, boy. Go with whoever is going to look after you in the future."

'Super League had a guarantee in their contract of employment after football, which was unheard of in the ARL. They would provide any training you chose, and you could be based where you chose. I told them I wanted to be based in Europe. Fine. The charity work I had always done on a voluntary basis, they were organising properly into a whole arm of the game. Basically any promotions work was to be paid for. For ten years I had been doing what was basically PR work for the ARL for nothing.'

Ian decided to sign with Super League and tried to appease the ARL and Manly. He went and saw Bozo Fulton, John Quayle and James Packer to tell them personally of his decision. An ARL source says he was practically the only player to sign with the new league, who had the courtesy to front up and explain what he was going to do and why, and I know that the blokes at the ARL really respected him for that. Bozo accepted Ian's decision gracefully. Then, on *The Footy Show* Super League guests John Ribot and Chris Johns from the Broncos were outnumbered on a guest panel, and given a bit of a hard time. Ray Hadley from radio station 2UE had hinted that Ian was being paid $1 million to move to Super League. Bozo suggested, on air, that he understood from Ian that it was $900,000.

At a press conference at Manly Beach, along with Manly Super League co-signee Matthew Ridge, and with Lachlan Murdoch sitting quietly in the background, a limping Ian was a bit concerned to be seen to be doing the right thing by everyone while feeling pissed-off that a private conversation should become the subject of a TV discussion.

'They are all friends of mine and I didn't want to leave thinking we couldn't remain friends. I know they believe in what they are doing and it is for the betterment of the game, but unfortunately we have a difference of opinion there.' (John Geddes, 11/4/95)

Big Ian Roberts—rated the toughest player in the game on field, and arguably the most sensitive off it—yesterday made a characteristically emotional entry to Super League ... A 110 kg front-rower posing nude in a gay magazine. Now this.

'I don't worry about what people think of me and I'd much prefer that no-one gets hurt, but with Super League it's all become a bit personal. I was really upset with "The Footy Show" that such serious

matters could, at times, be treated comically … Bob Fulton and I are good friends. But I am absolutely filthy my personal business was aired in public, and that I was used. What happens at the negotiating table should stay there.' (Steve Crawley, *Australian*, 11/4/95)

Matthew Ridge was more forthright. He said that when he was making up his mind who to sign with, 'At no stage did the Super League try to discredit the ARL, but I can't say the same for the other blokes. They [the ARL] have been making big, big bucks for a long time and the players haven't been getting a fair share of it. It just seemed a little bit on the nose when they were threatened they decided to look after the boys. But I bet you they wouldn't have done it if these guys [Super League] hadn't come along. I wish the other players had the opportunity to speak with them too because I think it would have cleared up a lot of misconceptions. It's not a matter of if it's going to happen, it's a matter of when. It will be global and we have the chance to become real stars.'

Ian signed on 10 April, and celebrated at breakfast with Lachlan Murdoch. But he was still contracted to Manly until the end of '97. On 7 April, Manly played Auckland. Ian shouldn't have played. His knee was giving him grief, but he didn't wanted the public to get the wrong idea. It was like the groin saga at Souths in '89 all over again. He made sure the press knew 'the reason I did [play] was because I didn't want people to think that because of the dramas leading up to that game, "he's not here, he's looking after his health".' So injured, he played and knocked himself out of contention for several weeks. Then the footy fan hate mail started up again, to add to his growing collection of homophobic hate mail.

'Over the years at Manly you can't help but get attached to some of the supporters, who are innocent when it comes to the business part of the game. They never get to see what's going on. They don't understand. Especially the kids. And it really hurts when they turn on you. They're like family.

'And I'm one of these blokes who'll sit there or stand there and sign everyone's stuff, and it's not that I'm always forcing myself to be polite to people, it's just the way I am.

'And in return, there are supporters, women like Joan Allen, Hazel and Helen, who don't care how successful the team is, as long as the players are well and doing well themselves. They appreciate it when you give them time in return.

'They would always send me cards and letters of encouragement. When I did the *Blue* spread they said how great it was, you know, "obviously there is more to you of stature than just a body", blah, blah, blah, and they would send birthday cards and Christmas cards, and I had never met this woman. When the papers quoted me saying that my opinion and the opinion of the ARL as to where the game should go was different, one of the supporters wrote to me. And she ripped right into me saying, "How could you say this and say that, and how dare you ..." I thought, well, "How shallow are you? Because someone has a different opinion, you wipe them."

'Anyway, one day a woman came up to me on the street and said, "Hi, I'm the one who writes to you all the time" and I was blank for a second. It didn't register, then I recalled all the nice birthday cards and things, and feeling warm and friendly I smile and go, "Yeeees! How *are* you. It's lovely to meet you!" Then she just launched! Swearing like crazy at me about my disloyalty. I didn't know what hit me. I had remembered about her angry letter by this time and I tried to calm her down. Eventually I explained my position to her, and my point of view and she was fine. She had been under a lot of misconceptions. She wrote to me to apologise, which was great.'

Theo was there. 'She went off. "HOW DARE YOU BETRAY RUGBY LEAGUE!?!" Security guards came over and everything!'

A series of features on Ian appeared in the mainstream press throughout '95. In *The Australian* newspaper Wanda Jamrozik credited him with having the strength and fortitude to lead a different lifestyle despite the pressure to conform. It was a congratulatory and pleasantly accurate article, and heartfelt. 'The culture of Rugby League does not encourage individualism. Yet Roberts is an individual,' she wrote, and then paid homage to the way Ian quietly copped abuse for his 'lifestyle', over the years, and to his 'choosing to let the jeers and insults wash over him, trusting to his incredible feats on the football field to stand as the best possible riposte'.

Ian would momentarily fire up if he felt someone betrayed his trust, though he found it hard to maintain his rage against people who committed white-collar deceit. They would only have to put their confusing verbal spin on things and in the end it looked like they were doing *him* the favour. In the melee that swam around him that year, Ian just said 'yes' to requests from a number of people who were politely persuasive, but without his best interests at heart.

Amidst the quagmire of requests, Ian was juggling his time amazingly, trying to fit everyone's charity in. There were AIDS fundraisers, kids fundraisers, Mardi Gras fundraisers, safe sex campaigns. Sometimes he committed to events or charities without knowing what they were for. Helping out became a full-time occupation for most of 1995. According to his sister Julie 'Ian's gullible because he wasn't born with a silver spoon in his mouth. He's always grateful when people did things for him. He feels like he's got to pay people back in some way. That's why he feels obliged to people.'

'I'm not comfortable speaking in public,' Ian confesses. 'It's a responsibility that I have been given sometimes, that I have to do. So I do it. When I do public speaking for gay causes or AIDS organisations, I don't like doing it, and I don't do it as well as I should. But people expect it of you, because of the situation you are in, and you have to help people out. If you can help, you should. I just have things thrust upon me now, expectations because, "Oh, he's out there."'

Ian attempted three comebacks for Manly in as many months—May, June and July. By the end of July his knee situation was tolerable. He could play well, though not without pain-killers, but he would make it through the season.

The problem with his knee was simple, the remedy complex. Neil Halpin explains, 'He had originally torn his posterior cruciate ligament, one of the stabilisers in the knee. He initially partly tore it, and then progressively he finished it off, so that by this time [in '95] he effectively was without a posterior ligament at all. It's a funny ligament. A lot of players tear them and have surprisingly little trouble. You can tear it and play for years without trouble. Ian wasn't one of those players, possibly because of his build, and height. He developed progressively more instability in his knee over many months. He also then started to wear down the back of his kneecap. Now, if you tear your posterior cruciate, one way that your body copes with it is to put more strain on your thigh muscles, and that's reflected in increased wear and tear at the back of the kneecap. That was his main problem. He wore that down to bone on bone, which was his current situation. Ian, of course, ignored the pain and played on pain-killers for two years, which didn't exactly help his cause. Bone on bone equals arthritis, and is extremely painful. He was heading to the stage where the pain was going to stop him from playing altogether. And his knee would be wrecked. We saw a few surgeons up here who weren't keen to touch it. The results of posterior cruciate surgery are variable, nothing near as good as the results of anterior cruciate surgery, and people are scared off it.'

After surgery there would be between three and six painful physio-filled months before the knee would regain any reasonable range of movement and running could be attempted. Neil had briefed Ian on these options and probabilities over the years since the knee became an issue. By 1995, living with pain *every* day, plus dealing with everyday life, if you can call it that, had started to take its toll. But for the '95 season, at least, the op had to be put on hold. Manly were premiership contenders, and there maybe weren't going to be chances as good as this again. With the uncertainty created by the Super League challenge, no-one knew where the game would be in '96.

Super League players were excluded from selection for the Origin series in 1995, and this raised a whole lot of ethical and legal questions.

Ian had his say:

'I want to say from the outset that I love the Manly club and would not want to leave the organisation under any circumstances. But by leaving Super League players out of the Origin series the league just wants to punish players for joining, even though they are not breaching their existing contracts.

'But if the players are not welcome to play rep football why

doesn't the League tell them they're also not needed to play for the clubs?

'*The League only wants us to bolster their competition now but if they really don't want us why not tell us to go now.*' (Peter Frilingos, *Telegraph Mirror*, 11/5/95)

This move by the ARL set in train legal action by players to ensure that Super League players weren't going to be ignored when it came to selection to play for Australia at the end of the year.

It also set in motion legal action by Super League, on Ian's behalf, to have him released from his contractual commitment to Manly for 1996 and '97. It was becoming uncomfortable for all concerned that he remained at Manly when he was becoming loyal to an organisation that, it was rumoured, would amalgamate Manly with Norths into a Super club, if they had their way. Ian began to get more resentful of his contract too. It was signed at a time of salary cap restrictions and bound him for two more years while other players went straight on to their new deals with the ARL or Super League, in what was now a free market.

When Ian signed his Manly contract, it was on the understanding that he would represent his state and country if he was good enough, and therefore earn additional income. If he was denied that income, surely, he thought, it was a breach of contract and a restraint of trade. So when he had said he wouldn't leave Manly for anything, he was talking impulsively. It was his old damage-control mechanism coming into play.

He made his third comeback attempt, when his knee had stabilised, against Cronulla on 28 July. Manly lost 10–17. This was Ian's only loss for the season, out of twelve premiership round games he played. He was relieved to be back to see the season out. Come what may.

On the field he was secure. It gave his life off the field substance and strength, and made him happier. He needed it this year of all years, and the fear of a repeat of '89 terrified him.

'In 1995, I heard him talk the most I've ever heard him, on the field,' says Terry. 'He was especially fired up, wanting to win. He always wanted to win, but especially in games this year, and we worked really hard.

'And when Ian talks, he inspires people. Like when David Gillespie talks. People listen. They don't say much but when they do say something, everyone listens. You hear it. And he gets fired up and you get fired up, and it's great.

'It was always constructive. All encouragement.'

Ian was already well known for the re-assuring pats on the back he gave teammates after they had made a tackle and were still down. They were small gestures that said and meant a lot, and energised a camaraderie needed for the crusade to the final. Nothing off field affected Ian's focus on.

Terry continues, 'He'd be "Come on, let's do it!", "Let's give it to these bastards!" Everyone says about Ian, "Ian's a tough bastard because he tackles so hard" or "Ian's a tough bastard because he works so hard", but I'll tell you right now, when you're under pressure, the biggest thing in his game which proves how tough he really is and how inspiring he is, is when you look round and Ian Roberts is *always* there ready to take the ball off you!

'He's *always* the first in line saying, "Give me the fucking ball!"

'I know further on down the field he'll get one or two guys a little bit wide and he'll hit them, he'll turn round, get the ball in the air, and flick it back and all that, but if you're ever looking for someone to take the ball up inside your own 22, he's always the first putting his hand up for the ball and taking it to them. And that's the thing a spectator wouldn't notice. But that is the most important thing because you've got to get out of there! Everything is like a couple of tackles and they'll get it out and kick it in. Mate! It's *real tough* work! It's the hardest thing to work the ball out from your own goal.'

Ian's revels in the battle, despite always being heavily marked.

Terry reckons, 'If you've got a nineteen-year-old forward on the field, he wouldn't attract players. But he's Ian Roberts. He attracts players. It doesn't matter who you are, you would want to mark Ian Roberts because he's a danger. I mean, he gets targeted. They'll even put players out there just to bash him. Now that's wrong. But it happens. It's just the way it is. That's been footy for years. And because he's marked he's often involved in plays as a decoy which he hates because he wants to be involved in the action all the time.'

In July, Shane and Ian organised a thirtieth birthday party for Ian at the Beresford Hotel in Bourke Street. It was an eclectic mix of people from all aspects of Ian's life. There were footballers, drag queens, gays, straights, as well as Ray and Jean looking a little bewildered in the middle of it. The place was packed. Jean was impressed by the crowd's behaviour. 'I couldn't believe that so many people could be in one hotel and everyone was polite and nice to each other. There were no fights!' Ian was sharing his real life with all his family for the first time. 'My brother and I never spoke about my sexuality until my thirtieth birthday party. We were always close-but-not-close. We would always show affection and that. He said to me, "I don't give a fuck what you do. I love you, will always love you." This comes from Mum in a way. She has always been so protective of her family, and possessive, and we were always shown that if you are a family, you are expected to be there for each other, no matter what.'

After the 28 July loss, Manly marched right through to the finals with a series of high-scoring wins. The first semi was a tough game against Cronulla on 3 September. Ian was instrumental in Manly getting up in the second half to eventually take out the game 24–20.

Ian determined to make '95 the crowning glory of his football achievement. After a season of good football, a grand final win for Manly could be topped off by representing Australia in the centenary World Cup in England. But after the exclusion of Super League players from Origin, a court decision was pending on whether it was legal to exempt players from other rep games. Any decision would leave matters a bit grey. The ARL could always say they considered everyone, and then make a selection that was just ARL players, and it would be difficult to prove a case against them.

Ian appeared at court just the week before Manly's first semi, to help plead the case for Super League players.

'I was badgered for 15 minutes about Steve Menzies and Geoff [Toovey]. He [the ARL barrister] was just trying to put me in an awkward position. I said, with the injuries he has had, Geoff wouldn't be in my [Test] side [if I was a selector]. As soon as I got to training I explained to Geoff what I'd said.' (RLW, 8/9/95)

After the semi final win against Cronulla, Ian told Darren Hadland from *Rugby League Week* that he had received feelers from England. Would he like to play for them in the World Cup? Testing the waters, as it were, he said, 'I told them I wouldn't even consider it until this court thing is resolved. But the World Cup is something that I want to play in desperately. You really want to be part of it.' England wanted everyone to be a part of it. The ARL only wanted some to. Ken Arthurson snapped back. 'He's not eligible to play for England; he can't change countries . . . There have been exceptions in some countries in the World Cup, but that is to help development of the sport.' A World Cup spokesperson disagreed saying that the rules allowed someone to play for the country of their birth.

A win against Newcastle at the Stadium on September 17, and Ian and Manly were on their way to the grand final! After exactly a decade of professional football, Ian now had a real chance to achieve the one thing that had eluded him. He wept tears of joy. 'When fulltime came and I realised what we'd done, I couldn't hold back the tears . . . I'm still coming to terms with it all.'

FIFTEEN

MAINTAINING THE RAGE

Ian played in his first grand final on 24 September. Much of the game resembled the dogged and persistent stalemate of trench warfare. The forwards were locked in combat and exhaustive inches were relinquished and gained. Ian worked. He threw his whole being in to the fray again and again and again. But Manly looked cautious for much of the game. There were nervous costly errors and few breaks, most of which went Canterbury's way.

The anti-climax of the loss against the Bulldogs, 4–17, was unbearable.

'I would never have thought that a game could affect me the way that it did. I still haven't been able to watch a video of it. Most of it is like a dream. A few highlights, but most of it a blur. Screaming inside my head when I came off a few minutes before the end was, "It's over! You've lost!" It became personal again. "You've lost your last chance to win. You've blown it!" Then you start thinking about all the disappointments in the past. They all flood back and catch up with you again.'

Back at Manly, Ian's devastation was exacerbated by his new-found ostracism within his own club. There was to be no commiseration. 'The World Cup side was announced when we were back at Manly. There were seven or eight Manly blokes in a second-string side. And everyone started carrying on about how fucking great it was to be in the World Cup, because so many guys from Manly got in, and

I was stunned. "We just lost the grand final and you guys are running round celebrating the World Cup as though the grand final didn't really matter! As if it was a means to an end to get to the World Cup." I thought, "Fuck you guys!" This was *my* one chance! A grand final. Anyone who's good enough will eventually get selection for Australia, but not everyone gets to be in a premiership team.'

In the end, Ian and fellow Super League outcast Matthew Ridge, along with Lachlan Murdoch and some other friends, went out and got obliterated. Shane spent a lot of the night holding Ian up. 'I hadn't seen him that upset before. He was just in tears, continually. He couldn't hold his head up. I mean Matthew was upset, but he was all right. Ian felt so hard done by, I think, because he played all year with an injury he should have had fixed ages ago.' Manly had to switch focus quickly after the game. A Super League team had beaten them in the grand final. It was a demoralising defeat. The ARL had lost a court case which would enable them to favour ARL players in their selection of the World Cup side. They chose, arguably, to ignore that ruling. If they were bad sports in selection, they were hardly going to be any different in their attitude to the final. Ian knew World Cup selection was out of the question, really. 'But I asked Frank Stanton if anyone had gone in to bat for me on the selection panel. I still considered myself one of the two best front-rowers, after Glen Lazarus. I still think I should have made the Australian side. I said, "I know this is an ARL club but I'm playing for you guys." I honestly believed I was performing well. I was happy with how I'd been playing. And he said, "You knew what the policy was." It was just a joke to them.'

Ian grieved for weeks and went on an extended bender. Terry was dragged into it. 'Ian said to me, "Will you come to the Sleaze ball?" And I said, "Yes, I'll come." Of course, a couple of mates, I think Jim Dymock and a couple of others, went back to my mother and said, "Did you know Terry's gay?" She said, "Why?", "Oh, because he was with Ian Roberts at a party." She rang me up. "A couple of people told me you were gay." I just told my mum, "Well, what's the drama? Anyway, I'm not gay, don't worry about that. I was out with Ian. Don't you give a fuck what they say." '

*

The guy leant out of the white van as it slowly passed Ian and Shane while they stood on the traffic island in the middle of Oxford Street. It was the afternoon of the Sleaze Ball dance party. Mucus was sliding down Shane's face for seconds before he realised that the guy had spat at them. Then he told Ian and pointed out the van.

'Come on, we'll chase him,' Ian said. The Gay Avenger!

He ran across to his car, jumped in and was off after the culprits. They lost the van, then found it again stuck in traffic in Woolloomooloo. Ian dived out of his car and stuck his head in the van driver's window.

'If you think you're going to spit, mate, well spit now!'

The driver put his fist into Ian's face.

'That's the worst thing you could've done, mate,' Ian snarled and dragged the guy from his van.

A passenger came around the back and king-hit Ian on the back of his head. That had little effect so then he tried to hold him. (What is it they say about a footballer's head?) There was blood everywhere. A terrified Shane jumped out of the car and tried to stop Ian. 'I'd never seen Ian fight till then. He just went berserk! I was trying to get him to stop, but he wouldn't.' Next thing, Shane was running around the car trying to get away from the passenger, who had decided to have a go at him. 'Ian was fighting the other guy still and yelling, "You fucking touch him and I'll kill you."'

And Shane was screaming, 'Don't you hit me, you bastard. Touch me, and he'll kill you, he'll kill you! Ian! Ian!'

It was Laurel and Hardy. No, Schwarzenegger and Pee-Wee Herman. At one stage it calmed down. Then one of the guys came up behind Ian and kinged him again, not convinced that a person could withstand two such hits. 'It was on again, then,' Shane continues. 'Then someone came over and said he had seen the whole thing if Ian needed a witness. By this stage traffic was banked up for miles. People were just sitting in their cars, mostly just watching. Some were driving around us. When it finished the van drove off. The guys were a mess. Ian wasn't going to press charges because he wouldn't want something like that in the papers.'

Ian had agreed to appear on stage during a show at the party that night and was on his way to rehearsals when the chase began. 'So off we went to rehearsals, Ian with a front tooth nearly hanging out, a split lip, and covered in blood. We got there and they were like, "What happened to *you*?", and he just told them he'd had a fall! Then he used his shirt to clean himself a bit and went through what he had to do.'

He was cheered by thousands of revellers when he appeared onstage that night, riding a motorcycle, before awkwardly lifting a drag queen into the air. Another obligation fulfilled.

He enjoyed recounting and embellishing that day's events for days after, unable to contain his laughter at the part where a terrified Shane was running round and round the car.

Meanwhile, across Sydney, gays who had been to the Sleaze Ball were holding post-mortems. Some thought Ian had looked stiff and ridiculous on stage. 'He'll do anything for attention.' 'Probably got paid a bundle.' 'You'd want to to look that stupid. *I* was embarrassed!'

The events that day confirmed Ian as an easily recognisable target. Now he represented homosexuality as a cause. He was standing tall and proud, and that angered some people. He was sent lovingly and painstakingly graffitied photographs of himself with knives drawn through his body and explicit descriptions of the fate that awaited him if he proceeded further on his pro-gay crusade. He would open hate mail, look at it, and throw it away. 'Fuckwits.' He focused on the thankyous.

He battled most of the clichéd and institutionalised prejudice against homosexuality. But for every time he stood his ground against a detractor, there were countless times he has walked away. Friends like Theo recall that many a pleasant day or evening was ruined by an incident. 'One beautiful balmy night, a month or two after *Blue* came out, Ian and I were just wandering back along Flinders Street to Taylor Square, to go home. We were laughing and relaxed, in that lovely mood, you know, when this guy came out of the Courthouse Hotel and starts yelling, "TAKE IT OFF! Take your clothes off now, you FUCKEN FAGGOT! Are you going to take them off now?" The guy was right in Ian's face, and he went on with some pretty nasty stuff. The usual. But he was out for a fight, this guy. A lot of guys are like that. They see Ian as a challenge now. Let's see how tough this faggot really is. And the guy wasn't alone of course. He had his mates backing him up, egging him on. There were three of four of them and I thought, "Oh no, we're going to get bashed." And it's not worth it. For what? And Ian was just staying cool this night. I was saying, "Forget it, Ian. Just leave it. Believe me, it's not even worth thinking about! Come on." It seemed the most reasonable thing to do. You could see he was getting tense. He just kept looking at them, turning back and looking.'

Ian recalls, 'The guy was blind drunk. I could've ripped his throat out. I wanted to. He was going "Yes, you fucking faggot, have a go NOW!" I couldn't be bothered ... But it ruined our night.'

'Ian would get so wound up,' says Theo. 'He'd always be going "The next person that does that ..."'

At the same time Ian came in contact with so many good and fair-minded people, the anger from the aggressive minority baffled him. That night at Taylor Square, the aggressive guy was dark-skinned. 'Why the hell is one persecuted minority picking on another, for fuck sake! I mean, that's lovely, isn't it.' But there's nothing like a good poofta bash when you're out of luck, or you're frustrated, broke, the world is out to get you.

Society provides the ammo, and the target, for the disgruntled and the fearful. These bigots don't form their attitudes independently. They get them from one sort of condoned authority or another.

One day, Ian was sitting alone at an outdoor cafe when a group of men with their girlfriends arrived. The cafe was busy, and one of the guys recognised Ian, walked up to him and demanded his chair. Ian was taken aback at first and kind of looked at the guy as if to say, what? 'We want your chair, mate. Get up!' The group hovering in the background found the situation amusing. Ian said, 'Mate, I'm *sitting* on it! Are you for real?' The guy said, 'We want to sit down!'

The guy felt safe in the pack, which didn't perturb Ian. 'Are you actually going to have a go at me because you want my chair ... you slimy piece of wog shit!' The guy exploded then, kicking Ian's table over, sending, coffee, sugar crystals and china everywhere. Ian stood up and eyeballed the guy. 'Oh good. Aren't you good! What can you do now? Can you kick me over too!? You lay a hand on me and I'll be down your throat before you know it!' The cafe owner was on the phone to the police and waiters were requesting the group leave, while Ian braced himself for the inevitable. But the group decided to move out and coaxed their mate away.

Ian developed a series of catch phrases for different situations. Quick retorts. He used to laugh when he'd repeat what he had said in sticky situations. 'I said to him, "Mate, you know me. I'll never know who *you* are . . ."' He was more impressed with the quality of his retort than what everyone else saw as the danger of the situation. Friends laughed at his laughter, but nervously, wondering if they'd be calm enough in similar situations to even *think* of witty or cutting things to say.

Because of a generous nature, a feeling of responsibility to people, and his public profile, Ian has inadvertantly become political. He was exposed to people and situations which required skills not developed in a world of football. He was required to impart information. To be responsible. 'You have a responsibility to the community, not a gay community, *the* community. Your main worries might be yourself and your family, but you have a wider responsibility because you are part of it. Whether you want to believe it or not. People always want to say, "Well, it doesn't affect me. I don't want anything to do with it." But it does affect you. You are part of it and you can help. And I say that knowing what I know now, and I say it to the people who should know better than me, intelligent and important people everywhere, gay and straight. Too many people are hung up on success. They forget to be a good person along the way. A good person *is* a successful person.'

He doesn't just mouth these words like snappy catch-phrases or sound bites. Ian's capacity for compassion never ceased to amaze Shane. 'With all that was going on in his own life, being with him all the time, the things he does amaze me. Just for an example, we were walking down Oxford Street one night. There was a guy who was on heroin, obviously, he was so off his face, and he recognised Ian and started calling out to him, "Oh, Ian Roberts", blah, blah, blah. He was working The Wall [as a prostitute], and Ian got really upset about it and tried to help him. We would see him quite a bit, and Ian would always be giving him advice, and saying to the guy that he'd like to help him, you know, like "Would you be interested in helping yourself, mate?" and the guy would say, "I've tried, but I can't." Ian wanted him to go into rehab. But in the end, there wasn't a lot he could do without the guy wanting to help himself. Ian would be affected when he saw what people had done with their lives, and being so young, going the wrong way, and it's like their life is wasted.'

One of the kids Ian used to visit in hospital years before, Darren, came to stay with Ian and Shane a few months later. They gave him keys and a room in the apartment, so he felt he had a stable home, and on condition that he attended school. Darren had first come to Ian's attention when Ian noticed that no-one from Darren's family was ever at the ward. 'I think over a period of months, his mother visited once or twice that I saw.' Darren was pretty much a street kid. He had little respect for authority and was always in trouble. Over the years, Ian was the only adult he had any respect for. Through Ian consistently being there to help him out of trouble, Darren has turned out to be a good kid, if somewhat too streetwise for his years.

'How can you promote *that* lifestyle?' was the question at the core of the abuse Ian encountered. 'People of a different lifestyle' had been the unfortunate wording chosen as a loose code for 'people of a different sexuality' in the *Blue* article that appeared in February. It was a bad choice. People can freely swap and change a lifestyle—like moving house, or redecorating—so it was too flippant when compared to how Ian felt about his sexual identity. The politeness of his reply to people when they asked questions like that, usually depended on the manner in which the enquiry was made, but the message is straightforward.

'I'm not promoting any lifestyle. I am promoting my right to live my life both as a good person *and* as I choose, as long as I do no harm to anyone by it. There is not just one correct way, one right way to live. Don't tell me it's healthy or better to live a lie. I've seen how it affects people, and all the people around them. I am not recruiting people into this "disgusting" lifestyle. If other people decide to live honestly as well, because of my example, good.'

One day, a comely and quiet-looking middle-aged woman left the group of friends at Circular Quay, where Ian was waiting to catch a water taxi. He heard one of them say, 'There's that footballer' and when he looked up to nod g'day, he saw her approach him. He tensed just slightly for the encounter. And then she was at him. 'You!' she exploded. 'Because of YOU, my son is GAY! NOW he doesn't mind admitting it to his FRIENDS!' She was becoming hysterical and increasingly loud! 'Love, it wasn't me that made your son gay,' Ian offered. He glimpsed at her friends just to see how many he would have to fend off. They seemed as shocked as he was, fidgeting and shuffling. 'What I really wanted to say was fuck off,' he thinks. 'I mean, you'd think as a mother you'd be happy now that your son feels free enough to tell you who he is.' So, he says, 'It's not my fault. I'm sorry if it upsets you. I'm happy for your son.' Her friends had rallied from their shock and sent assistance. For Ian. 'Come on, Sally. Just forget it. Come over here.' 'Because YOU came out', she spat. And Ian was left. Alone and very embarrassed. How often he felt very alone in those particular moments.

GOSSIP
Three weeks is a long time in football ... Ian Roberts said the world would have to wait for his autobiography for revelations about his personal life. Suddenly in a magazine called 'New Weekly', Roberts tells a love story that puts 'My Beautiful Laundrette' in the shade ...

'From the beginning I always knew it was special with Shane. From the outset I was very very keen. Still am. The way I feel I wouldn't swap Shane for anyone.'

What surprises could possibly be left for Ian's autobiography? (SMH)

If *The Advocate* article was Ian's accidental official outing, *The New Weekly* ran his accidental official Australian one. Nick Karandonis had approached Ian a few months earlier and offered to represent him. He had encouraged Ian to do some promotions for a clothing label (naked) against the advice of some friends. Then *New Weekly* appeared offering not unattractive quick money—$20,000, less Nick's commission. Never mind that it was supermarket journalism, definitely downmarket, lower than Lowe's and taking Ian beyond the reach of a quality advertising market. Ian was told that if he didn't cooperate with the magazine they were running with a story anyway. Better to take the money and at least have a say in the story. He understood he had final approval on the story. However, it appeared the contract enabled Nick to approve it, and the article hit the stands after Ian had left for a holiday in England. 'A Man and His Match' was about Shane and Ian's relationship. Shane was quoted extensively and both were explicit about their feelings for each other. 'I expect to be with Ian forever. I truly love him ... He walked up and gave me a kiss in front of everyone, full-on,' Shane was quoted as saying.

Most of Ian's friends thought the article was tacky. There were pros and cons. So what if the intimate talk about two men in love offended? People needed to be desensitised so this sort of thing didn't remain shocking. A similar exposé of straight lovers would hardly warrant comment.

After the article appeared, Ray says, 'We found out who our friends were!'

They worried, not just about Ian's safety, but for the grandchildren at school. 'The oldest is seven,' says Ray. 'She's no idiot. I suppose there'd be a few repercussions at school.'

'They don't understand what all the fuss is about Ian', adds Jean. To them, it's just Ian.'

Jean had seen enough of people's vileness first hand. 'I had a go at Ian and Shane about the article. "You keep your personal life personal, your private life private. We don't go round telling everyone what we do in the bedroom, so you shouldn't either!" It's just personal isn't it?' Bedroom details hadn't been revealed, of course. Just a public kiss.

Ray and Jean had weathered personal and public storms since Ian's revelation of his sexuality that night two years before.

But Ray concedes 'It's definitely been easier for us since he told us. One of Ian's main concerns was to protect his family, and in doing that, in the end, it wasn't good for him.'

Jean agrees 'Knowing diffuses the whole thing. It takes away people's thinking they've got something over you. "Yeah, so what!" you can say now.' Ray nods. "Tell us something we don't know!"

Jean says 'It's a pity young kids growing up don't know that if they let it out in the open, it's better … I wouldn't like Ian to be cuddling and kissing his boyfriend when the grandchildren are here. But they wouldn't do it. There's too many questions the grandchildren would ask. I know eventually they would ask, but … Ian's done a lot for me, when he played for Australia. For me, all those people that said those nasty things. I could think, "So what? Look what I've done. What have you done?" Then I could be proud. He'd made it, as far as I was concerned, when he'd played for Australia. He'd reached the top!'

Ian found himself closer to his siblings during the year. Paul, who he had fought with so much as a child, touched Ian's heart on his birthday. Julie, who had what she already knew confirmed by the *New Weekly* article, was happy for her brother. 'Every now and again a person has to say, "I'm number one." I got out of home at nineteen. I was doing what I wanted to do. It's taken Ian till 29 to be able to say he's doing what he wants to do, and he's happy about it.'

In 1995 Ian talked more about his sexuality than ever before. To everyone. He was sold, now, on the therapeutic value of talk. It broke down differences between people, and the chasm that silence can create. 'To just be able to say to your mother and father, "Oh, I'm pissed off" or "I'm upset today, because I had a fight with my boyfriend about such and such" makes such a difference. They can relate to what you are feeling, and you are not hiding anything from them.'

He was elated by the relief it had brought him. It was palpable. 'I just took it for granted my brother and sisters knew. Well, they did, but no-one spoke about it because they were too embarrassed to. For me, or whatever. That's what I've come to realise. You need to speak. If you can't talk about things, can't be yourself with your family, then it's not a family. And that's why gay people have to develop all these other close friends, who become a kind of family. The thing is, every-one knows at least one gay person in their lives. But they don't know it. It could be their child, their brother or sister. How can we change people's attitudes if we don't show them that a gay person is *anyone*? And how can we begin to get loved for who we are if we can't get it from our family? I know I've been lucky, with my family, who have been supportive.'

Ian was at the McDonald House Christmas party a couple of months after the *New Weekly* article appeared. Penny Douglas encountered parents who baulked at Ian's presence. ' "Isn't that Ian Roberts, the guy who just, you know?" I said, "Yeah, so what? He's still Ian Roberts the fantastic person the kids love." And they went "Oh, yeah. Yeah. But ..." "Look, he's still the same person. In your children's eyes he's still a hero. Nothing's changed." Most of the kids couldn't care less. But the problem is many parents still think everyone starts out the same in life and then get to a certain stage where they think, "Oh, I'm going to be gay now!" My own children I consider to have brought up very broadminded. They have been exposed to a whole realm of differences, and acceptance of those. But they were still, when the article came out, "Oh no. Oh, isn't that sad." And I said, "What is sad about him being gay, and finally being able to feel comfortable enough to say, look, I actually care about Shane a lot, that this is a relationship that means a lot to me?" It took a long time for them to realise, and I thought about it, and it's just that they are so pounded at school, and they're in that sort of society of an all-boys school, and they are pounded by this "gotta get out there and get 'em" kind of macho stuff. There are a couple of boys in their year, they are fifteen and sixteen, who I think are probably gay, and I'm sure they're having a very very difficult time at school. They are a bit more noticeable because of their natures, and I think the kids sort of get confronted by them, because that's not how you are supposed to be. And that in turn makes the less noticeable gay children retreat into themselves because they see how these boys are ostracised.

'It comes from parents, too. At one of my sons' football matches Ian was watching the game. One of the kids saw him during the game, and after that the kids just wanted to meet Ian Roberts. They lost interest in whether their team was going to win or not. That ceased to be important. And after the game, a couple of the parents were saying, you know, "That's Ian Roberts over there. I don't think it's a good idea if the kids go over there, do you?" They were really quite worried about it, you know!

'I have had two close friends over the past couple of years who have been married, one for fifteen and one for twenty years; it's taken them that long to be able to turn around and sort of say, "Look, I can't do this anymore." And they are both living in gay relationships now. But what they went through in realising that their lives were just facades, and in trying to do something about it at this stage, was just so traumatic. It took them such a long time to come to terms with how they really felt, because they were so rigidly locked in this idea that they were masculine men, and weren't supposed to be gay.

'It's been interesting for me. I'd been to a few Manly games since the *Blue* article, and what astounds me is sitting in the stands and hearing people around me saying, "Oh, you bloody poofter Roberts. We're gunna get you." And yet six months before, I mean supporters would say something about him, but they didn't say *that*, and I wonder what is it that's changed. He's still the same footballer but their attitude has changed. For Ian personally, I think now that he has come out, it frees him and it clarifies his position, and people can take him as they want. I think some people are finding it difficult still to accept that he *is* homosexual. But I can't see why he is a threat to anyone, unless people are responding to their own fears about their own lives.'

'It's funny, you know,' Terry Hill muses. 'I've seen players and blokes who've got girlfriends, and they'd be pissed or on ecstasy, and all of a sudden they'd be kissing blokes! Then the next day, you say, "You were at so and so", and they say, "No, I wasn't!" When they're off their faces, they forget, and they start expressing themselves. Then they're like "No, mate, no way, mate!" Their type is the first to point the finger, to bring gays down. They'll see a priest or something accused of molesting a kid and they go "Fucking poofter!" I just think, "What a sick *guy*." 'But they're so caught out, so they point the finger anywhere.'

George Piggins concurs. 'I respect the strength in Ian being able to come out and say, "This is what I am", more than that bloke who hides it and gets married and has kids. I think to myself, "Why weren't you strong enough to come out, instead of hurting yourself and other people?"'

Peter Fitzsimons applauded the message, and ignored the igno-minious messenger, when it came to Ian's *New Weekly* revelations. His pioneer had surfaced. In 'Roberts Does Hard Yards With Gay Abandon', he encapsulated the hope of all homosexuals and many het-erosexuals, for a better Australia, when he looked forward to a time when a person's homosexuality won't matter. When an outing doesn't get any reaction except 'so what?'

Roberts is not the first gay footballer, but he is the first with the courage to live it openly, and to hell with what anyone thinks. Against this will be the likely reaction of the Bible belt with the usual hand-wringing, wailing into the wind, and so forth. Spare us, please ... the reptiles of redneck radio will no doubt be equally straining to heap scorn on Roberts on the usual principle that if it doesn't fit into 1950s Australia—the way the country was before the last four decades of social progress—then it's a God-awful thing and should be done away with ... Surely the wretched schoolyard taunt of 'yer a poofta!' has lost an awful lot of sting already ... things have changed. (SMH, 10/10/95)

'The reptiles of redneck radio' and some of their illuminating phone-in listeners vomited generalisations, ignorance and misinformation across the airwaves, whenever the subject of Ian came up. The tabloids in London, meanwhile, were littered with front-page stories like 'Stone the crows, mate! One of the roughest toughest Aussies ever to rip the Poms apart has admitted he's a poofter' and 'Bugger Me, What Have We Queer'!

The gays on the street were divided in their reaction to the exposé. Some were concerned this would negate the work he had done in getting people on side. Others feared he would be over-exposed. People would be sick of him grandstanding, and the tide of his popularity would turn. Maybe the pack would turn on him, because he was a little too proud and public now. While Ian has the attitude that even-tually he'll be forgotten, like old news, a lot of gays, not surprisingly, have a siege mentality. History has seen enough cycles of persecution and liberalism. In Christian societies, hundreds of thousands have been put to death because of their sexuality, and more recently than Hitler's little round-up 50 years ago. Fear, and a feeling of isolation, colour the attitudes of many gay men, who don't dare to hope, or get too excited about advances in attitudes towards sexuality. Some of the more fearful and self-defensive and so-called Christians can always be relied upon to find a weapon of containment.

Gays don't form a homogeneous and united front against victimisation, either. They are dispersed throughout the whole community, pursuing a wide range of lifestyles. A shared sexuality doesn't equal allegiance, despite generalised talk of the 'gay community'. Gays have to struggle to maintain any organised grouping. Mardi Gras itself is miraculous for its momentary bringing together of scores of gay organisations and clubs. To assume gays form a loving and united community based on their shared sexual identity, is like starting a sentence with 'All heterosexual men are ... ' as in 'All heterosexual men swill beer and watch footy on tv'.

For gays, the persecution *is* the main bond, and most gays avoid that by minding their own business while they live in the mainstream community at large, as car salesmen, coin collectors, professors, soldiers, doctors, lawyers, you name it. Only a small percentage of gays, who are out, are actively pursuing the cause, battling the ongoing attempt to marginalise them, and living in a state of constant anxiety. And now AIDS and other concerns have led to far greater privation and sorrow than the average human encounters. Even sex has become a matter of life and death. Few want to *invite* persecution, and most gays just want to be able to live freely in *the* community, not just a gay community. The irony is that gays want to be an equal part of mainstream society, yet mainstream society seeks to force them into separateness and isolation as punishment for what is seen as nonconformity. So when gays want to be conformist, recognised as families, rear children, get married, there is outrage from some sectors. The media marginalise gays in their reporting: 'A gay community spokesman ...' 'The gay community is today ...' 'Leaders from the gay community expressed concern ...' 'Ian Roberts drew the applause of the gay community ...'

The only real community where gays can be truly happy is the wider one. That's where they exist. Ian laughs at many of the misconceptions. 'This fascination that I could succeed in football and then run back to take part in the gay community really intrigued people. I was seen as this Jekyll and Hyde thing . . . Hilarious.'

Ian's situation certainly didn't win unanimous support from politically active gays. He had blended in for years as a footballer and lied publicly about his sexuality. Yet he lived largely honestly according to his sexuality. There were some who weren't sure whether he should be embraced or chided, some who were suspicious that he came out when he did because it was safe and convenient and lucrative for him. And a number of gay men and women approached him to let him know they didn't think he was anything special. They were in the minority, but they represented a bitterness and resentment that this dumb football player was being treated like something special.

At a bar one day, after the knee operation, he asked to borrow a vacant stool near a group of gay guys. 'You're a big strong footballer,' one said. 'I'm sure you can stand, can't you?' There are gay people who will try to pick a fight in front of their boyfriend to prove Ian Roberts isn't such a hero. And there were gays who weren't as keen to know Ian because he was *too* out for them to be seen with. Theo recalls, 'There were guys who prided themselves on being butch men, who loved Ian once, were his best friend when they saw him, who basically didn't want anything to do with him when he came out. Because people knew Ian was gay now, they knew they would be identified as gay by being seen with him. That worried some. Everywhere you'd go somewhere with Ian there was always someone with something nasty to say. Ian feels a bit better if he is able to tell them off. He forgets about it, then. But it's not just straight people.'

A lot of high-profile gay men have copped flak for being simply that. Gay and high profile. All successful people have detractors, but for gay people who've had ugly experiences in the wide world, a ghetto mentality sharpens insecurities into cynicism, and suspicion of anyone who looks like they're making out with the 'enemy'.

Ian was frustrated and bewildered by such attitudes, and he had no power of reply when it came to caustic remarks made in the gay press. There seemed to be none of the parameters of fair play which he found in the manstream press, where journalists over the years grew to know and respect him, and feel protective of him.

It wasn't necessarily personal. Cynicism breeds scathing satire and some gay writers simply can't help themselves. Steve McLeod practically accused Ian of throwing away the first try in the '95 Grand Final, and then appearing at Gilligan's [a gay bar] that night with, 'the inestimably better looking Matthew Ridge ... Roberts, and number one fan Mike boyo Gibson may well resent the prissy side of gay life ... The growing iconisation of Roberts as a *Good Weekend* Greek god too big to ever get bashed up and too much of a footballer to ever get frocked up ... This game would make me a man? Fuck off. It's only made Roberts money. By the way, there are strong rumours that a Balmain league legend has recently left his wife, children and former lifestyle.' The *Star Observer* was never particularly kind to him, Ian felt.

McLeod was peeved about that phrase 'different lifestyle' which encouraged people like Gibson to differentiate between 'types' of gays, and which implied choice. A lot of people laboured under the misapprehension that their sons were being lured by a degenerate 'lifestyle'. McLeod's rage was a bit misdirected, which was seemingly not lost on readers, who swamped the paper with letters of support for Ian.

It is a depressing aspect of gay life how few gay men and lesbians in the public eye are willing to come out. Given Steve McLeod's bitchy whingeing treatment of Ian Roberts, I now understand why those closet doors stay shut ... Ian Roberts has been out in Oxford Street for a long time and never made any secret of his sexuality. This makes him unique as far as I can tell among top line professional sportsmen. He deserves respect and support for the stand he has taken. He should not have to put up with carping, which reads like it is driven by more than a hint of jealousy. (Robert Niemann, Paddington)

Once again, we are not impressed with an article in your paper about Ian Roberts. Why do we embrace gays in the arts, but not a gay person who plays a so-called hetero sport? Let's all get over the pretentiousness, loosen up and realise that Ian Roberts has done so much to show the heterosexual community that we are not in any way different from them. (Marc Kew, Dranne McFadzen, Greta Martin, *Redfern*)

I am tired of the cheap jibes made by various correspondents and columnists about the 'coming out' of Ian Roberts. I think that it was a very courageous act by a caring and intelligent young man. (Don Dudgeon, *Bomaderry*)

Steve McLeod's response in the 11 November issue was unrepentant:

Well. There are few things certain in this life, but I do know that this particular column will never arouse the frothing frenzy of abuse and condemnation that greeted my piece on that footy poof, who shall remain nameless, unless we pay his manager $16,000. Sad but true. Even though this column will deal with the issues of life and death, it will seem small marbles indeed to those who find the meaning of lifestyle in muscles, shorts and a crooked smile.

*

One night that same week, Ian and Shane were swimming in the pool at their apartment complex in Camperdown. 'We were diving in and swimming around and stuff and talking, and all of a sudden Ian starts speaking like he was speech impaired,' Shane recalls. 'I thought he was just being an idiot, you know how he always jokes around, and I told him to shut up because I didn't think it was in very good taste. Then I realised he was actually panicking, and half his face was just dropped and he was trying desparately to get out of the pool but couldn't. He was paralysed on one side. He was trying to say, "Shane, help me! Oh, my leg, my fuckin' leg." I tried to help him out and he ended up falling out onto the concrete. I was so fucking frightened because he was panicking and there was nothing I could do. After a good minute, he was just shaking, scared, but back to normal. The episode scared the shit out of him. This was something that hadn't happened since he was young and to suddenly be with him again, he was just freaked. The next day he went to see Neil Halpin and had a series of tests.'

MAINTAINING THE RAGE

It was diagnosed, after an MRI scan, as more than likely nothing major, a one-off recurrence, the result of a build up of stress and pressures in his life which weren't finding release in any other way. It was true that Ian bottled up and worried about so many little things he seemed so nonchalant about to any observer. So there was a physical toll after a year jampacked with change, with criticism and adulation, new responsibilities and expectations of him, and with good and bad choices which now seemed to increasingly affect those around him.

In December, the *Star Observer* hosted its 'Inaugural Media Matters Weasal Awards' and presented Jacqui Lang, who wrote the *New Weekly* article with 'The Scoop of the Year, or I'm Sorry, You Thought We Were Friends and I Wouldn't Use It? Weasel Award.'

In private, Ian railed against what he saw as unjust criticism. Eventually, he forgot himself and he lashed back more publicly. Probably his first terse public response to his gay detractors came in an interview he did for *Outrage* magazine, which appeared in their August 1996 issue.

I was told I was not doing enough [for gays] at one stage and then I was accused of doing too much. Then I was saying too little, then I was saying too much. The worst was when I didn't do it the way they thought it should have been done ... I really wanted to say to these people, 'What do you want?' Who the fuck are they, really, who the fuck are they?

Referring to one gay columnist he explodes, 'Has he ever copped a good hiding in his life? Might have sprained his ankle, the fucking maggot.' He blamed the nagging knee for the uncharacteristic lapse in his usual good grace. Plus we had been working continuously through his life, for this book, and it was dawning on Ian that he had been through quite a bit in a short life. He was bound to get pissed off sooner or later.

The volley of expletives and denunciation did not come out of the blue. Once again, the frustration came as a consequence of trying to do the right thing by everyone. In May of 1996, for example, a former member of the Sydney Gay & Lesbian Mardi Gras executive had asked Ian for his assistance with a charity fundraiser for Kids With AIDS. Ian had had a bit to do with them through Blake. He said yes.

He'd got back from a trip to New Zealand only a week before. He had flown there for an AIDS Education organisation. They'd wanted him to help with a phone-in aimed at educating men who have sex with men. Ian came back from that one, astounded how few gay issues reached people in the mainstream. 'Did you know that a lot of men who have sex with men don't identify as being gay and therefore don't believe they can catch HIV? There are actually all these guys out there who live in the closet with wives or whatever, and go to beats and have sex and don't think they have to have safe sex because they tell themselves they're not gay, and AIDS is a gay disease!'

Ian felt that he had been constructive in New Zealand, and so he said he'd help in any way he could with the KWAIDS fundraising.

'It turned out that what was involved was me being in a show. I said to the people putting the thing on, that under no circumstances would I do drag, and that I didn't want them using my name to publicise the whole event. 1995 had been exhausting and draining for me and I was as sick of everyone wanting a bit of me as everyone was sick of seeing me. I said they could say that a high-profile sportsperson was going to be there, but mate, over the years I've learnt what the media are like, so I knew where to draw the line. I was worried because I thought the media would make a big deal out of the thing if they knew I was going to be in a show. But I was happy to help.

'They wanted me to do some Elvis Presley impersonation, which was fine. One performer had arranged a really cool Elvis wig and stuff. Anyway, what do you know, the next day Channel Nine is on the phone asking me if it was OK by me if they came along to DCM nightclub, where the fundraiser was to be, and filmed my *drag* show! "What did you say?" I said. They repeated themselves and I've got to admit I saw red. I was pissed off. By the next day, every station, gossip column, newspaper, whatever, had rung to ask me about this drag number I was supposedly doing. I was fed up by the time Bryce from Page Thirteen called and I explained to him that there had been a huge misunderstanding and that, though I was helping, I was not dressing up as a woman. By that stage I decided I was pulling out of the whole thing, I was that pissed off. Anyway, Page Thirteen rang the organisers and told them what I had said, and this lady let loose against me saying how pissed off she was I'd pulled out after they'd done all the publicity around me. Then out of spite or something she said that the *dress* had been made and everything!

'I rang this woman to ask her why the hell she'd said those things to the media. She was a passionate fiery person. She goes all haughty like, and she has a Spanish accent or something, "Well why deed you tell them you were not doeeeng the show?" I couldn't believe it! She told the whole country I *was* doing a drag act to get me back for pulling out! I yelled as calmly as possible that I'd done that because she'd gone against everything I had requested in offering to appear at the show, and compromised me, and put me into a very uncomfortable situation with the media.

'Next, the guy who'd approached me in the first place, is on the phone to me saying I'd better try to patch things up with this woman because if I didn't it wouldn't reflect well on *me*! I mean, it's not like I hadn't done heaps of embarrassing stuff before to help out. I've made a fool of myself several times! But this time I thought he could forget it. I mean what the fuck did he expect would happen? I've been scorched by the media but I've learned a little bit about what to say and what not to say and I know what "no comment" means when it's appropriate. Most of all, though, I thought it was unreasonable that he didn't seem to care if the media beat up this whole thing at my expense, you know, "Oh yeah, here we are at last. Footballer 'turns' gay and now he's finally wearing the dresses." The old cliched stages that a lot of people seem to think a gay guy goes through. I couldn't believe he'd want me to continue that image. His response was like "Oh, I don't think that would matter" type thing. I thought, and I can't remember if I said, that it mattered a considerable deal, seeing as though this was *me* that was going to be selling this idea. This was me who was going to be selling this old myth, which wasn't going to help progress gay issues at all. I mean, even I could see there was more at stake here.'

SIXTEEN

HOPE SPRINGS
ETERNAL

'At Manly, not long after I signed with Super League, we had these two nights when Graham Richardson came and spoke to us, and made out as if Super League were all a pack of bastards, and that it was a shelf company and this, that and the other. The whole club was there, and I had even started to doubt Super League myself. Then, a long time after all their rhetoric about how *they* were doing the right thing by players, ARL player payments were published, so everyone got to see what everyone else got. I think a lot of players realised then what a joke all the talk had been. Everyone got to see that that [payment] scale they had talked about was a lot of bullshit. When I saw the salaries, I got really angry for the first time when I saw how many good players had been shafted, people like Des Hasler and Cliffy Lyons. They must have been on some scale of their own, because players of their calibre were getting heaps less than some players who had hardly played first grade and were not as good players, by far! And players who had at least a good three years left in them, were virtually told, "Well, your time is done. Fuck off!" Mind you, they had also been told before the salaries were published, that they were right up there at the top on that bloody scale! Loyalty went down the drain well and truly then, as far as I was concerned, and I really wanted out of Manly. I didn't care what I did after that. You are only meat, mate. You are only meat.'

On 7 December, Ian had one of his regular meetings with Frank Stanton. 'I had been going over to Manly regularly, after the final, out of courtesy, to have a chat, and update the guys there on progress with my knee. I had an obligation to try to fix it without major surgery and I was trying every possible means that they wanted me to.' But the court case to secure a release from his contract was pending, and Manly felt the friendly chats had got to the stage where they could have legal ramifications. 'Before I could chat to Frank, our chief exec, that day, I had to sign an affidavit saying, "Without prejudice, this conversation cannot be used in a court of law"! All the years I have known Frank, and I was happy there. But there is a line they won't step over.' He came out of that meeting incredulous. 'I can't believe that! I can't believe what just happened. "Mate, you've got to sign this. I just can't talk to you otherwise." And he wasn't joking and mucking around with me like he usually does. It was straight down the line. No friendliness. Whenever something like that happens I always go with the worst possible scenario in my head.' Despite Ian's bravado in a harsh business world, the innocent within could still not grasp some of the ugly necessities which drive that world. He was naive about the ramifications of his own actions, so he was affronted.

This made his decision to have the knee reconstruction easier. He had nothing to lose. His bad leg had wasted two inches in circumference. 'I said to Frank, "Look, I'm going down on the weekend to have this op." He said, "Oh, well, fair enough. I don't begrudge you that. You've waited long enough."' After exclusion from rep football, and after being offended on grand final night, and stewing on that for weeks, his meeting with Frank added to the cumulative effect of the league war. Eventually, it would lead to his private resolution not to play with Manly or the ARL again, if he could help it. He knew his knee would take several months to repair after the surgery, and he hoped his case against the ARL would come up before his recovery was complete.

When he was in hospital in Melbourne, Terry Hill rang a few times, to see how he was going. The next thing he knew, there were reporters ringing to ask him about their falling out. Terry takes the story up. 'It was the biggest disappointment of my whole life. I was at Port Macquarie on holiday when Ian was recuperating. Eight million people rang me saying, "You had a fight with Ian?" I said, "What over?" "Oh, you called his boyfriend, Shane, a poof." Yeah, right! So then Ian supposedly belted me and left me lying in the gutter. I spoke with Ian. "Mate, have you heard ..." and he said, "Mate, five people rang me today." It seemed like everyone in Australia was talking about it. That was first. Then, I'm supposed to be suing him! My dad rang. "What's going on? He's your mate!" "Of course we're mates, Dad. Don't worry." '

Ian was in surgery for three hours. For several days afterward, he was immobile and on pethidine. His knee was swollen and under the bandage looked brutalised by the incisions through which the new 'tendons' had been pulled and pushed, woven through the knee and bolted into place. He was tearing his hair out with pain and it was an added irritant to have to talk in depth about his life at this time. His responses were often brief and terse, especially when the pethidine wore off. Under close personal scrutiny, and obliged to be really honest, extremes of emotion like anger, rage, excitement, were conveyed with a profusion of expletives.

As '96 unfolded, his knee calmed down and the pandemonium of '95 grew more distant, Ian genuinely opened up and enjoyed working the knots out of his psyche. He would ponder on issues we raised and come back, sometimes days later, with a personal insight. It intrigued him, working his life out. Seeing it on paper was another thing. He cringed all the time at how he appeared or sounded. He hated the way he translated into print, just as he hates the way he appears in photographs. He will probably never be comfortable about those aspects of himself. But he is a tryer. He will do something he is uncomfortable doing when he thinks it is the right thing, or if it is a good personal challenge. In a couple of the interviews he did during the year, he answered questions by drawing on the character analysis that he had read in early drafts. At least if he didn't like it, he was absorbing it. Like a true adventurer, Ian is a genuine exponent of 'nothing tried nothing gained'. He still gives 100 per cent.

Ian's recovery from the knee reconstruction was a reminder that change for the better often comes slowly. More than six months after the operation he went in for another bout of surgery to try to improve his restricted mobility. He spent much of '96 aching his way through physio to achieve only incremental improvement. Ray knows Ian's determination. 'Ian will play for another few years. They're not limited, that type of player, who can bounce back, who has the drive, the ability, the fitness, everything. I put Ian in that class. Ian's the sort of player who can adapt. When you play with a bad groin injury for years, then a knee problem for four years, you are just playing on sheer ability.'

'I don't care what it takes,' Ian says, 'I'll be back. I've just got to. For me. I'm not ready to retire and I don't want to have come out and be honest about myself, and then disappear. It looks too much like I'm running away. And I'm definitely not doing that. I want to be able to enjoy a few more years of football.' George Piggins thinks Ian should have been able to retire by now, and blames John Wiseman for Ian's predicament. 'He's got through football in reasonable condition. But there's life after football. That's what you've got to look at. The money might be good, but the quality of life is important. You've got to get out when you can still go play a game of golf or tennis. If you get out and you're 35 and you've got the body of a 60-year-old, it's no good. It's like a prize fighter who's had one too many fights and he's ga ga. It's sad to think that Ian is in that position. To think you took all those bumps, you should have been out of there by now.'

If losing all his money was a contributing factor in Ian's predicament, it was also part of a chain of events and circumstances that led Ian on a journey of growth culminating in the events of '95. 'Last year ['95] was quite stressful. I felt like everyone wanted something from me, for their benefit. But a lot of what I did was for me, too. Now I want to enjoy that. I want to really enjoy not having to worry about hiding. I want to enjoy playing football with that feeling. And getting good money to do it. I miss playing because you get used to the energy of it. The rush of it. I miss the release it brings. I want to get back to doing what I do best.' While he waited to return to football he was in limbo, without a purpose. And totally frustrated, and frustrating, because his life was not on the move. 'I feel like I'm ready for the next stage in my life. My next adventure. I'm bored. I get bored easily. I hate just sitting still. I prefer to be moving ahead, doing new things, keeping busy.'

To have made the changes in his life that he had made, and then to not be able to live it fully, was a real fear for him, which reminded him of his epilepsy. Then he felt a pathetic helplessness when he had his fit in the spa late in '95. And his physical immobility was a constant reminder of his biggest nightmare. Then, like a self-fulfilling fear, came another series of fits. One seizure left him quietly crying in his car, on the side of the M4 freeway. He couldn't tell whether the wrenching was the same as it had been years before. It felt worse. Again, the diagnosis was that the fits were stress-related, but doubt lingered in his mind.

Ian's case against the ARL, to obtain a release from Manly, had been deferred and deferred. Super League resources were directed towards an appeal against Justice James Burchett's Federal Court ruling which banned them from holding their own competition until at least the year 2000. Finally, with Ian still off the field and Manly fielding a strong team at the top of the ARL ladder, they sent a telegram to Ian agreeing to release him. In September *Sports Weekly* magazine ran an article confirming Ian's angry defiance of the ARL and resolve to sit '96 out on the sidelines. As it was, circumstances allowed the man of principle his victory on that one.

He'd been to Townsville a few times to suss out a possible move there to play with the North Queensland Cowboys, deep in the heart of ... well, mainstream Australia. A couple of the directors of the Cowboys were reticent about having Ian play. At a meeting, one director, a bit aghast at what he thought was the lack of concern about Ian's personal life, apparently felt compelled to remind the others, 'You know what he is, don't you?' However, the representatives of News Corporation, which owns 50 per cent of the Cowboys, were keen to have Ian up there, and the idea was generally well received.

One weekend, Ian stayed at the Travelodge, Townsville. An 'insider' at the local paper, *The Bulletin*, contacted him via Nick Karandonis, back in Sydney, to advise that he was seen on security camera cuddling his boyfriend in the pool at the hotel. 'Some security guy must have got in touch with the paper. Probably thought it rated as a scandal. He said we were being "intimate". We were alone in the area and it was all very innocent. We were just basically jumping and diving around. And you know, it doesn't bother me any more. I'm just going to live my life. I'm not going to start ducking security cameras now.' But Ian was concerned for the new man in his life, who was terrified of public scrutiny, and it must have reminded him of his own terror of discovery for all those years.

Ironically, Ian had broken up with Shane just a few months after the *New Weekly* article was published, and had, by this stage, been seeing someone else for 5 months. In many ways Ian and Shane had grown over the years they were together, but in different directions. What started out as a somewhat co-dependent relationship, had evolved into something that was uncomfortable for both parties, even though the two had a difficult time admitting it for ages. As one friend observed, 'They were basically suffocating each other, and would punish each other, because they both resented the claustrophobia. I would tell Ian, "Look, this is fucked." It put a strain on my, and a lot of people's, relationships with Ian, it was so unpleasant to be around.' When Shane started working and becoming more independent, Ian felt more comfortable ending the relationship, though he still cared deeply for Shane. The move to Townsville would give the two breathing space from each other. 'Our breakup was very painful for me,' says Ian, 'because I still love and care for Shane and probably always will.'

Townsville was a far cry from Sydney, that was for sure. But the deal was lucrative for someone in the twilight of what has been a troubled career. By the time Super League won their appeal before the full bench of the Federal Court, and the previous ruling banning their competition was overturned, in early October, Ian was living up there. He looked at the move in a positive light. 'Part of me is actually looking forward to being away from Sydney for a while. Just for the change. I know I'll be lonely, but it will be a new challenge.'

Not that he has yet triumphed over all his other challenges. But, like a healing knee, some things take time. Take changing people's attitudes about homosexuality. Our society lumbers along shackled by ancient institutions, fearful of straying from a well-worn path, while daring individuals and groups, trying to implement change, scurry around it, trying to encourage it this way and that. Often they only succeed in scaring it. Eventually, after many attempts, there is a marginal altering of course, a reluctant change towards a road less travelled.

Change will probably always scare a lot of people. Australia had a taste of conservative reactionism with an election in 1996 that brought an end to some of the changes that were being wrought by a Labor government with liberal social policies. Just when you thought it was safe to assume Australia was working towards a multicultural wonderland, when the importance of working out a balanced national psyche on which to build a good and integrated future was being stressed, out it all goes, bathwater and baby. Political correctness was now an ugly phrase. It was again okay to be loudly hateful and narrow-minded, to be divisive, because that's freedom of speech. But no speech is free. The cost of informed speech is the education and knowledge that occurs beforehand. The price of ill-informed speech is the needless pain and disharmony afterwards. Ignorant talk about minorities, without an understanding of their difficulties often produced the plaintive cry 'What about the average Australian?' Forget the below-average Australian!

So many people claim to speak out for the average Australian, the so-called silent majority, most of whom may just be silently and appreciatively content with their lot. A good cross-section of them have silently written to Ian. He received literally thousands of letters during '95 and '96. It was uplifting that by far the majority of them from all kinds people were warm, thankful and supportive. There were hundreds of loving letters from Mr and Mrs Average, from concerned residents of 'middle' Australia who felt inspired to speak against the generalisations that were so often made in their name. Reading them, you could be buoyed and comforted by the capacity for love and acceptance which many people quietly have. Some letters left you feeling despondent, when you realise how many young homosexual people suffer at the hands of blind faith and ignorance. Still others sent a sharp chill through the body, a reaction to the capacity for hatred that is in people, leaving you violated and threatened.

Ian has kept some of the touching, supportive letters. He is still outwardly nonchalant about the nasty ones. 'Mate, to some people you are evil and there is no way around them. You can't afford to let their attitudes bring you down. If they want to live their life according to a set of myths and fairy tales that some blokes wrote thousands of years ago, then that's their right. I feel sorry for people that can't think for themselves and come up to me quoting from this and that passage in their Bible, supposedly proving that this is what their god thinks about me. What can I do?' It fascinates him, for a minute, that people can place so much much importance on what someone once said way back when humans were ignorant of just about everything to do with human existence. You wonder when someone will actually sue a religious instructor for damage to their mental well-being, and challenge the right of one human or institution to impose its beliefs on another. How a court of law would deal with the authenticity and source of God's supposed law would be interesting. The uncritical worship of ancient writings will perhaps remain an anomaly in a world that expects to update and improve just about everything in life, the more knowledge and technology that is acquired.

Ian was at a gay bar one night when a loud drunken voice called out to him. 'Hey, Roberts, get your arse over here!' Ian looked through the dim smoky light in the direction of the voice and barely recognised the overweight hulk it belonged to. He walked over, then broke into a smile when he saw there were a couple of other hulks he recognised. He kept smiling when they started to berate him, jovially slurring all over him.

'Just remember, matey, you weren't the first. You weren't the fuckin' first ... not by a fuckin' long shot.'

'Don't you worry about that, mate. I never doubted it for a fuckin' second,' Ian said, but he thought to himself, 'I was the first to stand up and admit it.'

Then a more chilling thought came to him as he contemplated the drunken men at that bar. 'What if I end up looking like them?' Ian was already starting to become obsessed with some theory that footballers' faces start ageing horrifically after thirty. Now that theory seemed to be all but proved. He felt sad for the drunks who were still arguing good-humouredly about whether some guy who just walked by was cute or not. It was hard to believe that he had feared one of them so much when he had faced him in games against Canterbury all those years ago.

In 1996 the producers of Channel 9's panel-format *Footy Show* had the ground-breaking courage to broach the subject of homosexuality, in a commonsense way. And Ian had the courage to front the show's panel. He didn't think twice about it. It was something he felt he should do, so on 30 May, he nervously fielded questions about his sexuality from some of league's staunchest heterosexuals. It was all a bit surreal, really. For thousands of gays watching, it was a spin-out. Acclimatised all their lives to separating their maleness into boxes, one for their sexuality and one for their love of sport, here was the unthinkable happening. Footy blokes chatting about poofs like they were nice guys. Paul 'Fatty' Vautin reverted to comfortable reality when he unconsciously skipped into a homophobic gaffe. At one point he jokingly mentioned that, while he continuously 'heard' about Ian being a poof, he doubted it because Ian was 'a good bloke'! But generally the questions and comments were intelligent and thoughtful. A great positive step forward for the hundreds of confused homosexual kids playing football who thought they were the only ones. And poor old Fatty had to take his foot out of his mouth, apologising on the next show for any homophobic impression his comments gave. In October, Vautin, along with Peter Sterling and Steve Roach, from the show, appeared as part of a poster campaign against homophobia being conducted by The Lesbian and Gay Anti-Violence Project. And you could be excused for thinking that Ian Roberts had a lot to do with sincere attempts by men such as these, to attempt to understand what it means to be gay in this society.

For every good action there is often an equal and opposite reaction. Often it is as tiny and good-humoured as Fatty's innocent joke on the footy show. Or Mike Gibson taking the micky out of the voluntary outing, in October '96, of prominent gay Australians, by 'outing' some heterosexuals in his column in the *Telegraph*. We should not lose sight of good humour, but many journalists are insensitive and blatantly ignorant of what it is like for gays growing up out there. With tongue in cheek Gibson, assessed the heterosexuality of his 'outees' by how they acted. 'There's just something about him, you know what I mean? The way he talks. Those telling mannerisms. The form guide sticking out of his back kick. Sorry, but it's a dead set give-away.' Is he for real? Has he been watching anything that's been going on around him? Obviously, the Ian Roberts he eulogised a year before for doing so much for the gay cause has had no influence on his thinking. The scare-mongering that prompts talk of a 'yellow peril' in respect of another minority in this country, still invades his slop as he absurdly states 'that it has almost reached the stage where you feel like asking would the last heterosexual in Darlinghurst please turn out the lights'. Gibson is a good argument for involuntary outing. He'd be very, very shocked!

Oh well. It had been another Gibson, actor Mel, whose pearls of stereotyping wisdom were quoted in the Spanish newspaper *El Pais*, after it was suggested he might be mistaken for being gay. 'With this look, who's going to think I'm gay? I don't lend myself to that type of confusion. Do I sound like a homosexual? Do I talk like them? Do I move like them?' Mel later claimed he had been quoted out of context.

But you are left wondering what society would do with a contemporary Leonardo da Vinci. As long as people try to narrow and define sexuality as a type of person, as a particular character, then children will continue to be oppressed and tortured, psychologically and physically, and many will have to fight immense odds, internal and external, in order to lead a fulfilling and productive life. And only a lucky minority of homosexuals who achieve great success will know what it is like to be truly successful and happy, to be both a known homosexual in the public eye, and to still be able to hold their heads up high.

Consistent with the new prevailing mood of the country, harking back to a time when some white Anglo-Celtic heterosexuals were comfortable and relaxed on a headland, the Wood Royal Commission in New South Wales in 1996 and even the Port Arthur massacre gave the media the chance to fire several homophobic salvos, to contain the 'menace'. The *Telegraph* deduced from the idle remarks of an ex-girlfriend of the Tasmanian mass murderer that Martin Bryant was possibly a homosexual who perved on, and lusted after, little boys. Not to mention the articles that all but equated homosexuality with pedophilia as journalists referred to alleged pedophiles as 'shameless homosexuals' and the grey area between someone going to a gay bar, and someone using the private rooms there for sex with teenage youths was boldly coloured in. The media were excused from differentiating between forced sexual encounters with pre-pubescent children, and consenting sex between post-pubescent males, or in other words, between criminal acts, and homosexuality. The tabloid media seemed to constantly salivate over the scandals they could whip up with a couple of ingredients that had a few homosexuals thrown in. At the end of it all how was any of this going to help the sexually-abused children, of whom statistically 90-odd per cent are abused hetero-sexually, and within their own families?

There was a real, growing fear among 'out' gays that a witch hunt was occurring, which was only really interested in putting gays back in their place. High profile 'out' gay men were wondering, often out loud, where it would stop. In the minds of many gays the ghetto/victim mentality slipped back into place, replacing any hint of euphoria that the positive effect Ian's outing had had on so many lives. It doesn't take much for such positive feelings to be quashed. For gays who don't busy themselves pursuing what looks, from the outside, a hedonistic lifestyle, it is too easy to imagine a return to a suppressed and horrific life, because the reminders of that life, which every gay person has lived at some stage, are never far away. For Ian, that feeling of dread of discovery was recent. He only really escaped it a couple of years ago. But, while he might be a worrier, a strong faith in his goodness and his right to be means he no longer fears fear itself.

Ian's immediate concern is to milk some enjoyment out of his day to day life, and his calls from Townsville reflect this. 'Mate, I don't know if I'm going to be able to handle this. I think I'll go crazy if he [his current boyfriend] doesn't move up here. And what's it been now, six days?' Then later. 'I'm going to have to buy a little shop or some-thing to fill in time. Do you like sleeping alone? Because I can't stand it. I'm just not used to sleeping alone. I can't sleep properly. I need to feel the breath of the someone I care about. That warm rush just makes me feel comfortable. Close. You just feel connected to something that, in the end, makes it all worthwhile. Like you are needed.' He's not as desperate as he lets himself sound. But he is free, because he can willingly admit his feelings and insecurities to close friends. All of them. And his new relationship is reflective, as Michael Gorman points out, of a mature Ian: 'He's finally found somebody who is his own person, who's coming into that relationship as an equal and not as someone to be protected.' And as much as that scares Ian in a way, he knows it's the best thing for him.

So what if he verbalises a few insecurities. 'Look, I'm fuckin' sure my face is just getting worse and worse. I look at these pictures that were taken and all I see is this ugly fuckin' ... thing! But anyway, what was I ringing for? Oh yeah, I'm coming to Sydney this weekend, but I need to hire a gorilla suit.'

So we rang round to see if we could get a gorilla suit for someone as tall as Ian. He had been sitting in his ninth floor apartment overlooking the sparkling tranquil blueness of Townsville's bay, chuckling to himself as he formulated a plan. All week he had been talking to his lover, in Sydney, dropping strange little comments into phone conversations like 'And what's all this monkey business I've been hearing about, going on down there in Sydney?' When asked what he was referring to, he just moved the conversation on. Then he'd say things like, 'Hang on, I'll just get rid of this banana peel' or, when asked about a noise he was making on the phone, he'd say 'I'm just eating a banana'. He hadn't told the guy he was coming to Sydney for the weekend. He wanted it to be a surprise. So much so in fact that he wanted to turn up at the cafe where he worked, dressed as a gorilla, order a banana split and just sit there and eat it before revealing himself to what he knew would be the excruciating embarrassment of his boyfriend. The only problem was that he couldn't get a gorilla head that fitted comfortably.

It was the middle of October, and the weight training program the Cowboys had started on had Ian enthused. 'It's funny, you know. The program is really intensive. It's a killer. But I watch some of the young guys going at it, and I can see myself back there at Souths, when I first started, trying my guts out, to prove to all the older guys in the team that I was as good as them. I was always right out there in front with everything, desperately trying to be first and best. It's a really nice feeling being able to relax and enjoy the training, and be able to encourage others, without having to run myself into the ground with panic. And without having to pretend to be anything else other than myself. Because there is nothing anyone can find out that can hurt me or my career. I've matured too much for that to happen. And so, I think, has the game.'

Cowboys' coach Tim Sheens offered Ian the captaincy of the team. The gesture moved Ian. 'I really appreciated Tim offering me the job. I know he probably had to put his foot down with a few people who would've been funny about it, but I respect that about Tim. He knows what he wants, and if he knows he's right he will put his foot down until he gets it. At first I thought I couldn't take it—I just didn't think it would be fair to the rest of the team. I didn't want to be the cause of them copping flak because I was their captain. And being captain, you have a lot of responsibility to the others, and I would want to have a positive effect, not a negative one. Tim had already considered the angles and told me to give it some thought.'

Ian Roberts celebrates his promotion to captain with an inspired performance as he led the North Queensland Cowboys to a 30–22 victory over Auckland ... The veteran former Manly prop ... who admitted he was inspired by the captaincy role, led his charges admirably. (Sydney Morning Herald, 28/4/97)

Ian finally decided to accept this new challenge, bearing in mind that the position, announced on April 23, 1997, was a genuine compliment, and a recognition that the person he had fought to honestly be, was after all, someone who could command respect in the wider community. And Ian can reflect with satisfaction on the fact that the maturation that has occurred in the sport in which he excels can be attributed in no small part to his own struggle and growth. That makes him an Australian pioneer.